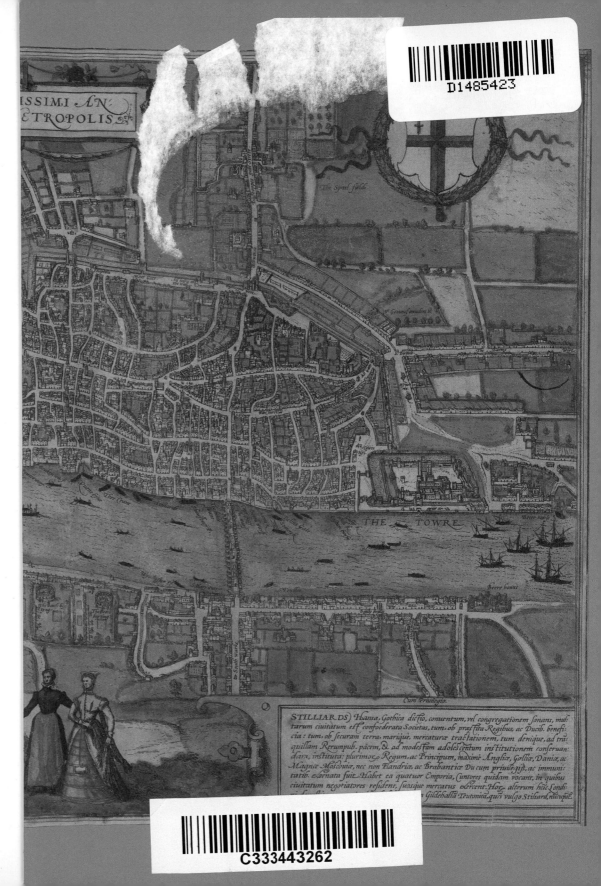

~ A London Year ~

~ *A LONDON YEAR* ~

365 Days of City Life in Diaries, Journals and Letters

Compiled by

Travis Elborough
&
Nick Rennison

FRANCES LINCOLN LIMITED
PUBLISHERS

Frances Lincoln Limited
74–77 White Lion Street
London N1 9PF

A London Year
Copyright © 2013 Frances Lincoln Limited

Introduction and compilation copyright © 2013
Travis Elborough and Nick Rennison
Edited and designed by Jane Havell Associates
Index by Marianne Ryan

A catalogue record for this book is available from the British Library
ISBN 978-0-7112-3449-9
Typeset in Walbaum
Printed and bound in China
2 4 6 8 9 7 5 3 1

∼ CONTENTS ∼

the Dutch Churche.

St. Michaels.

ange.

St. Peters.

Leaden hall

St. Hellen

St. Andrew

Fishmongers hall

THE BRIDGE

chester house

Warke

St. Mary Overis

St. Dunstan in the east

Alhallowes Borking

Hackny

Billingsgate

Bridge Gate

∼ INTRODUCTION ∼

LONDON. What better place is there, in all honesty, to write about? Or to keep a diary in? Should it really come as much of a surprise that Samuel Pepys, the first 'real' diarist, and the most famous diarist of all time, was a Londoner? Or that from his time to ours, and from John Evelyn to Chris Mullin, some of the greatest observers of daily life ever to put pen to paper (or fix a font on a screen) have turned their attention to London at one point or other? Even what we think of as the standard diary was actually invented in the city. It was in the opening decades of the nineteenth century that the London stationer John Letts first began selling a yearly almanack from his shop at the Royal Exchange, then home to numerous booksellers and coffee-houses and an area previously haunted by Pepys. The Letts Diary was an immediate success, attracting such devoted users as William Makepeace Thackeray – who favoured the 'three shillings cloth boards' No. 12 model – and continues to be published in a multitude of formats to this day.

Thackeray, alas, is not one of the contributors to this volume, an anthology that seeks to provide intimate snatches of London life for each and every day of the year. To include every celebrated diarist or letter writer who has ever considered London would be impossible. Some of the giants of the form are noticeable by their absence here, while some of our city scribes will be completely unknown to many readers. But London, home to monarchs, prime ministers, clergymen, artists, writers, movie stars and oligarchs, is equally a city populated by ordinary people getting on with extraordinary things. We hope we have captured some of their cadences amid the raised voices of the well-rewarded and self-important. Diaries, like family silver, do have something of a habit and a substantial history of being kept and passed on.

'London', the French-born New Yorker Louis Simond maintained in his journal of 1810, was a 'giant', a city so vast that 'strangers' such as himself could only ever 'touch its toes'. It has, of course, grown exponentially in size since then and the difficulty of getting much beyond its ankles is no less daunting for locals. Where does London really end? Or, for that matter, truly begin? Here, the names of certain famous districts, streets and buildings (ancient and modern) naturally enough occur and recur. Indeed, some names seem to come around with the same giddying regularity as the children George Orwell observed happily riding around the Circle Line during the Blitz. And arguably the topography of this book is as distorted and dishonest a picture of London as that proffered by Harry Beck's famous Tube map (but hopefully no less revealing or enduring for that). And similarly, just as the rhythm of city life frequently mirrors the clustering of red London buses, some days stuffed with historic events and others possessing barely an incident worthy of interest, our entries ebb and flow accordingly.

If diarists have their idiosyncrasies and preoccupations (money, say, in the case of Nathaniel Bryceson, or attractive women for James Boswell), so we as anthologists have our own hobby horses, blind spots and peccadillos. Some of those shortcomings we have done our best to rectify. Others we make no apologies for indulging. Our overall criteria for inclusion, however, was relatively simple. We were seeking diarists (and the odd letter writer) who'd managed to say something about London over the past five hundred years or so. What that 'something' was remained a somewhat inchoate concept. But we believe a certain essential Londonness, a quality that the writer and editor D. M. Low once termed 'Londinity', is discernible in each and every one of our selections. London is, of course, a city of many aspects and ages – and, it almost goes without saying, a very different place for residents from what it is for visitors. Love it or loathe it, hail from it or elsewhere, we all have our own London. Much like New York or Paris, it is also a metropolis whose cityscape is immediately familiar the world over from pictures, photographs, movies, television shows and the internet. It is somewhere whose basic reality is constantly coloured by, if not often at

odds with, those representations. Cities are both physical and imaginative entities, after all. But in gathering up particular first-person impressions, we feel a more identifiably universal city emerges here. A London
that not only belongs to us and our writers, but should belong to everyone who reads this compendium, whether you know the city well, or
hardly at all.

Inevitably, and quite compellingly to our minds, much of what is
encountered in these pages has since been lost to us. For the most part,
this is a London long before central heating and air conditioning, let
alone inside bathrooms, the Clean Air Act and underarm deodorants.
A London at the mercy of the elements and tied to the shifts in the
seasons in ways far more profound than they are now. A London of
winter Frost Fairs on the Thames and May Day feasts for apprentices
in Westminster. A bucolic-sounding London with fields around Blackfriars and sheep grazing on Green Park; if also a capital of open sewers,
plagues, fires (great and small), grisly murders and public executions.
And, later, of lethal smogs and filthy chimneys and deadly incendiaries.
But then, even a London with an oily working river and a soot-wreathed
hub of industrial production – a city, on the cusp of living memory,
where the aromas of vinegar from the Crosse & Blackwell pickle factory
in Soho Square hung in the air at St Giles's and High Holborn – today
feels nearly as unimaginably distant as the capital of footpads and highwaymen also recorded by Horace Walpole and Jonathan Swift.

And yet, while compiling *A London Year*, we were frequently
brought up short by sudden continuities between the past and the
present. Covent Garden may have lost its fruit and vegetable market,
animals are no longer for sale in Club Row, Bethnal Green, and postal
workers rather than impecunious poets prop up the bars in Fitzrovia.
But, as one of our more contemporary London diarists Dickon Edwards
is surprised to discover, there still is a windmill in Brixton. Hackney
retains its marshes, Wimbledon its common and the City of London
coffee-houses of a sort at least.

But ignoring these moments of geographical (or, possibly, psycho-
geographical) synchronicity, certain issues and tropes prove surprisingly
consistent over the centuries. The impossibility of getting around the
place. The dirtiness of London's streets. The unpredictability of the
weather. The expensiveness of food and lodgings. The snootiness of

shopkeepers, restaurateurs and/or publicans. The difficulty of finding somewhere decent to live, and interrelatedly, the worry about whether X or Y neighbourhood will go up or down. The feeling, memorably expressed by Charles Lamb way back in 1829, that the old place isn't what it once was. All of these concerns crop up, in various guises, again and again. And even some of the wilder events of yesteryear — the witch-hunts, earthquakes, floods and riots, say — are not without their obvious modern-day parallels, or reiterations.

We have edited many of the entries for clarity of sense and ease of reading and, on occasions, to help bring out their 'Londinity'. But *here* we believe is London — eternal but ever-changing, and vividly drawn first-hand by a floating cast of inhabitants as they go about their daily lives, at work and at play, and in pursuit of money, sex, entertainment, pleasure and power.

T.E. and N.R.

TAMESIS
Flumen

JANUARY

～ 1 *JANUARY* ～

NEW YEAR, NEW ALE AND NEW AILMENTS

Much disturbd with a guiddiness in my eyes and head after drinking new ale and eating a mutton pottage, slept a little after it. Better after eating pullet and drinking ale . . . after at Garways* was somewhat better after drinking tea and cleering right nostrill after Beet Juice . . . I took a clove of garlick in drink: at night I slept pretty well but had a strange noyse in right ear upon waking like or a horne or bell. Toward bed I spitt very much and my right nostrill was cleerd which I ascribe in part to the juice of beet and part to garlick swallowed.

Robert Hooke, *Diary*, 1672

* Garraway's, the coffee house.

A RUDE AWAKENING

Waking this morning out of my sleep on a sudden, I did with my elbow hit my wife a great blow over her face and nose, which waked her with pain, at which I was sorry, and to sleep again. Up and went forth with Sir W. Pen by coach towards Westminster, and in my way seeing that the 'Spanish Curate' was acted today, I light and let him go alone, and I home again and sent to young Mr. Pen and his sister to go anon with my wife and I to the Theatre. That done, Mr. W. Pen came to me and he and I walked out, and to the Stacioner's, and looked over some pictures and traps for my house, and so home again to dinner, and by and by came the two young Pens, and after we had eat a barrel of oysters we went by coach to the play, and there saw it well acted, and a good play it is, only Diego the Sexton did overdo his part too much. From thence home, and they sat with us till late at night at cards very merry, but the jest was Mr. W. Pen had left his sword in the coach, and so my boy and he run out after the coach, and by very great chance did at the Exchange meet with the coach and got his sword again. So to bed.

Samuel Pepys, *Diary*, 1662

TAKING IN A WEST END SHOW GIRL, OR TWO

Tonight I treated Lizzie and myself to extra nice seats to see Sid Field in *Strike it Again*. Field was just as amusing as he was in the days at the South London Music Hall long before he was discovered. Like a good many clever comics, he'd been round and round the halls for years without setting the Thames on fire, then he gets a break and does the *same* things in the same way at five times more salary and his name in lights at The Prince of Wales Theatre. Lizzie enjoyed the show and I enjoyed the very attractive lot of show girls.

Fred Bason, *Diary*, 1945

～ 2 *JANUARY* ～

THE PASSING OF A CAMDEN CHARACTER

Reg who kept the junk stall in the market has died. And today is his funeral. Where his stall stood outside The Good Mixer there is a trestle-table covered with a blue sheet, and a notice on a wreath of chrysan-themums announces that Reg Stone passed peacefully away on Boxing Day and that his cortège will be passing through the market at three o'clock. Until I read the card I'd never known his last name.

Reg's stall was a feature of the market long before I moved here in 1961. Then he had two prices, sixpence and a shilling. In time this went up to a shilling and five shillings, and latterly it had reached 50p and £1. To some extent he shaped his price to the customer, though not in a Robin Hood sort of way, the poorer customers often getting charged more, and any attempt to bargain had the same effect. I have two American clocks, both in working order, that were five shillings apiece, and an early Mason's Ironstone soup dish that cost sixpence and hangs on the wall in the kitchen. Local houses used to be full of treasures from Reg: model steam engines, maple mirrors, Asian Pheasant plates, rummers – all picked up for a song. Once I saw a can of film (empty) with 'Moholy-Nagy' round the rim, and only this last year Harriet G. got some Ravilious plates for 50p. Money didn't seem to interest Reg.

Scarcely glancing at what one had found, he'd take the fag out of his mouth and say, 'A pound,' then take a sip from his glass of mild on the pub window-sill and turn away, not bothered if one bought it or not.

I go down at three. The table is now piled high with flowers, mostly the dog-eared variety on offer at the cheap stall at the market, petals already scattering on the wind. One or two of the long-established residents stand about, old NW1 very much in evidence. Thinking that the cortège will arrive from the Catholic church, we are looking along Arlington Road when it comes stealing through the market itself. It is led by a priest in a cape and an undertaker bearing a heavy rolled umbrella that he holds in front of him like a staff or ceremonial cross. The procession is so silent and unexpected that it scarcely disturbs people doing their normal shopping, the queue at Terry Mercer's fruit stall gently nudged aside by the creeping limousines. The priest stops at the top of the street, turns, and stands looking down the market as if the street were a nave and this his altar. The flowers are now distributed among the various cars, more petals falling. In one of the limousines a glamorous blonde is weeping, and in the other cars there are children. Just as I never thought of Reg as having a name, so a family (and a family as respectable as this) comes as a surprise. And for a man I never saw smile or scowl, laugh or lose his temper, grief, too, seems out of place.

Alan Bennett, *Diary*, 1987

A TRIP TO A MUSIC HALL

On Friday night, our last in London, we went to the Tivoli. There were no seats except in the pit; so we went in the pit. Little Tich was very good and George Formby, the Lancashire comedian, was perhaps even better. Gus Elen I did not care for. And I couldn't see the legendary cleverness of the vulgarity of Marie Lloyd. She was very young and spry for a grandmother. All her songs were variations on the same theme of sexual naughtiness. No censor would ever pass them, and especially he wouldn't pass her winks and silences. To note also was the singular naiveté of the cinematograph explanation of what a vampire was and is, for the vampire dance. The stoutest and biggest attendants laughed at Little Tich and G Formby. Fearful draughts half the time down exit staircases from the street. Fearful noise from the bar behind, made chiefly by the officials. The bar-girls and their friends simply ignore the performance and the public. Public opinion keeps the seats of those who go to the bar at the interval for a drink. Going home, stopped by procession of full carriages entering the Savoy and empty carriages coming out of it.

Arnold Bennett, *Journals*, 1910

THE BENEFITS OF LONDON TRANSPORT

Cold bright day. No one about at 8.15 as I go to Bron. I like taking the bus (getting on at Great Western Road, after a walk of about half a mile). One of the unsung benefits of public transport: people relate to each other and have a chance to be nice to each other. It's a mobile version of the village well. Cars are the equivalent of private plumbing.

Brian Eno, *Diary*, 1995

~ 3 JANUARY ~

CHELSEA SOUP

Saw in Chelsea 'Leg of Beef Soup 2d per Bason', so had a bason for dinner, which make-believe bason was nothing more than a large saucer on a high stand, with a broad thick bottom with pieces of meat like so much twine. 'Remarks': no more Chelsea soup. Edward Heskett, fellow clerk, made me present of a very nice mince pie. A maidservant of all work, Catherine Bird, left her situation at the wharf this evening. Left off old black trousers, otherwise they would soon have left me off. Old Matthew Ward, father to the present Matthew Ward, if had lived would have completed his 96th year this day.

Nathaniel Bryceson, *Diary*, 1846

THE DEATH OF A COSTER QUEEN

Two days ago at Streatham there died Kate Carney, and a large slice of real old London has gone. She was the real Coster Queen, the exuberant Cockney. There was no one and there never will be another Kate Carney for her London is fast disappearing. She could hold her audience with that sad song 'Are we to part like this, Bill?' or get 'em laughing and joining in with '3 Pots a Shilling', and *no one* else could!

Her songs were almost tailor made for her. She made them her own and for 63 years she was a star of the GENUINE music hall. Indeed, she was singing ballads in Victorian days – and so she was a star through 5 reigns. She was a big fat plain looking woman with a big chest and a large heart. She was ALL big and there wasn't anything mean about her. She had a loud voice and loud ways – but she was a real dear old girl. She lived most of her life in Brixton and her home was like as if nothing had been changed in it for 40 years. It was all Edwardian and stout. Even the piano was of the 1912 period with fretwork inlaid with mother of pearl.

She must have appeared in many Royal Command Performances in her time. I understand she started on the Halls at Collins in Islington, and was friends with Marie Lloyd. Kate Carney was always larger than life. Her husband was George Barclay who owned a music hall at Stoke Newington called The Alexandra. I've never been there. They must have been married all of 40 years. He died in 1945 and we thought Kate Carney would retire – but not a bit of it. You couldn't keep Kate down – not that you wanted to.

I got her autograph first in 1922 (the same year I got Marie Lloyd's). She was fat in 1922. She was still fat in 1942. In between those 20 years I'd seen her 5 times in almost the same act – and the same resonant voice. She never needed a microphone. Her dress was coster in every way and her hat a blaze of Happy Hampstead feathers. She was REAL Cockney – everyone said that. But when I asked her where she was born she said it was a question she did not like to answer!

It's like I've said, a piece of real old Cockney London is gone and I'm downright sorry. I believe she had children. Will one of them carry on the tradition? I expect not. What's gone is gone forever!

Fred Bason, *Diary*, 1950

~ 4 JANUARY ~

THE UNFORTUNATE DR CLENCH

Dr. Clench the physitian was strangled in a coach: two persons came to his house in Brownlow street, Holborn, in a coach, and pretended to carry him to a patients in the citty: they drove backward and forward, and after some time stopt by Leaden hall, and sent the coachman to buy a couple of fowls for supper, who went accordingly; and in the mean time they slipt away; and the coachman when he returned found Dr. Clench strangled with a handkercheife tyed about his neck, with a hard sea coal twisted in it, and clapt just against his windpipe: he had spirits applyed to him, and other means, but too late, he having been dead some time.

Narcissus Luttrell, *Diary*, 1692

THE NEW EMBANKMENT

The Thames Embankment is (faults of ugliness in detail apart) the finest public work yet done. From Westminster Bridge to near Waterloo it is now lighted up at night, and has a fine effect. They have begun to plant it with trees, and the footway (not the road) is already open to the Temple. Besides its beauty, and its usefulness in relieving the crowded streets, it will greatly quicken and deepen what is learnedly called the 'scour' of the river. But the Corporation of London and some other nuisances have brought the weirs above Twickenham into a very bare and unsound condition, and they already begin to give and vanish, as the stream runs faster and stronger.

Charles Dickens, Letter to M. de Cerjat, 1869

∼ 5 *JANUARY* ∼

COMPANY IN THE KITCHEN

Got up at half past seven. Had a great deal of work to do this morning with cleaning lamps, knives and plate. All our people dine out. They go to the old lady's marreyd daughter who lives in Belgrave Square. Went at five o'clock and stayed until eleven. I went to see my friends; also got home at ten, found company in the kitchen, drank elder wine until eleven, went with the carriage and fetched home the gentry, got to bed by twelve.

William Tayler, *Diary*, 1837

POLICEMEN GETTING YOUNGER

Frost and fog today. Curious romantic scenes around the Round Pond, its centre lost in fog, and exotic birds wheeling in and out of the unseen, and slipping on the ice when grabbing at food thrown at them. Sparrows hopping amongst them. Chatted with a policeman at the corner this morning. Evidently very young. So young and fresh that the only really policemanish thing about him was his uniform. A sort of man dressed up as a policeman. I have noticed this before in young policemen, but have never defined it so well.

Arnold Bennett, *Journal*, 1908

AN ISLINGTON MUSIC HALL

In afternoon saw Nora [Stapleton] and we called on the Faasens at Spencer Park. Then we went to Islington to Manzi's for pies & mash. Then to the Collins Music Hall to see Peaches Page's Nude Show. It was crap. Hal Blue was the comic. Outrageous. The theatre is practically in ruins: the audience moronic. Alack a day.

Kenneth Williams, *Diary*, 1957

～ 6 *JANUARY* ～

CHASTISING POSTERIORS

There has been much discourse about the city of a Whipping Tom, who is used to bestow some pains in chastising the posteriors of severall females who have fallen into his hands: diverse have been severely handled by him; some of them have received great damage thereby; and there are two persons (one a haberdasher in Holborn) clapt up about it.

Narcissus Luttrell, *Diary*, 1682

EATING TWELFTH-CAKES

This was Twelfth-day, on which a great deal of jollity goes on in England, at the eating of the Twelfth-cake all sugared over . . . I took a whim that between St Paul's and the Exchange and back again, taking the different sides of the street, I would eat a penny Twelfth-cake at every shop where I could get it. This I performed most faithfully. I then dined comfortably at Dolly's Beefsteak-house. I regretted much my not being acquainted in some good opulent City family where I might participate in the hearty sociality over the ancient ceremony of the Twelfth-cake. I hope to have this snug advantage by this time next year.

James Boswell, *London Journal*, 1763

UNDER WATER IN WESTMINSTER

There was an unprecedented flood in London, owing to a high spring tide meeting the swollen river. Fourteen people were drowned, and the basement of the Tate Gallery, containing drawings by Turner and other matters, was submerged. The water swept over the Embankment and invaded the Houses of Parliament.

William Ralph Inge, *Diary*, 1928

～ 7 *JANUARY* ～

FROM THE TOWN TO THE CITY

Went through Temple Bar into the city in contradistinction to the West-end of London, always called town . . . If I looked with any feeling of wonder on the throngs at the West-end, more cause is there for it here. The shops stand, side by side, for entire miles. The accumulation of things is amazing. It would seem impossible that there can be purchasers for them all, until you consider what multitudes there are to buy; then, you are disposed to ask how the buyers can be supplied. In the middle of the streets, coal-waggons and others as large, carts, trucks, vehicles of every sort, loaded in every way, were passing. They were in two close lines, reaching farther than the eye could see, going reverse ways. The horses come so near to the foot-pavement, which is crowded with people, that their hoofs, and the great wheels of the waggons, are only a few inches from them. In this manner the whole procession is in movement, with its complicated noise. It confounds the senses to be among it all. You would anticipate constant accidents; yet they seldom happen. The fear of the law preserves order; moreover, the universal sense of danger if order were violated, prevents its violation. I am assured that these streets present the same appearance every day in the year, except Sundays, when solitude reigns.

Richard Rush, *Residence at the Court of London*, 1818

BEHIND BARS IN WANDSWORTH

I went to Wandsworth Jail yesterday morning. The Governor was a splendid type of person. He took me round himself through every cranny of the place. It is rather ghastly – not that they could make it better, but imprisonment is a ghastly thing. What is so touching are their possessions which they deliver up when they enter the prison. They take off their clothes and never see them again until they come out. But what is nice is that they clean and press the clothes for them before they are coming out so as to give them back their self-respect. I do not quite see how it could be more humane, but of course I went away feeling a beast and a brute.

Harold Nicolson, Letter to Vita Sackville-West, 1938

HAD UP FOR SPEEDING IN SOHO

Rotten and I are stopped walking through Soho. The police find some amphetamines on Rots, and he's bundled into a van and taken to West End Central.

Nils Stevenson, *Diary*, 1977

～ 8 JANUARY ～

MAKING LOVE ON THE FROZEN THAMES

Above Westminster the Thames is quite frosen over and the Archbishop came from Lambeth on twelfth day over the ice to the Court. Many fantasticall experiments are dayly put in practise, as certain youths burnt a gallon of wine upon the ice, and made all the passengers partakers; but the best is of an honest woman (they say) that had a great longing to have her husband get her with child upon the Thames.

John Chamberlain, Letter to Dudley Carleton, 1608

BUS TROUBLE

To the City. Omnibus horses, Ludgate Hill. The greasy state of the streets caused constant slipping. The poor creatures struggled and struggled but could not start the omnibus. A man next to me said: 'It must take all heart and hope out of them! I shall get out.' He did; but the whole remaining selfish twenty-five of us sat on. The horses despairingly got us up the hill at last. I ought to have taken off my hat to him and said: 'Sir, though I was not stirred by your humane impulse I will profit by your example'; and have followed him. I should like to know that man; but we shall never meet again.

Thomas Hardy, *Diary*, 1889

A CAR JOURNEY TO THE CAPITAL

Back to London by motor with Nelly, horrible method of getting about, train far better.

Viscount Sandhurst, *Diary*, 1915

THE DIFFICULTIES OF KEEPING A LONDON DIARY

Work fruitlessly superficially futilely upon the Londoner's Diary. The difficulty is that the only news I get is from friends and that is just the news that I can't publish.

Harold Nicolson, *Diary*, 1930

RUSHING TO OXFORD STREET

Malcolm [McLaren] rang with a 1000 things to do. End of quiet day at home. I just half sorted things then rushed off – if you can call a 137 bus rushing. Knightsbridge took about half an hour to get through & Oxford Street was as packed as before Christmas.

Sophie Richmond, *Diary*, 1977

～ *9 January* ～

A FROST FAIR

I went across the Thames on the ice, now become so thick as to bear not only streets of booths, in which they roasted meat, and had divers shops of wares, quite across as in a town, but coaches, carts, and horses passed over. So I went from Westminster stairs to Lambeth, and dined with the Archbishop: where I met my Lord Bruce, Sir George Wheeler, Colonel Cooke, and several divines. After dinner and discourse with his Grace till evening prayers, Sir George Wheeler and I walked over the ice from Lambeth stairs to the Horse-ferry.

John Evelyn, *Diary*, 1684

BURGLARS ABOUT IN THE WEST END

I could not go sleep last night till past two, and was waked before three by a noise of people endeavouring to break open my window. For a while I would not stir, thinking it might be my imagination; but hearing the noise continued, I rose and went to the window, and then it ceased. I went to bed again, and heard it repeated more violently; then I rose and called up the house, and got a candle: the rogues had lifted up the sash a yard; there are great sheds before my windows, although my lodgings be a storey high; and if they get upon the sheds they are almost even with my window. We observed their track, and panes of glass fresh broken. The watchmen told us to-day they saw them, but could not catch them. They attacked others in the neighbourhood about the same time, and actually robbed a house in Suffolk Street, which is the next street but one to us. It is said they are seamen discharged from service.

Jonathan Swift, *The Journal to Stella*, 1712

FEMALE MUDLARKS IN THE THAMES

Went across Hungerford Bridge and round by Blackfriars bridge at 3 . . . It was bitter cold. Yet some divers – noble looking fellows – were working at the piles of the new bridge, & down by Blackfriars several female mud-larks were wading, barefoot and thigh deep, under the barges through the frozen ice covered mud. One, a young woman, with simious face and creel on back, stood by me as I looked over the rails down the Whitefriars dock, considering her chances of stray coal; then . . . she waded through mire and water, among dead cats and broken crockery, towards the river, until, stooping almost double, she disappeared in the mud and darkness under the side of a coal barge.

Arthur Munby, *Diary*, 1861

METROPOLITAN MISERY

Days too miserable to chronicle. Weather foggy and rainy. Went to the British Museum, and there chanced to meet Joseph Anderton.

George Gissing, *Diary*, 1897

∼ *10 JANUARY* ∼

HATING THE LONDON CHARIVARI

Notwithstanding of all the caressing I have met with, which is perfectly ridiculous, I hate London, and I do not think that either flattery or profit can ever make me love it. It is so boundless that I cannot for my life get out of it, nor can I find any one place that I want. But there is one great comfort, and it is the only one that cheers me, I shall soon get out of it and return to my dear family, as my friends Cunningham, Lockhart, and Pringle are going to take the charge of the press off my hands, and I have arrangements made for each volume which will take some time, and which I can only do here where every scattered fragment can be laid hold of; but when my time has been so much cut up I have got very little done indeed. I never get home before three in the morning, and have been very much in the same sort of society . . . the list of the great literary names and those of artists would of itself fill up this whole letter . . . It is almost a miracle that I keep my health so well, considering the life I lead, for I am out at parties every night until far into the morning − great literary dinner − I am sure I have received in the last three days three hundred invitations to dinner, and I am afraid I have accepted too many of them − I positively won't come to London again without you.

James Hogg, letter to his wife Margaret, 1832

SHATTERED IN AMEN COURT

A terrific explosion at Woolwich, nine miles off, broke several windows in Amen Court, and shook down ornaments from chimney-pieces.

William Ralph Inge, *Diary*, 1917

SORDID OLD STREET

At 2 o'c. I walked through the city to Shoreditch & returned via Old Street, Goswell Road, and Mount Pleasant. Some of the areas are utterly sordid and the soulless concrete blocks which are replacing the old slums have an equally depressing effect on the environment. I saw one schoolboy wandering along, lost in a world of his imagination, & I thought, 'Romantic dreams have given such hope to so many young people who have to grow up in aesthetically revolting surroundings, and I ought to know, because I was one of them.' When you see the filth and squalor of the East End you marvel that the year is 1972! One has come all this way, and supposed there had been civic enlightenment, but here it is as dark as ever. Called at the chemist at King's Cross & the assistant said 'You are looking peaky!' which irritated me & I replied 'I have suffered many things.' She said 'What things?' & I said 'Things that cannot be discussed with you.' I got the Gerval & left.

Kenneth Williams, *Diary*, 1972

TOWING CARS IN CAMDEN

The newly privatized tow-away trucks are now operating in Camden and make regular visits to our street. The crews display fearsome zeal, scrambling to get the slings and chains around the offending car before the owner (just doing five minutes' shopping in the market) returns. They are like a gang of executioners hurrying the victim to his doom before a reprieve arrives.

The pound is only at the top of the street, and the crews find it handier (and, if they are on piecework, more profitable) to tow our cars away than go questing for them in the outlying areas of the borough.

That the operation is on the dubious boundary between commerce and law enforcement could be deduced from the jaunty demeanour of the policeman in charge, who wears his flat cap tilted to the back of his head. 'Distancing', the late Erving Goffmann would have called it, the cap enough to call the whole activity into question.

Alan Bennett, *Diary*, 1988

~ 11 JANUARY ~

HITTING THE DIRT AFTER HYDE PARK

We arrived yesterday at Richmond. This morning I set out myself for *town*, as London is called *par excellence*, in a stage-coach, crammed inside, and *herissé* outside with passengers, of all sexes, ages and conditions. We stopped more than twenty times on the road — the debates about the fare of way-passengers — the settling themselves — the getting up, and the getting down, and the damsels shewing their legs in the operations, and tearing and muddying their petticoats — complaining and swearing — took an immense time. I never saw any thing so ill managed. In about two hours we reached Hyde Park corner; I liked the appearance of it; but we were soon lost in a maze of busy, smoky, dirty, streets, more and more so as we advanced. A sort of uniform dinginess seemed to pervade everything, that is, the exterior; for through every door and window the interior of the house, the shops at least, which are most seen, presented as we drove along, appearances and colours most opposite this dinginess; everywhere was clean, fresh and brilliant. The elevated pavement on each side of the streets full of walkers, out of the reach of carriages, passing swiftly in two lines, without awkward interference, each taking to the left. At last a very indifferent street brought us in front of a magnificent temple, which I knew immediately to be St Paul's, and I left the vehicle to examine it. The effect was wonderfully beautiful; but it had less vastneess than grace and magnificence. The colour struck me as strange — very black and very white, in patches which envelope sometimes half a column; the base of one, the capital of another — here a whole row quite black — there, as white as chalk. It seemed as if there had been a fall of snow, and it adhered unequally. I had not time for any long examinations, and felt uneasy and helpless in the middle of an immense town, of which I did not know a single street. A hackney-coach seemed to be the readiest way to extricate myself.

Louis Simond, *Journal of a Tour and Residence in Great Britain, During the Years 1810 and 1811*, 1810

BREECHED IN SOUTHWARK

Morning, wore knee breeches for first time. A terrible bother we had to get them on and make them meet at the knee and button. Started for St John Southwark fully equipped (costume, beginning uppermost: high-crowned broad-brimmed hat, black frock coat, strait-collared waistcoat with brass buttons, drab breeches with covered buttons and silver buckles at knees, speckled worsted stockings, shoes with straps and buckles to the same, white neckhandkerchief with plain fronted shirt); but found that I had been to the church about three weeks previous, viz St John Horslydown. Returned home through the City, Clare Market etc, rather quizzed by some but minded it not. Afternoon, bullock's heart for dinner, after which I took walk with Ann Fox to Hyde Park and Kensington Gardens etc, returned home to tea about half past 6 o'clock. Eliza, otherwise Ann Thomas, came to Richmonds Buildings for a short time after which I accompanied her to an acquaintance at 101 Chancery Lane. There was I kept waiting half an hour after which I accompanied her to her home, 22 St James's Street. Pretty good sweating, walked in all about 22 miles. Met Mr Perry, father of the now celebrated John, in Newport Market. Paid into bank 20s, making total £15.

Nathaniel Bryceson, *Diary*, 1846

A DODO IN CAMDEN TOWN

Afterwards on to Camden Town to see some Moa bones at Mr Bartlett's, for sale, the price required £25. A good femur, tibia, and tarso metatarsal; the rest very poor; many seal's bones. Saw the admirable restoration of the Dodo by Mr B. made of feathers from various birds; claws, scales of the legs etc. ought to be in the British Museum.

Gideon Mantell, *Journal*, 1850

FOXES IN KENNINGTON

Awakened at 4am by terrible, murderous screeching. Put my head outside the door to find two foxes who had apparently been fighting, though neither seemed the worse for wear. A few minutes later a third fox put his head round the corner, but made off when he saw me. All this, only 50 yards from the national headquarters of the Countryside Alliance.

Chris Mullin, *Decline and Fall: Diaries*, 2006

∼ 12 January ∼

NO QUESTION OF MARRIAGE

With Mr. Martyr in his postchaise to London, to Clare, and drank tea with him. To Drury Lane playhouse, but could not get in, so we went to the Robin Hood Society, and stayed till after 10. The question was, whether the increase of unmarried people was owing to the men's greater bashfulness, or women's greater coyness, than formerly.

William Bray, *Diary*, 1756

ICED UP ON THE RIVER

Such a severe winter has not been known since 1814, when I remember my Mother taking me to see the Thames which was frozen over, and a Fair held upon it.

Louisa Bain, *Diary*, 1861

THE WASTES OF CROMWELL ROAD

Reading Gide – the best antidote possible to the triumphant commonplace of an English Sunday. Not even the Blitzkrieg has been able to break the spell which the Sabbath casts over the land. One could not fail by just putting one's head out of the window and smelling and looking and listening for two minutes to recognize that this is Sunday. In my mind's eye I can see the weary wastes of the Cromwell Road beneath a sullen sky where a few depressed pedestrians straggle as though lost in an endless desert. One's soul shrinks from the spectacle.

Charles Ritchie, *The Siren Years:*
A Canadian Diplomat Abroad 1937–45, 1940

～ 13 JANUARY ～

A DUE PLAGUE OF GOD

On Sunday the stage at Paris Garden fell down all at once, being full of people beholding the bearbaiting. Many being killed thereby, more hurt, and all amazed. The godly expound it as a due plague of God for the wickedness there used, and the Sabbath day so profanely spent.

John Dee, *Diary*, 1583

BARBARY HORSES IN HYDE PARK

The Morocco ambassador, with his attendants, went into Hide park, and mounted their Barbary horses, where they shewed great activity in managing the same, and their dexterity in shooting, his majesty doing them the honour to see them perform the same.

Narcissus Luttrell, *Diary*, 1682

A SMALLPOX EPIDEMIC

The Thames was frozen over. The deaths by smallpox increased to five hundred more than in the preceding week. The King and Princess Anne reconciled, and she was invited to keep her Court at Whitehall, having hitherto lived privately at Berkeley House; she was desired to take into her family divers servants of the late Queen; to maintain them the King has assigned her £5,000 a quarter.

John Evelyn, *Diary*, 1695

REGENTS PARK IS YOU

The other day I walked in, and all round, Regents Park. I hadn't for ages. Already small green buds are coming out on some of the bushes. I wish you and I'd made time to walk in this park when you were last in London. A particular gentle tract of our happiness belongs to it —

walks after lunch, walks when we were coming back here to this house for tea. So much so that the park has become you for me.

Elizabeth Bowen, Letter to Charles Ritchie, 1950

∼ 14 JANUARY ∼

MYSTERIOUS MURTHERS

A barbarous murther was committed in Brookstreet, by Ratcliffe, where an antient gentlewoman, a maid and a child, were all found killed and the house rifled; but not known by whom.

Narcissus Luttrell, *Diary*, 1691

PREACHING AT NEWGATE GAOL

I visited the condemned malefactors in Newgate, and was locked in by the turnkey, not with them, but in the yard. However I stood upon a bench, and they climbed up to the windows of their cells; so that all could hear my exhortation and prayer.

John Wesley, *Journal*, 1743

PANTO SEASON

In the evening I went with Thomas to the Alhambra formerly the Panopticon. It is now converted into a circus and is very different to what it was when last I saw it, but the organ is still there. I saw the two celebrated mules 'Pete' & 'Barney'. A reward of a guinea was offered to anyone who would ride round the ring three times. Several boys attempted it but they were all thrown off. There was afterwards a Pantomyme entitled the 'Miser of Bagdad' but it was very stupid.

Rafe Neville Leycester, *Diary*, 1859

HONEST POPLAR

A cyclist in Poplar dropped his wallet. Four boys saw the wallet dropped. They called out but the cyclist didn't hear so they took it to the post office. It contained forty pounds in notes. They were just leaving when in came the cyclist seeking his wallet. He was able to convince the post office people it was his. He gave the four boys one halfpenny each! Honesty is the *best* policy . . . outside Poplar?

Fred Bason, *Diary*, 1928

～ 15 *JANUARY* ～

A WALK ON WIMBLEDON COMMON

I corrected the last sheets of 'Adam Bede', and we afterwards walked to Wimbledon to see our new house, which we have taken for seven years. I hired the servant – another bit of business done: and then we had a delightful walk across Wimbledon Common and through Richmond Park homeward. The air was clear and cold – the sky magnificent.

George Eliot, *Journal*, 1858

DISAPPOINTING ISLINGTON

Yesterday afternoon I suddenly decided that I couldn't proceed with my story about Elsie until I had been up to Clerkenwell again. So at 4.50 I got a taxi and went up Myddleton Square. Just before turning left into this square I saw a blaze of light with the sacred name of Lyons at the top in fire, far higher than anything else; also a cinema sign, etc, making a glaring centre of pleasure. I said, surely that can't be the Angel, Islington, and I hoped it might be some centre that I had never heard of or didn't know of. However, the old chauffeur said of course it was Islington. Rather a disappointment.

Arnold Bennett, *Journal*, 1924

ST PAUL'S, EVER STABLE

I had a rest and then walked to St James, the Embankment, City, Fleet St., Clifford's Inn to Gray's Inn, bus from there to Gt. Portland St & walked home. The day was cold but not dauntingly so, and the sun shone bravely over Waterloo Bridge . . . St Paul's gleaming in the afternoon's glow . . . oh! it looked beautiful . . . it looked as if nothing could ever go wrong . . . utterly stable, tranquil & permanent.

Kenneth Williams, *Diary*, 1981

WINTER SPORTS

The 'Winter of Misery' (LBC this morning) is into its fifth day. Snow remains uncleared in Oak Village and there is no rubbish collection. Don the gloves and woolly hat and run into the bitter wind. Plenty of children on Parliament Hill sledging on everything from proper sledges (very rare) to plastic red and white striped barriers pinched from roadworks abandoned during the bad weather. Arrive home glowing.

Michael Palin, *Diaries*, 1987

∼ *16 January* ∼

SNAKE ABOUT BOND STREET

Rattle Snake I went to see in Bond St. It was caught 8th of May last in South Carolina. A maid servant with a child in her arms heard its rattle in her masters garden. It was caught alive by a noose being thrown over its head. It is about 9 feet long, and can coil itself up so as to be a foot in thickness round the Body. Its eyes are aways open it having no eye lids. The Rattle at the end of the tale is always erect. This Rattle is not formed so as to sound till the animal is 3 years old. The Bones which form the Rattle are a continuation of the Vertebrae, and it is not by shaking but by a thrilling irritation that the sound is caused. I thought the sound something like the chirping of a bird, but the man better observed that it resembled the running down of a clock. The Rattle Snake has upper teeth only formed in a Curve which when the mouth is closed are rec'd into sockets. The teeth of this Snake, are an Inch long. Sometime since a Rabbit was put into the Cage, which beginning to leap abt the Snake darted a bite at it, and the Rabbit falling died in a minute. The wounds were very small resembling such as would be made by large needles. Near the orifices of the wounds the flesh immediately smoked & fermented as if it were boiling. Some gentlemen wishing to dissect the Rabbit found when they attempted to clear away the Skin that the Flesh came away in pieces. The man told me that the bites of a Rattle Snake will produce their effect 10 or 11 times after which the poison is exchanged. Sometimes when enraged the animal will bite itself, which proves mortal. It appeared evident to me, as the man asserted, that this Snake had sagacity to know him, & to be sensible when required to rattle. This Snake is known by the number of his rattles to be abt. 11 years old. They have been proved to have lived 50 years. The Colour is dark and dusky, with black spots. The Rattle Snake only takes food once or twice a year. This Snake has not taken any food since it was caught in May last. A basin of water was placed in the cage which it drinks occasionally. Food has been offered it. It has no evacuations but by perspiration. The Scales on the belly are hard, those on the back softer.

Joseph Farington, *Diary*, 1797

A BUG RIFE AMONG BOBBIES

The Influenza was never known to be so bad as it is now. Seven hundred policemen and upwards of four thousand soldiers are ill with it about London, and many large shops and manufactorys are put to great inconveniences on account of it. I am obliged to stay within to help the sick. This is what I don't like as I like to get a run everyday when I can.

William Tayler, *Diary*, 1837

~ *17 JANUARY* ~

NATIVE AMERICANS IN LONDON

Being so close to the Egyptian Hall we took the opportunity of witnessing the exhibition of the Ojibbeway Indians in Catlin's rooms.* One of them was ill, so we only saw eight, viz. the two old men or chiefs, two younger warriors, the interpreter, two women, and a girl. They gave us some of their dances, sham fight etc but I must say I was disappointed at the result. The interpreter did not speak a syllable the whole time, and is one of the stupidest looking persons I ever saw. Altogether, it was a very dear five shillings worth. We remained about an hour and a quarter, and as soon as the ceremony of shaking hands commenced, we retreated, as I had no ambition to grasp the palm of a dirty savage.

Sir Frederic Madden, Diary, 1844

* The American artist and showman George Catlin, one of the first men to paint portraits of Native Americans, toured Europe with both his paintings and some of their subjects in the 1830s and 1840s.

A POSTCODE LOTTERY

A new regulation . . . London and its vicinity has been divided into 10 districts, North, South, etc.; ours is West, extending from New Road (Marylebone Road) to Piccadilly; and our letter is to be placed at the end of the address and on all letters and cards, etc. It has scarcely yet become universally attended to; tho' they say people are trying to do their duty!

Annie Elizabeth Fisher, unpublished journal, 1857

～ 18 JANUARY ～

A PANORAMA OF DUBLIN IN LONDON

Arose before seven. Read the fourth and fifth acts of 'The two Gentlemen of Verona.' Wrote a note to Mess. Fielding and Sharp, of Queenstreet, Cheapside. After breakfast read the first act of 'The Merry Wives of Windsor.' Went with Mrs. Cooke to the corner of Leicester Square, and viewed the Panoramas of Dublin and Gibraltar. They appear to be well executed. The first, taking in a view of the River Liffey, from Essex bridge to below the custom-house, with the shipping &c, Carlisle bridge, a small part of Trinity college, and another of the late Parliament house, Westmoreland street – the quays – Foundling hospital, &c. recalled the city strongly to my mind. The latter place I never saw, but it is a varied, and seems a beautiful view. During the evening finished 'The Merry Wives, &c.'

George Frederick Cooke, *Journal*, 1809

A LION IN DRURY LANE

I dined early with my sister at Alexander's, and went to Drury Lane to see Van Amburgh with his lions; but we stayed too long at dinner, and got there only just in time to see the man coming out of the den and the lion springing after him as he shut the cage. The beast seemed very savage, and what I saw of the strange sight made me wish to go again. I had to sit out a pantomime and farce and ballet, which I have not done for years. The dancing seemed much improved since I saw it last at Drury Lane, but I could make nothing of the farce.

John Cam Hobhouse, *Diary*, 1839

THE ITALIAN OPERA HOUSE IN COVENT GARDEN

I went to see Covent Garden Theatre, which is being newly constructed for an Italian Opera House. It was a very curious spectacle. M. Albano, the architect, showed it to me. It took them fourteen days to pull down the parts they wished to remove, so strongly was it built. Charles Kemble told me tonight the theatre had cost 300,000l.; that 100,000l. of this, his money and that of his family, had been sunk in the concern, and he should be very glad to sell his share of it for 10,000l.

Henry Greville, *Diary*, 1841

～ *19 JANUARY* ～

A BUSY DAY

To the Comptroller's, and with him by coach to White Hall; in our way meeting Venner and Pritchard upon a sledge, who with two more Fifth Monarchy men were hanged to-day, and the two first drawn and quartered. Where we walked up and down, and at last found Sir G. Carteret, whom I had not seen a great while, and did discourse with him about our assisting the Commissioners in paying off the Fleet, which we think to decline. Here the Treasurer did tell me that he did suspect Thos. Hater to be an informer of them in this work, which we do take to be a diminution of us, which do trouble me, and I do intend to find out the truth. Hence to my Lady, who told me how Mr. Hetley is dead of the small-pox going to Portsmouth with my Lord. My Lady went forth to dinner to her father's, and so I went to the Leg in King Street and had a rabbit for myself and my Will, and after dinner I sent him home and myself went to the Theatre, where I saw 'The Lost Lady,' which do not please me much. Here I was troubled to be seen by four of our office clerks, which sat in the half-crown box and I in the 1s. 6d. From thence by link, and bought two mouse traps of Thomas Pepys, the Turner, and so went and drank a cup of ale with him, and so home and wrote by post to Portsmouth to my Lord and so to bed.

Samuel Pepys, *Diary*, 1661

~ 20 *JANUARY* ~

SCOTCH GAME IN ST JAMES'S

Dined at Blake's Hotel, St James's, on grouse, which I killed myself on the borders of the Highlands of Scotland this very day week.

Colonel Peter Hawker, *Diary*, 1813

DEATH IN REGENT'S PARK

More than forty bodies have been got up from under the ice in the Regent's Park since last Tuesday when the fearful accident happened: it seems incredible, but while the drags are working to get up the dead bodies men are crowding on the ice, skating and sliding.

Louisa Bain, *Diary*, 1867

VANISHING NW5

The houses around Lismore Circus are fast disappearing – Gospel Oak is being laid waste. I get the feeling that Oak Village is like a trendy ghetto, hanging on for dear life, until the mighty storm of 'civic' redevelopment is over and we walk once again in a neighbourhood free of noise and mud and lorries and corrugated iron and intimate little rooms with pink flowered wallpaper suddenly exposed by the bulldozer. It will probably be another two years before there is any semblance of order from all this chaos – by then I'll be 28 and Helen will be 29 and Thomas will be three and going to nursery school.

Michael Palin, *Diary*, 1970

∼ 21 JANUARY ∼

FROST FAIR ON THE FROZEN THAMES

Afternoon I went to London Bridge & saw booths & shops as farr as the Temple but they say there is booths to Chelsey, & below Bridge from about the Tower booths & many huts & people crossed over. There was they say 2 oxes roasted.

Peter Briggins, *Diary*, 1716

SWARMING WITH GERMAN PRINCES

The town is swarming with German princes.* There are five or six Prussians, the Saxe-Coburgs, a Prince of Baden, and the King of the Belgians with his two sons. The Queen took them in sixteen carriages to the old Opera House, where the tragedy of *Macbeth* was drawled out by some third-rate actors, and last night gave a ball to which I was invited, but did not go.

Henry Greville, *Diary*, 1858

* For the wedding of Princess Victoria, eldest child of Victoria and Albert, to Frederick William of Prussia.

IT'S ONLY LONDON

To the Serpentine Gallery for an exhibition of photographs by André Kertesz. The park is empty, the sun warm, and the Albert Memorial is glinting through the trees. If this were New York I would be revelling in such a morning, but it's only London. Few people in exhibition, just one or two students and an old couple discussing the human interest of the pictures.

Alan Bennett, *Diary*, 1980

～ 22 *J* ANUARY ～

NOT SO MIGHTY LONDON

This Diary reads for all the world as if I were not living in mighty London. The truth is I live in a bigger, dirtier city – ill-health. Ill-health, when chronic, is like a permanent ligature around one's life. What a fine fellow I'd be if I were perfectly well. My energy for one thing would lift the roof off . . .

We conversed around the text: 'To travel hopefully is better than to arrive and true success is to labour.' She is – well, so graceful. My God! I love her, I love her, I love her!!!

W. N. P. Barbellion, *Diary of a Disappointed Man*, 1913

A CITY IN MOURNING FOR ITS MONARCH

Every flag was at half-mast yesterday except Buckingham Palace where there was no flag at all, there being no sovereign. The town like a Sunday; all theatres and cinemas closed and all public functions abandoned. Dined quietly at the Langham with Moray McLaren and Rose Troup and at 9.30 went across to Broadcasting House to hear the Prime Minister. Very good and well-delivered. Moray said the speech was for all Europe as well as England – 'Hitler and the boys will be listening.' When Baldwin spoke of the Prince of Wales and his tremendous responsibilities, there came into his voice or I thought so, just a hint of the Lord Chief Justice, of Henry IV, Part 2 Act V, Sc. 2.

James Agate, *Journals*, 1936

AN OLD BAILEY TRIAL

I have been – in fact still am, for there will be 2 more days of this week before it finishes – sitting through a murder trial at the Old Bailey. I am there representing the R Commission on CP [Capital Punishment]. This is not a thing anybody would do for pleasure, one would have thought, though as a matter of fact any spare accommodation in the

Court is packed with what journalists called well-dressed women. The thing I can't get used to is that the whole inside of the Court we're in is like the inside of Harrods – light oak panelling. Edwardian baroque plaster ceilings (extremely clean) and tasteful lighting. It's small, and doesn't hold many people. The acoustics are bad.

The man on trial is [Donald] Hume, 29-year-old, charged with the murder of [Stanley] Setty, a Jewish dealer in second-hand cars. I'm relieved to find that one is far less conscious of the prisoner, and that he – or at any rate this particular young man – is so riveted by the to-and-fro of the trial that he seems unconscious of himself. His head turns to and fro, as though he were watching tennis.

I don't know whether you read the Hume–Setty case? Everything happened early last October. Settty disappeared, and dismembered portions of him were found in the Essex marshes, having been parcelled up and dropped from a plane. Hume – who had been making a living by air-smuggling – admits to having dropped the parcels (to oblige friends who gave him cash down for the job) but swears he had no idea what was in the parcels. The police claim Hume stabbed Setty to death in his (Hume's) Finchley Rd flat, in order to rob him.

Elizabeth Bowen, Letter to Charles Ritchie, 1950

GOOD NEWS FOR LONDON

The London *Standard* has been bought by a Russian oligarch. Someone from *Guardian Online* rang to ask if I thought this was a threat to free speech. 'Can't be worse than the Rothermeres,' I replied. Later, in the Tea Room, Bruce Grocott held up the early edition of tonight's *Standard*. The headline was 'Good news: gas prices cut by 10 per cent.' 'When was the last time you saw good news on the front of the *Standard*?' When indeed?

Chris Mullin, *Decline and Fall: Diaries*, 2009

～ 23 *JANUARY* ～

A COVENT GARDEN COMEDY

Went to Covent Garden to see a new esteemed fashionable Comedy from the pen of Mr. Morton, Cure for the Heart Ache. If I did not know to what a miserable ebb The Drama is reduced, I should have been surprized to see so many people sit so long and patiently to hear such Stuff! – A collection of Trash just calculated to hit the depraved state of the Times. Coming from Bedford some weeks ago with Mr. Maddox, the Brewer, and speaking of Beer he said, 'As long as you continue to drink the Liquor which we give you for Beer, we shall never brew you better.' And so I fear it is with the drama. As long as the Town can listen to, and laugh at, such stuff as The Cure &c there is very little chance for the revival of chaste and ancient Comedy.

George Mackenzie Macaulay, *The War Diary of a London Scot*, 1797

NEW AMUSEMENTS IN MARBLE ARCH

I am making things much easier for myself in London by working hard and by not seeing more than two or three people each day. If I can keep this up & then if I can find a bedfellow this life should be quite bearable till May. It is infinitely better now that we have left that huge house. Bed-sitting rooms are much nicer than several rooms because one is always in same atmosphere, so I find I can always take up anything I am working at at anytime and go on with it . . . I spend most of my evenings in the Amusement Park near Marble Arch or the Haymarket. London seems much improved. The other day a cissy friend of Humphrey's got off a bus, and as he alighted the conductor smirked & said, 'What a short ride you've been,' so Eddy said 'Never mind, I'll come a longer one next time.' Two days later I went to Sadler's Wells with my sister. I didn't know whether we were in the right tube for Angel, so I held out our tickets to the collector and said 'Angel?' in a querying voice. 'I am,' he replied with an enticing smile.

Stephen Spender, Letter to Christopher Isherwood, 1933

～ *24 JANUARY* ～

THE INHABITANTS OF LONDON

We are at last established in London, in furnished lodgings, very near Portman Square, a fashionable part of town. A previous study of the map has made me sufficiently acquainted with the town to find my way to every part of it, by means of two principal avenues, Piccadilly and the Strand, Oxford Street and Holborn, which unite St Paul's, whence, as from a common centre, they separate again, to form two other great avenues, Cornhill and Bishopsgate Street: they are the arteries of this great body, and all other streets are the veins, branching out in all directions. It is easier to acquire a practical knowledge of the geography of London than Paris, which has not the same rallying points, except the Seine, which divides Paris more equally than it does London; the other side of the Thames is only an extensive suburb, whereas the other side of the Seine is half Paris. The people of London, I find, are quite as disposed to answer obligingly to the questions of strangers as those of Paris.

The inhabitants of London, such as they are seen in the streets, have, as well as the outside of their houses, a sort of dingy, smoky look; not dirty absolutely – for you generally perceive clean linen – but the outside garments are of a dull, dark cast, and harmonize with mud and smoke. Prepossessed with a high opinion of English corpulency, I expected to see everywhere the original of *Jacques Roast-beef.* No such thing; the human race is here rather of mean stature – less, so perhaps, than the true Parisian race; but there is really no great difference; and I have met more than once with Sterne's little man, when, in turning round to help a child across the gutter, he saw with surprise a visage of fifty where he expected to see one of five.

Louis Simond, *Journal of a Tour and Residence in Great Britain, During the Years 1810 and 1811*, 1810

HOPELESS SHADWELL

Went off with dear Father to the opening of 'Paddy's Goose' as a Mission by Rev. Peter Thompson. We got out at Shadwell Station, was struck by the hopeless look of the place, the despairing dissoluteness. Passing by St George's Chapel and the nice grounds now laid out for the people, we came into the notorious Ratcliffe Highway and to the equally notorious 'Paddy's Goose' or the 'White Swan' public house. We found Mr. Thompson there. What a cheery man he is. We saw the Coffee Bar and first Music Hall now fitted up for meetings, and the second Hall above where extensive preparations were going on for three tea meetings, women's, children's and men's. We saw on this floor the comfortable sitting-rooms fitted up for the young man workers, and above that, the bedrooms, and above again, the plank bridge over which many a thief has escaped! It was indeed thrilling! Father and I then strolled down to the Docks and looked around, then came back to the women's meeting . . . Serious rumours of a war on the continent.

Helen G. McKenny, *City Road Diary*, 1887

WAX WORKS IN MARYLEBONE

To Madame Tussaud's, with the Sheriffs, Miss Treloar, Miss Crosby, and Miss Dunn, to a poor children's treat. They had tea at many tables in the rooms with the wax figures. The children cheered loud enough almost to wake up the figures.

Sir William Treloar, *A Lord Mayor's Diary*, 1907

~ 25 JANUARY ~

GETTING OUT OF TOWN FOR THE DAY

Been to Hamstead with the carriage. It's about six or seven miles out of London. It's where a great many Cockneys goes to gipseying and to ride on the jackasses. It's a very plesent place.

William Tayler, *Diary*, 1837

SUBURBAN HIGHGATE

Went to Highgate to spend the evening. The suburbs! O, how dead they seem! We wonder, Jack and I, how we ever could have lived in them! Give us the City with its pulsating life, its need, its misery even, rather than the self-indulgent calm of suburban life!

Helen G. McKenny, *City Road Diary*, 1887

BORING ST PAUL'S

The annual St Paul's dinner. The speeches, including mine, were so bad that I hope we shall drop them. The Bishop of Kensington and the Dean of Rochester were the worst of a bad lot.

William Ralph Inge, *Diary*, 1922

CONTEMPORARY CAFE REPARTEE, CHARING CROSS ROAD

After viewing Mr Nicholson Senior's art at the RA, I sit in Borders Books Cafe, Charing Cross Road. The cafe is now a Starbucks, so I only use it if the one in Foyles (still an independent family business) is full up. And then, as I do in all Starbucks, I only ever order tea. Tea drinking as a revolutionary act, I like to think. The joke's on me, as their tea is revolting. Clever, very clever.

A young couple seated near to me are talking loudly to each other about 'gigs'.

It is only after some time that I realise it's not concerts they are discussing.

Neither is it 'gig' as in 'job', used in a spirit of matey modesty. As in 'I got the Spielberg gig.'

They are, in fact, discussing different types of *iPod*.

2005 London in a nutshell.

Dickon Edwards, *Diary*, 2005

～ 26 *JANUARY* ～

THE REMAINS OF OXFORD STREET

Yesterday afternoon went to London by Brighton to see Mrs Mantell, arrived at her mother's in Kentish Town at ten o'clock. Left her this morning at ten, with my brother Joshua; visited the Geological Society's rooms in Oxford Street, Covent Garden, and inspected the wonderful remains brought by Mr Crawford . . . They consist of vast quantities of silicified bones, teeth etc. of Mastodons, Crocodiles, Mammoths, Rhinoceroses etc., plates of turtle; vegetables etc.

Gideon Mantell, *Journal*, 1828

TRAVELLING ON THE DRAIN

Yesterday, Mary Anne and I made our first trip down the 'Drain'. We walked to the Edgware Road and took first-class tickets for King's Cross (6d each). We experienced no disagreeable odour, beyond the smell common to tunnels. The carriages hold ten persons, with divided seats, and are lighted by gas (two lights), they are also so lofty that a six-footer may stand erect with his hat on. Trains run every 15 minutes from six in the morning till twelve at night (with some slight variation) and about 30,000 are conveyed on the line daily: shares have risen, and there is a prospect of a large dividend.

Sir William Hardman, *Diary*, 1863

A GREAT GALE

Yesterday a great gale swept through London in the afternoon, tearing at roofs and scaffolding. The police, as usual, overreacted and closed off streets and by-ways at random, blocking motorists and shouting at pedestrians through loudhailers. The whole of Westminster and the West End went into 'gridlock' from tea-time until about nine pm, with angry and resentful drivers lurching and clutch-slipping up on to the pavement and abandoning their cars.

Alan Clark, *Diaries*, 1990

∼ 27 JANUARY ∼

CAPITAL PUNISHMENT

John Chapman told us that a woman convicted of clipping coin of the realm has been condemned and burned alive in the cattle market at Smithfield, London.

Sir Thomas Isham, *Diary*, 1672

A ROOM AT THE INN

Arrived in town about half-past nine; drove to the New Hummums, and had a warm bath . . . No room for me at my old lodgings in Duke Street; was forced to put up at the George, in Coventry Street. Dined in Paternoster Row . . . Rees and I went after dinner to the Sanspareil, and from thence to the pantomime at Covent Garden (Harlequin Munchausen), with which I was much amused.

Thomas Moore, *Diary*, 1819

A CHEQUE REMAINS UNCASHED

At a City branch of a certain bank yesterday morning two golden-haired girls with large feathered hats presented a piece of paper bearing a penny stamp and the words 'Please pay the bearer £2 10/- Henry T. Davies.' The cashier consulted his books and had to inform the ladies that Henry T. Davies had no account there. 'I don't know about that,' said one of them, 'but he slept with me last night, and he gave me this paper because he hadn't any cash. Didn't he, Clara?' 'Yes,' said Clara, 'that he did, and I went out this morning to buy the stamp for him.' The cashier commiserated with them, but they were not to be comforted.

Arnold Bennett, *Journal*, 1897

WITHDRAWING LABOUR IN W8

Holland Park School is on strike and there's a big poster in our window supporting the striking teachers. Hilary has written an article in the school magazine *Focus* and generally speaking we are right in the middle of it all, and *The Times* this morning made a reference to Hilary's article.

Tony Benn, *Diary*, 1970

~ 28 JANUARY ~

NEWGATE ORDINARIES

To-day Dr. Bedford, minister of Hoxton, came to see me, to complain of the scandal the playhouses give, by the blasphemous and obscene plays they act, also of the scandalous practice of the Ordinaries of Newgate and other prisons in obliging the prisoners to auricular confession, or declaring them damned if they refuse, which is only to extort from them an account of their lives, that they may afterwards publish the same to fill their printed papers and get a penny.

Earl of Egmont, *Diary*, 1730

OUT CLUBBING WITH A LONDON BEGGAR

To Infinity, for the club White Heat. The venue is in Old Burlington Street, a short walk from Piccadilly Circus. An unusual location for a nightclub, surrounded as it is by Mayfair offices, foreign embassies, and the homes of the impossibly wealthy . . .

I suppose I could score the art of nightclubbing on a budget with a points system. If I have to pay my way in and pay for all my own drinks, zero points. If I am on a discount list, where I still have to pay something, one point. Getting in for free: one more point. Free cloakroom treatment: quite rare, so three points. Being bought a drink, or given a free drink voucher, not nearly common enough for me, so two points per drink.

Tonight was a discount list affair, after some argument, plus a welcome drink from Ms Manga. I had to pay for the cloakroom. So, a three points evening. Not bad, and it means I can go out again this week . . .

Standing on Tottenham Court Road, snow starts to fall after all. It's really very beautiful, and Richard Curtis could put the scene in one of his popular films.

But then Real, Unfair, Cruel Life crashes into the frame. A bearded man collars me:

Man: Excuse me. I'm not a beggar, but . . . I've just got to get to Leyton. I only need TEN pee. Just TEN pee.

Me: Here you are, then. (Produces the coin.)

Man: . . . or a pound. Just a pound.

Me: You said ten pee! I don't have a pound!

Man walks off.

There's gratitude for you. Really, London beggars must learn a little consistency in their appeals. What can the unions be thinking of? I'm a London beggar myself, and all I ask is just one drink.

Dickon Edwards, *Diary*, 2004

∼ *29 JANUARY* ∼

THE ALLURE OF A NEW LIBRARY IN BRIXTON

A great public library is shortly to be opened in Brixton. One of Tate's gifts. They say it will be by far the best local library in London. Now that part, South Brixton, close to Clapham, is a high and healthy position, with tram and train to every part of town. Really, I don't know what to do. I simply must not go anywhere if there is not a good reading room to hand, as, in my personal isolation, I am so greatly dependent for material and suggestion of the daily and weekly papers.

George Gissing, Letter to his brother, 1893

FIRST NIGHT AT THE OPERA

First production of *Rosenkavalier* in England. Covent Garden. Began at 8.20 (20 minutes late) and finished at midnight with many cuts. Then 30 minutes' wait nearly, for motor in procession of motors. The thing was certainly not understood by stalls and grand circle. What its reception was in the amphitheatre and gallery I was too far off to judge. First act received quite coldly. Ovation as usual at end – and an explosive sort of shout when Thomas Beecham came to bow . . . An entirely false idea of this opera so far in England. Not sensual, nor perverse, nor depraved . . . It seemed to me to be a work of the first order.

Arnold Bennett, *Journal*, 1913

∼ *30 JANUARY* ∼

THE LONDON WATCHMEN

When the service was finished I took a walk on the other side of the river into the country as far as Stockwell which is a small village about 4 miles from London . . . Vauxhall Gardens are also here, which we passed by. We dined at Stockwell & returned home by another road. It was late in the evening & the lamps which extended from London to this place were lighted & formed a most august & beautiful appearance. At small distances watchmen armed with musquets are placed to prevent mischief & detect robberies & they have bells placed in such a manner as to give notice to each other by ringing them if any thing remarkable occurs, by which means they could readily come to each others assistance & be upon their guard to prevent the escape of any suspected person.

Joshua Wingate Weeks, *Diary*, 1779

ON PREFERRING LONDON TO
THE LAKE DISTRICT

I ought before this to have replied to your very kind invitation into Cumberland. With you and your sister I could gang anywhere; but I am afraid whether I shall ever be able to afford so desperate a journey. Separate from the pleasure of your company, I don't much care if I never see a mountain in my life. I have passed all my days in London, until I have formed as many and intense local attachments as any of you mountaineers can have done with dead nature. The lighted shops of the Strand and Fleet Street; the innumerable trades, tradesmen, and customers; coaches, wagons, playhouses; all the bustle and wickedness round about Covent Garden; the very women of the town; the watchmen, drunken scenes, rattles; life awake, if you awake, at all hours of the night; the impossibility of being dull in Fleet Street; the crowds, the very dirt and mud, the sun shining upon houses and pavements; the print-shops, the old-book stalls, parsons cheapening books; coffee-houses, steams of soups from kitchens; the pantomimes, London itself a pantomime and a masquerade, – all these things work themselves into my mind, and feed me without a power of satiating me. The wonder of these sights impels me into night-walks about her crowded streets, and I often shed tears in the motley Strand from fulness of joy at so much life. All these emotions must be strange to you; so are your rural emotions to me. But consider what must I have been doing all my life, not to have lent great portions of my heart with usury to such scenes?

My attachments are all local, purely local, – I have no passion (or have had none since I was in love, and then it was the spurious engendering of poetry and books) to groves and valleys. The rooms where I was born, the furniture which has been before my eyes all my life, a bookcase which has followed me about like a faithful dog (only exceeding him in knowledge), wherever I have moved; old chairs, old tables; streets, squares, where I have sunned myself; my old school, – these are my mistresses. Have I not enough without your mountains? I do not envy you. I should pity you, did I not know that the mind will make friends with anything. Your sun and moon, and skies and hills and lakes, affect me no more or scarcely come to be in more venerable characters, than as a gilded room with tapestry and tapers, where I might live with handsome visible objects. I consider the clouds above me but as a roof beautifully painted, but unable to satisfy the mind, and at last, like the pictures of the apartment of a connoisseur, unable to afford him any longer a pleasure. So fading upon me, from disuse, have been the beauties of Nature, as they have been confidently called; so ever fresh and green and warm are all the inventions of men and assemblies of men in this great city. I should certainly have laughed with dear Joanna.

Give my kindest love and my sister's to D. and yourself. And a kiss from me to little Barbara Lewthwaite. Thank you for liking my play!

Charles Lamb, Letter to William Wordsworth, 1801

OLD FASHIONED FULHAM

In the morning with father to Paddington where he took stage to Islington. I went to Gloster Coffee House, Oxford Street for the purpose of meeting Walmsley, who did not appear. Met my father at Gurney's. Called on Mortimer and Cocker and then to Walham Green. Papa left me at Carter's all night and as he and his daughter were to spend the evening at Fulham, I accompanied them to their friends there. It was quite dark when we arrived but I saw enough of the town to prepossess me strongly in its favour. I always loved anything ancient, and its old queer fashioned mansions with the irregular gables jutting into the street made me regret leaving the place without seeing more of it. We returned about 10 o'clk.

John Thomas Pocock, *Diary*, 1828

～ *31 January* ～

A CURE FOR LEPROSY

A very clear and pleasant day but cold. With Lord London's Dickens at Westminster Hall . . . Sir A King told me of a kinswoman of his which had a certain cure for a leprosy or Scaled head. She had £100 per annum of St Bartholomews hospitall to which she promised to leave receipt.

Robert Hooke, *Diary*, 1672

NO DECENT OLD WOMAN LEFT IN TOWN

We have variety of diversions this winter in town, operas, burlettas, (which are comic operas) are much admired, but I am so unfashionable to dislike them extremely. However, the girl that sings in them has charmed the Duke, but he has a powerful rival in Mr. Delaval, who declares he will give her his whole estate rather than lose her. You see what important affairs employ our great people here. Plays are in great perfection at Drury Lane, and my favourite diversion. As for fashions in dress, which you sometimes inquire after, they are too various to describe. One thing is new, which is, there is not such a thing as a decent old woman left, everybody curls their hair, shews their neck, and wears pink, but your humble servant. People who have covered their heads for forty years now leave off their caps and think it becomes them, in short we try to out-do our patterns, the French, in every ridiculous vanity. Lady Northumberland gave an entertainment last week, in which was an artificial goose in her feathers, and a hen with seven little chickens. The dessert was a landscape, with gates, stiles, and cornfields, but I have, I'm afraid, tired you with the account of such follies.

Lady Jane Coke, Letter to Mrs Eyre, 1754

A FIRST PEEP OF LONDON

I don't think you will ever forget that first peep of London, shall you? That walk about the City, the first glimpse of St Paul's with the sun on it, the view from the Hungerford Bridge, the view from the dome of St Paul's! You remember too, that glorious concert at the Albert Hall — perhaps that has slipped your memory?

George Gissing, Letter to his sister Ellen, 1886

GO TO SEA IN STEPNEY

Went to visit a group of Bengali women on the Ocean Estate, organized by Shaheda Chowdhury. As its name suggests, the Ocean Estate is seemingly endless. Row after row of enormous rectangular blocks, often ten storeys high, thrown up after the Blitz.

Oona King, *Diary*, 2005

FEBRUARY

～ 1 *FEBRUARY* ～

COCK-FIGHTING IN WESTMINSTER

We went to see a cock-fight, which lasted the whole of this week, where heavy bets, made by the Duke of Ancaster and others for more than 100 guineas, were at stake. The fight takes place at the Cock-pit, close to St. James's Park, in the vicinity of Westminster. In the middle of a circle and a gallery surrounded by benches, a slightly raised theatre is erected, upon which the cocks fight; they are a small kind of cock, to the legs of which a long spur, like a long needle, is fixed, with which they know how to inflict damage on their adversaries very cleverly during the fight, but on which also they are frequently caught themselves, so breaking their legs. One bird of each of the couples which we saw fighting met with this misfortune, so that he was down in a moment and unable to rise or to help himself, consequently his adversary at once had an enormous advantage. Notwithstanding this he fought him with his beak for half an hour, but the other bird had the best of it, and both were carried off with bleeding heads. No one who has not seen such a sight can conceive the uproar by which it is accompanied as everybody at the same time offers and accepts bets. You cannot hear yourself speak, and it is impossible for those who are betting to understand one another, therefore the men who take the bets, which are seldom even, but odds, such as 5 to 4, or 21 to 20, make themselves understood to the layers of the bets by signs.

Count Frederick Kielmansegge,
Diary of a Journey to England, 1762

A PENNY FOR THE (OLD) GUY

Morning, went to the Church of St Katherine Cree, Leadenhall Street. Had for dinner an unusual dish viz roasted hare, and I wish it to remain unusual, for it is poor, dry eating when compared with beef or mutton. Afternoon, took walk with Ann Fox up Maiden Lane to Highgate. From thence to Hampstead. Sat ourselves on a stone in the churchyard.

Returned by Hampstead Road etc. Homeward met George King and his brother Henry in Carlisle Street. He has lately left Nodes and is now in a lawyer's office. Saw a very aged man at the top of Maiden Lane near Copenhagen House, with a large placard on his breast stating his age to be 92 years. Gave him a penny for the curiosity of himself, for old age was written in his face and limbs. Paid into bank 20s, making total £16.

Nathaniel Bryceson, *Diary*, 1846

MANIPULATING LONDON RADICALS

London is in a ferment: strikes are the order of the day, the new trade unionism with its magnificent conquest of the docks is striding along with an arrogance rousing employers to a keen sense of danger, and to a determination to strike against strikes. The socialists, led by a small set of able young men (Fabian Society) are manipulating London Radicals, ready at the first check-mate of trade unionism to voice a growing desire for state action.

Beatrice Webb, *Diary*, 1890

～ 2 FEBRUARY ～

MARRIED IN THIS PARISH

My other dear daughter was this day married at Christchurch, St Marylebone, to the Rev. Lewis Playters Hird. I never felt anything more acutely than parting from this dear child, and may God be a Father to her wherever she goes. My family are now all disposed of, and I remain as the mere scaffold on which has for more than twenty years been building, as it were, the edifice of their education.

Colonel Peter Hawker, *Diary*, 1843

HORACE WALPOLE VISITS
THE COCK LANE GHOST

We set out from the Opera, changed our clothes at Northumberland-house, the Duke of York, Lady Northumberland, Lady Mary Coke, Lord Hertford, and I, all in one hackney coach, and drove to the spot: it rained torrents; yet the lane was full of mob, and the house so full we could not get in; at last they discovered it was the Duke of York, and the company squeezed themselves into one another's pockets to make room for us. The house, which is borrowed, and to which the ghost has adjourned, is wretchedly small and miserable; when we opened the chamber, in which were fifty people, with no light but one tallow candle at the end, we tumbled over the bed of the child to whom the ghost comes, and whom they are murdering by inches in such insufferable heat and stench. At the top of the room are ropes to dry clothes. I asked, if we were to have rope-dancing between the acts? We had nothing; they told us, as they would at a puppet-show, that it would not come that night till seven in the morning, that is, when there are only 'prentices and old women. We stayed however till half an hour after one. The Methodists have promised them contributions; provisions are sent in like forage, and all the taverns and alehouses in the neighbourhood make fortunes. The most diverting part is to hear people wondering when it will be found out – as if there was any thing to find out – as if the actors would make their noises when they can be discovered.

Horace Walpole, Letter to George Montagu, 1762

SNOWED UNDER

To London, through a bleak freezing landscape, though for once the north got off lighter than the south, which is under six inches of snow. Much of the capital paralysed. No buses, only half the Underground, even the Members' Tea Room closed because the staff could not get in. The *Evening Standard*, which has reverted to type after its brief flirtation with good news, was ranting on about 'chaos' but it all seemed quite peaceful apart from one or two minor inconveniences.

Chris Mullin, *Decline and Fall: Diaries*, 2009

~ 3 *February* ~

LESS POWERFUL IN LONDON

Thirteen days since I came to town, a time during which, in any situation such as Oxford or Felbrigg, considerable advance would have been made in some articles of study, or some habit of mental improvement. At the end of this time in London I find myself less powerful in every respect than at the beginning of it. I cannot have the smallest doubt that this would not have happened in the country. In what then does the difference consist? Is it from causes merely mental, occasioned by the difference in the habits of life, or from bodily causes dependent on the temperature of the air and want of opportunities of exercise? This should be ascertained by exact observation. I suspect that enough time might be found for most purposes, both of business and pleasure, if there was no intermediate state, and every moment not wanted for amusement was vigorously employed in business.

William Windham, *Diary*, 1785

PICTURESQUE STAMFORD HILL

From after breakfast, Josiah and I took a walk, and passing Shoreditch Church (where my two poor sisters are buried who died in one day of Hooping Cough shortly before my birth) we took the Tottenham Road and reached Lower Edmonton before we turned homewards. Here, near the Cross, Josiah went to school. The only part of the road which took my fancy was Stamford Hill which is very picturesque. I remember having been there once before with my brother George, though some years since. The road, however, is interesting from the circumstance of its being Johnny Gilpin's equestrian adventure which the poet Cowper has immortalized in verse.

We came home to dinner very tired, having walked 18 miles. Spent a pleasant afternoon with Josiah among his books. He walked me as far as the Diorama [east of Park Square, Regent's Park] on my return homewards.

John Thomas Pocock, *Diary*, 1828

COCKNEY WRESTLERS

In the evening saw some third-rate all-in wrestling at filthy little hall where the best seats cost half-a-crown. I judged it to be complete fake throughout, but fake very well done with some admirable tumbling. How little serious it was became obvious when one of the wrestlers threw the referee, and presently the ref. kicked the wrestler who was standing at full height in the face! By 'kicked' I mean he put the sole of his gym shoe over the man's mouth and nostrils and pushed him over, proving incidentally that the ref. was a bit of an acrobat too. Plenty of Cockney humour. Once when the proceedings were a bit slow a voice at the back said gloomily: 'Put a record on!' And when they livened up and one fellow bumped another's head against the floor the same voice said, even more gloomily: 'Summons 'im!'

James Agate, *Journals*, 1936

～ 4 *FEBRUARY* ～

GETTING AHEAD IN BOND STREET

I am this morning admitted a student at the Royal Academy; the figure which I drew for admittance was the Torso. I am now comfortably settled in Cecil Street, Strand, No. 23. I shall begin painting as soon as I have the loan of a sweet little picture by Jacob Ruysdael to copy. Since I have been in town I have seen some remarkably fine ones by him . . . Smith's friend, Clanch, has left off painting, at least for the present. His whole time and thoughts are occupied in exhibiting an old, rusty, fusty head, with a spike in it, which he declares to be the real embalmed head of Oliver Cromwell. Where he got it I know not; 'tis to be seen in Bond Street, at half a crown admittance.

John Constable, Letter to John Dunthorne, 1799

THE OPENING OF PARLIAMENT

The great day of the opening of Parliament. Soon after breakfast we prepared to go to the House of Lords – that is to say, we made ourselves great figures with feathers and finery. The day has been, unfortunately, rainy and cold, and made our dress look still more absurd. The King did not come till two, so that we had plenty of time to see all the old lords assembling. Their robes looked very handsome, and I think His Majesty was the least dignified-looking person in the house. I cannot describe exactly all that went on. There was nothing impressive, but it was very amusing. The poor old man could not see to read his speech, and after he had stammered half through it Lord Melbourne was obliged to hold a candle to him, and he read it over again. Lord Melbourne looked very like a Prime Minister, but the more I see him and so many good and clever men obliged to do, at least in part, the bidding of anyone who happens to be born to Royalty, the more I wish that things were otherwise – however, as long as it is only in forms that one sees them give him the superiority one does not much mind. After the debate, several of Papa's friends came to dine here. Lord Melbourne, Lord Lansdowne, Lord Glenelg, and the Duke of Richmond, who has won my heart – they talked very pleasantly.

Lady John Russell, *Diary*, 1836

ON THIN ICE

I walked with my daughter Charlotte across the Serpentine, much to the child's delight, although I own I did not like to hear the ice cracking under the weight of thousands.

John Cam Hobhouse, *Diary*, 1838

A LOCAL ELECTION CANDIDATE

As I have been foolish enough – or is it wise? – to stand here for the London County Council, I am horribly tied here, having to see local bores and busybodies every day. I never knew before how delightful good books and pictures were; after a few hours with these tedious creatures I find art or poetry an absolute and immediate necessity. By the way, I am standing for Deptford . . . my opponent is Sidney Webb.

John Cann Bailey, Letter to Arthur Hughes, 1892

~ 5 *FEBRUARY* ~

CURIOUS PRINTS IN SOHO

A letter directed to Mr Lloyd, postage unpaid, when opened proved to be a Valentine, supposed to be meant for me by my name being mentioned twice, or more, and which I suspect was sent by the nursery maid at Eccleston Wharf. If so, I feel obliged to her for directing it to Mr Lloyd, thereby saving me 2d. Her motive for so doing I know not, but she reversed the picture by sending an old house maid with mop and broom, thereby taking herself off rather than me. Bought five curious old prints at Miscellanous Repository in Princes Street, Soho, the subjects of which are as follows: a view of Privy Garden Westminster; a view of the Savoy from the River Thames; a perspective view of the new buildings at the Horse Guards; a view of the Foundling Hospital; a view of the Royal Hospital at Greenwich.

Nathaniel Bryceson, *Diary*, 1846

AN OFFICE WITH A VIEW

The day started with a visit to Douglas Jay in his office in the new Board of Trade building at the corner of Great Peter Street and Victoria Street. He really has a magnificent view, and you can see the dome of St Paul's behind the Tower of Big Ben.

Richard Crossman, *Diary*, 1965

∼ 6 *FEBRUARY* ∼

A MINER DEMONSTRATION IN TRAFALGAR SQUARE

Today I went to the miners' demonstration in Trafalgar Square in support of their wage claim, marching from Hyde Park with Jack Jones, Lawrence Daly and Alex Kitson . . . It was a marvellous demonstration although it was a little chilly and looked as if it was going to rain. I made a short speech which lasted about two and a half minutes and they were shouting at me part of the time. But I did get across that Heath was a cold, hard man and we ought to have an election.

Tony Benn, *Diary*, 1972

∼ 7 *FEBRUARY* ∼

A SLOW COACH TO SNOWHILL

Arrived at 11 this evening at the Saracen's Head, Snowhill. The usual time of arrival is 1 pm, but the coachman and the guard both got a little boozy, and each had a girl. Stopped every few minutes to drink. The coachman extremely insolent. With great difficulty got a very dirty bed, in a room with another, and, after an hour's perseverance, got a little fire and a glass of hot lemonade. Went below in the public room to smoke a pipe. No segars. Two very intelligent young men there. One a foreigner . . . They both made approaches for acquaintance, which, *pour des raisons*, I received distantly.

Aaron Burr, *Journal*, 1809

HATEFUL LONDON

I envy you – great lady as you are, you lead a quiet life; how far from quiet mine is and always must be, and how intensely I long that it could be more so, how completely worn out both mind and body often feel at the end of a common day, none can imagine but those who have become in one moment mother of six children, wife of the Leader of the House of Commons, and mistress of a house in London. You will suppose that I wish husband and children at the world's end, and you will call me a sinful, discontented creature; you will do anything but pity me, since my only complaint is that I have not as much leisure as so much happiness requires to be enjoyed. Well, say and think what you please; I must let you into my secret follies, in the hope of curing myself in so doing. London, hateful London, alone is at fault. Anywhere else my duties and occupations would be light, and my pleasures would be so not in name only . . . How could I beg Mama, as I used to do, to have more parties and dinners and balls! I cannot now conceive the state of mind which made me actually wish for such things. Now I have them in my power without number, and I detest them all.

Lady John Russell, Letter to Lady Mary Abercromby, 1843

FOGGY LONDON TOWN

Last Saturday week we had the worst day and night known in London for very long. After nine at night the street lamps were perfectly useless. You could scarcely see the light even standing directly under them. I had to go to Bertz that night, and in returning I was more than two hours making three miles, for I had *absolutely* and *literally* to grope with my stick, like a blind man, all the way. No 'buses dared to run, and the few cabs and carts which continued to voyage, did so with the driver walking at the horses' head, with a lantern in his hand. Boys made an admirable trade with links and lanterns, which were, however, of little use. I had to give such a boy a penny to be taken over King's Cross. I should *never* have found my way into the right street, though I am familiar with the place as with my own study. Another night it was nearly as bad and I took a lantern.

George Gissing, Letter to his brother, 1880

OUTCLASSED IN PICCADILLY

Intending to buy my usual 3d. packet of Goldflakes, entered a tobac-
conist's in Piccadilly, but once inside surprised to find myself in a classy
west-end establishment, which frightened my flabby nature into buying
De Reszke's instead. I hadn't the courage to face the aristocrat behind
the counter with a request for Goldflakes — probably not stocked. What
would he think of me? Besides, I shrank from letting him see I was not
perfectly well-to-do.

W. N. P. Barbellion, *The Journal of a Disappointed Man*, 1914

∼ 8 FEBRUARY ∼

A GOODLY SPORT?

Turner and Dun, two famous fencers, playd their prizes this day at the Banke side, but Turner at last run Dun soe far in the brayne at the eye, that he fell downe presently stone deade; a goodly sport in a Christian state, to see one man kill an other!

John Manningham, *Diary*, 1603

THE DESIGN FOR ST PAUL'S

The weather breake, a misty thaw all day. With Mr. Haux at Pauls Churchyard, at Dr. Wrens, told me the Designe of burying vaults under Paules and Addition of Library Body and portico at the west.

Robert Hooke, *Diary*, 1672

AN EARTHQUAKE HITS LONDON

It was about a quarter after twelve that the earthquake began at the skirts of town. It began in the south-east, went through Southwark, under the river, and then from one end of London to the other. It was observed at Westminster and Grosvenor Square a quarter before one. (Perhaps if we allow for the difference of the clocks, about a quarter of an hour after it began in Southwark.) There were three distinct shakes, or wavings to and fro, attended with a hoarse rumbling noise, like thunder. How gently does God deal with this nation! Oh that our repentence may prevent heavier marks of His displeasure!

John Wesley, *Journal*, 1750

A ROYAL RIDE

Riding through the Horse-Guards to-day I saw a great crowd waiting the arrival of Prince Albert, but H.R.H. (for so he is, and a Field-Marshal) went over Vauxhall Bridge, straight to Buckingham Palace.

It is said H.M. saluted him, on receiving him, and went down the hall steps to meet him. He was accompanied by his father and brother.

John Cam Hobhouse, *Diary*, 1840

THE ILL EFFECTS OF THE LONDON AIR

Charles is going on so well that one is sometimes tempted to think he might go out and behave just like a man in health, but every now and then some little bit of overtire and dissipation knocks him up, and shews that he must still be careful. Last night he was at the Athenæum Club ... They have soirées every Monday evening, and as all the literary and scientific men in London are in the Club they must be very pleasant, and I hope C. will soon be able to join them, but he is quite knocked up to-day.

The London air has a very bad effect upon our little boy's v's and w's, he says his name is 'Villy Darvin,' and 'vipe Doddy (which is his pet name) own tears away,' and 'open vindow,' &c . . .

Emma Darwin, Letter to her aunt Madame Sismondi, 1842

⌢ *9 FEBRUARY* ⌢

BIRDWATCHING IN ST JAMES'S PARK

Dined at my Lord Treasurer's, the Earl of Southampton, in Bloomsbury, where he was building a noble square or piazza, a little town; his own house stands too low, some noble rooms, a pretty cedar chapel, a naked garden to the north, but good air. I had much discourse with his Lord-ship, whom I found to be a person of extraordinary parts, but a valetu-dinarian. – I went to St. James's Park, where I saw various animals, and examined the throat of the Onocrotylus, or pelican, a fowl between a stork and a swan; a melancholy water-fowl, brought from Astrakhan by the Russian Ambassador; it was diverting to see how he would toss up and turn a flat fish, plaice, or flounder, to get it right into his gullet at its lower beak, which, being filmy, stretches to a prodigious wideness when it devours a great fish. Here was also a small water-fowl, not bigger than a moorhen, that went almost quite erect, like the penguin of America; it would eat as much fish as its whole body weighed; I never saw so insatiable a devourer, yet the body did not appear to swell the bigger. The solan geese here are also great devourers, and are said soon to exhaust all the fish in a pond. Here was a curious sort of poultry not much exceeding the size of a tame pigeon, with legs so short as their crops seemed to touch the earth; a milk-white raven; a stork, which was a rarity at this season, seeing he was loose, and could fly loftily; two Balearian cranes, one of which having had one of his legs broken and cut off above the knee, had a wooden or boxen leg and thigh, with a joint so accurately made that the creature could walk and use it as well as if it had been natural; it was made by a soldier. The park was at this time stored with numerous flocks of several sorts of ordinary and extraordinary wild fowl, breeding about the Decoy, which for being near so great a city, and among such a concourse of soldiers and people, is a singular and diverting thing. There were also deer of several countries, white; spotted like leopards; antelopes, an elk, red deer, roebucks, stags, Guinea goats, Arabian sheep, etc. There were withy-pots, or nests, for the wild fowl to lay their eggs in, a little above the surface of the water.

John Evelyn, *Diary*, 1665

SOMETHING ROTTEN IN COVENT GARDEN

Thursday last we went to London by car and ran into a coal car at 11 a.m. in Lea Bridge Road. Much excitement and crowd. It gave me a headache, which grew capriciously and lasted. Marguerite absolutely calm throughout. Back axle bent and much damage to the coachwork. Still we finished journey in car.

Afternoon 5 p.m., Parsifal at Covent Garden. Putrid performance. Bodanzky commonplace conductor. Poor orchestra. Appalling scenery, costumes and scenic effect. Ugly. Kundry, good singer. Rotten female chorus, amazingly ugly and ill-dressed. Also long stretches of dull music. I never saw uglier scenery. I went to sleep in the middle of each act. Over after 11.

Arnold Bennett, *Journal*, 1914

∽ 10 *FEBRUARY* ∽

POWER CUTS IN KENSINGTON

Eric suggested that we all be very naughty and go to see *Diamonds are Forever*, the latest of the James Bond films at the Kensington Odeon. After brief and unconvincing heart-searching, we drive over to Kensington – but, alas, have not been in the cinema for more than 20 minutes when the film runs down. After a few minutes there is much clearing of throat, a small light appears in front of the stage and a manager appears to tell us that we are the victims of a power cut (this being the first day of the cuts following four weeks of government intractability in the face of the miners' claim). For half an hour there is a brief, British moment of solidarity amongst the beleaguered cinemagoers, but as were were shirking work, anyway, it looked like a shaft of reprobation fron the Great Writer in the sky,

Michael Palin, *Diary*, 1972

∽ 11 *FEBRUARY* ∽

A PLAN FOR THE EMBANKMENT OF THE THAMES

Went to Covent Garden Theatre. A dull time of it, though I went in at half-price. The pantomime a fatiguing exhibition, but the scenery beautiful; and this is one of the attractions of the theatre to me. A panoramic view of the projected improvements of the Thames, by the erection of a terrace on arches along the northern shore, is a pleasing anticipation of a splendid dream, which not even in this projecting age can become a reality.

Henry Crabb Robinson, *Diary*, 1825

AN EVENING AT THE CHELSEA ARTS CLUB

Dinner at Chelsea Arts Club. Room long, low. Billiard Room. Rules and cues still hanging on walls. Some men in elegant evening dress; some in fair ditto, some in smoking jackets, some in morning coats, some in lounge suits. Frampton in the last, with rough hair. Shannon, in chair, très élégant.

New ventilation put in roof for this banquet. Ventilation bad. Dinner sound. Service mediocre. Man on my right who grumbled at most things.

Caricatures, drawings and paintings round the walls. Whitish walls. No elegance of furniture. The whole place rather like a studio.

After the regular speeches, comic speech read by Cavaliere Formih, interrupted by an arranged suffragette invasion. Coarse jokes here. Political opinions of majority seen at once. Invaders in costume, also policemen. One put his leg down a hole in roof . . . The professional humorist, Walter Emanuel, read out sham telegrams from people who couldn't come. One or two pretty good. The rest idiotic, in the conventional *Punch* manner. (He is 'Charivaria' of *Punch*.)

I had to go out here, as the chill caused by the opening windows for the invasion got into my guts. All fires let out in other rooms. I stayed near the bar, talking to various people. Konody [*Daily Mail* art critic], Conrad, Hardy, Turner, Cillick. We got colder and colder. I peeped into the big room sometimes. Ventriloquism, songs, piano, etc. Not quite full now. The distinguished Shannon still sitting there bravely enjoying, with his monocle.

Arnold Bennett, *Journals*, 1910

NEW YEAR IN CHINATOWN

It's Chinese New Year and the crowd spill out
Of Chinatown and on to the streets of Soho.
Paper dragons breathe fire on sticks.
Overweight mothers push Big Mac Kids.
Chinatown and Soho – the crowd starts to blend.
And the Old Compton Street habitués come to an end.
(It's the Year of the Rat meets the queers in a pack.)

The melting pot meets with surprising ease.
Queens cruise by in Abercrombie tees.
The first hint of sun brings the first hint of pec.
A heavyset lesbian couple aggressively neck.
A little Chinese girl, a badge with her name.
The leather queen who always dresses the same.
Firecrackers explode and we jump in our seats.
Chinese New Year on Old Compton Street.

Clayton Littlewood, *Goodbye to Soho*, 2008

∼ *12 FEBRUARY* ∼

A RUN ON THE BANK

The last three months have been remarkable for the panic in the money market, which lasted for a week or ten days – that is, was at its height for that time. The causes of it had been brewing for some months before, and he must be a sanguine and sagacious politician who shall predict the termination of its effects. There is now no panic, but the greatest alarm, and every prospect of great distress, and long continuation of it. The state of the City, and the terror of all the bankers and merchants, as well as of all owners of property, is not to be conceived but by those who witnessed it. This critical period drew forth many examples of great and confiding liberality, as well as some of a very opposite character. Men of great wealth and parsimonious habits came and placed their whole fortunes at the disposal of their bankers in order to support their credit. For many days the evil continued to augment so rapidly, and the demands upon the Bank were so great and increasing, that a Bank restriction was expected by everyone. So determined, however, were Ministers against this measure, that rather than yield to it they suffered the Bank to run the greatest risk of stopping; for on the evening of the day on which the alarm was at its worst there were only 8,000 sovereigns left in the till. The next day gold was poured in, and from that time things got better.

Charles Greville, *Journals*, 1826

THE SIAMESE TWINS

Went to see the Siamese Twins, who are exhibiting at the Egyptian Hall,* where they were forty years ago. It is strange to see a human being who is not completely rounded off from every other: but the apparent duality here is much less than I expected. You simply see two small elderly Mongolian men, grizzled & wizened, closely alike in feature & make & height, but each evidently in act and volition an individual. They lean on each other as they stand or walk, & the flesh bond that connects them (5 inches long and as thick as a strong man's wrist) is just seen through their open shirtfronts. With them was the daughter of one; a tall well-made young woman, good looking, and like an English farmer's daughter, though her father is an abnormal Siamese. But her mother is an American of English descent.

Arthur Munby, *Diary*, 1869

* Built in 1812 and demolished in 1905, this was an exhibition hall in Piccadilly.

CAMDEN IN BLOOM

I am buying daffodils in a shop in Camden High Street. An oldish woman asks for some violets, but they aren't quite fresh. 'Never mind,' she explains. 'I only want to throw them down a grave.'

Alan Bennett, *Diary*, 1985

～ *13 February* ～

HIGH LIFE AND LOW LIFE

I crammed my day pretty full. First did books; then went to Mrs. Humphrey's who took me to see their capital schools; mem. especially, a little school held in the roof of a mission-chapel lately built in a squalid street, where they get hold of wretched neglected children. At 12 I found myself with the Mesdames Talbot in their delightful soup-kitchen, which they have set up in Westminster. Poor people (not beggars) are given tickets, on showing which and paying a sum not exceeding 2*d.* they get good meat, soup, beef-tea, or pudding of at least twice the value of what they pay. Fred is going to be treasurer. Got home to luncheon, where we entertained Mr. St. Aubyn who is going to be married. May Lascelles came to see me about 4, after which I smiled for a few minutes upon a little tea-business at Auntie P.'s, and then drove off to S. Ann's National Schools, Limehouse, where a most charming, successful 'mission tea-party' was held, under the auspices of my dear Miss Lilley, and the other good folk. Was glad to see Sarah Dorrington the 2nd mission woman looking busy and bright, but, alas! not well. There were 210 women and 49 babies! I poured out for one table. Had to go off directly after tea, hearing only one chorus, to my grief: but as it was, in spite of getting home by superhuman exertions in 35 minutes, I arrived after 8, with His Grace the Duke of Devonshire, the Secretary of War, the Lord-Lieutenant of Worcestershire, and Mr. Charles Howard MP, to entertain at dinner. I was a little jeered. But would not have missed the tea-party.

Lady Frederick Cavendish, *Diary*, 1866

BLOOMSBURY'S GOLDEN GEORGE

On foot to see Bruce Hunter in Golden Square. Good to see how many Georgian and Victorian houses remain, all worth a squint. The blue plaques always elicit interest, even of the dreariest past inhabitants. In Golden Square I went to look at the statue of George II. Face like Malcolm Muggeridge, sadly worn and streaked with bird messes. On the head was perched a black crow, which I tried in vain to shoo away. An old woman earnestly scavenging in a litter bin – the sort of thing which I suppose will never be eliminated even in the best-regulated society.

James Lees-Milne, *Diary*, 1993

∼ 14 *FEBRUARY* ∼

TO LONDON WITH LOVE

Dear London! So vast and unexpectant, so ugly and so strong! You have been bruised and battered, your clothes are tattered and in disarray. Yet we who never knew that we loved you (who regarded you, in fact, like some old family servant, ministering to our comforts and amenities, and yet slightly incongruous and absurd), have suddenly felt the twinge of some fibre of identity, respect and love.

Harold Nicolson, *Diary*, 1941

A NIGHT ON THE TOWN

I found Percy Street immersed in an odd perplexity: Barbara [Bagenal]'s lavatory is out of order, and Sonia Brownell in the flat above dislikes hers being commandeered. The sudden importance of our excrement is a trifle ludicrous . . . Dined with Janetta at the Ivy: she looked happy, her face ironed out of strains, and was friendly and charming . . . Derek telephoned while we were dining and asked us to join him and Sonia at their restaurant. This we did, and drank brandy among a smart crowd in funeral black arm-bands . . . Sonia was keen to 'go on somewhere',

so on we went – first to the Gargoyle and then to Claridges, where the
Jacksons were staying en route to Khartoum, with a packing case of
scientific instruments, for Derek to do experiments on the total eclipse.
At the Gargoyle we ran into Francis Bacon, lit up with drink, reckless,
charming, giggling wildly. He joined our table, and turning to me asked,
'Don't you think Derek is the most marvellous person you know?' Next
we were joined by Lucian Freud, who began a serious conversation with
Derek about art and science, Derek's contribution to which was eager,
amusing and paradoxical. Champagne was ordered and when Sonia,
Lucian and I left Claridges it was two o'clock. Outside the front door
two handsome, well-educated policemen were standing to whom
Lucian remarked, 'I suppose you're here to prevent all the Kings getting
assassinated?' (There are seven Kings and Queens here for the funeral.)
The policeman looked down his nose and didn't deign to answer. We
three took a taxi to Percy Street, but even at the door Sonia couldn't
give up and they left me and drove on 'somewhere else'.

Frances Partridge, *Diary*, 1952

CYCLING IN KILBURN

Beautiful sunny morning: early to studio (8.15). On the way in I saw
Terry the greengrocer, the pleasantly weatherbeaten old jazzer who
stands out all day on the corner. 'Lovely day,' I said. He agreed, and I
said how I liked these cold bright days better than hot ones. 'Oh, I love
them all,' he said, 'I am just happy to be alive.' I think he is telling the
truth...

Went for a bike ride up Kilburn High Road. Saw a lady with her
nose smashed in, sitting dazed in a heap of bloody tissues with a policeman nearby. The scene had an African quality about it: the nonchalance
of the passers-by contrasted with the woman's plight. Like that festival
in Ghana when the amputee was attacked by a swarm of bees and, after
a few moments' helpless and hysterical bouncing round on the ground,
he just settled down and and let them cover him. Everyone was watching and laughing.

Brian Eno, *Diary*, 1995

A LONDON DERBY

Arsenal have their own Valentine's Day massacre when they beat Crystal Palace 5–1; they also create an unwelcome record for the English game, when they not only field a complete team of foreign players, but also five foreign subsitutes.

Russ Wilkins, *Diary of a Common Fan: My Year During Charlton AFC's Centenary Season 2004/5*, 2005

~ 15 FEBRUARY ~

FIRST IMPRESSIONS OF A NEW LONDON PARK

At two I took a ride with Preston in his gig, into Regent's Park, which I had never seen before. When the trees are grown this will be an ornament to the capital; and not a mere ornament but a healthy appendage. The Highgate and Hampstead Hill is a beautiful object, and within the Park, the artificial water, the circular belt or coppice, the bridges, the few scattered villas &c., are objects of taste. I really think this enclosure, with the new street leading to it from Carlton House, will give more glory to the Regent's government, which will be more felt by remote posterity than the victories of Trafalgar and Waterloo, glorious as these are.

Henry Crabb Robinson, *Diary*, 1818

A CLUB FOR ACTORS

Dine with the Garrick Club, a new society to bring together friends of the drama. The Duke of Sussex in the chair, and all the principal actors present: a droll scene, but nothing will make the actors gentlemen nor the gentlemen actors.

John Cam Hobhouse, *Diary*, 1832

FEVERISH IN SOHO

Tried to kiss her in a taxi-cab on the way home from the Savoy – the taxi-cab danger is very present with us – but she rejected me quietly, sombrely. I apologised on the steps of the Flats and said I feared I had greatly annoyed her. 'I'm not annoyed,' she said, 'only surprised' – in a thoughtful, chilly voice.

We had had supper in Soho, and I took some wine, and she looked so bewitching it sent me in a fever, thrumming my fingers on the seat of the cab while she sat beside me impassive. Her shoulders are exquisitely modelled and a beautiful head is carried poised on a tiny neck.

W. N. P. Barbellion, *The Journal of a Disappointed Man*, 1913

FEELING LOCAL IN LONDON

Decimal Day. Today, not only our old currency but a small portion of our everyday language dies forever and is replaced . . . Funnily enough, I find myself resenting the new decimal coinage far less than the postal codes (which I fear will one day replace towns with numbers – and after towns streets, and after streets . . .?), or the all-figure telephone numbers which dealt one mighty blow to local feeling in London and, in the process, made it practically impossible to remember phone numbers.*

* Our own area code changed from GULliver to the soulless 485.

Michael Palin, *Diary*, 1971

~ 16 *FEBRUARY* ~

A SERMON SOUTH OF THE RIVER

I went to Rotherhithe which used to be one of the most uncomfortable places in England. But it was far otherwise now. Many of the people seemed much alive to God and His presence was manifested in the congregation in a very uncommon manner.

John Wesley, Journal, 1787

A FIRE AT THE OPERA HOUSE

Last night the English Opera House was burnt down – a magnificent fire. I was playing at whist at the 'Travellers' with Lord Granville, Lord Auckland, and Ross, when we saw the whole sky illuminated and a volume of fire rising in the air. We thought it was Covent Garden, and directly set off to the spot. We found the Opera House and several houses in Catherine Street on fire (sixteen houses), and, though it was three in the morning, the streets filled by an immense multitude. Nothing could be more picturesque than the scene, for the flames made it as light as day and threw a glare upon the strange and motley figures moving about. All the gentility of London was there from Princess Esterhazy's ball and all the clubs; gentlemen in their fur cloaks, pumps, and velvet waistcoats mixed with objects like the sans-culottes in the French Revolution – men and women half-dressed, covered with rags and dirt, some with nightcaps or handkerchiefs round their heads – then the soldiers, the firemen, and the engines, and the new police running and bustling, and clearing the way, and clattering along, and all with that intense interest and restless curiosity produced by the event, and which received fresh stimulus at every renewed burst of the flames as they rose in a shower of sparks like gold dust. Poor Arnold lost everything and was not insured. I trust the paraphernalia of the Beefsteak Club perished with the rest, for the enmity I bear that society for the dinner they gave me last year.

Charles Greville, *Journals*, 1830

DEATH STALKS DRURY LANE

Terrible murder, 4 Pitts Place, Drury Lane. James Bostock, a working brass finisher, shot by his apprentice aged 20 (Thomas William Wicks) in fit of revenge. Murderer apprehended in the evening in coffee shop.

Nathaniel Bryceson, *Diary*, 1846

∿ *17 February* ∿

EAST IS EAST, BUT WEST IS MORE EXPENSIVE

London is a giant — strangers can only reach his feet. Shut up in our apartments, well warmed and well lighted, and where we seem to want nothing but a little of that immense society in the midst of which we are suspended, but not mixed, we have full leisure to observe its outward aspect and general movements, and listen to the roar of its waves, breaking around us in measured time, like tides of the ocean.

In the morning all is calm — not a mouse stirring before ten o'clock; the shops then begin to open. Milk-women, with their pails perfectly neat, suspended at the two extremities of a yoke, carefully shaped to fit the shoulders, and surrounded by small tin measures of cream, ring at every door, with reiterated pulls, to hasten the maid-servants, who come half asleep to receive measures as big as an egg, being the allowance of a family; for it is necessary to explain, that milk is not here either food or drink, but a tincture — an elixir exhibited in drops, five or six at most, in a cup of tea, morning and evening . . . Not a single carriage — not a cart are seen passing. The first considerable stir is the drum and military music of the Guards, marching from their barracks to Hyde Park, having at their head three or four negro giants, striking, high, gracefully and strong, the resounding cymbal. About three or four o'clock the fashionable world gives some signs of life, issuing forth to pay visits, or rather leave cards at the doors of friends, never seen but in the crowd of assemblies; to go to shops, see sights, or lounge in Bond Street — an ugly inconvenient street, the attraction of which was difficult to understand. At five or six they return home to dress for dinner. The streets are then lighted from one end to the other, or rather edged on either side with two long lines of little brightish dots, indicative of light, but yielding very little — these are the lamps.

From six to eight the *noise* of wheels increases; it is the dinner hour. A multitude of carriages, with two eyes of flame staring in the dark before each of them, shake the pavement and the very houses, following and crossing each other at high speed.

For two hours, or nearly, there is a pause; at ten a *redoublement* comes on. This is the great crisis of dress, of noise, and of rapidity — a universal hubbub; a sort of uniform grinding and shaking like that experienced in a great mill with fifty pairs of stones; and, if I was not afraid of appearing to exaggerate, I should say that it came upon the ear like the fall of Niagara heard at two miles distance! This crisis continues undiminished till twelve or one o'clock; then less and less during the rest of the night – till at the approach of day, a single carriage is heard now and then at a great distance . . . Such may be, it will be said, the life of the rich, the well-born, and the idle, but it cannot be that of the many people; of the commercial part, for instance, of this emporium of the trade of the universe. The trade of London is carried on in the east part of town, called, *par excellence*, the City. The west is inhabited by people of fashion, or those who wish to appear such; and the line of demarcation, north and south, runs through Soho Square. Every minute of longitude east is equal to as many degrees of gentility *minus*, or towards west, *plus*. This meridian line north and south, like that indicated by the compass, inclines west towards the north and east towards the south, two or three points, in such a manner, as to place a certain part of Westminster on the side of fashion; the Parliament House, Downing Street and the Treasury are necessarily genteel. To have the right to emigrate from east to west, it is requisite to have at least L. 3000 sterling a-year; should you have less, or at least spend less, you might find yourself slighted; and L. 6000 sterling a-year would be safer.

Louis Simond, *Journal of a Tour and Residence in Great Britain,
During the Years 1810 and 1811*, 1810

MIDNIGHT POVERTY

Coming home along the Embankment at midnight, with Arthur Pearson, from Blackfriars as far as Northumberland Avenue, we counted fifteen homeless couples, evidently married out-of-works. Three of them had children with them, and of these two were barefooted; which was unusual even in this haunt of the unfortunate. The Salvation Army people were handing out hot soup to the miserable folk. This midnight poverty of London is one of the most pathetic sights of the metropolis.

R. D. Blumenfeld, *R.D.B.'s Diary*, 1908

∼ 18 FEBRUARY ∼

TAINTED AIR

Dr. Jenner observed to Lawrence that he could by smelling at his hand-kerchief on going out of London ascertain when he came into an atmos-phere untainted by the London air. − His method was to smell at his handkerchief occasionally, and while he continued within the London atmosphere he could never be sensible of any taint upon it; but, for instance, when he approached Blackheath & took his handkerchief out of his pocket where it had not been exposed to the better air of that situation, − his sense of smelling having become more pure he could perceive the taint. − His calculation was that the air of London affected that in the vicinity to the distance of 3 miles.

Joseph Farington, *Diary*, 1809

ICE SKATING ON THE SERPENTINE

After dinner, my mother Tom Gurney and self walked to the Serpentine River in Hyde Park and were much amused by the skaters, many of whom received innumerable thumps on the upper storey from the ice.

John Thomas Pocock, *Diary*, 1827

A SOCIABLE CITY

We find London very sociable and pleasant . . . people all looking glad to meet, and fresh and pleasant from their country life, quite different from what they will be in July . . .

Lady John Russell, Letter to Mr Rollo Russell, 1868

THE MAYFAIR MEN TRIAL

The Old Bailey. This is the fourth and last day of the Hyde Park Hotel jewel robbery case, in which four young men, educated at the best public schools, receive sentences from eighteen months' hard labour to seven years' penal servitude with 20 strokes of the 'cat'. Crowded court. Celebrities – 'better than any play'. A horrid glamour about the whole affair. I am naturally fascinated by criminals, whose dreadful jauntiness haunts me for days.

James Agate, *Journals*, 1938

∼ *19 FEBRUARY* ∼

DR GRAHAM'S TEMPLE OF HEALTH

Evening at Dr. Graham's lecture on health, in his 'Temple of Health' in Pall Mall, near St James's.* The first room entered was properly a vestibule, from whence through folding-doors one passes into the apartment holding the electric bed, about seven feet square, raised three feet from the floor; over the frame at the head are fixed two balls gilded, of four inches diameter and one inch apart, to receive the electric spark from the machine above, continued down in a glass tube through the floor. Passing this, you enter the Room of Apollo, through a narrow entry, having on each hand two or three niches containing statues gilded, about half the natural size. The first object that meets the eye is the Temple of Apollo, being a round cupola five feet in diameter, supported by six fluted pillars of the Corinthian order and eight feet high, in imitation of scagliola; in the centre stands a tripodal frame with concave sides, on which rests in each angle a lion couchant supporting a long firaune for the branch of six or eight lamps, adorned (or rather over-charged) with crystals, whose tremulous motion by the company's walking adds great brilliancy to the appearance, the walls all around having many branches with three candles each, besides two more large central branches, suspended by gilt chains from the ceiling. The decorations in the frippery kind are in great profusion in this as well as in the other room, consisting of glass in various forms and sizes, inlaid and hanging; many gilt statues of Apollo, Venus, Hercules, Esculapius, etc., besides a few pictures. The master discovered a ready elocution, great medical knowledge, and appeared well qualified to support the character he assumes.

Samuel Curwen, *Journal*, 1783

* James Graham was a famous quack and pioneer sex therapist whose Temple of Health and its Great Celestial Bed, designed to improve female fertility and male virility, attracted crowds of the gullible and the fashionable.

LOOKING OVER THE UNDERGROUND

The new office is a capital place. It is on the first floor and on a terrace that overlooks the river. We can see from our window right across the Thames, and on a clear day every bridge is visible. Everybody says that we have a beautiful place.

To-day has been wretched. It was almost pitch dark in the middle of the day, and everything visible appeared the colour of brown paper or pea-soup . . . I tried the Underground Railway one day – Everything is excellently arranged.

Thomas Hardy, Letter to his sister Mary, 1863

VIEWING WAR PICTURES

I went up to the Scala Theatre to see some war pictures really taken at manoeuvres. A long talk with the manager – he showed me all the machinery, very interesting, All the apparatus is close to the entrance and behind the audience in a masonry box – two men to work it. Then a long walk as the rain had stopped, passed the Zeppelin gun on the Embankment guarded by R.N.R. How fine is the Embankment and Cleopatra's needle, well worth a study.

Viscount Sandhurst, *Day by Day*, 1915

ELEPHANT AND CASTLE, HONEST?

Sometimes right deep in my heart I wonder *if* honesty really *is* the *best* policy! I see the wide boys around the Elephant and Castle. They pay £20 for their suits – *cash!* My suit is seven years old and cost £3. They put £5 on the nose of a horse and if it loses they shrug their padded shoulders. I put 2s on a dog occasionally and me and Lizzie worry all night till the papers arrive next morning and we then know the result of our investment.

Fred Bason, *Diary*, 1951

～ *20 FEBRUARY* ～

SHELTERING IN SOUTH KENSINGTON

By evening I was very tired because I slept badly last night. On return-ing home was obliged to shelter in South Kensington tube during another severe and noisy raid. A lot more fires and a bomb dropped on the Treasury buildings. The Carmelite church in Kensington destroyed.

James Lees-Milne, *Diary*, 1944

PAINTING CAMDEN TOWN, BROWN

One of the pleasures of painting, even if it's only the wall which I'm currently engaged on, is to be able to visit Cornelissen's shop in Great Russell Street, which sells all manner of paints and colours and where I go this morning in order to find some varnish to seal the surface of the plaster.

After I'd finished putting on all the greenish-yellow colour yesterday I did some trial patches of varnish on it. I knew, though it's twenty years since I last stained a wall, how this transforms and enlivens the colour but I am astonished all over again at the depth and interest it gives to even the most ordinary surface. There's no literary equivalent that I can think of to this vernissage, no final gloss to be put on a novel, say, or a play which will bring them suddenly to life. Today when I go down to Cornelissen the assistant suggests that as an alternative to the gloss I try shellac, which has even more of a surface. It's one of the pleasures of the shop that you're served by people who know what they're talking about and who, one gets the feeling, go home from work, don a smock and beret and go to the easel themselves. Which reminds me how when I first stained some walls, back in 1968, I had no need to come all the way down to Cornelissen. Then I just went round the corner in Camden Town where Roberson's had a (long gone) shop in Parkway. They were old established colourists and had in the window a palette board used by Joshua Reynolds. Whatever happened to that?

Further to the painting, though, for which I scorn to don the Marigolds, I am buying bread in Villandry when I see the assistant gazing in horror at my hands, the fingers stained the virulent yellowish green I've been sponging on during this last week. As a young man my father smoked quite heavily and his fingers were stained like this by cigarettes – and a nice brown it was, and one which I wouldn't mind seeing on the wall; if he were alive still and the man he was when I was ten I could take him along to Cornelissen where I'm sure they could match his fingers in water, oil or acrylic.

And it stirs another memory from the 1970s, or whenever it was that the IRA conducted their 'dirty protests' at the Maze prison, smearing the walls of their cells with excrement. Occasionally one would see edited shots of these cells on television when I was invariably struck by what a nice warm and varied shade the protester had achieved. 'Maze brown' I suppose Farrow and Ball would tastefully have called it.

Alan Bennett, *Diary*, 2006

～ 21 *FEBRUARY* ～

A BOW STREET BRIDAL SUITE

Shrove-Tuesday. My son was married to Mrs. Martha Spencer, daughter to my Lady Stonehouse by a former gentleman, at St. Andrew's, Holbom, by our Vicar, borrowing the church of Dr. Stillingfleet, Dean of St. Paul's, the present incumbent. We afterward dined at a house in

Holborn; and, after the solemnity and dancing was done, they were bedded at Sir John Stonehouse's lodgings in Bow Street, Covent Garden.

John Evelyn, *Diary*, 1680

UNWELCOME NUPTIAL ARRANGEMENTS

The Prince of Wales's marriage is to take place on the 10th of next month, at Windsor, to the great disgust of the London public.

Louisa Bain, *Diary*, 1863

～ *22 FEBRUARY* ～

WAR OF THE OPERAS

In the mean time our most serious war is between two Operas. Mr. Hobart, Lord Buckingham's brother, is manager of the Haymarket. Last year he affronted Guadagni, by preferring the Zamperina, his own mistress, to the singing hero's sister. The Duchess of Northumberland, Lady Harrington, and some other great ladies, espoused the brother, and without a license erected an Opera for him at Madame Cornelys's. This is a singular dame, and you must be acquainted with her. She sung here formerly, by the name of the Pompeiati . . . Her taste and invention in pleasures and decorations are singular. She took Carlisle House in Soho Square, enlarged it, and established assemblies and balls by subscription. At first they scandalised, but soon drew in both righteous and ungodly. She went on building, and made her house a fairy palace for balls, concerts, and masquerades. Her Opera, which she called Harmonic Meetings, was splendid and charming. Mr. Hobart began to starve, and the managers of the theatres were alarmed. To avoid the act, she pretended to take no money, and had the assurance to advertise that the subscription was to provide coals for the poor, for she has vehemently courted the mob, and succeeded in gaining their princely favour. She then declared her Masquerades were for the benefit of commerce. I concluded she would open another sort of house next for the interests of the Foundling Hospital . . .

Horace Walpole, Letter to Sir Horace Mann, 1771

MORMONS IN LONDON

With L. Oliphant to a Mormonite meeting at a music hall in Theobald's Road. As strangers we were put in a little gallery opposite to the platform. Many persons addressed the meeting, some with exhortations, and others with spiritual experiences and relations of miraculous cures – all extremely tedious and tiresome. Special notice was taken of our presence, and we were told of the time and of the place to which we could go to be taught more of their mysteries. Bread and wine, in celebration of the Lord's Supper, was handed round to each person coming in, on a tray like tea and cakes at an evening party. We came away impressed with the want of interest and the mean features of all that we had seen and heard.

Sir Frederick Pollock, *Diary*, 1852

SWELL SIGHTS AT ROTTEN ROW

What an amazing Masque is Rotten Row on a Sunday morning! I sat on a seat there this morning and watched awhile.

It was most exasperating to be in this kaleidoscope of human life without the slightest idea as to who they all were. One man in particular, I noticed — a first-class 'swell' — whom I wanted to touch gently on the arm, slip a half-a-crown into his hand and whisper, 'There, tell me all about yourself.'

Such 'swells' there were that out in the fairway, my little cockle-shell boat was wellnigh swamped. To be in the wake of a really magnificent Duchess simply rocks a small boat in an alarming fashion. I leaned over my paddles and gazed up. They steamed past unheeding, but I kept my nerve all right and pulled in and out quizzing and observing.

It is nothing less than scandalous that here I am aged 25 with no means of acquainting myself with contemporary men and women even of my own rank and station. The worst of it is, too, that I have no time to lose — in my state of health. This accursed ill-health cuts me off from everything. I make pitiful attempts to see the world around me by an occasional visit (wind, weather, and health permitting) to Petticoat Lane, the Docks, Rotten Row, Leicester Square, or the Ethical Church. To-morrow I purpose going to the Christian Scientists'. Meanwhile, the others participate in Armageddon.

W. N. P. Barbellion, *The Journal of a Disappointed Man*, 1915

SNOWCAPPED HIGHGATE

As aesthetically pleasing snow falls upon Highgate, I walk home past a snowball fight between three teen boys. As I pass, they hit the small of my back with a snowball.

All very traditional, except that this happens at 2 a.m. at night.

Perhaps they're worried that the morning sun and urban activity will melt their ammunition beyond use (as the IRA phrase goes). That at 2 a.m. it's now or never for snowballing in N6 this year. Perhaps they're a bit drunk, coming back from a party.

Whatever the reason, I am immensely relieved that a single snowball is the limit of their attack, and walk quickly past, head down, not stopping, not reacting. Had this been daylight, there would be less fear involved. Snowballs or no, a group of shouting young men in a deserted street at 2 a.m. is still just that.

Dickon Edwards, *Diary*, 2005

∼ 23 *FEBRUARY* ∼

KISSING A QUEEN ON SHROVE TUESDAY

Up: and to the Office, where all the morning, and then home, and put a mouthfull of victuals in my mouth; and by a hackney-coach followed my wife and the girls, who are gone by eleven o'clock, thinking to have seen a new play at the Duke of York's house. But I do find them staying at my tailor's, the play not being to-day, and therefore I now took them to Westminster Abbey, and there did show them all the tombs very finely, having one with us alone, there being other company this day to see the tombs, it being Shrove Tuesday; and here we did see, by particular favour, the body of Queen Katherine of Valois; and I had the upper part of her body in my hands, and I did kiss her mouth, reflecting upon it that I did kiss a Queen, and that this was my birth-day, thirty-six years old, that I did first kiss a Queen. But here this man, who seems to understand well, tells me that the saying is not true that says she was never buried, for she was buried; only, when Henry the Seventh built his chapel, it was taken up and laid in this wooden coffin; but I did there see that, in it, the body was buried in a leaden one, which remains under the body to this day. Thence to the Duke of York's playhouse, and there, finding the play begun, we homeward to the Glass-House, and there shewed my cozens the making of glass, and had several things made with great content; and, among others, I had one or two singing-glasses made, which make an echo to the voice, the first that ever I saw; but so thin, that the very breath broke one or two of them. So home, and thence to Mr. Batelier's, where we supped, and had a good supper, and here was Mr. Gumbleton; and after supper some fiddles, and so to dance; but my eyes were so out of order, that I had little pleasure this night at all, though I was glad to see the rest merry, and so about midnight home and to bed.

Samuel Pepys, *Diary*, 1669

PROSPECTING IN WAPPING

After lunch I drive down to Wapping to see Chris Orr. Wapping High Street is the most unlikely high street left in Britain. Some fine houses remain, but mostly it's corrugated iron and mud and warehouses turned into wine stores. To Chris's room at New Crane Wharf. I look at his latest etchings. The humour and the style and skill and originality are all there. Now, instead of illustrating prose he's putting words as commentary on to prints. We walk downstairs and along cobbled streets past warehouses which other artists have moved into, but not greatly changed. Reminds me of Covent Garden just after the fruit market left. To a red-brick building opposite the Prospect of Whitby pub which announces that it was built in 1890 for The London Hydraulic Power Company. I'm shown around by a young man and an older character, who is quite marvellous and would be a superb TV presenter – a working man's Kenneth Clark. Very articulate, tells a good story, is never lost for words, ideas and references – all presented in a light and original fashion. He tells me about the use of hydraulic power in central London, pumped around a network of ten-inch cast-iron pipes below the ground which would now cost a fortune to lay. When the Hydraulic Power Co finally closed down – only four years ago – it had 3,000 subscribers, controlling the rise and fall of theatre safety curtains, lifts, the vacuum cleaners in the Savoy Hotel and, its star client, Tower Bridge.

Michael Palin, *Diary*, 1981

~ 24 *FEBRUARY* ~

DEATH OF A HISTORICAL PAINTER

Landseer called in the evening to invite me to hear his 3rd lecture on engraving. He mentioned the death of James Barry, historical painter. Abt. 10 days ago Barry attended at the Adelphi to vote for a Son of Dr. Coomber to be Secretary to the Society of Arts, &c. When he went there he had not on his thick Spenser which he usually wore, and the room being very warm owing to the crowd of persons who attended it is supposed he caught cold on going into the open air. From thence he went to an eating house, which he usually frequented, to dinner, & was found there in the afternoon by an Irish gentleman who knowing it to be his place of resort had gone in search of him. The gentleman found him leaning his head upon his hand & very unwell being scarcely able to speak. A coach was got & the gentleman took him to his own house in Castle Street but found the key hole of the door filled by mischievous boys with stones & dirt so that it could not be unlocked. The gentleman then got him a lodging at a pastry cook's in Mortimer Street, where he became worse. Mrs. Bonomi hearing of his condition had him removed to her house where at the end of about five days, on Saturday last, Febry 22nd, he died. Dr. Ferris, Mr. Carlisle, Surgeon, & another gentleman, thought it best not to report his death for a day or two, to give them time to remove his effects from his ruinous house in Margaret Street, which Landseer assisted them in doing.

Joseph Farington, *Diary*, 1806

CHOLERA IN LONDON

The news of the cholera being in London, has been received abroad. According to the feelings of the different nations towards England, France, who wished to court us, has ordered a quarantine in her ports of three days; Holland, who feels aggrieved by our conduct at the Conference, one of forty days. The fog so thick in London, that the illuminations for the Queen's birthday were not visible.

Thomas Raikes, *Diary*, 1832

ST. KATHARINE DOCKS.

WHEREAS unfounded Reports have been circulated of the prevalence of CHOLERA in the ST. KATHARINE Docks, *Notice is hereby given*, that no such Disease exists within the Walls of the Establishment.

By Order of the Board,
JOHN HALL,
July 20, 1832. Secretary.

RCHANT, PRINTER, INGRAM-COURT.

CLEANING UP SOHO

Seven minutes past midnight.

I'm by the window. All the lights off inside so no one can see in. And I'm listening to Hercules and Love Affair on my laptop.

Outside, the night road sweeper brushes the pavement: empty beer bottles and discarded G.A.Y. Flyers. He sweeps them into a small pile, then reaches toward his cart for his shovel. As he does a drunk walks through the pile and staggers on, oblivious. The road sweeper looks down at the scattered rubbish. Runs his fingers through his hair. Sighs.

On Old Compton Street crowds make their way home. Rowdy gangs, boisterous boys, gregarious girls. Like an embarrassing office party that you wish you could leave.

I stand up. Watch from the doorway.

Just by the door a group of businessmen congregate. They crack jokes about the gay couples, unconsciously deflecting the curiosity that draws them here. Patting each other on the back with each comment. Hugging. Whispering in each other's ears. Lips touching skin. Like lovers exchanging tender words. Ironically the most homoerotic presence on the street . . . the businessmen turn into Dean Street. They kick at the resurrected pile of rubbish as they pass, laughing. The road sweeper shouts back at them. They ignore him. Carry on. Then the loudest guy of the group kicks a bottle and slips, landing on the pavement. He picks himself up, curses the road sweeper and storms off to join his friends.

The road sweeper leans on his brush, dejected. He stares at the rubbish strewn across the pavement again and shakes his head. Then a flicker of a smile. What's he seen? Then I spot it, there amongst the flyers. A £20 note that must have fallen from the businessman's pocket.

Clayton Littlewood, *Goodbye to Soho*, 2008

～ 25 *February* ～

YOU LIVE AND LEARN IN LONDON

To Science Museum to join hordes of kids banging away at the do-it-yourself demonstrations, trying to elude the burglar alarm or catch the vanishing metal ball, filling and emptying the bladder in a vacuum jar, pulling a weight various ways. The principles involved seemed to escape them all, as they would me at their ages. Teachers and parents sat nearby snoozing and glancing at their watches. On the bus home, my wallet was stolen by an old lady sitting beside me as I nursed Dan on my lap.

Peter Nichols, *Diaries*, 1971

VICTORIA PARK, VARIABLE

Sunshine followed by snow blizzards. It never snows like it used to, but the snow is still spirited. As I walk along the canal to work, through Victoria Park, listening to 'California Soul' and watching the snowflakes fall, I'm momentarily overjoyed. Music is even better than coffee in the morning, especially in contrast to the addiction of the Today Programme. A gaggle of geese eye me in a guarded way, so close I could offer my hand to peck. Or hack. They're like Government Whips. Every now and then they can be vicious, but it not their fault. It's in their nature.

I walk past a newsagent on Old Ford Road. A billboard for the local paper says, 'Crackdown on Yobs Urges MP Oona.' I'm listening to Brazilian Jazz. I would really like to see a billboard that says, 'Everyone Should Have a Little Dance Urges MP Oona.'

Oona King, *Diary*, 2005

～ 26 *FEBRUARY* ～

INSULTING NELL GWYN

Mrs. Ellen Gwyn being at the dukes playhouse, was affronted by a person who came into the pitt and called her whore; whom Mr. Herbert, the earl of Pembrokes brother vindicating, there were many swords drawn, and a great hubbub in the house.

Narcissus Luttrell, *Diary*, 1680

ON MANOEUVRES

Had job to move the Grenadier Guards from the Barracks near Charing Cross to the Railway Terminus, Paddington, which occupied nearly eight hours. This job is most annoying as there is no remuneration made it. We care not how seldom it comes.

Nathaniel Bryceson, *Diary*, 1846

～ 27 *FEBRUARY* ～

PLANNING FOR THE GREAT EXHIBITION

Rode a little; very fine day. Looked at an old Elm in Hyde Park, which I will not sacrifice to the site of the Exhibition of '51.

George Howard, *Journals*, 1850

STRANGE SPECIMENS IN THE EAST END

I spent the evening in the east end on Saturday. It is a strange neighbourhood, totally different from the parts of London in which my walks generally lie. The faces of the people are of an altogether different type, and even their accent is not quite the same as that of the poor of the west end. I rambled till midnight about filthy courts and backyards and alleys, and stumbled over strange specimens of humanity. I had a long conversation with a curious Welshman. He informed me that he was 'something of a scholar', for he constantly read the newspapers. He was rambling about the crowded streets in his slippers, looking for his wife.

George Gissing, Letter to his sister Ellen, 1883

THE ADVANTAGES OF LATE SNOW
FOR THE CAPITAL

We are simply buried in snow! It is the first real winter weather we have had, and it has come as quite a shock to us, for we thought spring had nearly come. But one blessing of the snow and wintry gales is that it keeps the Zeppelins from coming over.

Hallie Eustace Miles, *Diary*, 1916

THE LONDON LIBRARY BOMBED

Read the papers in Brooks's and walked to the London Library in my corduroy trousers and an old golfing jacket. Joined the volunteers for two exhausting hours in salvaging damaged books from the new wing which sustained a direct hit on Wednesday night. They think about 20,000 books are lost. It is a tragic sight. Theology (which *one* can best do without) practically wiped out, and biography (which *one* can't) partially. The books lying torn and coverless, scattered under debris and in a pitiable state, enough to make one weep. The dust overwhelming. I looked like a snowman at the end. One had to select from the mess books that seemed usable again, rejecting others, chucking the good from hand to hand in a chain, in order to get them under cover. For one hour I was perched precariously on a projecting girder over an abyss, trying not to look downwards but to catch what my neighbour threw to me. If it rains thousands more will be destroyed, for they are exposed to the sky.

James Lees-Milne, *Diary*, 1944

~ 28 FEBRUARY ~

SOCIALISTS AT ST PAUL'S

My French friend went yesterday to St Paul's and saw a large procession of socialists. It is a strange move of the socialists to visit all the Churches. The Archdeacon of London preached to them from: 'The rich and poor meet together, and the Lord is the maker of them all.' A noble sermon. They behaved fairly well.

Helen G. McKenny, *Diary*, 1887

THE ARTISTIC AIR OF HAMPSTEAD

Hampstead still has that air of concealing just around the corner the house I read about in some old book when I was a child, a different life. I know some day I shall find that family whose smell is in the very Hampstead mists, behind the clipped hedge, under the arched doorways where Keats walked with Leigh Hunt, or the whole Sanger family sitting in the sunshine in an untidy studio making music in the middle of the afternoon.

Elizabeth Smart, *Journals*, 1937

THE MOORGATE TUBE DISASTER

In Stanhope Street they were drilling the road and I notice the blond man handling the pneumatic was v. handsome . . . then his friend along-side saw me & and called out 'Hallo Ken! You're looking well!' and they both chorused greeting to me. I loved it & and simpered my 'Thank you very much' like a schoolboy receiving unexpected praise. O! I do adore these kind of men. God sent that incident to me . . . We saw on TV news the account of a bad accident at Moorgate . . . the train accelerated & crashed into the wall of the tube tunnel . . . about 30 people dead. One of the firemen spoke to a cameraman and he was so utterly absorbed in doing his job, but finding time to say 'They've got a lot of courage down there . . .' about the victims, that it made me cry.

Kenneth Williams, *Diary*, 1975

∼ *29 FEBRUARY* ∼

EXPLOSIVES FOUND IN LONDON RAILWAY STATIONS

Henry bought the paper with the account of dynamite being discovered both at Charing Cross and Paddington. Too horrible it is, and as Lord Randolph says it seems hardly a time to talk of extending the franchise when our railway stations are flying in the air! – Mr Gladstone spoke very well and clearly and on the whole I sympathise with the extention [of the vote to town-dwellers] which is likely to bend towards the improvement of the working classes.

Julia Cartwright, *Diary*, 1884

EXOTIC ISLINGTON

A few days before I left London I went to lunch with Raymond Mortimer and his chum Paul, in their wonderful and exotic Georgian house in Canonbury – uphill above Islington. The surrounding ground was covered with snow.

Elizabeth Bowen, Letter to Charles Ritchie, 1956

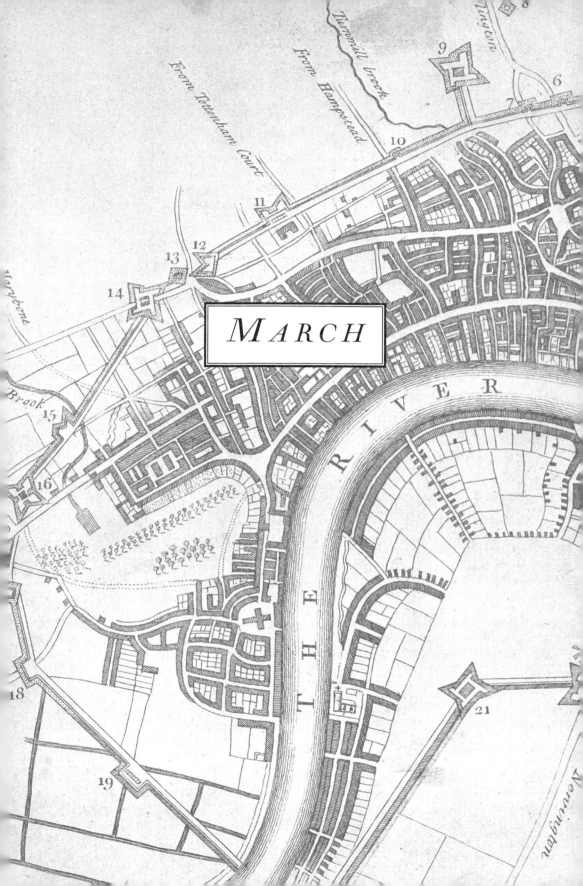

MARCH

~ 1 MARCH ~

A WELSH PROCESSION

The Welsh procession from St. Andrew's Church, Holborn, to the Crown and Anchor Tavern in the Strand to dine; the members, and all of that nation, adorned with leeks and ornaments resembling them, stuck on the button-band of their hats, as is usual on this day, called in the Roman calendar St. David's Day; still continued in his honour, who is the titular saint of the nation. This society is established for the support of the poor, for which they have a fund, schools, etc.

Samuel Curwen, *Journal*, 1782

A GIRL IN GLASSES

In Portland Street, about 10.30 a.m., I saw a bare-armed servant girl on her knees in the street . . . As I passed her, she happened to look up; and I saw that she wore *spectacles*. The first time I ever saw a girl of her class and calling do so.

Arthur Munby, *Diary*, 1880

THIS SUBHUMAN LIFE

The B.s, who only came up to London a few weeks ago and have seen nothing of the blitz, say that they find Londoners very much changed, everyone very hysterical, talking in much louder tones, etc., etc. If this is so, it is something that happens gradually and that one does not notice while in the middle of it, as with the growth of a child. The only change I have definitely noticed since the air-raids began is that people are much more ready to speak to strangers in the street . . . The Tube stations don't now stink to any extent, the new metal bunks are quite good, and the people one sees there are reasonably well found as to bedding and seem contented and normal in all ways – but this is just what disquiets me. What is one to think of people who go on living this subhuman life night after night for months, including periods of a week or more when no aeroplane has come near London? . . . It is appalling to see children still in all the Tube stations, taking it all for granted and having great fun riding round and round the Inner Circle.

George Orwell, *Diaries*, 1940

∼ 2 MARCH ∼

A GREAT FIRE IN THE HAYMARKET

I was wakened at three this morning, my man and the people of the house telling me of a great fire in the Haymarket. I slept again, and two hours after my man came in again, and told me it was . . . Sir William Wyndham's house burnt, and that two maids, leaping out of an upper room to avoid the fire, both fell on their heads, one of them upon the iron spikes before the door, and both lay dead in the streets. It is supposed to have been some carelessness of one or both those maids. The Duke of Ormond was there helping to put out the fire. Brother Wyndham gave 6,000 pounds but a few months ago for that house, as he told me, and it was very richly furnished . . . Wyndham's young child escaped very narrowly; Lady Catherine escaped barefoot; they all went to Northumberland House. Mr. Brydges's house, at next door, is damaged much, and was like to be burnt. Wyndham has lost above 10,000 pounds by this accident; his lady above a thousand pounds worth of clothes. It was a terrible accident.

Jonathan Swift, *The Journal to Stella*, 1712

SIX GROWN MEN STAND ON ANOTHER

After dinner I went to the Haymarket playhouse, where among other representations I saw the strong man show one of his feats. Two chairs were placed on the stage at such a distance as that laying himself along, his head and a small part of his shoulders rested on one, and his feet on the other, so that his body and legs were suspended in the air. Then six grown men (two of whom I observed to be remarkably tall) go up, and stood perpendicular upon his body, two on his chest, two on his body and two on his legs. He bore them all a quarter of a minute, and bending his body downward till it almost touched the ground between the chairs, with a surprising spring and force raised his body with all that weight upon it, not only level as he lay at first, but higher in the air. The mob of the gallery not satisfied with this, hissed, whereupon he refused to show any other of his tricks. This man is about thirty years old and married. He was born in a neighbouring village and by trade a carpenter. His father was 70 years old, and his mother 52 when they begot him. When 13 years of age he beat at boxing boys of 19. He is very fond of music and goes a note lower than Montagnana, the deep voiced Italian now here, wherefore he is now learning to sing. He will bend a kitchen poker round his neck like a withy, or break it by a blow on his arm. He formerly ran vastly swift, till resisting the draught of three cart horses, they by a sudden jerk pulled him over, by which accident he broke his thigh.

Earl of Egmont, *Diary*, 1734

~ 3 March ~

A GRAND DESIGN FOR LONDON

Went to Leicester Square with Mr. Ames, and saw Mr. Vertue there, and had some discourse about his grand design of an Ichnographical Survey, or Map of London and all the suburbs; but Mr. Rocque and he are not yet come to an agreement.

William Oldys, *Diary*, 1738

VERY SLOBBERY STREETS

It hailed more than once in the forenoon, and it rained almost all the afternoon, so the streets were very slobbery. The atmosphere over London is above measure heavy, impregnated so strongly with coal, that the lower part of St. Paul's and other churches are blackened prodigiously.

Thomas Campbell, *Diary of a Visit to England*, 1775

A PLAYWRIGHT AT THE STRAND

This night at the Strand Theatre I saw a great play called *Rope* by Patrick Hamilton. It's a thriller and everyone cheered it. Will soon sell and be seen by the public and how they will like it. Got the author's autograph and by the way he signed I could guess no one had ever before asked him for his signature. Nice sort of bloke . . . quiet and almost shy. But knows his onions.

Fred Bason, *Diary*, 1929

THE OPENING OF THE BARBICAN CENTRE

The Barbican Centre was like a sleeping beauty. One was always aware that something or other was going on in the City but the sheer size of it was totally unexpected: a vast concert hall, huge theatre, studio theatre, cinema, restaurant and art gallery. The opening went like clockwork as far as we were concerned. We found our way to the car park C as instructed and decanted ourselves along with a steady stream of other people in black tie and trailing dresses, and were put on a bus for the Centre. It seemed quite a long drive but after fifteen minutes it became apparent that we had gone more or less round in a circle. The whole affair was a terrific feat of organisation; thousands of people cramming every auditorium were moved this way and that, given endless drinks and finally a buffet supper. The

Arts and City world were there in force, a plethora cascading over seemingly acres of concourse. One appreciated the space and facilities but did it have to be like a Holiday Inn? Garish in colour, splodgy orange ceilings and check carpets, and obtrusive signposting.

Sir Roy Strong, *Diary*, 1982

～ 4 MARCH ～

IMITATING THE BIRDS

It rained almost all the day. That day I left the Hummums, and took a lodging at the Grecian Coffee House, where, after coming from Drury Lane, I heard a fellow imitate the black bird, thrush, lark and canary birds so exactly, that had I heard the same sounds, at proper times, and places, I should never have suspected them to be any other than original: he also did equally well the mewing, and caterwauling of cats, barking of dogs, and dogs hunting cats, &c.

Thomas Campbell, *Diary of a Visit to England*, 1775

A MELANCHOLY VISIT

I have just returned from a most melancholy visit to Newgate, where I have been at the request of Elizabeth Fricker, previous to her execution to-morrow morning, at eight o'clock. I found her much hurried, distressed, and tormented in mind. Her hands cold, and covered with something like the perspiration preceding death, and in an universal tremor. The women who were with her, said she had been so outrageous before our going, that they thought a man must be sent for to manage her. However, after a serious time with her, her troubled soul became calmed. But is it for man thus to take the prerogative of the Almighty into his own hands? Is it not his place rather to endeavour to reform such; or restrain them from the commission of further evil? At least to afford poor erring fellow-mortals, whatever may be their offences, an opportunity of proving their repentance by amendment of life. Besides this poor young woman, there are also six men to be hanged, one of whom has a wife near her confinement, also condemned, and seven young children. Since the awful report came down, he has become quite mad, from horror of mind. A strait waistcoat could not keep him within bounds – he had just bitten the turnkey, I saw the man come out with his hand bleeding, as I passed the cell.

Elizabeth Fry, *Journal*, 1817

WIGEON GOING CHEAP

London swarming with wild fowl; wigeon as low as 1/- a couple in the streets.

Colonel Peter Hawker, *Diary*, 1837

∽ 5 *March* ∽

NOT GOING SOUTH OF THE RIVER

One may live in a vast capital, and know no more of three parts of it than of Carthage. When I was at Florence, I have surprised some Florentines by telling them, that London was built, like their city, (where you often cross the bridges several times in a day), on each side of the river: and yet that I had never been but on one side; for then I had never been in Southwark.

Horace Walpole, Letter to the Miss Berrys, 1791

A BAND OF MECHANICAL MUSICIANS

Visit Weeks's Museum, in Tichborne Street, which consists chiefly of specimens of mechanism. There were birds that not only sung, but hopped from stick to stick in their cages; there were mice made of pearl, that could run about nimbly; there were human figures of full size playing on musical instruments, in full band though neither musicians, nor mice, nor birds, had a particle of life in them. There were silver swans swimming in water, serpents winding themselves up trees, tarantulas running backwards and forwards all equally without life; in short, a collection too numerous and curious for me to attempt to describe . . . The outside of this museum, looks like a common shop for umbrellas and other small wares; as, in fact, it is in front. No one in passing along would ever dream of what it contains as you advance inside, and get towards the rear.

Richard Rush, *Residence at the Court of London*, 1819

RUSHING UNBIDDEN INTO GOD'S PRESENCE

A melancholy event indeed − my poor friend Henry B. destroyed himself this morning in his room at Limmer's Hotel, Conduit-street. Continued losses at play and other pecuniary embarrassments drove him to despair, and he cut his own throat after shaving and dressing himself completely, while the breakfast was preparing by his servant. It was an infatuation of long standing; his father had twice paid his debts to a large amount, and they were unfortunately not on speaking terms for some time past. His poor mother was burnt to death not two months ago, and he never saw her in her last moments. This sad event, and the recollection of his intimate friend ——, who last year drowned himself in the Serpentine from the same dreadful cause, most probably accelerated this catastrophe. He left no letter to any one, − merely the following words, scribbled on the back of a kind note which he had received the preceding evening from his friend the Duke of Dorset: 'I cannot pray, and am determined to rush unbidden into the presence of my God!'

Thomas Raikes, *Journal*, 1832

HAVING A FIT IN BELGRAVIA

Saw a poor miserable girl lying quite rigid on her back in a fit in a smart part of Belgravia; if we had not come up, I suppose she would be there now, everybody 'passing by on the other side' like priests and Levites! We sent for a policeman, who brought her round, and after a time she was well enough to walk feebly away, refusing to go in a cab: only lately out of an infirmary.

Lady Frederick Cavendish, *Diary*, 1868

∼ *6 March* ∼

A STRANGE METEOROLOGICAL PHENOMENON

An extraordinary light in the sky, described to me since by Dr. Clarke, who saw it from the beginning. First appeared a black cloud, from whence smoke and light issued forth at once on every side, and then the cloud opened, and there was a great body of pale fire, that rolled up and down, and sent forth all sorts of colours like the rainbow on every side; but this did not last above two or three Minutes. After that it was like pale elementary fire issuing out on all sides of the horizon, but most especially at the North and North-west, where it fixed at last. The motion of it was extremely swift and rapid, like clouds in their swiftest rack. Sometimes it discontinued for a while, at other times it was but as streaks of light in the sky, but moving always with great swiftness. About one o' clock this phenomenon was so strong, that the whole face of the heavens was entirely covered with it, moving as swiftly as before, but extremely low. It lasted till past four, but decreased till it was quite gone. At one the light was so great that I could, out of my window, see people walk across Lincoln's Inn Fields though there was no Moon . . . All the people were drawn out into the streets, which were so full one could hardly pass, and all frighted to death.

Lady Cowper, *Diary*, 1716

CRUISING ON GOLDERS HILL

A wet Sunday afternoon, and A. and I walk round the edge of Inverforth House on Golders Hill. Noting a number of condoms in the bushes I assume it's a Lovers Lane, but gradually we become aware of a number of single men wandering slowly round and realize we have hit a cruising-ground. We walk up into the gardens, empty on this cold, grey afternoon, and up the steps to the huge pergola that stretches round the house and which is now threatened with demolition. From here we have a grandstand view of the wood below.

A young man in white with a rucksack, whom we saw outside, is still hanging about. He is passed by three or four men, none of whom go far but wait and look back so that eventually he is ringed by admirers, all of them at a radius of twenty yards or so. But nobody actually approaches him, and he seems unaware that he is being watched and eventually drifts away. Occasional decorous family groups pass through the middle of this cruising-ground, civilians crossing a battlefield under the white flag of respectability, but no one who watches for more than two minutes could fail to be aware of what is going on. Though nothing *is* actually going on – just men watching and waiting. Driving home, we speculate why no one approached the young man in white and decide it was because he was (or was thought to be) a policeman.

Alan Bennett, *Diary*, 1988

～ 7 MARCH ～

WATCHING LOVERS IN HYDE PARK

The streets were full of tulips and narcissus and daffodils and it was spring – really. I passed by that little pool in Hyde Park by the Serpentine, cut off from the bridge by bushes. A heron was standing dark and blue grey by the edge and there were sky and bushes shining in its bottom. The grass was bright green and fresh looking and on all the little hillocks purple and white and yellow crocuses are coming up.

I walked along the Serpentine – not on the bank because there were too many people there. Why do people when they go for a walk look at each other? – but up on the other side of the road – and there was a breezy wind enough to blow your hair and make you feel a little like the mascots on motor cars – so I took my loose, loose hat off before the wind did. Before I came to the end, I took a new path across – on my right were two lovers walking away – he bending over and around her with his arm and head. The sparrows were making so much noise that I took off my gloves and scarf in spite of the brick red dress showing, and stuffed them in my purse. And then just as I thought I was alone I saw two more lovers on my left who thought they were alone. They were sitting on a seat under a gigantic trunk of a tree.

I had to walk across that long bare path trying to think of other directions to look in besides theirs. Even painful things pass and that did. It was not that they embarrassed me – I was afraid of embarrassing them and having them send unpleasant thought waves after me. 'Why did she have to come along then?' 'Why can't she get a lover of her own?' Very disconcerting.

The path ended at a little dark house or group of them – with a fence between that and the hard path. The space was a hillock covered with unbelievable crocuses, some just suggestions of colour and others splashes. There was an old tree that began down somewhere low and grew up above the hill and it was so old that two of its frail branches – winding branches – rested on the hill. There was a swarm of policemen coming from one of the houses in the group – some on bicycles – some walking – some with coats or macintoshes slung over their backs. I didn't look at them. Everybody flirts with policemen – they're too used to it.

Elizabeth Smart, *Journals*, 1933

TWO POUNDS FOR THE AFTERNOON

I dressed myself tidily and made my way over Westminster Bridge for a walk to Shepherd's Bush via Oxford Street and the Bayswater Road. I did not hurry. When a shop window attracted my attention I paused and gazed at the things for sale. I read the posters and all manner of advertisements. Looked at the stills in cinemas: and several times went into shops to ask the price of unmarked things in the windows – out of sheer curiosity and without the slightest intention of buying them. For instance I enquired at a jewellers the price of a handsome engagement ring. It was one hundred and fifty-six pounds. I was tempted to ask if they threw in a woman as well at that price, since I had no woman to buy it for. But it was a smart shop and they might not have seen the funny side of my enquiry.

I had long passed Marble Arch and was a good way along the Bayswater Road – indeed within two hundred yards of Notting Hill Gate. It was exactly 2.30 p.m. and the sun was shining brightly. Suddenly a youngish lady with very high heeled shoes and expensive nylons stopped me. 'Hello, dearie,' she said. 'Would you like to come along with me? Only two pounds for the whole afternoon. You can have my mate – look she's just across the road – for an extra thirty shillings. We will give you very good value. You look nice. It will be nice for *all* of us.' This she said without a single pause. I think I must have shown my feelings in my eyes. 'Look at the sunshine,' I said. 'I've come out for *sun*, not *sex*. Don't you think you'd better enjoy the sun as well? There is a time for everything – and not at 2.30 on a lovely afternoon . . .' At Notting Hill I got on a bus to Shepherd's Bush where I called on my friends in the market. They were delighted to see me and we had a nice chat. After some tea, I walked back the way I had come and was near Queensway tube station, when I was asked, 'Like a little time with me? Only two pounds. Do you good. You can have my mate as well for another thirty-five shillings. Both of us will make you happy. She's just across the road.' Lo and behold, although at least two hours had passed, I'd bumped into the girl who'd been across the road on my outward journey, only this one wanted an extra five shillings for her mate. I shook my head. But *why* the extra five shillings? Diary, I hadn't the guts to ask that woman why their tariffs had not agreed. Well, that's what happened. Another side of London life.

Fred Bason, *Diary*, 1953

⌒ 8 MARCH ⌒

SHROVE TUESDAY RIOTS

On the 4th of this month, being our Shrove Tuesday, the 'prentices, or rather the unruly people of the suburbs, played their parts in divers places, as Finsbury Fields, about Wapping, by St. Catherine's, and in Lincoln's Inn Fields, in which places, being assembled in great numbers, they fell to great disorders, in pulling down of houses, and beating of guards that were set to keep rule, specially at a new playhouse, some time a cockpit, in Drury Lane, where the queen's players used to play. Though the fellows defended themselves as well as they could, and slew three of them with shot, and hurt divers, yet they entered the house and defaced it, cutting the players' apparel into pieces, and all their furniture, and burnt their play-books, and did what other mischief they could. In Finsbury, they broke the prison, and let out all the prisoners, and spoiled the house by untiling and breaking down the roof and all the windows. And at Wapping they pulled down seven or eight houses and defaced five times as many, besides many other outrages, as beating the sheriff from his horse with stones, and doing much other hurt too long to write. There be divers of them taken since and clapped up, and I make no question but we shall see some of them hanged next week, as it is more than time they were.

John Chamberlain, Letter to Sir Dudley Carleton, 1617

ELECTION DAY IN BRENTFORD

The election for the county of Middlesex. Sir Francis Dashwood, Messrs. Furnesse, Breton, and I went in Sir Francis's coach, at eight o'clock, to Mr. Cooke's in Lincoln's Inn Fields – A great meeting there – We set out with him about nine; (my coach following) and went through Knightsbridge, Kensington, by the gravel pits to Acton, and from thence to Stanwell Heath, which was the general rendezvous. From thence to Brentford Butts, which was the place of poll. It began about one, I polled early and got to my coach, which was so wedged in, that after much delay, I found it impossible to make use of it; so that Mr. Breton and I were forced to take two of my servants' horses, with livery housings, and ride, without boots, ten miles to Lord Middlesex's at Walton, to meet their Royal Highnesses at dinner.

Bubb Dodington, *Diary*, 1750

～ 9 MARCH ～

AVOIDING THE MOHOCKS

I was at Court to-day, and nobody invited me to dinner, except one or two, whom I did not care to dine with; so I dined with Mrs. Van. Young Davenant was telling us at Court how he was set upon by the Mohocks, and how they ran his chair through with a sword. It is not safe being in the streets at night for them. The Bishop of Salisbury's son is said to be of the gang. They are all Whigs; and a great lady sent to me, to speak to her father and to Lord Treasurer, to have a care of them, and to be careful likewise of myself; for she heard they had malicious intentions against the Ministers and their friends. I know not whether there be anything in this, though others are of the same opinion. The weather still continues very fine and frosty. I walked in the Park this evening, and came home early to avoid the Mohocks.

Jonathan Swift, *The Journal to Stella*, 1712

A BLIND MAN PLAYS CARDS

A wet morning, but cleared up in the middle of the day, but again it rained hard at night. I dined this day with my friend T— B—, whose wife is, I think, the ugliest woman I ever beheld, and at least three-score. There dined with us two old maids, her contemporarys, the sad emblems of a single life, and a rich cit talking vulgar nonsense before dinner, and falling asleep after it; but in the evening, I was fully compensated for this woful set by the company of a blind man – Stanly, the leader of the Oratorio band in Drury lane. This was a very agreeable person, and comely for a blind man. He sat down to cards after tea, and played with as much ease and quickness as any man I ever saw. He had the cards however marked by pricks of a pin; I could not from my cursory examination make the key whereby he marked them. A very stormy night, – now near eleven so that we have not had twenty-four hours together fair, since I came to London.

Thomas Campbell, *Diary of a Visit to England*, 1775

SHOWERED WITH FILTH

A man standing in the pillory* in Oxford Street, at the end of our street, completely knocked me up, never having seen the operation before. I looked out of the window for the instant that the wretched man was putting in, and for one instant afterwards, when he was assailed by such a shower of every sort of mud, filth, and horrors, as to give every part of him and the machine one and the same hideous composition. The horror of seeing a wretched, degraded being, already exposed to the scorn and contempt of the multitude, thus treated by beings like himself; and to see the human form thus vilified, and human creatures – and those mostly women – thus treating it, seized upon my irritable nerves in such a manner as almost to give me what in my life I never had before – an hysterical affection between crying and screaming. We both fled from the window, and took refuge in my back room, to hear as little as we could of the noise of the crowd. It was over, thank heaven, at one o'clock, and nothing should ever bribe me to see such a sight again.

Mary Berry, *Journal*, 1811

* The last person to stand in the pillory in London was Peter Bossy in 1830.

A MATCH AT FOOTBALL

Went to Fulham with Sheriff Dunn to see a match at football between the Corinthians (amateurs) and Newcastle United (professionals), the latter winning by 5 goals to 2. I presented the shield and medals to the winners, and both teams dined with me at the Mansion House in the evening.

Sir William Treloar, *A Lord Mayor's Diary*, 1907

～ *10 March* ～

AN ODD FRAY

I know not whether I told you in my former, of an odd fray that happened much about that time near the Temple, 'twixt one Hutchison of Grays-Inn, and Sir German Pool; who, assaulting the other upon Advantage, and cutting off two of his Fingers, besides a Wound or two more before he could draw, the Gentleman finding himself disabled to revenge himself by the Sword, flew in upon him, and, getting him down, tore away all his Eyebrow with his Teeth, and then seizing on his Nose, tore away all of it, and carried it away in his Pockett.

John Chamberlain, Letter to Sir Ralph Winwood, 1613

HELPING A DISTRESSED DAMSEL

Prince of Wales's wedding. In the evening I went out with Tyndall to see the illuminations. In Pall Mall, at the bottom of the Haymarket, the crowd and crushing were frightful. We were for some time, jammed against the lamp-post in the middle of the roadway, without being able to move, and sustaining a severe pressure. It must have been very bad and dangerous for people not as tall and strong as we were . . . In front of Northumberland House two opposing torrents of people met, and there was a surging vortex of struggling humanity, in which Kenneth was helplessly torn away from me. The next moment a young man of short stature begged me to assist him in protecting his sisters from the crowd, and I had only time to say I would do what I could when another violent rush separated us, and I found myself with the distressed damsel on my hands. I got her out of the thick of the people as soon as possible, and we took refuge under the statue of Charles I, where it seemed likely the brother might come to look for her. Here we waited some time, until my charge said she thought she had better go home. Home might have been Clapham, or Bow, or some distant suburb, and I was glad to find it was no farther than over Blackfriar's Bridge. So we walked quietly in that direction along the Strand, till we got as far as Somerset House. Then there were cries of 'Oh, John!' and 'Oh, Jemima!' The damsel flew to her brother, who had been taking home the other sister, and was now going in search of the lost one; the two disappeared, without a word of thanks, and I went on my way rejoicing at being safely relieved of my responsibility.

Sir Frederick Pollock, *Diary*, 1863

LONDON'S IMMENSITY

I may say that up to this time I have been crushed under a sense of the mere magnitude of London – its inconceivable immensity – in such a way as to paralyse my mind for any appreciation of details. This is gradually subsiding; but what does it leave behind it? An extraordinary intellectual depression, as I may say, and an indefinable flatness of mind. The place sits on you, broods on you, stamps on you with the feet of its myriad bipeds and quadrupeds. In fine, it is anything but a cheerful or a charming city. Yet it is a very splendid one. It gives you here at the west end, and in the city proper, a vast impression of opulence and prosperity.

Henry James, Letter to his sister Alice, 1869

∼ 11 MARCH ∼

AN EARTHQUAKE IN TOWN

As far as earthquakes go towards lowering the price of wonderful commodities, to be sure we are overstocked. We have had a second, much more violent than the first; and you must not be surprised if by next post you hear of a burning mountain sprung up in Smithfield. In the night between Wednesday and Thursday last (exactly a month since the first shock), the earth had a shivering fit between one and two; but so slight that, if no more had followed, I don't believe it would have been noticed. I had been awake, and had scarce dozed again – on a sudden I felt my bolster lift up my head; I thought somebody was getting from under my bed, but soon found it was a strong earthquake, that lasted near half a minute, with a violent vibration and great roaring. I rang my bell; my servant came in, frightened out of his senses: in an instant we heard all the windows in the neighbourhood flung up. I got up and found people running into the streets, but saw no mischief done: there has been some; two old houses flung down, several chimneys, and much chinaware. The bells rung in several houses. Admiral Knowles, who has lived long in Jamaica, and felt seven there, says this was more violent than any of them: Francesco prefers it to the dreadful one at Leghorn. The wise say that if we have not rain soon, we shall certainly have more. Several people are going out of town, for it has nowhere reached above ten miles from London: they say, they are not frightened, but that it is such fine weather, 'Lord! one can't help going into the country!'

Horace Walpole, Letter to Sir Horace Mann, 1750

∼ 12 March ∼

LIFE IN NW1

Keith and Susan Kyle gave a party in their house on Primrose Hill. This is living NW1 style which has no respect for a period house. At the bottom of the stairs a gate had been fixed to cage in the child, the walls vanished beneath swathes of paperbacks, the kitchen cum dining room was scrubbed pine, the drawing-room lined with a particularly hideous gold-striped wallpaper. Everything was very NW1 including the dress of the guests. There was Peregrine Worsthorne in cuddly woollen buttoned down the front and baggy trousers. A. J. Ayer in a tatty suit desperately in need of an expedition to the dry cleaners with Dee Wells, all cleavage, like a vampire on her night off. Vanessa Lawson was like a nymph gone mad in a dress of black nothing while Nigel, thicker than of yore, frustrated and clever, told me he had a constituency waiting for him in the coming election. The food matched the ambience: piles of cold meats, salad and cheese, washed down with rivers of cheap wine.

Sir Roy Strong, *Diary*, 1972

～ 13 MARCH ～

THE FRENCH IN WAX

To-day I went to see Mr. Gosset's* representation of the court of France in wax, as big as the life and clothed in the habits the court of France wore last year, being given to him for that purpose. Nothing can be finer done, nor more like, though only the Duke of Bourbon's face was taken off in plaister of paris. He was so content that he gave Mr. Gosset a complete suit and eighty louis d'ors.

Earl of Egmont, *Diary*, 1731

* Isaac Gosset, born into a family of French Huguenot refugees, was a well-known artist and modeller in wax.

EGYPTIAN ANTIQUITIES AT SOTHEBY'S

Arrived at the Salopian Coffee House at Charing Cross, soon after three. Went to Sotheby's and inspected a fine collection of Egyptian anti-quities: to Somerset House: returned to my Inn to dinner. At nine went to the Meeting of the Geological Society, and returned home at midnight.

Gideon Mantell, *Journal*, 1833

RAIN KEEPS THE PEACE

The day fixed for a meeting at Kennington Common; all the young men of London were made special constables; however, the best peace preserver was a drenching rain, which sent the few thousands that met very quietly home.

George Howard, *Extracts from a Journal*, 1848

～ *14 March* ～

A GIANT BREWERY

This day I called at Mr. Thrale's, where I was received with all respect by Mr. and Mrs. Thrale. She is a very learned lady, and joyns to the charms of her own sex, the manly understanding of ours. The immensity of the Brewery* astonished me. One large house contains, and cannot contain more, only four store vessels, each of which contains

fifteen hundred barrels; and in one of which one hundred persons have dined with ease. There are beside in other houses, thirty-six of the same construction, but of one half the contents. The reason assigned me that porter is lighter on the stomach than other beer is, that it ferments much more, and is by that means more spiritualised. I was half suffocated by letting in my nose over the working floor, for I cannot call it vessel; its area was much greater than many Irish castles. Dined alone, having refused an invitation from Mr. Boyd, in order to see Garrick, and I saw him, which I could not have done, if I had stayed half an hour longer, the pit being full at the first rush. Nor was I disappointed in my expectations, tho' I cannot say he came up to what I had heard of him, but all things appear worse by being forestalled by praises. His voice is husky, and his person not near so elegant, as either Dodd's or King's; but then his look, his eye, is very superior. Lear however was not I think a character, wherein he could display himself.

Thomas Campbell, *Diary of a Visit to England*, 1775

* Henry Thrale, an MP and friend of Dr Johnson, owned a large brewery in Southwark.

ALMS AT PUTNEY

Walked to Mr. Legge's at Putney; a strong cold N.E. wind. Went into the long Putney almshouse, in which are ten old widows and two old men; 2/5 allowed from the charity, 1/6 from the parish, the whole amounting to £6 a year; Miss Pettyward of Putney the patroness.

William Hervey, *Journals*, 1811

A NATIONAL PORTRAIT GALLERY

Dined yesterday with Jerseys and met Lord Stanhope, who is busily employed in the establishment of a National Gallery of Portraits, for which he has obtained a grant from Parliament and a Commission. No portrait of any living person or of one who has died within ten years can be admitted but by the unanimous consent of the Commission. The portraits of criminals are not to be admitted, although Macaulay wished those of Felton, Bellingham, and others of that stamp should be included. He told me what I was not aware of, that Ellesmere had given to the Gallery his famous portrait of Shakespear.

Henry Greville, *Diary*, 1857

～ 15 MARCH ～

AN ATHLETIC HATTER

Yesterday morning at 7 o' clock, a young man, an apprentice to a hatter in the Borough, started for a wager of 20 guineas, to run 19 times round the railing of St. Paul's Cathedral, within the hour, which he performed with much apparent ease in 55 minutes, being 5 minutes under the time. He performed the first 4 rounds in 10 minutes, & then finding he had so much the best of it, he rather slackened his pace, & came in the distance, which is moderately rated at 9 miles, in the time we have mentioned.

Joseph Farington, *Diary*, 1808

A DESCENDANT OF BUNYAN

Wet morning. After breakfast went to the Church of St Lawrence Jewry, near Guildhall, a rather grand church, the first stone whereof was laid April 12th 1671, as stone in the church states. Dirty walking in the City. Saw a gilded coach, with ditto coachmen and footmen, in Holborn going towards the City, which I suppose to be the Lord Mayor's with a gentleman and lady inside – the Mayor and Mayoress 'Alderman Johnson'. After dinner took walk alone to Bunhill Fields Burial Ground to see (not the first time) the tomb of John Bunyan. While there fell into conversation with an elderly lady who came on the same errand, and from her learnt that there is now living an old lady, a descendant and the last remaining of that great man, who is also a member of a dissenting chapel in King's Head Court, Shoreditch, one end whereof leads to the High Street, and the other to Cumberland Street, Curtain Road, and she liveth somewhere in John's Row, Clerkenwell or St Luke's. This same lady has had tea with her twice, and the said descendant by name Skillicker has now in her possession a painting of him . . . I must see this lady if there is a possibility and that next Sunday morning if the weather is fine, and nothing particular prevents and see if the same be true, her age is somewhere about 83 years. Returned home to tea rather lame from the pinch I received upwards of two months back from wearing stockings too large and doubled underwards. Took walk in the evening to meet Ann in Tottenham Court Road and walked together about Bloomsbury and Oxford Street.

Nathaniel Bryceson, *Diary*, 1846

～ 16 MARCH ～

MURDERING ENGINES

I saw a trial of those devilish, murdering, mischief-doing engines called bombs, shot out of the mortar-piece on Blackheath. The distance that they are cast, the destruction they make where they fall, is prodigious.

John Evelyn, *Diary*, 1687

A READING BY DICKENS

To reading by Dickens at St. James's Hall.* He gave Boots at the Holly Tree, the scene between Bill Sykes and Nancy, and a bit of Mrs. Gamp. What an actor he would have made! What a success he must have had if he had gone to the bar! His power of reproducing a scene and bringing to the very eyes of his audience its exact features and the relative bearings of its composing parts has never been equalled.

Sir Frederick Pollock, *Personal Remembrances*, 1869

* A concert hall between Piccadilly and Regent Street, opened in 1858 and demolished in 1905.

THE STENCH OF BILLINGSGATE

To Fishmongers' Hall and found a lecture on Oysters proceeding . . . Then went with the Clerk to St. Magnus: found a man trying the organ which is splendid, and the church apt for rolling melody . . . Then we went on to Billingsgate – strange passages to right opening on wharfs, and to a half-demolished house . . . The stench of Billingsgate, which was deserted and being swabbed out, was appalling – concentrated centuries of bitter briny fishiness. The market is from 4.30 a.m. to 9.0. We keep an inspector and office here, and I saw the 'condemned' barge, officered by a merry pigeon-fancier, in which the condemned and refuse fish is taken away in iron tanks to be made into poultry food at Wapping. But the smell in the whole place made me feel almost faint, and remained with me all day. We then went and inspected Knill's Wharf, under the Hall: the great granite catacombs very fine, and the dark up-towering bridge, and the swirl of the flood-water round the prows of moored barges . . .

A. C. Benson, *Diary*, 1925

～ 17 MARCH ～

THREE TUDOR DEATHS

One master Lynsey armourer dwelling in Bishope-gate street did hang himself in a privy house within his own house for he had his office taken away from him by one that he had brought up. The same day there was a maid dwelling in Hay lane with master Campyon . . . did falle out of a window and break her neck. The same day at the Well with 2 buckets in saint Martens there was a woman dwelling there took a pair of shearers for to have cut her throat, but she missed the pipe in her sickness and madness, and within a day after she died and was buried there in the parish.

Henry Machyn, *Diary*, 1563

A COACH OVERTURNED

Went to see *The Foundling* at Drury Lane Playhouse, farce *Dragon of Wantley*; coming home at night our coach was overturn'd but thank God met with no greater harm than a slight bruise upon my forehead, my sister was not hurt at all.

Miss Ireland Greene, *Diary*, 1748

DRAWING A TOOTH

London. Busy in the City. Tortured with a toothache. Whipped in to the dentist, who ridded me of a tooth like a three-legged stool, which he hung fire at drawing. But I would have it out, and a blessed delivery too!

Colonel Peter Hawker, *Diary*, 1842

A BOMB EXTINGUISHED

An attempt was made yesterday to blow up the Mansion House. A lot of gunpowder was put in a box with a fusee inserted and placed under the painted window of the Egyptian Hall. The paper wrapping was ignited but a policeman saw the smoke and extinguished the flame just in time and before it reached the fusee. A grand banquet which was to have taken place that evening had been countermanded on account of the murder of the Czar.

Louisa Bain, *Diary*, 1881

AN ANTI-AMERICAN RIOT

The afternoon, for us, passed tranquilly, and no strangers ventured up to the gates, which were locked. Meanwhile, in Grosvenor Square, the largest disturbance ever witnessed in London took place. Viewing it on television, it looked for a time as if the police would be unable to withstand the onslaught of the demonstrators, who at their starting point in Trafalgar Square were estimated to number 15,000 people, of whom I regret to say almost 1,000 were said to be Americans. Potential troublemakers have flown in from Germany, Holland, France and some from the United States. By the time they had foot slogged their way to the vicinity of the Embassy, the crowd had somewhat diminished, and probably amounted to no more than 10,000.

David Bruce, *Diary*, 1968

～ 18 MARCH ～

WHIPPED AT A CART'S ARSE

Hugh Weaver, a fishmonger and servant by covenant with Rafe Surbot, was whipped at a cart's arse about London, with a paper set on his head, for misusing the mayor at the stocks and striking his officer in the open market when he was for his misbehaviour commanded to warde; and also had after that long prisonment in the Counter for the same.

Charles Wriothesley, *Chronicle*, 1545

VIOLETS IN CLAPHAM

Walked to Clapham with the children and picked Violets in plenty as we returned.

George Macaulay, *The War Diary of a London Scot*, 1797

OPERA IN COVENT GARDEN

London. I was till now an invalid, but being this day a little better, I went (wrapped up) in the evening to Covent Garden Theatre in order to hear my favourite overture of 'Der Freischütz' conducted by the immortal composer himself, Carl Maria Von Weber. Nothing could be more sublimely beautiful, and the applause that was drawn forth by the appearance of this great composer was no less flattering than just.

Colonel Peter Hawker, *Diary*, 1826

MARMALADE AND BACON THEFT

Opened the Sessions at Central Criminal Court at 10 . . . The first case actually disposed of was that of George Sidney Bodimead, a cook, who pleaded guilty to stealing marmalade, bacon, and other articles belonging to his employer, a coffee-house keeper in Fetter Lane. He was sentenced by the Recorder to twelve months' hard labour.

Sir William Treloar, *A Lord Mayor's Diary*, 1907

∽ 19 MARCH ∽

PEPYS BEHIND THE SCENES

Here we dined, and Sir J. Minnes come to us, and after dinner we walked to the King's play-house, all in dirt, they being altering of the stage to make it wider. But God knows when they will begin to act again; but my business here was to see the inside of the stage and all the tiring-rooms and machines; and, indeed, it was a sight worthy seeing. But to see their clothes, and the various sorts, and what a mixture of things there was; here a wooden-leg, there a ruff, here a hobbyhorse, there a crown, would make a man split himself to see with laughing; and particularly Lacy's wardrobe, and Shotrell's. But then again, to think how fine they show on the stage by candle-light, and how poor things they are to look now too near hand, is not pleasant at all. The machines are fine, and the paintings very pretty.

Samuel Pepys, *Diary*, 1666

∽ 20 MARCH ∽

CRAWLING UP HAYMARKET

Dined out and went to the opera, from whence I had to crawl* all the way up the Haymarket without being able to get a conveyance home; and then had to sit in a house while a fellow with a wooden leg went in search of a Jarvey.**

Colonel Peter Hawker, *Diary*, 1810

* Hawker had been wounded in the leg during the Peninsular War and the wound frequently gave him trouble.
** A slang term for a cab driver.

BAD TEETH

Presided at a meeting of the International Congress of School Hygiene at 3 . . . Dr. Macnamara said that on an examination of 245 boys and girls in a Board School in South London, only three had absolutely sound teeth, and only three had ever used a toothbrush.

Sir William Treloar, *A Lord Mayor's Diary*, 1907

～ *21 MARCH* ～

A SPECIMEN OF ENGLISH FREEDOM

A sweet, soft, and fair day. Strolled into the Chapter Coffee-house, Ave Mary Lane, which I had heard was remarkable for a large collection of books, and a reading Society. I subscribed a shilling for the right of a year's reading, and found all the new publications I sought, and I believe, what I am told, that all the new books are laid in, some of which, to be sure, may be lost or mislayed. Here I saw a specimen of English freedom, viz., a whitesmith* in his apron, and some of his saws under his arm, came in, sat down, and called for his glass of punch and the paper, both which he used with as much ease as a Lord – such a man in Ireland (and I suppose in France too, or almost any other country) would not have shewn himself with his hat on; nor any way unless sent for by some gentleman: now, really every other person in the room was well dressed.

Thomas Campbell, *Diary of a Visit to England*, 1775

* In contrast to a blacksmith who works mostly with iron and steel, a whitesmith works on light-coloured metals such as tin and pewter.

WELCOME LONDON!

It being a foggy day we are disappointed in our expectations of enjoying a distant sea view of England. However, as we draw near, Dover rises to view with its old castle. In a moment we are along-side the splendid wharf; in another moment we are led into a railway carriage which carries us in two hours to Charing Cross Station, London. Welcome London! The Lord be glorified! Directly we reach the station, I am glad to see two Bengalees standing on the platform, B.— and R.—. Accompanied by the former we proceed in cabs to the lodgings of K.—, in Albert street. How great is my joy to find on my friend's table a batch of letters from home! The joy of safe arrival is ten-fold aggravated by sweet news from home! We engage at once two rooms on the first and two on the second floor of the house where our friend is staying.

Keshub Chandra Sen, *Diary in England*, 1870

BAD NEWS FOR A BIGAMIST

I went by invitation to the Old Bailey to hear the recorder administer Justice. A young man of twenty-seven, who had eight sentences for burglary, was bound over to keep the peace. A bigamist got five years. I was rather shocked.

William Inge, *Diary*, 1928

～ 22 MARCH ～

A STAGNANT SUNDAY

In the afternoon, took a 'bus to Richmond. No room outside, so had to go inside – curse – and sit opposite a row – curse again – of fat, ugly, elderly women, all off to visit their married daughters, the usual Sunday jaunt. At Hammersmith got on the outside, and at Turnham Green was caught in a hail storm. Very cold all of a sudden, so got off and took shelter in the doorway of a shop, which was of course closed, the day being Sunday. Rain, wind, and hail continued for some while, as I gazed at the wet, almost empty street, thinking, re-thinking and thinking over again the same thought, viz., that the 'bus ride along this route was exceptionally cheap – probably because of competition with the trams.

The next 'bus took me to Richmond. Two young girls sat in front, and kept looking back to know if I was 'game.' I looked *through* them.

Walked in the Park just conscious of the singing of Larks and the chatter of Jays, but harassed mentally by the question, 'To whom shall I send my essay, when finished?' To shelter from the rain sat under an oak where four youths joined me and said, 'Worse luck,' and 'Not half,' and smoked cigarettes. They gossiped and giggled like girls, put their arms around each other's necks. At the dinner last night, they said, they had Duck and Tomato Soup and Beeswax ('Beesley, you know, the chap that goes about with Smith a lot') wore a fancy waistcoat with a dinner jacket. When I got up to move on, they became convulsed with laughter. I scowled . . .

On the 'bus, coming home, thro' streets full of motor traffic and all available space plastered with advertisements that screamed at you, I espied in front three pretty girls, who gave me the 'Glad Eye.' One had a deep, musical voice, and kept on using it, one of the others a pretty ankle and kept on showing it.

At Kew, two Italians came aboard, one of whom went out of his way to sit among the girls. He sat level with them, and kept turning his head around, giving them a sweeping glance as he did so, to shout remarks in Italian to his friend behind. He thought the girls were prostitutes, I think, and he may have been right. I was on the seat behind this man and for want of anything better to do, studied his face minutely. In short, it was fat, round, and greasy . . . I sat behind him and hated him steadily, perseveringly.

At Hammersmith the three girls got off, and the bulgy-eyed Italian watched them go with lascivious eyes, looking over the rail and down at them on the pavement − still interested. I looked down too. They crossed the road in front of us and disappeared.

Came home and here I am writing this. This is the content of to-day's consciousness. This is about all I have thought, said, or done, or felt. A stagnant day!

W. N. P. Barbellion, *The Journal of a Disappointed Man*, 1914

PARTIES, NOTHING BUT PARTIES

Last night, *party* at Lansdowne House. To-night, *party* at Lady Charlotte Greville's − deplorable waste of time, and something of temper. Nothing imparted − nothing acquired − talking without ideas: − if anything like *thought* in my mind, it was not on the subjects on which we were gabbling. Heigho! − and in this way half London pass what is called life. To-morrow there is Lady Heathcote's − shall I go? yes − to punish myself for not having a pursuit.

Lord Byron, *Journal*, 1814

～ 23 MARCH ～

SPECULATING ON POLYBIUS

In solitary rambles which I took in Hyde Park and Kensington Gardens on several days at this period, I was occupied in speculations upon Polybius, whose remains I had now nearly finished. I completed the whole 1495 pages in sixty-two days, in the midst of many other occupations, or about 750 pages in a month.

Henry Fynes Clinton, *Literary Journal*, 1811

HOUSES DESTROYED

I walked to the Mansion House, the last part of the way with Macaulay; he remarked on 18,000 houses having been destroyed in the great fire of London, and 10,000 being proposed to be taken down for the Metropolitan Junction Railways.

George Howard, *Extracts from a Journal*, 1846

SHOPPING IN HARVEY NICKS

I have spent the morning shopping in Harvey Nichols, which practically adjoins this hotel so is convenient – minor spring clothes. I bought a rather nice banana-coloured heavy-ribbed knitted jacket, and a tangerine Italian cotton shirt, nice and voluminous. I shall look like a plate of dessert. I also bought a toast-coloured woollen suit: I do hope this is a colour you like, as you'll see it often enough.

Elizabeth Bowen, Letter to Charles Ritchie, 1956

WALKIES

Drove to Hampstead for nocturnal walkies.

Ossie Clark, *Diary*, 1990

GLOWING COLOURS IN PICCADILLY CIRCUS

Driving home tonight, I'm staring at the bright lights and plasma screen of Piccadilly Circus. For the first time ever, due to a fluke combination of pastel glowing colours and original graphics, it looks tasteful. In fact, it looks like an art installation.

Oona King, *Diary*, 2005

～ 24 MARCH ～

ELIZABETH IS DEAD, LONG LIVE JAMES

This morning about three at clocke hir Majestie departed this life mildly like a lambe, easily like a ripe apple from the tree ... Dr. Parry told me that he was present, and sent his prayers before hir soule; and I doubt not but shee is amongst the royall saints in Heaven in eternall joyes.

About ten at clocke the Counsel and diverse noblemen having bin a while in consultacion, proclaymed James the 6, King of Scots, the King of England, Fraunce, and Irland, beginning at Whitehall gates; where Sir Robert Cecile reade the proclamacion which he carries in his hand, and after reade againe in Cheapside. Many noblemen, lords spirituell and temporell, knights, five trumpets, many heraulds. The gates at Ludgate and portcullis were shutt and downe, by the Lord Maiors commaund, who was there present, with the Aldermen, &c. and untill he had a token besyde promise, the Lord Treasurers George, that they would proclayme the King of Scots King of England, he would not open.

Upon the death of a King or Queene in England the Lord Maior of London is the greatest magistrate in England. All corporacions and their governors continue, most of the other officers authority is expired with the prince's breath. There was a diligent watch and ward kept at every gate and street, day and night, by housholders, to prevent garboiles: which God be thanked were more feared than perceived.

The proclamacion was heard with greate expectacion and silent joye, noe great shouting. I thinke the sorrowe for hir Majesties departure was soe deep in many hearts they could not soe suddenly showe anie great joy, though it could not be lesse than exceeding greate for the succession of soe worthy a king. And at night they shewed it by bonefires, and ringing. Noe tumult, noe contradicion, noe disorder in the city; every man went about his busines, as readylie, as peaceably, as securely, as though there had bin noe change, nor any newes ever heard of competitors. God be thanked our king hath his right!

John Manningham, *Diary*, 1603

～ 25 MARCH ～

THE BOY JONES

A little scamp of an apothecary's errand-boy, named Jones, has the unaccountable mania of sneaking privately into Buckingham Palace, where he is found secreted at night under a sofa, or some other hiding place. No one can divine his object, but twice he has been detected and conveyed to the Police office, and put into confinement for a time. The other day he was detected in a third attempt, with apparently as little object.

Thomas Raikes, *Journal*, 1841

A BEAUTIFUL GYPSY AT BATTERSEA

I called on Collinson on my way to see Hunt, and the latter himself came in while I was there. He has been on a foraging expedition to Battersea Fields after Gipsies, on the recommendation of one who sat to him for his Druid's head, and as he wants to get some woman with good hands of a proper savage brownness. He finds himself quite disabused of old ideas concerning 'sloshiness' and commonplace of gipsies, having fallen in with some of the most extraordinary-looking people conceivable. He found a very beautiful woman for what he wants, fit for Cleopatra; she consented to sit for 5 an hour, but finally came down to a shilling, and fixed a day to come. His Cleopatra asked him for a pot of beer, over which she and a most hideous old hag, her mother, made their bargain.

William Michael Rossetti, *The P. R. B. Journal*, 1850

PANHANDLING PAM

11 a.m. I'm outside the little coffee shop on the corner of Old Compton Street and Frith Street, writing in my notebook. It's the perfect spot to sit and watch the ebb and flow of Soho life. Within seconds Pam spots me and trots over.

Now, anyone who has ever seen Pam in action will know that she has been blessed with extrasensory powers. She is able to detect a potential pound coin at 50 paces, and once her nose has sniffed out coin, she homes in on it like a shark to menstrual blood. Here she comes now.

'I've missed you,' she sighs, gazing down at the change on the table as if it's the coins she's addressing.

'Ahhhhh. That's nice of you, Pam.'

She tears her eyes away from her long-lost loves and stares at me. ''Ave you got two pound?'

'So much for small talk.'

'Wot?'

'Whatever happened to "Have you got a pound?"'

'Well I haven't seen you for ages, 'ave I?' she fires back with twisted logic.

Feeling suitably chastised, and in one of my 'what goes around comes around' moods, I fish the £2 coin from the table and hand it to her. Without so much as a goodbye, she beats a hasty retreat, chasing a lone businesswoman on Frith Street like a lesbian Benny Hill.

Clayton Littlewood, *Goodbye to Soho*, 2008

～ 26 MARCH ～

SATYRS IN THE NATIONAL GALLERY

After writing in my journal I went out at twelve, and visited, for the first time, the National Gallery . . . There were a great many people in the gallery, almost entirely of the middle, with a few of the lower classes; and I should think that the effect of the exhibition must at least tend towards refinement. Nevertheless, the only emotion that I saw displayed was in broad grins on the faces of a man and two women, at sight of a small picture of Venus, with a Satyr peeping at her with an expression of gross animal delight and merriment. Without being aware of it, this man and the two women were of that same Satyr breed.

Nathaniel Hawthorne, *English Notebooks*, 1856

FIRST SIGHT OF SNOW

After breakfast we drive out in a cab with Rev. Mr. Spears in order to engage lodgings in a more central part of the city than Regent Square where we are at present staying and which lies at an inconvenient distance from the principal institutions and places of importance. After some search we succeed in securing very comfortable rooms in Norfolk Street, Strand, known as 'Mrs. Sampson's Private Hotel' . . . This day for the first time in my life, I see snow falling in beautiful flakes. It is a shower of snow; within a short time everything becomes white — streets, house-tops, trees and even the umbrella and dress of those who are going about. I am so highly delighted with this wonderful natural phenomenon that I cannot resist the temptation of going out into the veranda and receiving a good sprinkling of flakes on my overcoat.

Keshub Chandra Sen, *Diary in England*, 1870

HUMAN SKIN IN SELFRIDGE'S

I was walking in Selfridge's basement yesterday afternoon, idling between two appointments, when I met Selfridge in rather old morning suit and silk hat. He at once seized hold of me and showed me over a lot of the new part of his store. Cold-storage for furs — finest in the world. Basement hall 550 feet long. Sub-basement with a very cheap restaurant where they serve 3,000 to 4,000 customers a day. He introduced me to the head of his baby-linen department: 'Here is a gentleman wants things for three of his children, one is three months, another ten months, and another a year old.' Then up his own private lift to the offices and his room, where I had to scratch my name with a diamond on the window — with lots of others. He showed me a lot of accounting. Then downstairs to book department. Fine bindings etc. His first remark was, taking up a book: 'Human skin.' I had to hurry away. He kept on insisting that it was wonderfully interesting. And it *was*.

Arnold Bennett, *Journals*, 1925

∼ 27 March ∼

NOT KNOWING WHERE HE WAS

Lay long in bed wrangling with my wife about the charge she puts me to at this time for clothes more than I intended, and very angry we were, but quickly friends again. And so rising and ready I to my office, and there fell upon business, and then to dinner, and then to my office again to my business, and by and by in the afternoon walked forth towards my father's, but it being church time, walked to St. James's, to try if I could see the belle Butler, but could not; only saw her sister, who indeed is pretty, with a fine Roman nose. Thence walked through the ducking-pond fields; but they are so altered since my father used to carry us to Islington, to the old man's, at the King's Head, to eat cakes and ale (his name was Pitts) that I did not know which was the ducking-pond nor where I was.

Samuel Pepys, *Diary*, 1664

A SUBLIME HALLELUJAH

Strolled with Mr Flucker in St. James Park until 2 o'clk. Took a dish of Chocolate at the Coffee house & read the papers until 3. Dined at the Crown & Anchor on Cronip Cod & oyster sauce & had to pay for it. In the evening went to Drury Lane to hear the Oratorio of the Messiah, composed by Handel. It is impossible for me to express the pleasure I received. My mind was elevated to that degree, that I could almost imagine that I was being wafted to the mansions of the blest. There were more than one hundred performers, the best in England. The chorus 'Hallelujah! for the Lord God omnipotent reigneth', is the most sublime piece of music in the whole world.

Edward Oxnard, *Diary*, 1776

CRYING OVER NELSON

Where shall I spend the day? decided on Greenwich, arrived there at 1; lunched; everything fell out pat; smoked a cigarette on the pier promenade, saw the ships swinging up, one, two, three, out of the haze; adored it all; yes even the lavatory keepers little dog; saw the grey Wren buildings fronting the river; & then another great ship, grey & orange; with a woman walking on deck; & then to the hospital; first to the museum where I saw John Franklin's pen & spoons (a spoon asks a good deal of imagination to consecrate it) – I played with my mind watching what it would do, – and behold if I didn't burst into tears over the coat Nelson wore at Trafalgar with the medal which he hid with his hand when they carried him down, dying, lest the sailors might see it was him. There was too, his little fuzzy pigtail, of golden greyish hair tied in black; & his long white stockings, one much stained, & his white breeches with the gold buckles, & his stock – all of which I suppose they must have undone & taken off as he lay dying. Kiss me Hardy &c – Anchor, anchor, – I read it all when I came in, & could swear I was there on the Victory – So the charm worked in that case. Then it was raining a little, but I went into the Park, which is all prominence & radiating paths; then back on top of a bus & so to tea.

Virginia Woolf, *Diary*, 1926

∼ 28 MARCH ∼

LECTURES FOR WORKING MEN

Have, during the last few months, been much connected with F. D. Maurice, T. Hughes, and others, who have set on foot an Educational Institution, to which they have given the name of 'The Working Men's College'. It has been established in a house in Red Lion Square, No. 31, and I gave to-night my first lecture or lesson there, upon Physical Geography.

Mountstuart Grant Duff, *Notes from a Diary*, 1855

THE REAL DEAL

I am not sure what its name is. This coffee shop. The blue one on the corner of Old Compton Street and Frith Street. But there's something about it that I like. It feels like the real deal, and it's been here for years. Plus, you can always get a seat. And this is where I sit when I want to get away from the shop, tucked away in the corner, by the window, watching Soho life drift by . . .

Clayton Littlewood, *Goodbye to Soho*, 2008

∼ 29 MARCH ∼

OWLS FOR SALE

Dined at the Athenaeum with Kinglake and Bunbury . . . The latter mentioned that some friend of his having maintained that London was the best place to buy everything, some one present had said, 'Well not everything; I wanted to buy an owl the other day, and of course I had to send to the country for that.' 'Had you?' replied the other; 'come with me to Leadenhall market, to-morrow.' They went, and the advocate of

London, walking up to a stall, asked whether he could have an owl. 'No, sir,' replied the man, 'not to-day, this is Wednesday. Tuesdays and Fridays are the days for owls!'

Mountstuart Grant Duff, *Notes from a Diary*, 1881

∼ *30 March* ∼

LEWD, DEBAUCHED SPARKS

A certain barbarous sect of people arose lately in London, who distinguish themselves by the name of mohocks. There are great numbers of them, and their custom is to make themselves drunk, and in the night-time go about the streets in great droves, and to abuse, after a most inhumane manner, all persons they meet, by beating down their noses, pricking the fleshy parts of their bodies with their swords, not sparing even the women whom they usually set upon their Heads and committ such Indecencies towards them as are not to be mentioned ... They are found to be young, lewd, debauched sparks, all of the whiggish gang, and the whiggs are now so much ashamed of this great scandal, (provided whiggs can be ashamed) that they publickly give out there have been no such people, nor no such inhumanities committed, thereby endeavouring to persuade people out of their senses.

Thomas Hearne, *Diary*, 1712

HANDKERCHIEF STOLEN

I went with [Clowes] to the Vine Tavern while he dined on a beef steak; thence through Lincoln's Inn fields ... thence to the bookseller's by Temple Bar; thence to Richard's, coffee 2d; thence to Paul's Church Yard, had my handkerchief picked out of my pocket very strangely about Ludgate Hill, for I had my hand in my pocket most part of the way, and was resolved it should not go; Mr. Foulkes, Graham, Jurin, Sloane, Hauksbee, Brown, White, at the Club; we had cold ham and veal for nothing, but had the supper besides, which we had bespoke.

John Byrom, *Journal*, 1725

～ *31 March* ～

A PANORAMA AT RICHMOND

Nothing Remarkable happened the forenoon of that day. My Aunt were Buisey so After Dinner I crosst the water to Kew, took a walk between Kew Gardens and Richmond till I came to richmond green. Its a Sweet pleasant place, Tis much like a Square. from thence I went by the waters Side up to Petersham, turn up to the left Hand Up the Hill to Richmond park, which park I do Realy beleive is the pleasants Spot of Ground in the Known World for Sight. On that park you can see the River Thames 30 miles. You can See the countary every way as far as you can see for sight. You could Look East Nothing but Housen and Steeples, London, Westminster, With many other places Round. To look North was Brentford, Acton &c. In Short to Look North and east It was Like one City. To Look West was the River Thames, Vast Numbers of Villages and Gentleman's Seats. Looking south you could see all the country of Surrey. It Look like a Wood, but here and there a Space where was a Gentlemans Seats, theres Vast number of them there.

John Yeoman, *Diary*, 1774

A HECTIC DAY OF SIGHTSEEING

Mr. Davison breakfasted with me. I afterwards called at Mr. Pratt's, thence on to Mr. Barber at the British Museum, thence at Boosey's music shop in Holles Street, then on to Thomas Phillips, Esq., Professor of Painting, about Sir John Swinbourne's portrait, and then at the Papier Mache Manufactory in Edgware Road. I next called on Mr. Orel of Whitfield, then went through the museum of the Zoological Gardens in Bruton Street, and a very admirable museum it is. I next spent an hour at the Western Bazaar, and saw Haydon's pictures of Eucles and Punch, with which I was much pleased, and also with the sculptured figures of Tam o' Shanter and Souter Johnnie, which Mrs. Locker had particularly recommended to my notice. I then visited the beautiful and extensive exhibition of paintings, models, and sculpture at the galleries of the Society of British Artists; and after much too hasty an inspection of these, which well deserve a whole day's examination, I went to the Royal Menagerie at Charing Cross (removed from Exeter Change), – I saw the lions and other principal animals fed. The collection is very interesting, and the ravenous disposition excited by hunger, in most of the animals, is truly terrible. I returned by Fleet Street, where I purchased a very good pantographer.

Thomas Sopwith, *Diary*, 1830

WALKING MILES AND MILES

Very fine, hot day. Spent the whole of it on foot. First went to explore Brixton. Walked up Brixton Hill to Streatham Hill, and by a long circuit through Clapham back to Kennington Park, making a lunch of oranges on the way. Then concert at St James's Hall, but was too late for the cheap tickets. Again walked miles and miles. Home at 10.30, and then kept awake all night by bugs, fleas and crowing of cocks.

George Gissing, *Diary*, 1893

Sion House
One of the Seats of
the Right Honble
the Earl of
Northumberland

New Brentford

Kitchen
Garden

SION HOUSE

APRIL

RIVER THAMES

Ground

35

27

～ 1 APRIL ～

ELECTION RIOTS

The spectre is the famous Wilkes. He appeared the moment the Parliament was dissolved. The Ministry despise him. He stood for the City of London, and was the last on the poll of seven candidates, none but the mob, and most of them without votes, favouring him. He then offered himself to the county of Middlesex. The election came on last Monday. By five in the morning a very large body of Weavers, &c., took possession of Piccadilly, and the roads and turnpikes leading to Brentford, and would suffer nobody to pass without blue cockades, and papers inscribed 'No. 45, Wilkes and Liberty'. They tore to pieces the coaches of Sir W. Beauchamp Proctor, and Mr. Cooke, the other candidates, though the latter was not there, but in bed with the gout, and it was with difficulty that Sir William and Mr. Cooke's cousin got to Brentford. There, however, lest it should be declared a void election, Wilkes had the sense to keep everything quiet. But, about five, Wilkes, being considerably ahead of the other two, his mob returned to town and behaved outrageously. They stopped every carriage, scratched and spoilt several with writing all over them 'No. 45', pelted, threw dirt and stones, and forced everybody to huzza for Wilkes. I did but cross Piccadilly at eight, in my coach with a French Monsieur d'Angeul, whom I was carrying to Lady Hertford's; they stopped us, and bid us huzza. I desired him to let down the glass on his side, but, as he was not alert, they broke it to shatters. At night they insisted, in several streets, on houses being illuminated, and several Scotch refusing, had their windows broken . . . At one in the morning a riot began before Lord Bute's house, in Audley Street, though illuminated. They flung two large flints into Lady Bute's chamber, who was in bed, and broke every window in the house. Next morning, Wilkes and Cooke were returned members. The day was very quiet, but at night they rose again, and obliged almost every house in town to be lighted up, even the Duke of Cumberland's and Princess Amelia's. About one o'clock they marched to the Duchess of Hamilton's in Argyle Buildings . . . She was obstinate, and would not illuminate, though with child, and, as they hope, of an heir to the family, and with the Duke, her son, and the rest of her children in the house. There is a small court and parapet wall before the house: they brought iron crows, tore down the gates, pulled up the pavement, and battered the house for three hours. They could not find the key of the back door, nor send for any assistance. The night before, they had obliged the Duke and Duchess of Northumberland to give them beer, and appear at the windows, and drink 'Wilkes's health'. They stopped and opened the coach of Count Seilern, the Austrian ambassador, who has made a formal complaint, on which the Council met on Wednesday night, and were going to issue a Proclamation, but, hearing that all was quiet, and that only a few houses were illuminated in Leicester Fields from the terror of the inhabitants, a few constables were sent with orders to extinguish the lights, and not the smallest disorder has happened since. In short, it has ended like other election riots, and with not a quarter of the mischief that has been done in some other towns.

Horace Walpole, Letter to Sir Horace Mann, 1768

A MALTESE CALLED VINCENT

Hassling with a Maltese character called Vincent for El Paradise strip club. Track him down to a Soho gambling club. Malcolm knocks on the door and, as it opens, he pushes me inside a small smoky room with card tables. A group of very pissed-off heavy bastards are not amused by this interruption. I think I am going to get my head kicked in. Vincent obviously just wants to defuse this embarrassing situation. He jostles me out of the room and agrees to £90 rent for the club. Malcolm later complains that it's extortionate and that I am useless.

Nils Stevenson, *Vacant: A Diary of the Punk Years*, 1976

~ 2 *APRIL* ~

A MONUMENTAL CLIMB

I then went up to the top of the Monument. This is a most amazing building. It is a pillar two hundred feet high. In the inside, a turnpike stair runs up all the way. When I was about half way up, I grew fright-ened. I would have come down again, but thought I would despise myself for my timidity. Thus does the spirit of pride get the better of fear. I mounted to the top and got upon the balcony. It was horrid to find myself so monstrous a way up in the air, so far above London and all its spires. I durst not look round me. There is no real danger, as there is a strong rail both on the stair and balcony. But I shuddered, and as every heavy wagon passed down Gracechurch Street, dreaded that the shaking of the earth would make the tremendous pile tumble to the foundation.

James Boswell, *London Journal*, 1763

SHAKESPEARE FORGERY STAGED

Ireland's play of Vortigern I went to. Prologue spoken at 35 minutes past 6: Play over at 10. A strong party was evidently made to support it, which clapped without opposition frequently through near 3 acts, when some ridiculous passages caused a laugh, which infected the House during the remainder of the performance, mixed with groans. Kemble requested the audience to hear the play out abt. the end of the 4th act and prevailed. The Epilogue was spoken by Mrs Jordan who skipped over some lines which claimed the play as Shakespeare's. Barrymore attempted to give the Play out for Monday next but was hooted off the stage. Kemble then came on, & after some time, was permitted to say that 'School for Scandal would be given,' which the House approved by clapping.

Sturt of Dorsetshire was in a Stage Box drunk, & exposed himself indecently to support the Play, and when one of the stage attendants attempted to take up the green cloth, Sturt seized him roughly by the head. He was slightly pelted with oranges. Ireland, his wife, son and a daughter and two others were in the center Box, at the head of the Pitt. Ireland occasionally clapped, but toward the end of the 4th act he came into the front row, and for a little time leant his head on his arm & then went out of the Box & behind the scenes. The Play house contained an audience that amounted to £800.

Joseph Farington, *Diary*, 1796

FLYING OUT AT BOTH ENDS

Saterday, about 9 o Clock I set out for the City of London by Water, but the Wind and Tide was against each tother that the Waves did roll and it was Very Dangerous. I Landed att Hungerford Stairs about Eleven O Clock, from Thence I went to Mr. Forresters att the Seven Stars, Market Lane. Dined there, from thence I went with Mr Forrester to South-molten Street to my Cousen Ambrose Bools, but he being not at home We Wente to Sir Rich Suttons, where my cousen John Bool lives, where we made free with the Juce of the Vine. Mr. Forrester Was quite full, went home to his house Where he was so Sick that it flew out att both ends like a Bedlamite. We had Some Tea and my cousen John come to see where we was safe arrived. He and I drank two pots of Porter, Smokt a pipe of Tobacco and also claret. I went to Bed for that night.

John Yeoman, *Diary*, 1774

POLL TAX RIOTS

Last night there were riots in London. All the anarchist scum, class-war, random drop-outs and trouble seekers . . . There is this strain in most Western countries, but it is particularly prevalent in Britain, where this rabble have – confirming their middle-class social origins – their own press in *The Grauniad* [sic] and *The Independent*.

Alan Clark, *Diaries*, 1990

~ *3 April* ~

SETTING A BAD EXAMPLE

Snowball, our beadle, told us at the Vestry that five a clock in the morning one day this week the Duke of Bedford, Mr. Spencer, brother to the Duke of Marlburow, and Lord Beaumont, the Duke of Roxburow's son, together with two others he knew not, came from a tavern in Pall-Mall with three ladies (as he called them) to the watch house and stayed there till seven, drinking wine they brought with them, after which the gentlemen went away, leaving the ladies. Two of them were so drunk that the watchmen found it difficult to prevail on them to go home, they being desirous to sleep there. A rare example for the commonalty!

Earl of Egmont, *Diary*, 1736

NOT WORTH FIVEPENCE

Fair. I went to the British Museum. The sight was so various, that it was hard to remember any thing distinctly, but what pleased me most was the ruins of Herculaneum. The original Magna Carta of King John was in the Harleian, I think. The shell for which a Cardinal give five pounds, I would be sorry to give five pence for, unless merely because it is a specimen of human folly. The magnitude of the crocodile (twenty feet) and the horn (five feet at least) growing out of the nose of the unicorn fish were extraordinary to me.

Thomas Campbell, *Diary of a Visit to England*, 1775

∼ 4 *April* ∼

PAPIST FOPPERIES

I went to see the fopperies of the Papists at Somerset-House and York-House, where now the French Ambassador had caused to be represented our Blessed Saviour at the Pascal Supper with his disciples, in figures and puppets made as big as the life, of wax-work, curiously clad and sitting round a large table, the room nobly hung, and shining with innu-merable lamps and candles: this was exposed to all the world; all the city came to see it: such liberty had the Roman Catholics at this time obtained!

John Evelyn, *Diary*, 1672

VERY LIKE THE SANSKRIT COLLEGE

Rev. Mr. Spears accompanies us to the British Museum to-day. There, after seeing the central library room, which contains a large number of high book-shelves arranged in a circle, we pass on from department to department and hurriedly glance over the various animal, mineral, geological, collections. The front of the building is very much like that of the Sanskrit College at Calcutta. On our way home we go into a photographer's shop and sit for a 'group' of our whole party.

Keshub Chandra Sen, *Diary in England*, 1870

～ 5 *APRIL* ～

AN OLD INN IN WHITECHAPEL

After dinner took walk alone to Whitechapel to see the remains of an old inn called White Hart near Somerset Street, which was built before the reign of Henry VIII. Had very imperfect view – the house was partly razed to the ground and on its site is to be erected a more spacious building. Made for own neighbourhood and had tea at coffee shop corner of Grafton and Sussex Streets, after which took Ann for walk about Hyde Park. It may not be unworthy of remark that at the present time there is a little cherry tree growing on the City side of London Bridge, and a rookery in a tree corner of Wood Street and Cheapside. Paid into bank 20/-. Total £18.

Nathaniel Bryceson, *Diary*, 1846

A NOBLE BUT PURPOSELESS BUILDING

In the afternoon I went by omnibus to Hammersmith, passing the newly opened Albert Hall, a noble but purposeless building. Opposite, men were railing off a piece of Hyde Park into Kensington Gardens, and making a wide approach to the Prince Consort's monument, now nearly ready.

Arthur Munby, *Diary*, 1871

~ 6 *April* ~

STRENGTHENING THE TENDONS

I took my usual sweat, which made me well, and strengthened my tendons, so that the next day I went to London, and walked much up and down the streets, without any pain; at night I became hot and slept ill.

Elias Ashmole, *Diary*, 1681

DR HALE'S VENTILATOR

I went to the Hospital at Hide Park Corner where we agreed some matters for building a chapel and enlarging the house, and in my return visited my brother Percival who is still laid up with the gout. At the Hospital, I saw Dr. Hale's ventilator, or engine for recruiting the sick persons' apartments with fresh air, for he had fixt one there, which on occasion will draw the tainted air of three stories out in the space of half an hour, and supply its place with fresh air.

Earl of Egmont, *Diary*, 1744

A VISIT TO MILLBANK PENITENTIARY

I left off in the Millbank Penitentiary, but what more I was going to say I cannot recollect; so, my dear mother, you must go without that wisdom. All that I know now is that I saw a woman who is under sentence of death for having poisoned her sister. She appeared to me to be insane; but it is said that it is a frequent attempt of the prisoners to sham madness, in order to get to Bedlam, from which they can get out when *cured*. One woman deceived all the medical people, clergyman, jailer, and turnkeys, was removed to Bedlam as incurably mad, and from Bedlam made her escape. I saw a girl of about eighteen, who had been educated at Miss Hesketh's school, and had been put to service in a friend's family. She was in love with a footman who was turned away:

the old housekeeper refused the girl permission to go out the night this man was turned away: the girl went straight to a drawer in the house-keeper's room, where she had seen a letter with money in it, took it, and put a coal into the drawer, to set the house on fire! For this she was committed, tried, convicted, and would have been hanged, but for Sir Thomas Hesketh's intercession: he had her sent to the Penitentiary for ten years. Would you not think that virtue and feeling were extinct in this girl? No: the task-mistress took us into the cell, where she was working in company with two other women; she has earned by her constant good conduct the privilege of working in company. One of the Miss Wilbrahams, when all the other visitors except myself had left the cell, turned back and said, 'I think I saw you once when I was with Miss Hesketh at her school.' The girl blushed, her face gave way, and she burst into an agony of tears, without being able to answer one word.

Maria Edgeworth, Letter to her mother, 1822

~ 7 *APRIL* ~

TWO BOYS IN A DITCH

I dined with my Aunt Allanson. After Dinner we went to Sir Godfrey Kneller's to see a Picture of my Lord which he is drawing, and is the best that was ever done for him. It is for my dressing-room, and in the same posture that the dear fellow watched me so many weeks in my great illness. From thence I went to the New Exchange* and bought a Teaboard, and came home to wait upon my spouse, who came about an hour after. As he came along, the people were pulling two Boys out of a Ditch, that had been stript and flung there by Footpads.

Lady Cowper, *Diary*, 1716

* The New Exchange was a kind of early version of a shopping mall which was built on the south side of the Strand in 1608 and stood there until 1737.

AN EIGHTEENTH-CENTURY ELECTION

Passed a crowd attending procession in Parliament street, going to take the Westminster candidate, Charles J. Fox, from his lodgings to the hustings under St Paul's, Covent Garden portico. First marched musicians two and two, then four men supporting two red painted poles having on top the cap of liberty of a dark blue color; to each was fastened a light blue silk standard about nine feet long and five wide, having inscribed thereon in golden letters these words, 'The Man of the People'; followed by the butchers with marrow-bones and cleavers; then the committee two and two, holding in their hands white wands; in the rear the carriages. They stopped at his house in St James's-street, where taking him up, he accompanied them in Mr. Byng's carriage through Pall Mall and the Strand to the hustings, when the election proceeded; made without opposition, no competitor appearing against him.

Samuel Curwen, *Journal*, 1783

A HAT FROM LOCK'S

Lunched at White's, and did some shopping in the neighborhood. I replaced my battered felt grey hat with a new one from Lock's. Buying a hat at Lock's requires about one half hour of time. First, either the customer's head or present hat is measured, thereafter the measurer vanishes into the cellar, applies heat to whatever headgear he selects there, then reappears on the main floor and insinuates it on to one's head. Since the first presentation is seldom successful, there is a great going back and forth between floors before the mission is accomplished. As Lock's is famous for never having made two hats alike, the numbered sizes have little relevance.

David Bruce, *Diary*, 1967

~ 8 APRIL ~

A CAT HANGED IN CHEAPSIDE

Was a villainous fact done in Cheape early before daylight. A dead cat having a cloth like a vestment of the priest at mass with a crosse on it afore, and another behind put on it; the crown of the cat shorn, a piece of paper . . . put between the forefeet of the said cat bound together, which cat was hanged on the post of the gallows in Cheape beyond the Cross in the parishe of St. Matthew, and a bottle hanged by it; which cat was taken down at vi of the clock in the morning and caried to the Bishop of London, and he caused it to be showed openly in the sermon time at Paul's Cross in the sight of all the audience there present. The Lord Mayor, with his brethren the aldermen of the City of London, caused a proclamation to be made that afternoon that whosoever could utter or show the author of the said fact should haue 6l 13s. 4d. for his pains, and a better reward, with hearty thanks. But at that time, after much enquiry and search made, it could not be known, but diverse persons were had to prison for suspicions of it.

Charles Wriothesley, *Chronicle*, 1554

FREE FROM OUTRAGE

Saw Mr. Hatchet, who lives at the corner of Clarges Street; he reported Piccadilly to be full of people,* but free from outrage, owing to the presence of the Horse Guards; the people, however, getting into the Green Park, had pelted them through the iron rails, upon which a troop was dismounted and marched by with their bayonets fixed on their carabines, through the little gate into the Green Park, and driving the people without mischief to the walk on the other side of the pond, and keeping that next the street clear. I walked to Lady G. Morpeth's, with whom I sat an hour; it was a cold dry day, and the streets were uncommonly full, but no apparent disposition to rioting or anything more than general curiosity, and a general fabrication and belief in lies at the corner of every street.

Mary Berry, *Journal*, 1810

* People were in the streets protesting against government plans to arrest the Radical MP Sir Francis Burdett.

THE WILDNESS OF THE WORLD

I am under the impression of the moment, which is the complex one of coming back home from the South of France to this wide dim peaceful privacy – London (so it seemed last night) which is shot with the accident I saw this morning & a woman crying Oh oh oh faintly, pinned against the railings with a motor car on top of her. All day I have heard that voice. I did not go to her help; but then every baker & flower seller did that. A great sense of the brutality & wildness of the world remains with me – there was this woman in brown walking along the pavement – suddenly a red film car turns a somersault, lands on top of her, & one hears this oh oh oh.

Virginia Woolf, *Diary*, 1925

∼ *9 APRIL* ∼

DEAD MAN WITH REPTILES

Went to Guy's Hospital, and found my friend Dr Hodgkins examining the body of a man who had died suddenly. Went over the Museum of Anatomy, and afterwards looked at the skeletons of some reptiles.

Gideon Mantell, *Journal*, 1833

SEEING OFF A SON AT THE DOCKS

In Town. Sallied forth after breakfast, Bessy, Russell, and myself, to visit the ship in which our poor boy is to be taken away from us. Called at

Lubbock's, in whose hands I had placed the 339l. remaining of the sum destined for the outfit, &c. Went from thence to the East India Docks, where the ship was lying. The operation of getting Bessy up the step-ladder that led us on board added not a little to my exceeding nervousness on the occasion. Had never myself been on board so immense a vessel; the accommodations for passengers almost as roomy as those in a good-sized house . . . But our dear Russell's berth was, of course, the chief object of our attention, and I was most agreeably surprised by its roominess. We had determined from the first, that though increasing so much the expense, he should have a cabin to himself, and we now had all his things brought and stowed away under the mother's eye comfortably.

Thomas Moore, *Diary*, 1840

PANDEMONIUM

Usual scenes in town to-night after Oxford and Cambridge Boat Race, in which Oxford won by two and a half lengths, the fastest time on record. Empire, Alhambra, Trocadero, and Tivoli music-halls jammed with rollicking semi-riotous mobs of students. The Strand at 9 p.m. was pandemonium.

R. D. Blumenfeld, *R.D.B.'s Diary*, 1892

~ 10 APRIL ~

ALL PASSING OFF SMOOTHLY

Rather a fine morning. All looked very fine from Grosvenor Place; I walked across to the Office, which I found more animated than usual, the clerks receiving their truncheons as special constables, under the captaincy of Charles Gore. John Gardiner came in from Kennington Common, where he thought there were about twenty thousand people; all going on quietly.* Very soon the streets filled with the returning crowds; all was over, the meeting dispersed, the procession abandoned, the Petition sent to the House in three hack cabs . . . It has been a memorable day for England; after such long announced threats, such general apprehension, all has passed smoothly off, without a single soldier being seen, or one of the 150,000 special constables being called into action.

George Howard, *Extracts from a Journal*, 1848

* This was a mass meeting called by the Chartist Convention to form a procession to take a petition to Parliament demanding various electoral reforms. In a year of revolutions across Europe, the government was greatly concerned by the gathering and had sworn in more than 100,000 special constables to support the police but, as Howard reports, the meeting passed off peacefully.

PARADISE A VERY DULL PLACE

A horrible thick orange fog after a night of rain. Last night I went to Apsley House, where a few persons were assembled to see a conjurer of the name of Taylor, who professes to show up the humbug of spirit-rapping. I came too late to see this part of the performance, though I was told by people who were present that he was very successful in the attempt. I don't know if Sir Edward Lytton Bulwer, who is supposed to believe in 'mediums' and all the toggery of spirit-rapping, was convinced. It would be well if anything could put a stop to this subject of conversation, which has become a great bore, and which seems to have taken strong hold of the minds, not only of foolish women, but even of men whom one should not have supposed capable of being occupied with and deluded by such palpable humbug. Somebody said, 'Really Paradise must be a very dull place if spirits can so readily leave it to converse here below on the most frivolous subjects with the weakest of men and women.'

Henry Greville, *Diary*, 1862

A LAST VISIT TO LONDON

Feeling absolutely awful I nevertheless go to London for day. Not a success. Went First Class for once. Full of businessmen glued to telephones, very irritating. Failed to find a cardigan, chief object of expedition. Nearest approach to what I wanted was priced at £430 in Burlington Arcade . . . Was almost made gaga by dodging the blazing sun and blinding shadows of the streets. Tired to death. I fear I can never go to London again. Just not up to it. Found the weight of my rolled umbrella and overcoat almost too much for my feeble shoulders and stick-like arms.

James Lees-Milne, *Diary*, 1997

~ 11 APRIL ~

SHIPS SHOOTING OFF THEIR GUNS

The King removed from Westminster by water to Greenwich; and passed by the Tower, and there were a great shot of guns and chambers, and all the ships shot off guns all the way to Ratclyff, and there the 3 ships that was rigging there, appointed to go to the Newfoundland, and the 2 pennons shot guns and chambers a great number.

Henry Machyn, *Diary*, 1553

GARIBALDI IN LONDON

We spent a notable aftn in a window of the Privy Council Office; Atie P., Agnes, and I, with Ld. Frederic and Mr. Palgrave, waiting to see Garibaldi pass, on his way to Stafford House, which takes him in. We waited, and so did the great crowd that had assembled, till 6½, when at last, some time after a long procession of Working Men's Clubs and societies, with banners, had passed, the great man appeared in a carriage-and-six, wearing a blue-and-red cloak and wideawake. I suppose such a scene as has greeted him has never before been known, and never could be but in England. All the working people, of their own free will and enthusiasm, turned out in his honour; nobody directed or controlled them (very few policemen), and to be sure it is grand to feel and see the perfect trust that may be placed in the mighty free action of Englishmen and their sympathy with what is high-minded and disinterested. They poured and flocked round the carriage, shaking hands, waving hats and handkerchiefs; and he was accompanied all up the street by unbroken cheers.

Lady Frederick Cavendish, *Diary*, 1864

A PLAQUE IN ST PAUL'S, COVENT GARDEN

Family outing to *Popeye*. We ate excellent hamburgers in Covent Garden and the sun came out and shone on us as we walked through the Garden, past the escapologist, through St Paul's churchyard, where trees have been planted in memory of actors buried there. One rather undernourished little shrub was ironically plaqued 'In memory of Hattie Jacques'. Home to hear that there was burning and looting going on in Brixton as we had wandered through the quiet bustle of the West End on this sunny Saturday afternoon.

Michael Palin, *Halfway to Hollywood*, 1981

～ 12 APRIL ～

A HANGING IN THE CLINK

A priest hung himself in the Bishop of Winchester's palace, at the Clink, which priest was of the new sect, and there in the prisoner's ward was put in the bishop's house to have been examined by the bishop.

Charles Wriothesley, *Chronicle*, 1540

A HUGE GUN IN BAYSWATER

Had a grand day from six in the morning till twelve, with Joe Manton and his myrmidons firing with, and regulating the new elevated sights of, my huge double swivel gun, which we wheeled down to Bayswater, to the astonishment of the gaping multitude and idle followers.

Colonel Peter Hawker, *Diary*, 1827

COUNCIL ON ITS BEST BEHAVIOUR

Camden Council are sweeping the roads an awful lot these days. One thing Thatcher has done by introducing legal restraints on both the GLC (abolition) and Camden (rate-capping) is to stimulate both authorities into an orgy of PR. Nary a day goes by without a petition to be signed, or a new sticker to be stuck up, or a fresh slogan – Camden vehicles now carry: 'A Camden Service' 'Too Good to Lose'. Suddenly they're all on their best behaviour.

Michael Palin, *Halfway to Hollywood*, 1984

∽ 13 APRIL ∽

THESE WRETCHED BEINGS

I went on Friday morning to the Old Bailey to hear the trials, particularly that of the women for the murder of the apprentices;* the mother was found guilty, and will be hanged to-day – has been by this time. The case exhibited a shocking scene of wretchedness and poverty, such as ought not to exist in any community, especially in one which pretends to be so flourishing and happy as this is. It is, I suppose, one case of many which may be found in this town, graduating through various stages of misery and vice. These wretched beings were described to be in the lowest state of moral and physical degradation, with scarcely rags to cover them, food barely sufficient to keep them alive, and working eighteen or nineteen hours a day, without being permitted any relaxation, or even the privilege of going to church on Sunday. I never heard more disgusting details than this trial elicited, or a case which calls more loudly for an investigation into the law and the system under which such proceedings are possible. Poverty, and vice, and misery must always be found in a community like ours, but such frightful contrasts between the excess of luxury and splendour and these scenes of starvation and brutality ought not to be possible; but I am afraid there is more vice, more misery and penury in this country than in any other, and at the same time greater wealth. The contrasts are too striking, and such an unnatural, artificial, and unjust state of things neither can nor ought to be permanent. I am convinced that before many years elapse these things will produce some great convulsion.

Charles Greville, *Diary*, 1829

* Two women, mother and daughter, both called Esther Hibner, were tried for the killing of a ten-year-old boy who had been apprenticed to them.

LATE AT DOWNING STREET

Dined at Downing Street after a really frightful day of trivial but insistent pressures – compounded by that special sense of angst and frailty that affects one's birthday. No cards or tributes (fortunately I am not on The Times list. I say 'fortunately' because I do not like people knowing how old I am). I was exhausted, as there was a tube strike and no cabs so earlier I had to *walk*, carrying a full two gallon can of petrol, from the House of Commons to Albemarle Street where I finally got a taxi by *force majeure* and then on to Sussex Gardens where the faithful Citroen had puttered to a halt on Friday while I rushed to catch the Plymouth train. The only bonus was that she had stood unharmed and unticketed on a resident's parking space throughout the weekend. She started instantly, as always, and I drove back to the Albany so that Jane could use her to pick me up at the Commons. We arrived at Number 10 a little late . . .

Alan Clark, *Diaries*, 1981

∽ 14 *A*PRIL ∽

DANCING ON A WIRE

I went to the Royal Exchange & the New England Coffee-house, where I was invited to go with a number of gentlemen to Sadler's Wells to see the performances there, the dramatic & musical parts of which were very low & indifferent. The first thing curious which we saw was jumping & tumbling which they did in a surprising manner turning heels over head two or three times without stopping. But the most curious thing which next succeeded this was playing a tune on the Glassicord in a most melodious affecting strain. The next thing was dancing on a wire. There then came a man, who swang him backward & forward 15 or more feet, he standing all the time on one leg. There was then a long board bro't that was pliant, which wou'd not rest upon the wire before he put his feet upon it, and then kneeling down on one knee took a glass & held the foot of it in his mouth, then taking a sword & placing the point in the glass swang back & forward. Then placing a pewter plate upon the hilt of the sword, whirl'd the sword round very swiftly. There were many other things, which he perform'd with surprising agility, as fixing a hoop upon a pipe in such a manner as to stand steady; then fixing the small end of the pipe upon the hoop, one part of which he held in his mouth. He then took a French horn & placing it to his mouth, stretched forth both his hands horizontally & blew very well a minuet. He plac'd his cane upon the top of his head & a hat upon the end of that, then swinging about, threw his cane off so as it fell upon his head; this he repeated twice.

Joshua Wingate Weeks, *Diary*, 1779

SHOPPING FOR CLOTHES IN COVENT GARDEN, EIGHTEENTH CENTURY STYLE

As I go out of town for the summer to morrow, I have only time to tell you I have seen all the new lute-strings,* that three shops produce, those made for this summer are all clouded, I think vastly ugly and dear, for they are all dark, colours. In short I would not venture to buy one for you, if I was in your place I would have a plain one, and if you write to Mr. Hinchliffe, mercer at the Hen and Chickens, in Henrietta Street, Covent Garden, and say I recommended you, he will send you some patterns. I send inclosed one of the only striped I've bought for this summer, which I think a pretty one, but I know you dislike yellow, it was bought at Swan and Bucks, mercer at the Wheat and Sheaf in King Street, Covent Garden. Mrs. Dantin the sack-maker lives in Mount Street, near Grosvenor Square; and now as for caps, I have got you one of blonde which I bespoke, and one I intend as a present to Madam Sal, but do not know how to send them, 'tis too small to go by the carrier, and yet if they are tumbled they are spoiled, and I have set my heart upon your liking them; pray let me know how they are to be conveyed.

Lady Jane Coke, Letter to Mrs Eyre, 1755

* Lute-string here means not, as one might immediately think, the string of a musical instrument but a type of glossy silk fabric.

～ 15 APRIL ～

A GREAT TRAIN OF CHARITY CHILDREN

Wrote a little till ten; then walked to Mr. Gale's, and Mr. Harper's, but missed of both; in return met the Lord Mayor in all his pomp, with the Aldermen, Sheriffs, with a great train of charity-children, going to St. Bride's Church, all decently habited, some in blue coats with yellow vests, others brown, most with blue caps, but some with white hats and mathematical instruments in their hands.

Ralph Thoresby, *Diary*, 1723

BUT LITTLE PLEASED

Went to the ball at the Mansion house in company with Mr. Knight, a lady unknown, and Miss Pownall, all of River Terrace. At the said ball only two things worthy of notice occurred viz. the meeting of an old crony and schoolfellow (Edward Howard) whom I had not seen or heard of for upwards of 13 years; and the not being able to procure the least refreshment of any kind for our almost fainting ladies. We got home by about ½ past 2, and but little pleased with our expedition.

J. Williams, *Journal*, 1816

A HORRID CLUB

Went to dine at the Garrick Club, saw two or three persons with whom I have a slight acquaintance, but not to speak to them. Was disgusted by a most filthy and offensive speech made by a man whose name I do not know whilst I was dining; it *is a horrid club*!

William Charles Macready, *Diary*, 1837

A NEW RESTAURANT

Diana and I dined at a new restaurant called The Ivy. We discussed our future at length. It seems to me that in many ways it would be wiser to wait but I don't like to press this view on her. She is so anxious to be married in the spring. And I have myself an uneasy consciousness of the dangers of postponement . . . We went to see Katherine after dinner whom we found with Conrad. Diana wanted morphia as she had to battle with her mother again, who had promised to speak to the Duke today. But when she got in she found her mother had gone to bed with a headache and had shirked taking any action at all.

Duff Cooper, *Diary*, 1919

～ *16 April* ～

A NEW PRINCESS OF WALES

In the morning went to Mrs. Dawson's, the famous milliner in Pall Mall, to see the new Princess of Wales* go for the first time to the drawing-room in her new state coach. The crowd, as one might suppose, was immense; no carriages allowed to go up or down Pall Mall; but as it was a fine day, the companies who could not get into the houses walk'd for some hours up and down, and when the Prince's carriages came, made a lane for them to pass. It certainly was a fine sight, tho' almost too gaudy to be pleasing. On Saturday, we being out in the carriages, were stopped by another procession of eighteen carriages, the Lord Mayor and Sheriffs going with the address on the Prince's marriage.

Mrs Philip Lybbe Powys, *Diary*, 1795

* This was Caroline of Brunswick whose marriage to the Prince of Wales, later George IV, was a disaster.

THE NIGHT SHRIEKS LIKE
AN AFRICAN JUNGLE

Dine with Sibyl at the Dorchester. I get away as early as I can, but have to walk the whole way back to the Ministry. There is a hot blitz on. To the south, round about Westminster, there is a gale of fire, as red as an Egyptian dawn. To the north there is another fire which I subsequently see at closer quarters. The stump of the spire of Langham Place church is outlined against pink smoke. I walk on under the guns and flares and the droning of the 'planes. I fall over a brick and break my glasses. I limp into the Ministry to be told that we have sunk a large convoy between Sicily and Tripoli. This is the news we wanted.

After typing this I go to bed. I get off to sleep all right, but the blitz gets worse and worse, and the night shrieks and jabbers like an African jungle. I have never heard such a variety of sounds – the whistle of the descending bombs, the crash of anti-aircraft, the dull thud of walls collapsing, the sharp taps of incendiaries falling all around. The British Museum opposite my window turns rose-red in the light of a fire in the University. Every now and then it turns sharp white when a magnesium flare descends. Then rose-red again. It goes on all night and I sleep fitfully.

Harold Nicolson, *Diary*, 1940

∼ *17 April* ∼

BOMBS IN ST JOHN'S WOOD

Very heavy raid last night, probably the heaviest in many months, so far as London is concerned . . . Bomb in Lord's cricket ground (school-boys having their exercise at the nets as usual this morning, a few yards from the crater) and another in St John's Wood churchyard. This one luckily didn't land among the graves, a thing I have been dreading will happen . . . Passed this morning a side-street somewhere in Hampstead with one house in it reduced to a pile of rubbish by a bomb – a sight so usual that one hardly notices it. The street is cordoned off, however, digging squads at work, and a line of ambulances waiting. Underneath that huge pile of bricks there are mangled bodies, some of them perhaps alive.

George Orwell, *Diary*, 1941

DEATH OF A POLICEWOMAN

Emerging from Piccadilly Circus station found St James's Square cordoned off. At Brooks's was told that the so-called diplomats in the Libyan People's Bureau had opened fire on a harmless anti-Gaddafi demonstration, killing a poor little policewoman and injuring about ten others. All streets in area cleared of traffic and armed police on watch . . . It is horrifying that these savages should rake the streets with bullets from their embassy window, in our London. Bloody people. When they come out, I hope the assassins will be caught and tried, and the rest packed off. But Gaddafi has the effrontery to announce to the world that England has insulted his embassy officials and that our police did the shooting. Is it likely? The *fiancé* of the little policewoman killed is one of them.

James Lees-Milne, *Diary*, 1984

IRA BOMBS

The police had cordoned off the bottom of St Martin's Lane, Charing Cross Road and part of Trafalgar Square. A suspected terrorist bomb. People stood in groups by the police tapes, gazing and waiting – but for what? An explosion? Or at any rate some sort of drama. Tourists with their open maps were obviously very confused and kept revolving in a nonplussed way. Buses were nose to tail, empty and idling. At 10 p.m., while Sam and I were toying with our crème brulées, a bomb went off in The Boltons near Earl's Court. No casualties. The work, they say, of the IRA.

Alec Guinness, *Diary*, 1996

~ 18 *APRIL* ~

A NEW BEDLAM

I went to see new Bedlam Hospital, magnificently built, and most sweetly placed in Moorfields, since the dreadful fire in London.

John Evelyn, *Diary*, 1678

IS THAT THE KING?

Went in one of the Brentford coaches to Kew Bridge, walked from thence along the Thames, (N.B. – A smart shower then) to Richmond, near which I met the King with a single gentleman, and two of the Princes. I did not know him till I was cheek for jowl with him, (jowl here I apply to his Majesty) and then I took off my hat; sometime before I met the King I overtook a boy of fifteen or sixteen, dressed in flannel, or something of that sort. I asked him several questions, to all which he answered with English curtness, he was however glad of a penny for carrying my coat. After passing the King I asked him if he knew who that was, he answered in the negative. I then told him, that is the King;

he showed no emotion, but turned round and said leisurely, 'Is that the King?'

Thomas Campbell, *Diary of a Visit to England*, 1775

THIS ENORMOUS CAPITAL

Though London increases every day, and Mr. Herschell has just discovered a new square or circus somewhere by the New Road in the Via Lactea, where the cows used to be fed, I believe you will think the town cannot hold all its inhabitants; so prodigiously the population is augmented. I have twice been going to stop my coach in Piccadilly, (and the same has happened to Lady Ailesbury), thinking there was a mob; and it was only nymphs and swains sauntering or trudging. T'other morning, i.e. at two o'clock, I went to see Mrs. Garrick and Miss Hannah More at the Adelphi, and was stopped five times before I reached Northumberland-house; for the tides of coaches, chariots, curricles, phaetons, etc. are endless. Indeed, the town is so extended, that the breed of chairs is almost lost; for Hercules and Atlas could not carry any body from one end of this enormous capital to the other.

Horace Walpole, Letter to Miss Berry, 1791

SNUFFING THE LORD MAYOR'S HEALTH

In consequence of some misunderstanding with our landlady, a woman of bad temper, we remove this day to a more quiet and healthy place, 4 Woburn Square. Several small gardens are adjacent to us besides the one just facing our window, Russell Square, Gordon Square, Euston Square, Torrington Square and Bedford Square. The Lord Mayor's Dinner comes off this evening at the Mansion House, known also as the Egyptian House. The building is a splendid specimen of architecture and is very richly painted in an oriental style. Toasts are proposed and received, there are formal speeches, the goblet is passed round, the toast master announces every speech and toast in an imperious tone, at intervals there is music, the liveried attendants look like illustrious personages of a bygone period; the whole thing passes off in a most fashionable style. I of course respond to the various toasts with a glass of lemonade, and instead of drinking the Lord Mayor's health I snuff it!!

Keshub Chandra Sen, *Diary in England*, 1870

~ 19 *APRIL* ~

THE PRICE OF MUFFINS

Breakfasted with James at Johnstone's Coffee House, Charing Cross. Paid for chocolate and muffin, 2.5d.

William Bray, *Diary*, 1758

DRIVEN INTO A CUL DE SAC

Coming home, an Irish coachman drove us into a *cul de sac*, near Battersea Bridge. We were obliged to get out in the rain. The people admitted us into their houses, where they were having their bit of supper, assisted with lights, etc., and, to the honour of London, neither asked nor expected gratification.

Sir Walter Scott, *Journal*, 1828

THE INNOVATION OF WAITRESSES

Walked in the Temple Gardens, and on by Queen Victoria Street into the City, to dine in Milk Street, at a large restaurant which announces itself to me by circular as having 'a staff of quiet and well conducted *waitresses*' instead of waiters. A wholesome innovation, and we may as well see whether it is 'attended with good results', as it should be. It was nearly 6 when I got there, and folk dine early in the City; so the first room I entered was empty, and its waitresses, all alone, were sitting at a table, making up accounts & getting their tea: four decent looking young women, all drest alike in striped cotton gowns of fashionable cut, and dainty aprons, and broidered capless hair. They civilly explained that I could still dine, in another room; and one of them rose and showed me the way to The Saloon, a large well-appointed room, in which were three more waitresses, drest in the same livery; all of them girls of twenty or so; and three men, dining or about to dine. One of the waitresses sat making up her reckoning; another came forward to wait on me; the third and prettiest was standing by one of the three diners, who bent over her, holding both her hands and saying to her such soft endearing insults as 'gentlemen' bestow on damsels who have grace but not position. The girl, accustomed perhaps to such treatment, received his caresses with passive simpering acquiescence; her companions took no notice; and neither he nor she was disturbed by the entrance of a stranger. The other two men, who were young, dined quietly, but afterwards went and sat by the waitresses and gently flirted with them awhile: the first man, who seemed about forty and looked like a dissipated dragoon, continued his attentions to all the three girls; kissing his hand to them, seizing their hands & their skirts, begging them to sit down by him. And after dinner, when the waitresses began to collect knives & forks & fold up tablecloths, he went and joined the group, and 'chaffed' them, making indecent allusions. They laughed and did not resent these; perhaps they did not understand them. I, however, made a demonstration of disgust, which silenced him: and with an audible 'Damn' he left the room, shaking hands with the girls, who evidently bore him no ill will. Apparently the City is not yet ripe for female waiters . . .

Arthur Munby, *Diary*, 1872

∼ 20 *April* ∼

NO ENTHUSIASM FOR THE KING OF FRANCE OR THE PRINCE REGENT

I went this evening to see Lady H. Leveson, to arrange our going to her sister's empty house to see the entry of the King of France. The streets and the park were, before twelve o'clock, filled with people and carriages; the latter were not allowed to enter the park. At five o'clock we saw seven carriages of the Prince Regent's pass, drawn by six horses, in dress livery, preceded by several hundreds of gentlemen on horseback, and accompanied and followed by a detachment of Light Horse and the Blues; but that was all we saw, because from Park Street the distance was too great to see well into the carriages, and, if we could have seen so far, the people on foot, and the crowd on the rails and walls of the park, would have prevented our doing so. The people took off their hats and saluted the carriages as they passed with much goodwill, but without the least enthusiasm.

Mary Berry, *Journal*, 1814

BETJEMAN REMEMBERS

I can just remember the horse trams which were open on top and I longed to clutch one of those bobbles that hung temptingly near from the plane trees. Hampstead Heath then had buttercups and daisies and dandelions in the grass at the Parliament Hill Fields end. Daniel's was a kind of Selfridges and it was from the corner of Prince of Wales's Road, or very near that corner. There was a cinema higher up on the same side where I saw my first film, very early animated pictures, it was called the 'Electric Palace'. Then a grander cinema was built between Daniel's and Prince of Wales's Road. My father who was deaf very much liked going to silent films here and took me with him. The Bon Marché was an old-fashioned draper's shop with about three fronts north of the cinema, and opposite Kentish Town underground station was a Penny Bazaar and next to that was Zwanziger which always smelt of baking bread. Here too was the tram stop for the last stage of the route north. Then there was an antique dealer and picture framer called Yewlett and a public house. My father visited the former but not the latter.

Then there was some late-Georgian brick houses with steps up to their front doors, then the always-locked parish church of Kentish Town . . . It was rebuilt in the Norman style in 1843 by J. H. Hakewill and seems to have no dedication. It was very Low. Then there was Maple's warehouse always rather grim, then some squalid shops and a grocer's called Waile's which was very old-fashioned. Then came Highgate Road station with a smell of steam and very rare trains which ran, I think, to Southend from a terminus at Gospel Oak. Then were some grander shops with a definite feel of suburbia; Young the chemist on the corner . . . Pedder the oil and colourman; French for provisions; the Gordon House, grim behind its high grey walls. I remember thinking how beautiful the new bits of Metroland Villas were in the newly built Glenhurst Avenue, and my father telling me they were awful. Then there were the red-brick gloom of Lissenden Gardens and Parliament Hill Mansions. I was born at 52 but moved to West Hill as a baby so cannot recall the flats. Where the school is now there were trees, but they were not part of Parliament Hill Fields.

I could go on like this for ever, but I must stop or I shall arrive at 31 West Hill. It was very countrified. My greatest thrill was to walk with my father down to a place called Faulkner's Lane, I then thought it was a slum, but now realise it was charming Middlesex cottages. It was a little village south of the Great Eastern and on the east side of Kentish Town Road. I remember going with my mother to visit a 'poor family' in Anglers' Lane, Kentish Town. The only toys the children had to play with were pieces of wood from a bundle of kindling.

John Betjeman, Letter to Coral Howells, 1971

~ 21 April ~

EASY DAYS

We left London, and returned to Welwyn. We have passed exactly eight weeks in Dean's Yard; and these were passed at my father's house in his absence. Our increasing numbers now make it inconvenient that we should be inmates of his house when he inhabits it with his family; and we must take leave of those cheerful and pleasant days in London, free from domestic cares, which we enjoyed for so many years through the liberal kindness and hospitality of my father, who entertained us . . . for many weeks in each year. I look back upon these periods with pleasure, with gratitude, and with regret. I have carried on at those times useful portions of my literary labours, or have prepared the materials for pursuing them with effect. I have had the enjoyment of my own time and leisure without question or hindrance. These easy days of tranquillity, and security, and satisfaction, cannot be repeated.

Henry Fynes Clinton, *Literary Journal*, 1821

EARLY TRADES UNIONISTS ON THE MARCH

The Trades Unions' procession marched from Copenhagen Fields to Whitehall. I saw them; they were in good order, six abreast, and were about two hours and a half passing Whitehall. They were quite orderly, and did not shout. Dr. Wade, in full canonicals, marched before them, accompanied by Owen, the philanthropist, as some called him. The petition, signed, it was said, by 100,000 names, was carried by five bearers to the doors of the Home Office.

Lord Melbourne refused to receive it. The procession moved on over Westminster Bridge, and halted in the open space in front of the new Bedlam. After learning what Melbourne's decision had been, they separated quietly. The police and the soldiers were kept out of sight; so were all the special constables; and the usual sentries at the Horse Guards were withdrawn.

Joseph Hume was foolish enough to ride down Parliament Street by the side of the procession, but was not noticed. The numbers that marched in procession were calculated at from 25,000 to 30,000. Some of them were fine-looking fellows, and well-dressed; but the great majority very poorly clad, and meagre-looking. All sorts of absurd rumours were afloat as to these poor people. A near connection of mine told me that 15,000 of them carried stilettoes; I did not believe that 15,000 stilettoes could be found in all England no, nor in all Europe.

John Cam Hobhouse, *Diary*, 1834

SMASHING UP VICTOR HUGO

Went . . . into the City to see the Emperor and Empress of the French returning from Guildhall after the presentation of the address to them. The crowd not very great, nor the cheering of Napoleon and his spouse very vociferous. The applause more hearty in favour of the Duke of Cambridge, who followed with Prince Albert in the next carriage. The Emperor put his head close to the carriage window, and kept bowing backwards and forwards steadily all the time; only saw him in profile – a grave, disagreeable, designing-looking man. A placard respecting Victor Hugo was exhibited at one window; but the mob took part against the exiled poet, and in the presence of the Emperor smashed the glass to pieces.

George Harris, *Autobiography*, 1855

∼ *22 April* ∼

A SYNAGOGUE IN RESTORATION LONDON

Lately having a desire to spend some of my time here in learning the Hebrew tongue, and inquiring of some one that professed to teach it, I lighted upon a learned Jew with a mighty bush beard, a great Rabbi as I found him afterward to be, with whom after once or twice being together, I fell into conference and acquaintance; for he could speak Latin, and some little broken English, having as he told me been two years in London . . . A very modest man, and once with much ado I got him to accept of an invitation to take part of a dinner with me: at which time he told me that he had special relation as Scribe and Rabbi to a private Synagogue of his nation in London, and that if I had a desire to see their manner of worship . . . he would give me such a ticket, as, upon sight thereof, their porter would let me in upon their next Sabbath Day in the morning being Saturday. I made show as though I were indifferent, but inwardly hugged the good hap.

When Saturday came, I rose very early, the place being far from my lodging; and in a private corner of the City, with much ado, following my directions, I found it at the point of nine o'clock, and was let come in at the first door, but there being no Englishman but myself, and my Rabbi not being there then (for they were but just beginning service) I was at first a little abashed to venture alone amongst all them Jews; but my innate curiosity to see things strange spurring me on, made me confident even to impudence. I rubbed my forehead, opened the inmost door, and taking off my hat (as instructed) I went in and sate me down amongst them; but Lord . . . what a strange, uncouth, foreign, and to me barbarous sight was there . . . for I saw no living soul, but all covered, hooded, guized, veiled Jews, and my own plain bare self amongst them. The sight would have frighted a novice . . .

Every man had a large white vest, covering, or veil cast over the high crown of his hat, which from thence hung down on all sides, covering the whole hat, the shoulders, arms, sides, and back to the girdle place, nothing to be seen but a little of the face; this, my Rabbi told me, was their ancient garb, used in divine worship in their Synagogues in Jerusalem and in all the Holy Land before the destruction of their City: and though to me at first, it made altogether a strange and barbarous show, yet me thought it had in its kind, I know not how, a face and aspect of venerable antiquity. Their veils were all pure white, made of taffeta or silk, though some few were of a stuff coarser than silk; the veil at each of its four corners had a broad badge; some had red badges, some green, some blue, some wrought with gold or silver, which my Rabbi told me were to distinguish the tribes.

Joseph Greenhalgh, Letter to Samuel Crompton, 1662

At the time of this letter, it was only six years since Oliver Cromwell had allowed Jews to settle in England for the first time since 1290.

～ 23 APRIL ～

CHARLES II CROWNED IN WESTMINSTER ABBEY

About 4 I rose and got to the Abbey, where I followed Sir J. Denham, the Surveyor, with some company that he was leading in. And with much ado, by the favour of Mr. Cooper, his man, did get up into a great scaffold across the North end of the Abbey, where with a great deal of patience I sat from past 4 till 11 before the King came in. And a great pleasure it was to see the Abbey raised in the middle, all covered with red, and a throne (that is a chair) and footstool on the top of it; and all the officers of all kinds, so much as the very fidlers, in red vests. At last comes in the Dean and Prebends of Westminster, with the Bishops (many of them in cloth of gold copes), and after them the Nobility, all in their Parliament robes, which was a most magnificent sight. Then the Duke, and the King with a scepter (carried by my Lord Sandwich) and sword and mond before him, and the crown too. The King in his robes, bare-headed, which was very fine. And after all had placed themselves, there was a sermon and the service; and then in the quire at the high altar, the King passed through all the ceremonies of the coronacion, which to my great grief I and most in the Abbey could not see. The crown being put upon his head, a great shout begun, and he came forth to the throne, and there passed more ceremonies: as taking the oath, and having things read to him by the Bishop; and his lords (who put on their caps as soon as the King put on his crown) and bishops come, and kneeled before him. And three times the King at Arms went to the three open places on the scaffold, and proclaimed, that if any one could show any reason why Charles Stewart should not be King of England, that now he should come and speak. And a Generall Pardon also was read by the Lord Chancellor, and meddalls flung up and down by my Lord Cornwallis, of silver, but I could not come by any. But so great a noise that I could make but little of the musique; and indeed, it was lost to every body. But I had so great a lust to piss that I went out a little while before the King had done all his ceremonies, and went round the Abbey to Westminster Hall, all the way within rayles, and 10,000 people, with the ground covered with blue cloth; and scaffolds all the way. Into the Hall I got, where it was very fine with hangings and scaffolds one upon another full of brave ladies; and my wife in one little one, on the right hand. Here I staid walking up and down, and at last upon one of the side stalls I stood and saw the King come in with all the persons (but the soldiers) that were yesterday in the cavalcade; and a most pleasant sight it was to see them in their several robes. And the King came in with his crown on, and his sceptre in his hand, under a canopy borne up by six silver staves, carried by Barons of the Cinque Ports, and little bells at every end. And after a long time, he got up to the farther end, and all set themselves down at their several tables; and that was also a brave sight: and the King's first course carried up by the Knights of the Bath. And many fine ceremonies there was of the Heralds leading up people before him, and bowing; and my Lord of Albemarle's going to the kitchin and eat a bit of the first dish that was to go to the King's table.

Samuel Pepys, *Diary*, 1661

LE ROI IN LONDON

The King of France left London at nine o'clock this morning. If about the same interval elapses between the visits of the Kings of France to London, we shall not see another for 500 years.

Mary Berry, *Journal*, 1814

～ 24 *April* ～

A TEPID MASS OF FLESH

On Easter Monday we went up to visit the Murrys & see Hampstead Heath. Our verdict was that the crowd at close quarters is detestable; it smells, it sticks; it has neither vitality nor colours; it is a tepid mass of flesh scarcely organised into human life. How slow they walk! How passively & brutishly they lie on the grass! How little of pleasure or pain is in them! But they looked well dressed & well fed; & at a distance among the canary coloured swings & roundabouts they had the look of a picture. It was a summers day – in the sun at least; we could sit on a mound & look at the little distant trickle of human beings eddying round the chief centres of gaiety & filing over the heath & spotted upon its humps. Very little noise they made; the large aeroplane that came flying so steadily over head made more noise than the whole crowd of us. Why do I say 'us'? I never for a moment felt myself one of 'them'. Yet the sight had its charm: I liked the bladders, & little penny sticks, & the sight of two slow elaborate dancers performing to a barrel organ in a space the size of a hearthrug.

Virginia Woolf, *Diary*, 1919

∼ 25 APRIL ∼

A LAST-MINUTE REPRIEVE

The 25th day of April were hanged at Wapping at the low-water mark 5 for robbery on the sea, and there was one that had his halter about his neck and yet a pardon came betime.

Henry Machyn, *Diary*, 1562

SEND FOR SIR CHRISTOPHER WREN

Our work at the west end of St Paul's is fallen about our ears.* Your quick eye discerned the walls and pillars gone off from their perpendiculars, and I believe other defects too, which are now exposed to every common observer. About a week since, we being at work about the third pillar from the west end on the south side, which we had new cased with stone, where it was most defective, almost up to the chapitre, a great weight falling from the high wall so disabled the vaulting of the side-aisle by it, that it threatened a sudden ruin, so visibly, that the workmen presently removed, and the next night the whole pillar fell, and carried scaffolds and all to the ground.

The second pillar (which you know is bigger than the rest) stands now alone, with an enormous weight on the top of it; which we cannot

hope should stand long, and yet we dare not venture to take it down
. . . What we are to do next, is the present deliberation, in which you
are so absolutely and indispensably necessary to us, that we can do
nothing, resolve on nothing, without you. It is, therefore, that, in my
Lord of Canterbury's name, and by his order . . . we most earnestly
desire your presence and assistance with all possible speed. You will
think fit, I know, to bring with you those excellent draughts and designs
you formerly favoured us with; and, in the mean time, till we enjoy you
here, consider what to advise that may be for the satisfaction of his
Majesty and the whole nation . . .

William Sancroft, Dean of St Paul's,
Letter to Sir Christopher Wren, 1668

* After the Great Fire of London, there were originally hopes that the old
St Paul's could be repaired and reconstructed. This letter marks the point
at which the church authorities realised that this was impossible and that
an entirely new building was needed.

NOTHING TO DO AT THE CRYSTAL PALACE

To the Crystal Palace. None but holiday people there: ten thousand of
them. They showed more interest in the art Courts and other refreshments than usual: but I doubt the advantage, the rightness, of offering
them such exquisite food . . . They are not refined, but blunted and
vulgarized still more by eating sandwiches (and they *will* eat sandwiches) on the tombs of Kings, and drinking pots of porter in the Courts
of the Alhambra; these are mighty influences for good, wasted altogether by being exercised upon those who have never been taught to
feel them. Today I heard a wench exclaim, standing by the avenue of
Sphinxes, before the statues of Rameses the Great, 'Come on Bill, let's
cut: I'm sick of this place – there's nought to do . . .'

Arthur Munby, *Diary*, 1859

～ *26 April* ～

TWENTY-FOUR-HOUR BACKGAMMON

About 10 a clock in the evening I was at Toms Coffee house, Covent Garden, where in the little room I saw playing at Back Gammon one Mr. Glanville and Mr. Swiney. They begun about 10 or 11 the night before, and had continued playing ever since, and one, Mr. Pentlow, sat by all the while.

Sir Justinian Isham, *Diary*, 1712

CHELSEA SILK WORMS

Wrote till nine; then walked to Mr. Harper's and coached it from Holborn to Hanover-square, to wait upon Mr. Molyneux, the Prince of Wales's secretary, who was very respectful; but his library and curiosities being at Kew, I was in part disappointed, though he invited me earnestly, but cannot possibly have time to go thither; visited also Colonel Bladen, who was very courteous; dined at Mr. Gale's; had his kind emendations, in a few places, of my quarto manuscript. I saw there a sample of the satin, lately made at Chelsea, of English silk-worms, for the Princess of Wales, which was very rich and beautiful.

Ralph Thoresby, *Diary*, 1723

NEW SQUARES IN SWAMPY MEADOWS

My friend Mr. Littleton having invited me to take up my quarters at his house in Grosvenor Place, I proceeded there accordingly, and met a welcome reception from him and his beauteous wife, with most comfortable accommodation. We left Birmingham at half-past seven, and got to Grosvenor Place soon after nine next morning. I was perfectly astonished on observing the extraordinary extent of the new squares, streets, places, etc., on the back of Grosvenor Place, which I recollect wet, low, swampy meadows.

General William Dyott, *Diary*, 1829

~ 27 *APRIL* ~

THE DANGER OF FIREWORKS

Evening went to Mr. Winford's house in Sackville Street to see the Fireworks in the Green Park . . . The Fireworks continued about an hour, was intend'd to have been 3 but the Pavilion at one end catching fire they was oblig'd to put a stop to 'em.

Miss Ireland Greene, *Diary*, 1749

THE FA CUP FINAL

Final of the English Football Association Cup. The streets were full of charabancs carrying football enthusiasts, men and women, to see the sights of London before seeing the match. The Albert Memorial had great popularity. And indeed as a fact there are much worse architectural evils in London than the Albert Memorial . . . Most of the visitors had conspicuously labelled themselves. One charabanc bore the announcement: 'Reckitt's Canister Factory.' I admired this esprit de corps, this industrial pride. There was something fine in it.

Arnold Bennett, *Journal*, 1929

∼ 28 APRIL ∼

A FIRE IN HELL

This morning I went as early out as I could to the fire that broke out in St. James' House and consumed three houses. My purpose was to see which way the flame drove, that I might send my servants to assist such friend or acquaintance of mine as was in the greatest danger. I found it conquered by the great diligence of the firemen, animated by the presence of the King and Prince, who were there from half an hour after five till half an hour after seven, to give direction, and encouraged them with money. It begun in White's Chocolate House in a gaming room called Hell.

Earl of Egmont, *Diary*, 1733

NOTHING BUT MIDDLING PEOPLE

Went with Mrs. Locke to Kensington Gardens. They were as full as possible. Neither she nor I saw a single face that we knew, till we met Lord Aberdeen, and Mr. Ward, who joined us. The complexion of the company in these gardens is altered since I was there of a Sunday – always crowded with middling people, yet all the fine ladies used to come and show off their charms to the admiring mob; but now they have nothing to admire but one another.

Mary Berry, *Journal*, 1811

A FAMOUS MAD DOCTOR

Conversation with Dr. Conolly, the famous mad doctor, at Hanwell. He said that two in every thousand persons in England are mad, and that in his experience the chief causes are, among the lower classes, worry, the necessity for providing for the day that is passing over them, but in the upper classes, especially among women, drink and Calvinistic religion.

Mountstuart Grant Duff, *Notes from a Diary*, 1860

AN IRRECOGNIZABLE CITY

I am sorry to say I am about to leave Chelsea. You will be surprised to hear this. It is difficult to do, but self-preservation renders it unavoidable. This house has become very full of people, and the position of my room leaves me scarcely ever in quiet during the evening; my work has for some time been at a stand-still owing to this, and that really won't do. I shall go back to the old N.W. district, probably somewhere in St John's Wood; that is the true Bohemian locality.

Alas, the north side of Holywell Street is disappearing; the glorious old Wych Street houses are no more. I wonder if it were possible to photograph them. I fear not, on account of the narrowness of the way. We shall live to see London an irrecognizable city.

George Gissing, Letter to his brother Algernon, 1884

~ 29 *APRIL* ~

PREACHING ON SATAN'S OWN GROUND

I preached at Sadler's Wells, in what was formerly a playhouse. I am glad when it pleases God to take possession of what Satan esteemed his own ground. The place, though large, was extremely crowded; and deep attention sat on every face.

John Wesley, *Journal*, 1754

A CHAT WITH A BRICKLAYER

Walked to Hammersmith and back. On my way home I fell into chat with a shabby-looking fellow, a master-bricklayer, whose appearance was that of a very low person, but his conversation quite surprised me. He talked about trade with the knowledge of a practical man of business, enlightened by those principles of political economy which indeed are become common; but I did not think they had alighted on the hod and trowel. He did not talk of the books of Adam Smith, but seemed imbued with their spirit.

Henry Crabb Robinson, *Diary*, 1822

A SPEAKING MACHINE

Went out, and hastened down to King's College, where I saw Professor Wheatstone, who showed the persons present his electric telegraph, and his speaking machine, which uttered clearly the words, 'Mamma, papa, mother, thumb, summer.'

William Charles Macready, *Diaries*, 1840

∽ 30 APRIL ∽

A MISCHANCE WITH GUNPOWDER

A gunpowder house in Hogg-lane, beyond the Tower-hill, toward Stepney, about the houre of vi of the clock in the afternoon, by mischance of the beating of gunpowder, ix persons were cast away and burnt, whereof vi of them died out of hand, and three other sore burnt and in danger of death.

Charles Wriothesley, *Chronicle*, 1552

VISITING MADAME TUSSAUD'S

Saw Madam Tussaud's collection of wax figures. Sat for more than half an hour in front of the figure of Sir Walter Scott. The likeness was so good that I could scarcely keep my eyes off him.

Sir Michael Connal, *Diary*, 1836

MAY

~ 1 *MAY* ~

MAY DAY CELEBRATIONS IN THE CITY

The first day of May there was two pinnaces was decked with streamers, banners and flags, and trumpets and drums and guns, going a-Maying, and against the Queen's place at Westminster, and there they shot and threw eggs and oranges one against another, and with squibs, and by chance one fell on a bag of gunpowder and set divers men afire, and so the men drew to one side of the pinnace, and that did overwhelm the pinnace, and many fell in the Thames, but, thank be God, there was but one man drowned . . .

Henry Machyn, *Diary*, 1559

THE OPENING OF THE GREAT EXHIBITION

The great day dawned for the opening of the Great Exhibition, and with the promise of bright sun and soft airs, which was realized, for the day; the young green of Spring, the boats on the Serpentine, the flags round the top of the long crystal roof, were all full of life and flutter;

the scene was beautiful, gorgeous, unparalleled, inspiring; it looked like Ormuz, and Bagdad, and Florence and Fairyland; the *coup d'oeil* was most admirable, the whole idea most thrilling, the thought all the time even exceeding the sight, and the immense, orderly, pleased masses without, were as striking as all the rest.

George Howard, *Journals*, 1851

TRADITIONAL FESTIVITIES IN BLACKHEATH

In the afternoon in chilly sunlight and sudden cloud, The Blackheath Fayre with a 'y'. The village, as they call it, only goes back to the advent of the railway and never more than a stop for commuters. Now it's a traffic jam by day and a morgue by night. The tone of idiot nostalgia is carried through by the Romford Drum and Trumpet Corps ('I need this like an 'ole in the 'ead,' said a bystander) a jazz band, a Punch-and-Judy, the Blackheath Male Voice Choir in Victorian top hat and, main attraction, The Sealed Knot. This has 1,400 members who make their own costumes, though there is a Gentleman Armourer who will provide reproduction breastplates and greaves to order. Dan and I had a position near the ropes for the Mock Battle, re-enactment of a sham fight that the programme says was actually put on during the real Civil War. A space had been cleared and some booths representing houses erected at the base of the triangle. A Ford 1100 saloon was cruising with a loud-speaker on its roof and a man in Caroline clothes and horn-rimmed glasses was sitting with a mike and a lapful of notes. 'Please keep the opening clear,' he kept saying, 'this is for the entry of the cavalry. We don't want anyone hurt during the battle.' For the next chilly quarter of an hour there was only the Lady Mayor's arrival to divert us . . . At last some troops mustered with pikes, making a good – or goodly – sight. They marched towards the 'houses' and, would you credit it, children from the local dance academy were tripping round a maypole. The other instance of Merrie Englande we could see from our place was a slapstick rape by two Cavaliers of a village maid. Desultory cheers. They did an encore but by this time we were all pressing to see some mounted Parliamentarians . . . Cannons went off and the roisterers left the maides and set about defending their plywood homes. A chorus of Lewisham women were like the crowd at the coronation in Shakespeare's Henry VIII. As the captain of the horses urged his men to another charge, one said, 'I'll bet he never gets a word in at home.' 'Look,' said her friend, 'there's another house on fire. Bring it a bit closer, love, we're like brass monkeys here.' 'Hullo, Mrs Mayor's had enough, she's getting in her car. No stamina some of them.' But it was all in a good cause – or a variety of causes, ranging from the South Thames Referees to The Sydenham Guild of Handicapped Scouts.

Peter Nichols, *Diary*, 1971

~ 2 MAY ~

WAITING FOR A HANGING

Went to Newgate; crowds in the street opposite the gaol, some close to the walls; windows opposite open, with placards stuck up, 'Seats here'; smoking, drinking, laughing vagabonds waiting the public execution of James Greenacre the murderer.

Sir Michael Connal, *Diary*, 1837

INFANTICIDE AT BATTERSEA BRIDGE

Very unfortunate with our horses. The young mare taken suddenly ill while out with a load of coals, which makes the third that is queer, one whereof is in great danger. Woman committed murder by throwing her three children off Battersea Bridge, two perished, one saved.

Nathaniel Bryceson, *Diary*, 1846

A BEAUTIFUL BOW FROM THE PRINCE OF WALES

Rode with Agnes. As we cantered up Constitution Hill, we saw a young man riding in front of us, who proved to be the Prince of Wales; only one gentleman with him, and a groom. And near the Marble Arch, a little phaeton with pair of ponies driven by a very pretty young lady, passed us: somebody in deep mourning was with her. The carriage looked like a Royal one; and we have nearly made up our minds that the young lady was the Princess; the only objection being that she was not very like her! Coming back, the Prince of Wales passed us, and made us a beautiful bow. We saw him within the gates of Marlborough House, where they are just established.

Lady Frederick Cavendish, *Diary*, 1863

THE SIGHTS OF PICCADILLY

A girl held a long-stemmed narcissus to my nose as we went by each other. At the Circus, among the wily crew, there was a little innocent family standing waiting, I suppose for an omnibus. How pure they looked! A man on a stretcher, with a bloody bandage round his head, was wheeled past by two policemen, stragglers following. Such is Piccadilly.

Thomas Hardy, *Diary*, 1891

～ 3 MAY ～

KNOCKED DOWN BY A CAB-HORSE

I had a narrow escape in the evening, on my way to hear a lecture . . . as I was crossing the top of Torrington Square, with my umbrella up, I was knocked down by a cab-horse, and, luckily, was knocked out of his path. I fell flat, and was not run over; so that I may venture to say no serious injury has arisen. The splinters of my umbrella have cut my hand; and my knees are bruised. I was stunned, but in a few minutes recovered. I went on to the University College; heard part of the lecture; but was conscious of being very muddy, so I stole out again.

Henry Crabb Robinson, *Diary*, 1853

THE FLOTSAM AND JETSAM OF KING'S CROSS

Back in London I woke to brilliant sunshine. I spent a couple of hours filming around King's Cross Station – the grandeur of Cubitt's building still marred by 'improvements', glitzy pavements, and the jumble of ticket offices.

Stations attract all those who have no journey to take, they provide warmth, a roof in a sudden storm, and the illusion of being at the hub of things. Brueghel would have recorded this: a shrunken man in a wheelchair driving around in circles; old men shuffling past in shabby suits, demob refugees lost in time; tense, pale clerks, their ill-fitting trousers shiny with wear, threadbare briefcases; bleach-blonde mismatched office girls, hairdos and bulging jeans.

A boy with black nail varnish and tarnished jewels limps across the concourse. He stops and rummages through a litter bin. A bulky man on crutches with a lopsided theatrical turban heaves into view, cast adrift by a charity shop. A lean boy stripped to the waist walks back and forth with a pinched accusing face and wild darting eyes. A tragic tide spirals round gurgling like water disappearing down a plug hole.

I carry on filming. No one notices, except the lonely ice-cream boy with a straw boater and striped apron. He is stuck under the large advert that reads The Warhol Diaries: if you're not in it, you're in it.

Derek Jarman, *Journal*, 1989

～ 4 MAY ～

A GREAT REPOSITORY OF NATURAL CURIOSITIES

This morning by particular favour I gain'd admittance into the British Museum, one of the greatest repositories of natural curiosities perhaps in the world. The place containing them is Montague House, a large spacious elegant building, containing as many windows as there are days in the year. To see the whole took up two hours. It would be very tedious to relate all the natural rarities that strike one with wonder & admiration. There is the incombustible purse made out of stone, the large horns found in the bogs of Ireland, the water snake 16 feet long, the ostrich's egg as big as a quart pot, the artificial crab made out of precious stones & by its clock work would crawl very naturally, the first Bible ever printed in English, a cherry stone found in a man's body. Din'd with Dr. Burton, after which Mascarene & I went up to the Physic Gardens, Chelsea.

Joshua Wingate Weeks, *Diary*, 1779

LODGINGS IN A FASHIONABLE STREET

Our lodgings in London are in a narrow street, and are dirty, sooty, and uncomfortable. The paper of the sitting-room has glaring yellow roses upon a red ground, and the bedrooms are musty and airless. They say, to make things better, that it is a very fashionable street, but what is fashion? I can't tell, but you may 'ask of Folly, for she her worth can best express.' I sat moping and exclaiming against London all the rest of the evening.

Anne Chalmers, *Journal*, 1830

A NEW RESTAURANT OPENS

What do Japanese earthquakes or Chinese floods mean to anybody reading about them in Hampstead? The swallowing of Austria needs bringing home to one who had never been even to Vienna. Lunch to-day with Jock and Rayner of the Express at the Mirabell Restaurant, which has just been kicked out of Salzburg and reopened in Curzon Street. The very personable and well-educated young man who is running it showed me the old Visitors' Book, on whose first pages are the names of Reinhardt, Moissi and Jannings. Never can there have been a book of its kind so celebrity-crammed, from heads crowned and uncrowned down to mere fashionables and film-stars. Jock gazed long and rapturously at the handwriting of Richard Strauss and I confess to being sentimental about Edward, Hertzog von Windsor. Schussnigg was there also. To-day they started a new page headed 'London' and I was the first to sign. I won't pretend this didn't tickle my vanity!

James Agate, *Journals*, 1938

∽ 5 MAY ∽

NOT SO PRETTY POLLY

Perhaps I am a genius too, as well as my husband? Indeed, I really begin
to think so – especially since yesterday that I wrote down a parrot! which
was driving us quite desperate with its screeching. Some new neighbours, that came a month or two ago, brought with them an accumulation of all the things to be guarded against in a London neighbourhood,
viz., a pianoforte, a lap-dog, and a parrot. The two first can be borne
with, as they carry on the glory within doors; but the parrot, since the
fine weather, has been holding forth in the garden under our open
windows. Yesterday it was more than usually obstreperous – so that
Carlyle at last fairly sprang to his feet, declaring he could 'neither think
nor live'. Now it was absolutely necessary that he should do both. So
forthwith, on the inspiration of conjugal sympathy, I wrote a note to
the parrot's mistress (name unknown), and in five minutes after Pretty
Polly was carried within, and is now screeching from some subterranean
depth whence she is hardly audible. Now if you will please recollect
that, at Comely Bank, I also wrote down an old maid's house-dog, and
an only son's pet bantam-cock, you will admit, I think, that my writings
have not been in vain.

Jane Welsh Carlyle, Letter to Margaret A. Carlyle, 1839

FOREIGNERS IN LONDON

The Queen has written a letter to John Russell, expressing her great
satisfaction at the manner in which she was received, and in which
everything was conducted on the 1st of May. There had been all sorts
of rumours of probable disturbances and riots which were to be got up
by foreign emissaries, &c., but for which there does not seem to have
been any foundation.

The foreigners now in London were immensely struck by the order
of the vast crowds which perambulated the streets, and which was
maintained solely by the police.

Prince Albert dined at the Royal Academy for the first time, and
made an excellent speech.

I never remember a colder spring. It constantly hails and rains, and the sun rarely shines!

Henry Greville, *Diary*, 1851

WORSHIPPING IN CHEAPSIDE

Morning. Sunday. To Bow Church, Cheapside. The classic architecture, especially now that it has been regilt and painted, makes one feel in Rome. About twenty or thirty people present. When you enter the curate from the reading-desk and the rector from the chancel almost smile a greeting as they look up in their surplices, so glad are they that you have condescended to visit them in their loneliness.

Thomas Hardy, *Diary*, 1889

A MANSION HOUSE BANQUET

To the Lord Mayor's farewell banquet to Mr Choate at the Mansion House. Thought of the continuity of the institution, and the teeming history of the spot. A graceful speech by Arthur Balfour: a less graceful but more humorous one by Mr Choate.

Thomas Hardy, *Diary*, 1905

∼ *6 MAY* ∼

A LONELY PLACE

Now I am here again how solitary I feel. Hardly know anybody. Home is the place for little people who are little known. No living in London without servants and a carriage.

The Reverend W. J. Temple, *Diary*, 1780

THE CRIES OF LONDON

Heard as usual in the morning the varied intonations of the London cries, from the staccato of the old clothes man to the long of the men selling boxes. To-day for the first time I saw a Bishop in his lawn apron. He was a fine-looking man, upon whose countenance a pleasing smile was lighted up as he crossed the street to speak to a gentleman. This last turned out to be Mr Lockier, who called on us and told us it was the Bishop of London we had seen, a very talented man. Walked through the Horse Guard House and by the side of St James's Park and through the court of St James's Palace, where Papa showed us the identical spot at which he had received a curtsey to himself alone from Queen Charlotte many years ago.

Anne Chalmers, *Journal*, 1830

AND A NIGHTINGALE SANG . . .

To the Horticultural.* Exhibition Road crowded with vehicles, some for the Exhibition, some for the Gardens. The band played, and the many gay dresses in the sunshine were a pretty sight . . . To the Meringtons' to dinner. On the way home at 11 p.m. heard the nightingale sing in Kensington Gardens within a few yards of the road.

Walter White, *Journals*, 1871

* Between 1861 and 1882, the Royal Horticultural Society had gardens in South Kensington.

LOW LIFE AT THE LONDON DOCKS

This morning I walked along Billingsgate from Fresh Wharf to the London docks. Crowded with loungers smoking bad tobacco, and coarse, careless talk with the clash of a halfpenny on the pavement every now and again. Bestial content or hopeless discontent on their faces. The lowest form of leisure – senseless curiosity about street rows, idle gazing at the street sellers, low jokes – and this is the chance the docks offer.

Beatrice Webb, *Diaries*, 1887

～ 7 MAY ～

A THOROUGH EXPLORATION OF ST PAUL'S

Miss Elizabeth Cowan and Mr. Charles Virtue breakfasted with us. We had the loan of Mr. Murray's carriage to go to Walworth. We called on Mr. Chalmers and saw Mrs. Chalmers and her grandson, but Uncle was not at home. On our return we went to St. Paul's, which I explored very thoroughly. I went nearly as far as the ball that is, I ascended three ladders, but not the perpendicular steps. The monuments are beautifully arranged, and almost all bear some sculptured allegorical device. They are mostly the tombs of those who died for their country in battle. After leaving St. Paul's we went to a confectioner's, where we had ice, gingerbeer, cakes, and a number of those things that I like. From St. Paul's we have a very good view of the city. Although the houses appear so crowded that one can hardly imagine that they are separated, still when seen from a height they have a neat aspect, and the brick and red tiled houses are clean looking, if not handsome. This was the first time I had been in the city. We passed along Ludgate Hill and the Strand and went out by the Temple Bar, which the King cannot pass without permission from the most worshipful the Lord Mayor of London.

Anne Chalmers, *Journals*, 1830

PINK TULIPS AT THE RITZ

I lunched with E in the downstairs grill at the Ritz. There were pink tulips on the tables and a pinkish light . . . The unreality suited my mood and we talked as we used to when we first knew each other. It was one of those times which we shall both remember afterwards and say to each other, 'That fine windy Sunday in Spring when we lunched underground in the Ritz.' Our queer kind of love came alive.

Charles Ritchie, *Diary*, 1944

SEXY HIPSTERS

Hooked up with St Martin's student Fernandez: gathering material for this thesis on the influence of the Polish School on British film-makers. Told him there wasn't any, and attempted to sell him on the Czechs. On the loose and with that 'work completed' feeling bought a pair of exciting, sexy denim hipsters in Shaftesbury Avenue – then brown leather belt in posh leather shop in Piccadilly – discover gum gives one the feeling of casual assurance . . . Also Bob Dylan record – 'Times a-Changin' (EXCELLENT).

Lindsay Anderson, *Diaries*, 1965

～ 8 *MAY* ～

TO THE TOWER

I began to work on my new task – a history of the Tower of London – going by the underground from Earl's Court to Mark Lane, thence on to the Tower where I gave my letter from Sir Daniel to General Clerk whom I found at the Governor's, or the 'Queen's' House, for it is known by both appellations, which is in itself a building of historical interest; for there – but I am not now or here writing the story of the Tower. They – for Mrs Clerk was also there, and as full of interest as the General in the history of the place – took me all over the building. Mrs Clerk reminded me of portraits of Queen Elizabeth, an almost startling resemblance to find in the very house in which that Queen was sometime an inmate.

Lord Ronald Gower, *Old Diaries*, 1897

VE DAY IN LONDON

This is VE DAY at last . . . At midnight I insisted on our joining the revels. It was a very warm night. Thousands of searchlights swept the sky. Otherwise there were no illuminations and no street lights at all. Claridge's and the Ritz were lit up. We walked down Bond Street passing small groups singing, not boisterously. Piccadilly however was full of swarming people and littered with paper.

We walked arm in arm into the middle of Piccadilly Circus which was brilliantly illuminated with arc lamps. Here the crowds were yelling, singing and laughing. They were orderly and good-humoured. All the English virtues were on the surface. We watched individuals climb the lamp posts, and plant flags on the top amidst tumultuous applause from bystanders. We walked down Piccadilly towards the Ritz. In the Green Park there was a huge bonfire under the trees, and one too near one poor tree caught fire . . . One extraordinary figure, a bearded, naval titan, organised an absurd nonsense game, by calling out the Navy and making them tear around the bonfire carrying the Union Jack; then the RAF; then the Army; then the Land Army, represented by three girls only; then the Americans; then the civilians. If we had been a little drunker we would have joined in. The scene was more Elizabethan than neo-Georgian, a spontaneous peasant game, a dance around the maypole, almost Brueghelian, infinitely bucolic . . . I thought if we could have a V-night once a month, and invite the Poles, Germans and even the Russians to do what we were doing now, there might never be another war.

James Lees-Milne, *Diary*, 1945

This is V. E. Day and the war is over. Peace at last. I ought to report here that I had a great day but I did nothing except have two double whiskeys with Lizzie and then go out and get the autograph of Randolph Sutton, who has been on the halls for around thirty years . . . Thursday is always my AT HOME day to everyone. Being early closing day it's the only day there's a little silence in Walworth.

Fred Bason, *Diary*, 1945

∽ 9 MAY ∽

AN ATTEMPT ON THE CROWN JEWELS

At 7 in the morning the King's crowne endeavoured to be taken away by (Thomas) Bloud and his son and 3 others out of the Tower of London, but 3 of them were taken. The said Bloud and his son, who call themselves by the name of Hunt, were 2 of those 6 that set upon the duke of Ormond a little before last Xtmas, and they now confess that they had a designe to sell him to the Turks, because that by his meanes they had lost their estates in Ireland while he was Lord Deputy.

Anthony Wood, *Diary*, 1671

PICTURING SOUTH LONDON

We had a delicious drive to Dulwich, and back by Sydenham. We stayed an hour in the gallery at Dulwich, and I satisfied myself that the St. Sebastian is no exception to the usual 'petty prettiness' of Guido's conceptions. The Cuyp glowing in the evening sun, the Spanish beggar boys of Murillo, and Gainsborough's portrait of Mrs. Sheridan and her sister, are the gems of the gallery. But better than the pictures was the fresh greenth of the spring – the chestnuts just on the verge of their flowering beauty, the bright leaves of the limes, the rich yellow-brown of the oaks, the meadows full of buttercups. We saw for the first time Clapham Common, Streatham Common, and Tooting Common – the two last like parks rather than commons.

George Eliot, *Journal*, 1859

AN EXCURSION TO EPPING FOREST

I hope you are enjoying yourselves in the country; how I wish I could be there too, away for a short time from these dark streets. I had a pleasant walk the other day with a friend of mine. We went right out to Epping Forest, which is some twelve miles from London, and where, you will remember, lies the scene of 'Barnaby Rudge'. There is an inn called 'The Maypole', but the sight of it grievously disappointed us; it was nothing but a hideous 'gin-palace' built the other day.

George Gissing, Letter to his sisters, 1880

~ 10 MAY ~

THE DANGERS OF A FEATHER IN THE HAT

The citizens and common people of London had then so far imbibed the customs and manners of a Commonwealth, that they could scarce endure the sight of a gentleman, so that the common salutation to a man well dressed was ' French dog,' or the like. Walking one day in the street with my valet de chambre, who did wear a feather in his hat, some workmen that were mending the street abused him and threw sand upon his clothes; at which he drew his sword, thinking to follow the custom of France in the like cases. This made the rabble fall upon him and me, who had drawn too in his defence, till we got shelter in a house, not without injury to our bravery and some blows to ourselves.

Sir John Reresby, *Diary*, 1658

SICK OF KENSINGTON

This morning I visited my brother Percival. Dr. Couraye dined with me, and in the evening my wife and we walked in Kensington Gardens, where my wife was again taken ill of her stitch and the colic, and obliged to send for Dr. Hollins.

Earl of Egmont, *Diary*, 1731

A LIAISON ON WESTMINSTER BRIDGE

At the bottom of the Haymarket I picked up a strong, jolly young damsel, and taking her under the arm I conducted her to Westminster Bridge, and then in armour complete did I engage her upon this noble edifice. The whim of doing it there with the Thames rolling below us

amused me very much. Yet after the brutish appetite was sated, I could not but despise myself for being so closely united with such a low wretch.

James Boswell, *London Journal*, 1763

PASSING DICKENS IN THE STREET

Near Covent Garden this afternoon I met Charles Dickens, walking along alone and unnoticed. A man of middle height, of somewhat slight frame, of light step and jaunty air; clad in spruce frockcoat, buttoned to show his good and still youthful figure; and with brand new hat airily cocked on one side, and stick poised in his hand. A man of sanguine complexion, deeply lined & scantly bearded face, and countenance alert

and observant, scornful somewhat and sour; with a look of fretfulnes.
vanity; which might however be due to the gait and the costume. Thus
he passed before me, and thus, in superficial casual view, I judged of
him.

Arthur Munby, *Diary*, 1864

~ 11 MAY ~

UNDIGNIFIED MPs

We proceeded to Walworth and dined with my Uncle, and immediately
after dinner went to the House of Commons, found Mr. Hay waiting
for us, who conducted us to the ventilator where ladies can hear the
speakers and even see them sometimes through the holes in the roof.
We found a good many ladies there, among others two very gay ones
who laughed in convulsions at some of the members who came under
their scrutiny. 'Oh! Good God! What a pair of eyes! I declare he is
looking up! La! what frights in boots! I could speak better myself!' and
various similar instructive and amusing exclamations formed the tenor
of their conversation. But to return to the business of the house. Its
members do not sit gravely and sedately on their benches as wise legislators ought to do (I beg their pardon if I had said so in their presence
they would have bawled out 'Order! Order!' until I had said 'as I should
have supposed wise legislators would have done from their well-known
prudence and discretion in all other matters'). They walk about and
talk to each other unless an interesting person is speaking, and call out
'Hear! hear! Order!' I suppose at random, for they certainly do not seem
to pay much attention. Then they like so much to exercise their privilege of wearing their hats, and appear constantly in boots, so that their
general appearance is by no means dignified.

Anne Chalmers, *Journal*, 1830

DEFIANT BEAUTY

It was a particularly idyllic early evening. Cyril Connolly paid a visit. London was looking defiantly beautiful, its parks with their blue vistas of Watteauesque trees – so different from the trees that grow in the country – and its gardens behind the railing a mass of lilac and blossoming trees. As Cyril stood at the front door enjoying the opalescent evening light, the sun made the barrage balloons very bright gold, and the Gothic towers of the Victoria and Albert museum at the end of the road and the peach blossom trees in the Emlyn Williams's garden opposite were seen in an apricot haze . . .

Cecil Beaton, *Diary*, 1940

EYEING UP A NEW HOME IN ISLINGTON

Showed Highbury Terrace to the children. They played on the green with Sylvia while we walked to look at another for sale in Cross Street, noting the general decay of the area. It could go up or down and I'd say down's more likely. Alive and pretty in parts and on the Victoria Line. Sized up schools, shops and traffic. All okay. The girls are happy with their nearby schools, Lou's is called 'The Home and Colonials for Girls'. Dan hated the prospect having played football with some of the local boys and found them 'thick', which probably means they made fun of him.

Peter Nichols, *Diary*, 1974

～ 12 MAY ～

A RIOT AGAINST GERMAN RESIDENTS

The rioting in E. London continued with great violence today – any German shops being wrecked and in some cases any with a foreign name; Russians and Belgians suffered. Porters and carriers at Smithfield have joined in the boycott, one supposed to have declared he wouldn't move a German meal if a carcase was hung round with diamonds;

German butchers', bakers' and tobacconists' shops demolished and looted; troops and 30,000 special constables called out and a great deal of scuffling and many heads broken with batons, one German ducked in a horse trough at Smithfield . . . Rumours that the Germans in London are to set up a-light, – and indeed after and since the Lusitania the public nerve has been very much on the stretch.

Viscount Sandhurst, *From Day to Day*, 1915

END OF THE GENERAL STRIKE

The Strike was settled at about 1.15 – or it was then broadcast. I was in Tottenham Court Road at 1 & heard Bartholomew & Fletcher's megaphone declaim that the T.U.C. leaders were at Downing Street; came home to find that neither L. or Nelly had heard this: 5 minutes later, the wireless. They told us to stand by & await important news. Then a piano played a tune. Then the solemn broadcaster assuming incredible pomp & gloom & speaking one word to the minute read out: Message from 10 Downing Street. The T.U.C. leaders have agreed that Strike shall be withdrawn. Instantly L. dashed off to telephone the office . . . I saw this morning 5 or 6 armoured cars slowly going along Oxford Street; on each two soldiers sat in tin helmets, & one stood with his hand at the gun which was pointed straight ahead ready to fire. But I also noticed on one a policeman smoking a cigarette. Such sights I dare say I shall never see again; & don't in the least wish to.

Virginia Woolf, *Diary*, 1926

THE QUESTION OF SOHO

Two old queens walking down Old Compton Street arm in arm.

They walk in silence, past customers with takeaway bags spilling out of Ed's Diner, past dinner tables laden with baskets of bread and olive oil on Moor Street, past the pub that is The Spice of Life, witness to decades of musical greats, until they're standing amongst the bustling crowd outside the Palace Theatre, the grand imposing red brick building on Cambridge Circus.

'I am not quite sure what to say,' says the queen with the pinched face, knowing full well what he will say.

'Me neither,' replies the smaller, squarer one.

'I mean, it's very easy to pass judgement when you are middle aged, but wait until you're our age.'

'But the question is,' his friend says, 'what if he's right?'

'What do you mean, what if he's right?'

'What I mean is — what if we are wastin' our lives?'

'You were the one who said — '

'I know what I said!' interrupts his friend. He takes the other's hand and looks directly into his eyes. 'But what if I was wrong?'

Clayton Littlewood, *Goodbye to Soho*, 2008

∼ 13 MAY ∼

GOT TO PICK A POCKET . . .

To old Slaughters — to Westminster Hall. Stood some time at foot of King's Bench — a little squeezing, but one fellow behind me seemed to press more than ordinary, which I even thought odd then, and soon after missed my Spa snuff box.

John Baker, *Diary*, 1775

A BLOODY CONVENTION IN COLDBATH FIELDS

A public meeting held in Coldbath Fields to form a National Convention. The Government having previously issued a proclamation declaring such assemblage illegal, the numbers did not amount to more than 2000 or 3000; but the language held and the banners exhibited on the occasion proved that their object was nothing short of revolution. They were ultimately dispersed by the police; but not till three or four of that body had been stabbed by concealed daggers; one of whom died on the spot. Some of the ringleaders are now in custody.

Thomas Raikes, *Journal*, 1833

DASHING WEST END FASHIONS

I rushed into a whore's shop in Leicester Sqre and bought a coat.

Virginia Woolf, Letter to Vita Sackville-West, 1927

THE DEMOLITION OF THE ADELPHI HOTEL
ON THE STRAND

I got back for lunch today and you can't think what a state of squalid demolition the Adelphi has reached in these two days. All the opposite roofs in Robert Street are smashed. Roof in tatters, windows gone, great holes in walls. At this rate one feels all will be gone in a week or two. Workmen are crawling everywhere with hammers and every blow brings down a chunk. The noise is not as deafening as you might expect. The chief feeling is that it is disreputable to be here.

J. M. Barrie, Letter to Lady Cynthia Asquith, 1936

HOT IN THE CITY

London has been subjected for days to what is termed here a 'heat wave'. This means the temperature in the sun reaches about 75 degrees. The parks are filled with half naked bodies taking advantage of this unusual boon.

David Bruce, *Diary*, 1961

～ 14 MAY ～

PARTIES EVERY NIGHT

I am just going out to dinner, and then to two parties in the evening – Mrs. Harwood's and Dr. Grant's. This is the way we live in London, no less than three every evening. Vive la bagatelle! 'Away with melancholy.'

Thomas Moore, Letter to his mother, 1800

THE OPENING OF THE PEOPLE'S PALACE,
MILE END

At half-past three left Windsor for the opening of the People's Palace, accompanied by Beatrice and Liko. At Paddington we entered an open landau with four horses and postillions, in Ascot livery. Lenchen joined us, and she drove with Beatrice and me, the two sisters sitting opposite and I alone in the front seat. From the moment we emerged from the station the crowds were immense and very enthusiastic with a great deal of cheering; in the City especially, it was quite deafening.

Still, what rather damped the effect of the really general and very enthusiastic reception to me, was the booing and hooting, of perhaps only two or three, now and again, all along the route, evidently sent there on purpose, and frequently the same people, probably Socialists and the worst Irish. Everyone says it was wonderful that the reception was so cordial and enthusiastic, considering the masses of Socialists of all nationalities, and low bad Irish, who abound in London. In the City where the crowd was densest, and the cheering tremendous, there was nothing to be heard of this. There were a great many festoons, decora-

tions, and inscriptions on the houses, but hardly any arches.

The drive was a very long one, and at times the officer commanding the escort could hardly get between the carriage and the crowd. At Holborn Hill especially, there was a tremendous crush, where the Lord Mayor was waiting with his coach and got out to present me with the sword which I returned. This caused a delay, and a terrible rush; fortunately however, they were all kept back, and we went on, preceded by the Lord Major and four coaches to the boundaries of the City at Aldgate, where they stood on either side and let us pass. I cannot exactly describe where the People's Palace is, and there have been new openings and broad streets made there, but it is called Mile End. At first the building does not look very imposing, but after ascending a few steps one comes into a very fine hall.

Queen Victoria, *Journals*, 1887

DRAB LONDON

Goodness, London looked drab today: just enough of the Coronation decorations are up to have a fussy and sad, rather than cheerful effect. Regent Street was particularly disastrous, decked in enormous pink waxy-looking Bedalian roses, through which the grey faces of the houses are anxiously peering.

Frances Partridge, *Everything to Lose: Diaries*, 1953

∼ 15 MAY ∼

5,748 STEPS TO CHELSEA

My walk to town to-day was after ten, and prodigiously hot . . . My way is this: I leave my best gown and periwig at Mrs. Vanhomrigh's, then walk up the Pall Mall, through the Park, out at Buckingham House, and so to Chelsea a little beyond the church: I set out about sunset, and get here in something less than an hour; it is two good miles, and just five thousand seven hundred and forty-eight steps; so there is four miles a day walking, without reckoning what I walk while I stay in town. When I pass the Mall in the evening, it is prodigious to see the number of ladies walking there; and I always cry shame at the ladies of Ireland, who never walk at all, as if their legs were of no use, but to be laid aside.

Jonathan Swift, *The Journal to Stella*, 1711

CUT AND RUN

The riots seem to have died down, but a hairdresser just off Pall Mall, the Royal servants are customers, who is German or has German aid, is warned (they say) to clear out.

Viscount Sandhurst, *From Day to Day*, 1915

SHABBY LONDON

After days of rain, brilliant summer. London shabbier and shoddier in the sunlight than in the shadows. The crowds uglier and more aimless, horrible groups of soldiers in shabby battle dress with their necks open, their caps off or at extravagant angles, hands in pockets, cigarettes in the sides of their mouths lounging about with girls in trousers and high heels and filmstar coiffures. I never saw so many really ugly girls making themselves conspicuous. Restaurants crowded; one is jostled by polyglot strangers, starved, poisoned, and cheated by the management; theatres at an early hour of the afternoon when it is inconvenient to go; even so they are all crowded.

Evelyn Waugh, *Diaries*, 1943

～ 16 MAY ～

BOSWELL'S FIRST MEETING
WITH DR JOHNSON

I drank tea at Davies's in Russell Street, and about seven came in the great Mr. Samuel Johnson, whom I have so long wished to see. Mr. Davies introduced me to him. As I knew his mortal antipathy at the Scotch, I cried to Davies, 'Don't tell where I come from.' However, he said, 'From Scotland.' 'Mr. Johnson,' said I, 'indeed I come from Scotland, but I cannot help it.' 'Sir,' replied he, 'that, I find, is what a very great many of your countrymen cannot help.' Mr. Johnson is a man of a most dreadful appearance. He is a very big man, is troubled with sore eyes, the palsy, and the king's evil. He is very slovenly in his dress and speaks with a most uncouth voice. Yet his great knowledge and strength of expression command vast respect and render him very excellent company. He has great humour and is a worthy man. But his dogmatical roughness of manners is disagreeable.

James Boswell, *London Journal*, 1763

PRAISE IN PALL MALL

Breakfasted, on my return, at the London Coffeehouse; then took a warm bath in Pall Mall; the young lady of the house playing and singing my songs all the time, and her mother meeting me as I came out of the room . . . saying, 'Oh sir, are you *the* Mr. Moore whom I have been admiring these thousand years? When will you come to bathe again, sir?' etc. etc.

Thomas Moore, *Diary*, 1819

HEADING SOUTH

 I have arranged to take the upper part of a house in Brixton; if you are really going to London get a lodging in that same neighbourhood?

George Gissing, Letter to his brother, 1893

～ *17 MAY* ～

A SURGICAL MUSEUM

To the College of Surgeons to meet Professor Owen, who showed us over their Museum, and added infinitely to its interest by his luminous expositions. The things are arranged altogether physiologically on the idea which Hunter first struck out and worked on, that there is a certain analogy of structure running throughout Nature, vegetable as well as animal; a hyacinth, for instance, has its fibres, but no internal stomach, so the earth in which it is embedded acts as one. Owen believes that no animal has sensation unless furnished with a brain, therefore the cuttlefish is the lowest creature which can be effectively treated with cruelty. Examined a long series of skulls; those of babies so much phrenologically better than grown persons – which Owen thinks quite natural, as they came uncontaminated from the Author of all Goodness, and degenerate after contact with the world.

Caroline Fox, *Journal*, 1842

A ROMANTIC JOURNEY

Had very indifferent night last night, Mother being very ill, which broke my rest. Rose about half past 6 o'clock and met Ann corner Rathbone Place and Oxford Street. At half past 7 sent her onwards to Paddington whilst I breakfasted at coffee shop in Oxford Street. Overtook her in Edgware Road and went to Great Western Railway station and took place for Ealing at half past 8 o'clock. Arrived there quarter before 9, walked from thence to Hanwell, first round the back of asylum by canal; afterwards made for Greenford where we arrived about 12 o'clock and after service dined in the church porch as the doors were left open (bread and beef). Afterwards cut initials and date (NB 1846) on the paving of the same (paved with red tile) very distinct. Kissed Ann on every stile. She afterwards same to me. Returned through Hanwell and whilst walking thereabouts met Richard Bond junior with a young woman in gig opposite asylum gate. Left Hanwell half past 4 for Ealing Station and started from thither to Paddington where arrived 6 o'clock and walked home by the New Road etc. Weather very cloudy in morning. 12 o'clock some rain. After 2 cleared off and remained fine.

Nathaniel Bryceson, *Diary*, 1846

HOW TO LIVE AND LET LIVE IN NW1

Sitting outside a cafe in Regent's Park Road, A. and I see a transvestite striding up the street with a mane of hennaed hair, short skirt and long, skinny legs. It's the legs that give him/her away – scrawny unfleshed and too knobbly for a girl's. He/she has also attracted the attention of someone in the snooker hall above the pub, and there's a lot of shouting. Later, as we are getting into the car, Gary, a young man crippled with arthritis, calls out to A. from the snooker hall. She knows him and asks if it was him that was doing the shouting. 'Yes,' he says proudly. 'You shouldn't.' 'Why?' he asks. 'Because,' I put in weakly, 'it's a free country.' 'No, it isn't.' 'Well you shouldn't.' A. says again: 'I should think about it,' – meaning, I suppose, that if it's all right to shout at transvestites, next on the list will be cripples with arthritis. This is lost on Gary, who starts to shout at us too. It's a comic encounter, and the liberal dilemma it poses impenetrable. We mustn't abuse sexual deviants, but we must also be tolerant of the handicapped who do.

Alan Bennett, *Diary*, 1990

∼ *18 May* ∼

VAUXHALL AND PIGEON PIE

Breakfasted at home; James dined here; he fetched a pigeon pye; afterwards to Prosser's, where Pitts came to me; at 6 Emily came; we took boat at the Temple, landed at Lambeth, and walked to Vauxhall; supped there. Home about 12; very pleasant evening; paid for supper at Vauxhall, 2/-; going in, 1/-.

William Bray, *Diary*, 1758

QUEEN VICTORIA VISITS BUFFALO BILL

The Queen arrived soon after five p.m. with the Battenbergs. I had to present the American President of the Exhibition, Colonel Russell, and Mr Whitley, the Director-General, to Her Majesty, and the Secretaries, Messrs Speed and Applin. Some of us went in the Deadwood Coach, which, driven at a great rate round the arena, is attacked by mounted Indians, and much firing takes place from within and outside that vehicle. The Queen seemed delighted with the performance; she looked radiant. At the close of the performance, Buffalo Bill, at Her Majesty's desire, was presented, as well as the Indian Chief, 'Red Skin', and two of the Squaws with their 'papooses', whose little painted faces the Queen stroked. I hope that Melton Prior, who was there, will make a drawing of that scene, as it would make quite a pretty picture. Her Majesty, who had driven into the Exhibition in a carriage-and-four, with outriders in scarlet, left soon after six en route for Windsor.

Lord Ronald Gower, *Old Diaries*, 1887

A SHOPPING SPREE IN SELFRIDGE'S

. . . just to tell you about the arrival of darling Yves . . . He's sweet. Seldom have I been gladder to have anyone in the house. He seems happy so far . . . He liked his room very much . . . I think he appreciates having a gas fire . . . His work in the house is heaven: done with all-out passion and concentration. His cooking also seems to be in good form. He required, in order to truly express himself, saucepans, vegetable-grinders, ladles, etc. other than we have. In fact what used to be called 'the kitchen battery' in this house had run extremely low, and I had been hanging on before buying anything to know what Yves would want when he arrived. So he and I spent the morning riotously (and hellishly expensively) shopping in Selfridges's kitchen-outfitting department. 2 or 3 minor objects he'd wanted were not to be had: I don't believe they exist in England at all . . . We collected round us, in the course of our shopping, almost the entire staff of Selfridges, who were I think convinced that a master chef of international reputation had arrived in London. Certainly Selfridges went all out – 'We must do our best to satisfy him,' the assistants kept murmuring in my ear, while Yves examined object after object, tapped it, blew through it and put it down again, with a courteous indulgent but slightly pessimistic air. Finally I think I got the equivalents of what he'd wanted: he seemed very gay about it all. We emerged from Selfridges clattering all over with aluminium objects, like the White Knights. Then we raced home and unpacked them all on the kitchen table, to the amusement of Nancy.

Elizabeth Bowen, Letter to Charles Ritchie, 1950

∼ *19 May* ∼

A NEW DEFINITION FOR A COCKNEY

To the Office and then to the Post Office Tower for the public opening
with Billy Butlin. I said that there was a new definition of a Cockney:
'someone born within sight of the new Post Office Tower.' We went and
looked around with a party of people.

Tony Benn, *Diary*, 1966

UNFAIR WEATHER IN BLACKHEATH

'Blackheath Fayre this afternoon', said Thelma. 'How can it be? The
sun's shining.' But by two p.m. when it started, the drizzle was gently
falling. We trudged about in our anoraks. 'Get your tickets,' said a
tannoy voice, 'for the Eltham Light Opera's *Pirates of Penzance* in aid
of South London League of Limbless ex-servicemen.' The drizzle
became a downpour and we came home for tea with the Frayns, John
Hopkins and Shirley Knight.

Peter Nichols, *Diary*, 1973

A QUIET CORNER OF LONDON

Spend the first part of the day lying in bed wishing the world would
go away. Thankfully, Mr Hughes comes by, and passes on the results of
a photo session we had in Highgate the other day. Myself posing against
trees, reading 'The Lady' on a bench in Pond Square, loitering with
arch intent outside the public lavatory, that sort of thing. I can never
have too many photos taken of myself.

The Men's loos in Pond Square are marked with a Camden Council
sign in shockingly bad English: 'GENTLEMENS'. I wouldn't be at all
surprised if this has been the subject of angry letters to the editor of
the Ham and High.

Mr Hughes shows me a tree in a quiet corner of Hampstead Heath
where he used to come and sit in his schooldays, some thirty to forty

years ago. We languish there in the balmy afternoon, quoting Keats and playing I-Spy Cruisers with the occasional passing lone man, who passes again rather too often.

With birdsong the only background noise, it's difficult to remember we're in the middle of a metropolis. It's moments like this that remind me why I love London, and how best to deal with it on hot days if one is lucky enough to be one's own boss. The ability to quickly find a quiet leafy space, or in the case of the Heath an actual field, and settle down beneath the shade of a tree to read, write and think, or not think.

Dickon Edwards, *Diary*, 2004

～ 20 MAY ～

LONDON ON A SUNDAY

Went to Mrs. Wright, Turner Street, Whitechapel in the morning. Walked through the City, nothing can exceed the miserable monotony and dead appearance of London on a Sunday, especially a wet Sunday. Saw Josiah, who went with his sister Caroline to take tea with her 'affianced' Mr. Brown, the worthy citizen of Cheapside. Remained with Mrs. W. until it was time to return home.

John Thomas Pocock, *Diary*, 1827

THE PRICE OF BAD TASTE

. . . as for our Buckingham Palace yesterday – never was there such a specimen of wicked, vulgar profusion. It has cost a million of money, and there is not a fault that has not been committed in it. You may be sure there are rooms enough, and large enough, for the money; but for staircases, passages, &c., I observed that instead of being called Buckingham Palace, it should be the 'Brunswick Hotel'. The costly ornaments of the state rooms exceed all belief in their bad taste and every species of infirmity. Raspberry-coloured pillars without end, that quite turn you sick to look at; but the Queen's paper for her own apartments far exceed everything else in their ugliness and vulgarity . . . The marble single arch in front of the Palace cost £100,000 and the gateway in Piccadilly cost £40,000. Can one be surprised at people becoming Radical with such specimens of royal prodigality before their eyes? to say nothing of the characters of such royalties themselves.

Thomas Creevey, Letter to Elizabeth Ord, 1835

THE HORRID ATMOSPHERE OF LONDON

We avoided the City altogether, going by the New Road, through Regent's Park. I was altogether disappointed in the Park, I had expected at least to see fine timber. No such thing. The horrid atmosphere of London checks all vegetation. As far as I could see, there was not a tree in Regent's Park to compare with the greater part of those in White-wood. Besides, the sky is smoky and dingy; there is no freshness in the air, nor the bloom of spring everywhere, as in the country. It has also a formal look; it is intersected with wide public roads, which are inclosed by hedges or railings. These roads were full of carriages, cabs, horsemen, and pedestrians, which are supposed to give so much liveliness to the scene; so they do, but I like a retired, unfrequented park much better. On leaving Regent's Park we entered Portland Place. Here I was much struck with the grandeur of the buildings, surpassing anything I ever saw in the shape of private houses. If London had all been like this, it would have been a magnificent city. But I believe not many parts are so noble as this.

Emily Shore, *Journal*, 1835

LOCKED IN REGENT'S PARK

In the evening I often bike round Regent's Park. Tonight I am mooning along the Inner Circle past Bedford College when a distraught woman dashes out into the road and nearly fetches me off. She and her friend have found themselves locked in and have had to climb over the gate. Her friend, Marie, hasn't made it. And there, laid along the top of one of the five-barred gates, is a plump sixty-year-old lady, one leg either side of the gate, bawling to her friend to hurry up. I climb over and try to assess the situation. 'Good,' says Marie, her cheek pressed against the gate. 'I can see you're of a scientific turn of mind.' Her faith in science rapidly evaporates when I try moving her leg, and she yells with pain. It's at this point that we become aware of an audience. Three Chinese in the regulation rig-out of embassy officials are watching the pantomime, smiling politely and clearly not sure if this is a pastime or a predicament. Eventually they are persuaded to line up on the other side of the gate. I hoist Marie over and she rolls comfortably down into their outstretched arms. Much smiling and bowing.

Marie's friend says, 'All's well that ends well.' Marie says she's laddered both her stockings and I cycle on my way.

Alan Bennett, *Diary*, 1983

～ 21 MAY ～

BEATING THE BOUNDS OF WESTMINSTER

Saw sight never saw before – the charity boys of St Margaret's West-minster beating the boundaries of their parish. Met them at Elliot's Brewery gate, which is shown to be one of the boundaries by a stone there fixed. There they formed a ring, and after singing a hymn they all set up an hurrah! beating the stones with long canes, which they carried whilst those outside beat their canes over those inside, some with violence (though all in fun), which they inside endeavoured to return, which amidst sticks flourishing, boys hallowing, and masters chiding, presented a novel scene. After which they marched in procession, three beadles with maces and cocked hats taking the lead, preceded by men with ladders to get over any walls where necessary. After came the master and teachers of the several schools carrying rods and canes, then the Green Coat boys, the Black Coats and the Blue Coats, followed by divers schools in the said parish, all carrying long canes. I followed them to the boundary in William Street, Knightsbridge, which separates Westminster from St Luke Chelsea, where I left them, having already exceeded my dinner hour.

Nathaniel Bryceson, *Diary*, 1846

EAT LIKE THE RICH

Yesterday had luncheon at the Hyde Park Hotel with Mr N. from Estoril in Portugal. It was a wonderful luncheon and do you know I had for the first time ever GULLS eggs! They cost 5/- each. God! Talk about eating money. On my oath I couldn't tell the difference between them and eggs of Walworth at 3d each. But my host said he liked them and they made a difference as he couldn't get 'em in Portugal.

Fred Bason, *Diary*, 1958

UNIMPRESSED BY A NEW THEATRE ON THE SOUTH BANK

At 8 o'c. I walked to the National Theatre – it's like a terrible municipal housing estate & is nothing to do with the theatre.

Kenneth Williams, *Diary*, 1977

HOUSING IN TOWER HAMLETS

My obsession with housing and affordable homes (lack thereof) continues. The average income in Tower Hamlets today is £12,000, while the average home in Tower Hamlets costs £180,000. What that means, as I ranted in the Chamber to Stephen Byers, the minister responsible, is that no ordinary person can buy a house in my constituency. The way house prices are going in London, soon it will only be the very poor or the very rich who live here, i.e. those who qualify for social housing, or those who earn ten times the average income. We need housing schemes that allow people in the middle to get their foot on the housing ladder.

Oona King, *Diaries*, 2000

～ 22 *MAY* ～

ANIMAL MAGIC

We walked to the Zoological Garden in Regent's Park. It is a most delightful spectacle, the animals have so much more liberty than in common menageries. The enclosures are large, and all except the wild animals are kept in the open air during the daytime. The tiger seemed to feel annoyed at being looked on in what it esteemed a state of degradation, and walked up and down its narrow prison as if it would fain increase its boundaries, and the lion lay asleep perhaps dreaming of its own native forests, or of a delicious banquet which it tasted only once, but remembers with continued zest, consisting of a young negro which had been brought to it by its mother. Many more animals and birds were there than I can enumerate, but I shall mention the monkeys, whose tricks were very diverting. I brought them some nuts and biscuits, and whenever they saw them there was a commotion in their cages, and paws were stretched out in all directions for them. While I was bending to give a weak one a nut, which a superior was taking from it, my bonnet was seized from a cage above and the front nearly torn from it. The keeper let them out from their confinement into large arbours in the open air, where were hung swings and ropes, and certainly the gymnastics of the Greenwich boys were far exceeded by these agile creatures. They flung themselves from rope to rope and to the side of the cage with immense celerity. Next in agility to the monkeys were the bears, though in a more clumsy style. They begged for buns, and clambered up a long pole to amuse the bystanders, who rewarded them with cakes. Mamma was quite pleased with the beaver for showing itself both on land and water, she said it was very obliging and exceedingly gentlemanly of it.

Anne Chalmers, *Journals*, 1830

A LONELY BACHELOR DINES

Passing through Leicester Square, meet Alan Skinner, and walk with him in the flower avenue of Covent Garden, talking of the Home trial, the Eyre case, etc. Then we dine at Bertolini's pleasantly. I show him the local curiosity, old Mr. Seymour, now eighty-two, who has dined here every day for the last forty-three years : he comes at 5, stays till 8, sits always in the box on the left-hand of the fire-place as you go up the room, which is kept for him at this time of day; has the joint, college pudding, a gill of Marsala; puts his feet up and sleeps or snoozes for about twenty minutes, then reads the *Daily News*, fidgeting a good deal with it, for his hands tremble. Finally he puts on hat, buttons coat up to the throat, straightens his spine and walks down the middle of the room very stiff and wooden, driving off, the waiter says, to his house some-where near the Regent's Park. I should mention that when he comes in every evening the waiter who receives him invariably says, 'Good evening, Mr. Seymour: you are looking very well this evening, Mr. Seymour.' Looks like a solitary old bachelor, lawyer or attorney, dried up, penurious; the daily tavern dinner a sort of loophole glimpse of the outside world. Save a word or two to the waiters he never speaks to any one at Bert's. Skinner departed and I went into the Alhambra and see some good dancing, but the opera-glass is a terrible disenchanter. Next me a bald civil quiet gentleman with his wife and daughters. Leotard on the 'trapeze' wonderful.

William Allingham, *A Diary*, 1868

∼ 23 MAY ∼

SUSPECTS AT THE OLD BAILEY

Went Old Bailey – heard the trial of one Storer, a farrier's man, for poisoning a horse of Mr Whitebread, a brewer – (on the Black Act which makes it death). Jury went out. Little boy of 11 or 12 began to be tried for stealing 6 table spoons, but I came away. Charles and house-maid and cook to Sadlers Wells.

John Baker, *Diary*, 1776

AN UNQUIET GRAVE IN THE EAST END

I spent several hours at home, looking over reports &c., then walked to Clapton. I had a fine walk home over Bethnal Green. Passing Bonner's Fields, a nice boy, who was my gossiping companion pointed out to me the site of Bishop Bonner's house, where the Bishop sat and saw the Papists burnt; such is the accuracy of the traditional tales. He further showed me some spots in which the ground is low: here the poor burnt creatures were buried it seems; and though the ground has been filled up hundreds of times, it always sinks in again.

Henry Crabb Robinson, *Diary*, 1819

∼ 24 MAY ∼

THE THIEF-TAKER GENERAL
ON HIS WAY TO BE HANGED

Rose after nine; breakfast, milk porridge, 3d. Jo. Clowes called on me about eleven to go see Jonathan Wild, who went by to be hanged to-day; I stood at Abingdon's coffeehouse door. Jonathan sat in the cart between two others, in a nightgown and periwig, but no hat on, a book in his hand, and he cried much and the mob hooted him as he passed along. I wrote a letter of verses to Mr. Leycester at Barnet; had a mess of milk porridge to dinner, 3d.

John Byrom, *Journal*, 1725

BUYING A NEW COACH

Tooke and Toovey, Coachmakers, Great Queens Street, Lincoln's Inn, I bought of them a complete strong Crane neck coach which they warrant to be quite new and never used, to which they will add a pr. of neat wheels, harness, and will paint and fit up the whole in the most genteel and complete manner, and to have the same ready, with the arms painted, lining, straps, etc., by Saturday next for 115 guineas.

Thomas Wale, *My Grandfather's Pocket Book*, 1773

GETTING A TASTE FOR LONDON

I congratulate you on your change of quarters from Cheltenham to Kingscote, though my own goût paysager is not so strong as it used to be, or my taste for London is stronger. London is full of dirt and ugliness and vulgarity, but London is London after all, and it is something to have the freshest news and the freshest fish, and to see everybody and everything. Here am I, a Staffordshire man, 150 miles from home . . . What greater advantages should I enjoy at Hanley or Cowbridge or Burslem or Tunstall? The country is a very good place to see good company in, but is very blank by itself.

Harry Wedgwood, Letter to his mother
Mrs Josiah Wedgwood, 1827

∼ 25 MAY ∼

PRESERVED FOR SCIENCE

Nell bought me an abortive child from Blackfryers – which I put in Spirit of Wine in two shade glasses. Not out all day.

Robert Hooke, *Diary*, 1674

LOSING AN EVENING IN KENSINGTON

Went after dinner to Kensington Gardens, I think rather to my loss. Proceeded to Francis's, thence to Manchester Square again. How fairly may such evenings be called lost when no duty is fulfilled, no improvement made, no enjoyment felt. I had in my mind the question agitated by Priestley, about the impenetrability of matter, but was too much upon the confines of sleep to be able to carry it on.

William Windham, *Diary*, 1788

RUSSIAN MUSIC AT THE RUSSIAN EXHIBITION

Squire and Desmond McCarthy lunched with me at the Reform. At night . . . I went to Russian concert at Russian Exhibition and it was very good. The pianissimos of the Balalaika Orchestra were marvellous, especially with music like Borodin's. On the other hand I had little use for Tchaikowsky's *Grand Trio* (A minor). Place pretty full.

Arnold Bennett, *Journal*, 1917

A WRITE-OFF AT SOTHEBY'S

Sale at Sotheby's of Arnold Bennett's manuscripts and correspondence. Went expecting the world to be there and saw nobody I knew. Fifty or sixty booksellers, looking like the commissaries-priseurs out of a Balzac novel, bid unemotionally for incalculable treasures going at five or six pounds a bundle.

James Agate, *Journals*, 1936

～ 26 *MAY* ～

THE OPENING OF RANELAGH GARDENS

Today calls itself May the 26th, as you perceive by the date: but I am writing to you by the fire-side instead of going to Vauxhall, if we have

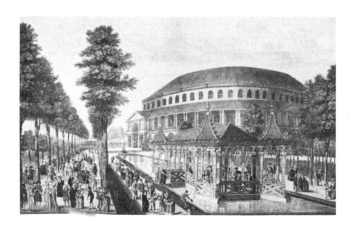

one warm day in seven, 'we bless our stars and think it luxury'. And yet we have as much waterworks and fresco diversions as if we lay ten degrees nearer warmth. Two nights ago Ranelagh-gardens were opened at Chelsea; the Prince, Princess, Duke, much nobility, and much mob besides, were there. There is a vast amphitheatre, finely gilt, painted and illuminated, into which everybody who loves eating, drinking, staring, or crowding, is admitted for twelve-pence. The building and disposition of the gardens cost sixteen thousand pounds. Twice a-week there are to be Ridottos, at guinea tickets, for which you are to have a supper and music. I was there last night, but did not find the joy of it. Vauxhall is a little better; for the garden is pleasanter, and one goes by water.

Horace Walpole, Letter to Sir Horace Mann, 1742

THE HOTTEST TICKET IN THE WEST END

Rainy. Went to Mr Johnston at the stage door of Drury lane theatre and took out two tickets for the play to be acted this evening toward raising funds for superannuated players. It is The History of King Lear, the part of Lear by Garrick. This play being advertised a month ago, all the places were taken long before I thought of making application; and if it had not been by means of Mr Garrick himself I could not possibly have got places, as the demand for them was prodigiously great . . .

Our seats were as convenient as we could wish. Garrick's action in this most difficult character transcends all praise. The many tears shed by the audience bore ample testimony to his and to Shakespear's merit. After the play he spoke an Occasional Epilogue with infinite propriety and humour. Mrs B & I came out when the tragedy was over: and got home about eleven, Mr. T Beauclerc have done us the favour to lend us his coach. – A french gentleman, M. De La Luc, whom I had seen at Lady Mary Coke's, sate next to me at the play: was transported wt. admiration of Garrick's action.

James Beattie, *Diary*, 1773

INCONVENIENT LONDON

The great extent of London makes visits or business very inconvenient to me. Never wish to be here without a carriage. Neither strength nor spirits to run about here. Should stay at home and be content. How provoking is it to take a long walk and then not find the person you want. No attachments here. Everyone is indifferent to one another. Neither literature nor anything appears of consequence.

Reverend W. J. Temple, *Diary*, 1783

～ 27 MAY ～

AN ACCIDENT AT CHARING CROSS

I do as unwillingly put my pen to tell you, as I am sure you will be to hear, what hath befallen my nephew Albertus this week. He was going on Friday last towards evening in a coach alone, whose driver alighting (I know not upon what occasion) hard by Charing Cross, the horses (being young) took some affrightment, and running away so furiously, that one of them tore all his belly open upon the corner of a beer cart; my nephew (who in this meanwhile adventured to leap out) seemeth to have hung on one of the pins of the boot, from whence struggling to get loose, he broke the waist-band of his hose behind, and so fell with the greater violence on the ground, hurting only the hindermost part of his head, by what possibility we cannot conceive, unless the motion of the coach did turn him round in the fall. The force of the concussion took from him for some hour or thereabouts, the use of his voice and sense, which are now well restored; only there yet remaineth in his left arm a kind of paralytical stupefaction, and his right eyelid is all black with some knock that he took in the agitation of the coach, which peradventure may have been the motive to make him leap out. But these external evils do not so much trouble us as an inward pungent and pulsatory ache within the skull, somewhat lower than the place of his hurt; which hath continued more or less since his fall, notwithstanding twice letting blood, and some nights of good rest, and shaving of his head for the better transpiration; which we doubt the more because it cometh *sine ratione*, his hurt being only in the fleshy part, and very slight, without fracture of the skull, without inflammation, without any fever, and all the principal faculties, as memory, discourse, imagination, untainted.

Sir Henry Wotton, Letter to Sir Edmund Bacon, 1613

SAPPED BY HOLBORN

Here I am, terribly swanky and snobby, but utterly penniless, unable to afford all the things I would like to do. I loathe my existence at the office, the drabness of the underground and Holborn saps my vitality. I'm in an awful groove and don't know how to get out of it. I know it's silly and wrong, but I believe I enjoy wallowing in my dejection.

Cecil Beaton, *Diary*, 1926

A HYDE PARK VISTA

If the weather is fine, quite a lot of men and women bathe at Lansbury's Lido on the Serpentine. How amusing are the garish tents in which the swimmers undress – formerly yellow, now green – a guffaw, as it were, at the riders in the Row and at those grey-top-hatted gentlemen who occasionally drive through on Dickensian coaches with terrific dignity.

George Buchanan, *Passage through the Present*, 1932

～ 28 MAY ～

A MAN VOMITING BLOOD

Called at Fox's to know whether attendance at the House was necessary. I was detained by the case of the poor man who was vomiting blood in St. James's Street and with Mr. Ferguson, of the House of Commons, who took his full share in the act, continued occupied in finding means of relief, till we determined finally in sending him to his home in Bishopsgate Street. When this was done, instead of going to the House . . . I proceeded to the Club at the Globe.

William Windham, *Diary*, 1790

THE KING AND QUEEN OF THE
SANDWICH ISLANDS VISIT LONDON

At half past ten o'clock I went with the Prince and Princess Lowenstein, their son, and my sister, to Mr. Canning's, the Secretary of State, who received for the first time the King and Queen of the Sandwich Islands! They arrived in the midst of a numerous assembly of all the best society, and all *en grande toilette* for a large assembly given at Northumberland House. Mr. Canning entered, giving his hand to a large black woman more than six feet high, and broad in proportion, muffled up in a striped gauze dress with short sleeves, leaving uncovered enormous black arms, half covered again with white gloves; an enormous gauze turban upon her head; black hair, not curled, but very short; a small bag in her hand, and I do not know what upon her neck, where there was no gauze. It was with difficulty that the Minister and his company could preserve a proper gravity for the occasion. The Queen was followed by a lady in waiting as tall as herself, and with a gayer and more intelligent countenance. Then came the King, accompanied by three of his subjects, all dressed like him in European costume; and a fourth, whose office I did not know, but he wore over his ordinary coat a scarlet and yellow feather cloak, and a helmet covered with the same material on his head. The King was shorter than his four courtiers, but they all looked very strong, and, except the King, all taller than the majority of those who surrounded them. The two ladies were seated before the fire in the gallery for some time . . . From the gallery Mr. Canning, still holding the Queen's hand, conducted them through the apartment and under the verandah of the garden, where the band of the Guards regiment in their full uniform was playing military airs. Her savage majesty appeared much more occupied by the red-plumed hats of the musicians than by the music. She ought to have been pleased to see that the officer's helmet of her court surpassed them as to colour. From there they were conducted into the dining-room, where there was a fine collation. The two ladies were seated alone at a table placed across the room, and ate some cake and drank wine. They appeared awkward in all their movements, and particularly embarrassed in their walk; there was nothing of the free step of the savage, being probably embarrassed by the folds of the European dress. After another walk under the verandah, we left them there about twelve o'clock, and returned home.

Mary Berry, *Journal*, 1824

ROARING LONDON

Waiting at the Marble Arch while Em called a little way further on ... This hum of the wheel – the roar of London! What is it composed of? Hurry, speech, laughter, moans, cries of little children. The people in this tragedy laugh, sing, smoke, toss off wines, etc., make love to girls in drawing-rooms and areas; and yet are playing their parts in the tragedy just the same. Some wear jewels and feathers, some wear rags. All are caged birds; the only difference lies in the size of the cage. This too is part of the tragedy.

Thomas Hardy, *Diary*, 1885

～ 29 MAY ～

GOING ON A BEAR HUNT

The Ambassadors had a fair supper made them by the Duke of Somerset and afterwards went into the Thames and saw both the Bear hunted in the River and also Wildfire cast out of boats and many pretty conceits.

Edward VI, *Journal*, 1549

MEMBERS ONLY

Went to London Library. A meeting of members was being held up-stairs . . . I stood by the door while Gladstone was speaking near the fire place. Gladstone, a dusky-complexioned spare middle-sized man, with grey hair, thin and straggling; eyes very black and rather bright; earnest expression; with a sort of approach to a slouch in his manner and bearing. He spoke fluently but not at all rapidly; sentences rather winding and long drawn out like honey you must twist the spoon to break off. When he had spoken, an old benevolent looking aquiline-nosed stooping man (the Archbishop of Dublin) made a few remarks, in the course of which, Gladstone quietly took his hat and sloped out stealing close by me to the door.

Alfred Domett, *Diary*, 1877

HATING LONDON'S BANK HOLIDAYMAKERS

Yesterday, I had a long walk with a friend out to Richmond Park, and saw some of the most beautiful country scenery one could wish to revel amongst. In the midst of the splendid woods and fields which border the Thames in that part, one could think any large town was at least a hundred miles away. It is Bank Holiday to-day, and the streets are over-crowded with swarms of people. Never is so clearly to be seen the vulgarity of the people as at these holiday times. Their notion of a holiday is to rush in crowds to some sweltering place, such as Crystal Palace, and then sit and drink and quarrel themselves into stupidity. Miserable children are lugged about, yelling at the top of their voices, and are beaten because they yell. Troops of hideous creatures drive wildly about the town in gigs, donkey-carts, cabbage-carts, dirt-carts and think it enjoyment. The pleasure of peace and quietness, of rest of body and mind, is not understood. Places like Hampstead Heath and the various parks and commons are packed with screeching drunkards, one general mass of dust and heat and rage and exhaustion. Yet this is the best kind of holiday the people are capable of.

George Gissing, Letter to his sister Margaret, 1882

～ 30 MAY ～

A CAPITAL LIQUID

Drank Dulwich water and mightily it refreshed me.

Robert Hooke, *Diary*, 1675

CHANGING INNS

We got to London about 2 o'clock in the afternoon all safe and well, thank God for it. To coachmen from Norwich gave 0.4.0. We did not like the inn where the coach put up (which was the Swan and 2 Necks in Lad-Lane) therefore we got into a Hackney coach and drove to the Bell Savage on Ludgate Hill and there dined, supped and slept. Mr Du Quesne went with us there and dined and spent the afternoon with us – in the evening he went to the Archbishops at Lambeth where he supped and slept. Nancy bore her journey very well as did Will and myself. We were all very glad to get to bed to-night, being tired.

James Woodforde, *Diary*, 1782

AN OASIS ON THE EUSTON ROAD

Lately, I've found myself keen to find out more about Quakers; it's the one religion I've always been the most intrigued about. They're anti-war, anti-aggression, anti-hierachy, anti-priests, anti-waste, anti-Making A Fuss, pro-environmentalism, pro-honesty. They commune with The Divine in utter silence. Meditation with a centuries-old English tradition behind it, as opposed to a self-help fad. They see other religions as something to learn from rather than rival, and actually rent out their properties to other faiths when they're not using them. And apparently, some Quakers really do describe themselves as agnostics or even atheists. That's a pretty tolerant religion.

The Friends House on Euston Road includes a public garden. I like how this oasis of humanist reflection is on one of the noisiest streets in London.

Dickon Edwards, *Diary*, 2007

~ *31 May* ~

CHANGING THE GUARD AT
ST JAMES'S PALACE

We breakfasted, dined and spent the afternoon at our inn. Before we breakfasted, I hired a coach and we went in it to St. James Park. Will also went with us. From the Horse Guards we all walked up the Park to St. James's Palace and saw the Guards relieved at 9 o'clock — a very pretty sight. We also saw most of the state rooms in the palace. Gave to people at St. James's Palace 0. 3. 6. From thence we walked up the Park to the Queens Palace but did not go into that — the Royal Family being there. After that we walked down the Park back to the Horse-Guards and there took a Hackney coach and returned to our inn to breakfast.

James Woodforde, *Diary*, 1782

ASSES AT HAMPSTEAD

After breakfast we proceeded to Mr. Hoare's at Hampstead, where we were to spend a day and a night. The country is very pretty at Hampstead, and one wonders to see so rural a situation so near London. We saw an immense number of asses saddled, which are let out for shilling

rides. After calling on the Hoares, we set out to visit Mr. Coleridge, the Lake poet, and saw the asses we had before observed cantering and trotting with children on them, in a style which severe blows would not have induced our ass to display last summer. We staid half an hour with Coleridge, and I can give no idea of the beauty and sublimity of his conversation. It resembles the loveliness of a song. He began by telling of his health, and of a fit of insensibility in which he had lain thirty-five minutes, three weeks before. Just as he came to consciousness, and before he had opened his eyes, having heard the voice of his physician, he uttered a sentence, which I regret that I do not remember exactly, but it was about the fugacious nature of consciousness and the extraordinary nature of man. His nephew was quite amused to find the ruling passion strong in death, when he heard him utter a piece of metaphysics. From this he went to a discussion on the soul and the body, and brought in an ingenious little interlude about a bit of wire. I did not understand him always, but I admired him throughout.

Anne Chalmers, *Journal*, 1830

WEST END SHOPLIFTING

Went to Selfridges in the afternoon and I saw a woman take shampoo & steal it, a child take bits of jewellery, and a student walk with a sweater into the hall of the foyer, take off his jacket, don the sweater & then put the jacket over it! I have never seen such blatant theft before. I felt disgusted & then thought 'That store deserves it . . . the place invites thieves . . .'

Kenneth Williams, *Diary*, 1980

JUNE

∼ 1 JUNE ∼

SLACK ON SOUTHAMPTON STREET

very slack day owing to the Whitsuntide holidays. Coals sold only 24 tons. Met James Smith's wife and son in St Martin's Lane, having not seen them for a considerable time since. Surprising news from Granny Shepard this evening that her son John Shepard, who is my uncle, who has nearly completed his 43rd year, bathed today for the first time in his life at the Metropolitan Baths, High Holborn, opposite Southampton Street. Wrote a letter for Charles Waters to Viscount Canning for an order to fish in the ornamental waters of the Regent's Park. Mr Edwards commenced travelling for orders for Eccleston Wharf — brought us one to begin with, though of very little account being low in price. (He was Morris's former clerk).

Nathaniel Bryceson, *Diary*, 1846

A DARING YOUNG MAN
ON HIS FLYING TRAPEZE

I was persuaded to go with Severn and his friend to the 'Alhambra', where some thousands of people had gathered to see a man fling himself, in a highly dangerous & thrilling manner, from one swing to another across the building. The man himself, Léotard,* was beautiful to look upon; being admirably made & proportioned; muscular arms shoulders & thighs; and calf ankle and foot as elegantly turned as a lady's. His feat also was wonderful and done with ease and grace.

Arthur Munby, *Diary*, 1861

* Jules Léotard gave his name to a type of gymwear and was the inspiration for the 1867 song, 'The Daring Young Man on the Flying Trapeze'.

POSH SOHO

I treated myself to a seat in the circle tonight to see again the wonderful Ruth Draper at the Vaudeville Theatre and have supper afterwards all posh in Soho. This was a luxury and I had to save up quite a time to get the money for this do, but it does me good. Makes a change.

Fred Bason, *Diary*, 1931

~ 2 JUNE ~

HIGHS AND LOWS OF THEATRELAND

Saw 'Beggar's Opera' at Drury Lane. Pit and gallery so full no place; went into front-box où much mob – low sort of people had tickets given them – side boxes almost empty.

John Baker, *Diary*, 1776

CHARITY AT ST PAUL'S

On Thursday morning I went to St Paul's to see the charity children assembled, and hear their singing. Berlioz says it is the finest thing he has heard in England; and this opinion of his induced me to go. I was not disappointed: it is worth doing once, especially as we got out before the sermon.

George Eliot, Letter to Sara Hennell, 1852

QUITE HOGARTHIAN SCENES

I walked home about 4 a.m. – broad daylight. The street scenes at that hour, especially at the top of the Haymarket, were quite Hogarthian. The last stragglers were just reeling out of the 'Pic', & talking or squabbling outside: two gentlemen in evening dress, a few unwashed foreigners, several half-drunken prostitutes, one of whom, reeling away, drops her splendid white bonnet in the gutter, & another dances across the street, showing her legs above the knee: languid waiters in shirt sleeves stand looking on from their doors: two or three cabmen doze on the box behind their dozing horses: and a ragged beggarwoman skulks.

Arthur Munby, *Diary*, 1859

A WINDMILL IN BRIXTON

The venue is The Windmill, a delightful little place near the nineteenth century landmark of the same name. To my shame, I've lived in London for ten years and never realised there WAS a windmill in Brixton. As it's still daylight outside, I go to take a good, tilting look. The windmill is in a small park, with Brixton Prison on one side and a children's playground on the other. A group of small boys are playing football, and as I approach their ball falls over the separating railings and lands at my feet. I try to affect an air of jovial, avuncular mateyness, as I loosely imagine one is supposed to do in such situations. I make some remark about the prison and not being able to kick a ball to save my life sentence, and throw the thing over to them. They have become completely silent and are staring at me in utter terror. I walk back to the venue, glance over my shoulder and see they are still looking at me. I do hope they got to resume their game. Perhaps I represent the sort of Stranger they've been told to not speak to.

Dickon Edwards, *Diary*, 2004

~ 3 *JUNE* ~

A WHALE IN THE THAMES

A large whale was taken betwixt my land butting on the Thames and Greenwich, which drew an infinite concourse to see it, by water, coach, and on foote, from London and all parts. It appeared first below Greenwich at low water, for at high water it would have destroyed all the boats; but lying now in shallow water, incompassed with boats, after a long conflict it was killed with a harping yron, struck in the head, out of which it spouted blood and water by two tunnells, and after a horrid grone it ran quite on shore and died. Its length was fifty-eight foote, height sixteen, black skin'd like coach-leather, very small eyes, greate taile, and onely two small finns, a picked snout, and a mouth so wide that divers men might have stood upright in it; no teeth, but suck'd the slime onely as thro' a grate of that bone which we call whale-bone; the throate yet so narrow as would not have admitted the least of fishes. The extremes of the cetaceous bones hang downwards from the upper jaw; and was hairy towards the ends and bottom within-side; all of it prodigious; but in nothing more wonderful than that an animal of so greate a bulk should be nourished onely by slime through those grates.

John Evelyn, *Diary*, 1658

DEAN STREET VETERANS

Saw old Mr Walker of Dean Street for first time – a very old man and dresses very old fashion. He was present when Margaret Nicholson attempted to stab George III. Bad works these holidays – men nearly all absent. Odd men in, very drunk and very saucy – one named Whiffin, in answer to a question, told me to 'Ax his ass.'

Nathaniel Bryceson, *Diary*, 1846

CAMDEN ACCIDENTAL

A bizarre accident in Camden Town. Shooting the lights at the foot of Chalk Farm Road, a fire-engine swerves to avoid a car and plunges straight through the front of a shop. It happens first thing in the morning and no one is hurt – the call turned out to be hoax. All day the fire engine has been stuck inside the shop, and so neatly, long ladder and all, with only the rear wheels visible, it's as if it had been deliberately garaged. Scaffolders toil till dark to shore up the building lest, when the engine is withdrawn, it will fetch the building down with it. Were thc shop a newsagent's or a greengrocer's it would be bad enough, but the premises in question are those of an extremely select antique shop, which fastidiously confines itself to art deco. There are mirrors tinted a faint pink, lamps in frail fluted skirts. Suddenly in the pearly light of dawn in bursts this red, bullying monster.

Alan Bennett, *Diary*, 1985

～ 4 *JUNE* ～

SPLENDID SHOPS

The large and splendid shops in Regent-street, with their enormous plate-glass windows and looking-glasses in gilt frames, are truly magnificent exhibitions! The perpetual movement and life in the streets, at once so wonderful and exciting! When I think of Paris and compare it with London, it now leaves on my mind the impression of a small town!

C. G. Carus, *The King of Saxony's Journey*
Through England and Scotland, 1844

KNOCK 'EM DEAD DOWN BY THE DOCKS

By train to Blackwall, where having ordered our dinner at the Hotel we strolled about going over one of the Docks in which were many fine vessels – & so to dinner which comprised the usual fish, winding up with chicken & cheese, we had two bottles of capital champagne, & one of sherry, & then sat a long time looking over the river (which was lighted by a jolly moon) until nearly 11 o'clock. Talked to many things, Norris telling me that the other day he went to a private 'spiritual séance' where he saw the most extraordinary things which he would not have believed had he not seen them: table rapping, musical instruments floating about in the air, tables rising & falling & so on. All this is wonderful no doubt but I should certainly require the evidence of my own senses before I put my faith in anything of that sort.

Rafe Neville Leycester, *Diary,* 1865

LUNCH IN THE PARK

Glorious hot June day. I had a 'workman's lunch' of smoked sausage and a bottle of red wine in Regent's Park with E. We sat on the river's bank and watched the swans go by in slow indignation . . . We are happiest in this dreamlike state, watching, talking, drifting, and when we are happy it always seems as though we were figures in a tapestry.

Charles Ritchie, *Diary,* 1942

THE SUMMER OF '76

Another glorious morning. Does London have the finest weather in England? Always look out of that little lavatory window behind the Corinthian columns of the RA.

Alan Clark, *Diaries*, 1976

~ 5 *JUNE* ~

DO THE STRAND

It has a strange appearance – especially in the Strand, where there is a constant succession of shop after shop, and where, not unfrequently, people of different trades inhabit the same house – to see their doors or the tops of their windows, or boards expressly for the purpose, all written over from top to bottom with large painted letters. Every person, of every trade or occupation, who owns ever so small a portion of a house, makes a parade with a sign at his door; and there is hardly a cobbler whose name and profession may not be read in large golden characters by every one that passes. It is here not at all uncommon to see on doors in one continued succession, 'Children educated here', 'Shoes mended here', 'Foreign spirituous liquors sold here', and 'Funerals furnished here'; of all these inscriptions, I am sorry to observe that 'Dealer in foreign spirituous liquors' is by far the most frequent. And indeed it is allowed by the English themselves, that the propensity of the common people to the drinking of brandy or gin is carried to a great excess; and I own it struck me as a peculiar phraseology, when, to tell you that a person is intoxicated or drunk, you hear them say, as they generally do, that he is in liquor.

Karl Philip Moritz, *Travels in England*, 1782

UNUSUAL MUSIC AT KING'S

Found yesterday Professor Wheatstone's card, with a note requesting a call to-day at King's College.* Therefore, after a quiet morning, went there and found Uncle Charles with the Professor inspecting his electric telegraph. This is really being brought into active service, as last week they began laying it down between London and Bristol, to cost £250 a mile. He then showed us his 'Baby', constructed in imitation of the human organs of speech; it can beautifully pronounce some words and can cry most pathetically. He treated it in a most fatherly manner. His 'Syren' is an extraordinary little instrument, so called because it will act under water; its object is to measure the intensity of sound. He then played the Chinese reed, one of the earliest instruments constructed, exhibited the harp, or rather sounding-board, with additaments, which communicates with a piano two stories higher, and receives the sound from it quite perfectly through a conductive wire. Wheatstone has been giving lectures, and in fact is in the middle of a course. No ladies are admitted, unluckily; the Bishop of London forbade it, seeing how they congregated to Lyell's, which prohibition so offended that gentleman that he resigned his professorship. We left our friend, promising to repeat our visit, when he will have some experiments prepared.

Caroline Fox, *Journal*, 1838

* Charles Wheatstone was Professor of Experimental Physics at King's College, London, founded nine years before Caroline Fox's visit.

∽ 6 *June* ∽

THIEF-TAKING WITH BLUNDERBUSSES

Last Sunday night, being as wet a night as you shall see in a summer's day, about half an hour after twelve, I was just come home from White's, and undressing to step into bed, I heard Harry, who you know lies forwards, roar out, 'Stop thief!' and run down stairs. I ran after him. Don't be frightened; I have not lost one enamel, nor bronze, nor have been shot through the head again. A gentlewoman, who lives at Governor Pitt's next door but one to me, and where Mr. Bentley used to live, was going to bed too, and heard people breaking into Mr. Freeman's house, who, like some acquaintance of mine in Albemarle-street, goes out of town, locks up his doors, and leaves the community to watch his furniture. N. B. It was broken open but two years ago, and all the chairmen vow they shall steal his house away another time, before we shall trouble our heads about it. Well, madam called out 'watch'; two men who were centinels, ran away, and Harry's voice after them. Down came I, and with a posse of chairmen and watchmen found the third fellow in the area of Mr. Freeman's house. Mayhap you have seen all this in the papers, little thinking who commanded the detachment. Harry fetched a blunderbuss to invite the thief up. One of the chairmen, who was drunk, cried, 'Give me the blunderbuss, I'll shoot him!' But as the general's head was a little cooler, he prevented military execution, and took the prisoner without bloodshed, intending to make his triumphal entry into the metropolis of Twickenham with his captive tied to the wheels of his postchaise. I find my style rises so much with the recollection of my victory, that I don't know how to descend to tell you that the enemy was a carpenter, and had a leather apron on.

Horace Walpole, Letter to George Montagu, 1752

THE GORDON RIOTS

In the midst of the most cruel and ridiculous confusion, I am now set down to give you a very imperfect sketch of the maddest people that the maddest times were ever plagued with. – The public prints have informed you (without doubt) of last Friday's transactions – the insanity of Lord George Gordon, and the worse than Negro barbarity of the populace; – the burnings and devastations of each night you will also see in the prints . . . There is at this present moment at least a hundred thousand poor, miserable, ragged rabble from twelve to sixty years of age with blue cockades in their hats – besides half as many women and children, all parading the streets – the bridge – the Park – ready for any and every mischief – Gracious God! What's the matter now? I was obliged to leave off – the shouts of the mob – the horrid clashing of swords – and the clutter of a multitude in swiftest motion – drew me to the door – when every one in the street was employed in shutting up shop . . . Lord S——h narrowly escaped with life about an hour since; the mob seized his chariot going to the house, broke his glasses, and, in struggling to get his lordship out, they somehow have cut his face – The guards flew to his assistance – the light-horse scowered the road, got his chariot, escorted him from the coffee-house, where he had fled for protection, to his carriage, and guarded him bleeding very fast home. This – this – is liberty! genuine British liberty! – This instant about two thousand liberty boys are swearing and swaggering by with large sticks – thus armed, in hopes of meeting with the Irish chairmen and labourers – All the guards are out – and all the horse – the poor fellows are just worn out for want of rest, having been on duty ever since Friday. – Thank heaven, it rains; may it increase as to send these deluded wretches safe to their homes, their families, and wives! About two this afternoon, a large party took it into their heads to visit the King and Queen, and entered the Park for that purpose – but found the guard too numerous to be forced, and after some useless attempts gave it up.— It is reported, the house will either be prorogued, or parliament dissolved, this evening, as it is in vain to think of attending any business while this anarchy lasts.

Ignatius Sancho, Letter to a friend, 1780

～ 7 JUNE ～

VISITING A FAT MAN

Daniell Lambert, the big man, I saw at a house in Piccadilly. He weighs upwards of 50 stone, is 36 years old . . . He told me he began to grow fat at an early age. He repeatedly said 'no man had better health', and that he can take as much exercise as his size requires. He said his appetite is a common one. I observed that his eye had a heavy look & his countenance the same, though not unhealthy. The breadth of his shoulders was great, his belly swagging, and his legs and thighs without form, rolls of flesh indented. His answers were blunt and direct. On the whole his appearance gave me pain. His feet were scarcely to be seen. His head moved easily.

Joseph Farington, *Diary*, 1806

A PORTRAIT IN CHELSEA

Went to keep appointment with W. Rothenstein, at his studio, Glebe Place, Chelsea. He made two drawings of me; one sitting, the other standing – latter I liked best. Max Beerbohm came in and had lunch with us.

George Gissing, *Diary*, 1897

QUEER MAIL FROM KENSINGTON

Extract from a letter from an entirely unknown lady living in Kensington today, Saturday 7th June: 'Neither I nor any of my six sisters would think of going to bed with a man unless we were married!' I do get a queer mail. And from Kensington at that!

Fred Bason, *Diary*, 1958

A GAY SOHO PUB

Comptons is a loud pub – no, the loudest bar in town. By eight you are pressed so tightly against your neighbours that to get out of the place is a major feat of concentration and negotiation.

When Sir Francis Rose brought me here many years ago, to find his lost son, it was dimly lit and half empty, a few Soho regulars propping up the bar. One of them, John, was a large man with a squashed face. He and Francis talked about the good old days before the war, when John had been a smashing boxer. The rubdown sexuality of those 'good old days' still pervaded the place, with its smattering of rent boys who had stopped off on their way to the Golden Lion from the White Bear in Piccadilly Underground (it was there that we later tracked down Francis's son).

Comptons had an underworldly atmosphere. You half expected the Krays to drop in with cash to spare on a night West drinking with old friends.

Francis looked the perfect punter – though Comptons was not a renters' pub, just the sleazy mix of that Soho now almost lost in Brasserieville. A pub for old pros of both sexes, its walls were covered with play bills and signed photos from the fifties: Tommy Steele, Henry Cooper, Diana Dors. That sort of thing. Here boys-in-the-band, faded stars of Physique Pictorial, Drummer spliced themselves with busy blondes.

Nowadays at 6:00 Comptons is still quite empty. At this moment the bar staff pull down the venetian blinds to shut out the street and the curiosity of passers-by; the heat, nicotine count, and decibels gradually mount.

Much has changed — and then nothing really. The only real difference is the tidal wave of terrible music. I discover the pub is still used by professional boys on their way to work — although in Mrs T.'s England, unlike Harold Wilson's, they are no longer waifs and strays from up North or the East End. These boys have passed their 'A' levels, have an arts degree and have opted for an easier life of the massage parlour and escort agency rather than a career in mortgageville.

Their attitudes and accents put the clients in Mayfair health clubs at ease, where for an extra £40 their hands slip under the towel. I have to admit I've never been interested in this world, except as a voyeur; even pushing fifty I would like to retain the illusion that I'm desired, if not for my body then perhaps for my conversation, or even memories!

I declined the offer of a young Portuguese lad, who, as he rubbed his crotch against my thigh, suggested I could do with some healthy exercise in his club. With their Jimmy Dean hairstyles and frayed, faded, blue jeans, these boys can make up to £1000 a week. They are forward and charming.

The Portuguese lad says 'I love your films' with an ever-so winsome twinkle in his dark eyes — 'though I've never seen any of them.' The boy standing next to him chips in 'I'm going to see them all at the Scala tomorrow. I am a painter and would love to talk to you.' Should I give him my phone number? I don't know. Perhaps they were all on the game, but it was quite exciting.

I left them all in the street debating whether to go to L'Escargot or an even more expensive Soho restaurant. I'm glad they can afford it; those places are pretty dull, and they'd cheer them up no end.

Derek Jarman, *Journal*, 1989

～ 8 *JUNE* ～

A VISIT TO BEDLAM

Hence I drove to Bethlehem Hospital, commonly called Bedlam . . . I
passed through several of the large, airy corridors, off which were cells
for single patients, or for two, three, and four together. Every thing was
very clean, but the black bars and doors produce a melancholy effect
against the white-washed walls. In several court-yards were patients
walking or working in the open air. A separate division is here made of
criminal patients, i.e. such persons as have committed crimes, of which
insanity was considered the reason or the excuse. Thus I saw Oxford,
who made an attempt on the life of the queen, and who has been shut
up here, although he did not appear to me to be insane. He is a person
of very ordinary appearance. Another person, really insane, a literary
man from Hanover, had already troubled the queen with the most
various requests before he was sent to this asylum. Also an elderly
German lady, who appears to have addressed Prince Albert on several
occasions. Both these persons spoke to me, and I had some difficulty in
getting away from them. Certainly it is very comprehensible that a
young couple, like this royal pair, standing upon a pinnacle, and represented every day to millions as an ideal of happiness, should become
the object of the passionate wishes of several of these unhappy persons.
Bedlam may yet have to open its doors to many others of the same kind!

C. G. Carus, *The King of Saxony's Journey*
Through England and Scotland, 1844

LIGHT UP THE TOWN

The 'Jubilee' was amazing. At night all the great streets were packed
from side to side with a clearly divided double current of people, all
vehicles were forbidden. You walked at the rate of a funeral horse from
top of Bond Street to the Bank, by way of Pall Mall, Strand, etc. Such
a concourse of people I never saw. The effect of illuminated London
from the top of our house here was strange. Of course I didn't try to
see the daylight proceedings.

George Gissing, Letter to his brother, 1887

UNDERWEAR PULLED DOWN ON
NEW OXFORD STREET

A paper I write for under a pseudonym wanted me to notice the Camargo Ballet at the Savoy . . . Beecham conducting. Would like to see this but will not write about it if I can help it. Strongly object to igno-ramuses writing about drama, and realise that I know nothing about ballet.

The advantage of a male secretary is that you can go on working while you are dressing or undressing. Worked out an entire theory of ballet when I was in my pants, dressing for the play. Jock says that in my pants I look exactly like those monstrosities which used to advertise Horne's, or somebody's, underwear on the coping of the building at the corner of Tottenham Court Road and New Oxford Street pulled down.

James Agate, *Journals*, 1932

~ *9 June* ~

THE GORDON RIOTS

At past ten I went to General Conway's, in a moment we were alarmed by the servants, and rushing to the street-door saw through little Warwick-street such an universal blaze, that I had no doubt the Mews, at least St. Martin's-lane was on fire. Mr. Conway ran and I limped after him to Charing Cross, but though seemingly close, it was no nearer than the Fleet Market; at past twelve I went up to Lord Hertford's, two of his sons came in from the Bridge at Blackfriars, where they had seen the Toll Houses plundered and burnt. Instantly arrived their cook, a German Protestant with a child in his arms, and all we could gather was that the mob was in possession of his house, had burnt his furniture and had obliged him to abandon his wife and another child. I sent my own footman for it was only in Woodstock-street, and he soon returned and said it had been only some apprentices who supposed him a Papist on his not illuminating his house, and that three of them and an Irish Catholic chairman had been secured, but the poor man has lost his all! I drove from one place to another till two, but did not go to bed till between three and four, and ere asleep heard a troop of horse gallop by. My Printer whom I had sent out for intelligence came not home till past nine the next morning, I feared he was killed, but then I heard of such a scene. He had beheld three sides of the Fleet Market in flames, Barnard's Inn at one end, the prison on one side and the distiller's on the other, besides Fetter and Shoe lanes, with such horrors of distraction distress &c., as are not to be described; besides accounts of slaughter near the Bank . . . Yesterday was some slaughter in Fleet-street by the Horse Guards and more in St. George's Fields by the Protestant Association, who fell on the rioters, who appear to have been chiefly apprentices, convicts and all kinds of desperadoes, for Popery is already out of the question, and plunder all the object. They have exacted sums from many houses to avoid being burnt as popish. The ringleader Lord George is fled. The Bank, the destruction of all prisons and of the Inns of Court, were the principal aims . . . The night passed quietly, and by this evening there will be eighteen thousand men in and round the town. As yet there are more persons killed by drinking than by ball or bayonet. At the great popish distiller's they swallowed spirits of all kinds, and Kirgate saw men and women lying dead in the streets under barrows as he came home yesterday.

Horace Walpole, Letter to the Reverend William Mason, 1780

A PIECE OF COXCOMBRY

Went with Edward and Patty to Sir John Soane's house or museum, a quaint piece of coxcombry and gimcrackery, absurd I think to be left as it is, alone, for it is scarcely worth the trouble of going to see.

William Charles Macready, *Diary*, 1848

LOST IN NOTTING HILL GATE

Some days ago sent a personal advertisement to the newspaper to try to find my little Irish girl who lives at Notting Hill Gate. To-day they return me the money and advert., no doubt mistaking me for a White Slave trafficker. And by this time, I'm thinking, my little Irish girl can go to blazes. Shall spend the P.O. on sweets or monkey nuts.

W. N. P. Barbellion, *The Diary of a Disappointed Man*, 1914

SCANDALOUS TALK

Dined at the British Embassy with the Ormsby Gores. There was much talk of the Profumo case. Dr Stephen Ward was indicted in London yesterday on the charge of receiving money from the physical exertions of call girls. He is expected to 'sing' freely and it is not a pretty tune.

David Bruce, *Diary*, 1963

～ 10 *JUNE* ～

A SPLENDID CREATURE IN LEICESTER SQUARE

Went in to the Circus in Leicester Square for a while on my way home, to see 'Ella'; a splendid creature, tall and well made, with large bright eyes, fine features, and dark abundant hair. She is said to be a man in disguise: but there is nothing to favour such a suspicion except her height and the boldness of her riding: which, like herself, is the most admirable thing I ever saw in a circus.

Arthur Munby, *Diary*, 1859

THE ALLY PALLY ALIGHT

We were told on Saturday what a beautiful place the Alexandra Palace was, and Sissy passed it on her way to town yesterday and admired it exceedingly. It could not have been more than twenty minutes later when all of a sudden flames burst out of the Dome, and the whole building was like a furnace. There was no water whatsoever, all arrangements made for it, but none yet laid on. The loss is tremendous, the place being filled with valuable paintings and china lent by the owners.

Louisa Bain, *Diary*, 1873

THE POLISH CLUB

Park by the Serpentine Gallery and walk down to the Polish Club in Exhibition Road. Always struck at this time of year by the sheer weight of greenery – the thickness of the crowns on the trees, the lushness of bushes and shrubs, the deep, thick pile of grass cover. It's June, it's raining and England puts on its own impression of a Continental rainforest. At the Polish Club I sit with a Perrier and wait for Tristram. Dark, smiling eyes of the girls at the bar – friendly, curious. It's like being in a very benevolent foreign country. Hardly anyone else dining there, except for a few very smart, grey-suited Polish men, well-preserved, with interestingly aged faces. Tristram tells me that they're the Polish Government in Exile.

Michael Palin, *Halfway to Hollywood*, 1987

~ 11 JUNE ~

A BURNING DOWNRIVER

After a long drought, we had a refreshing shower. The day before, there was a dreadful fire at Rotherhithe, near the Thames side, which burned divers ships, and consumed nearly three hundred houses.

John Evelyn, *Diary*, 1699

THE LORD MAYOR IN HIS ENTERTAINING GOWN

Went to St. Paul's, preceded by the City Musick . . . The Artillery
Company met me at St. Paul's, and marched before me through Cheap-
side and down King Street to my Hall. They were led by Col. Deacon.
They drew up before the Hall and fired three volleys, One at the King's
Health, One at the Prince and Princess of Wales', and the other at mine.
I afterwards entertained the Officers with a cold dinner. I received them
in the Entertaining Gown, and gave the Soldiers a Bottle of Wine
between three.

Micajah Perry, *Lord Mayor Perry's Diary*, 1739

A CANING IN THE COMMONS

One Gourlay, a turbulent and discontented Scotch gentleman farmer,
who had become a democrat in Canada, and a Radical in Somersetshire,
caned Mr. Brougham in the lobby of the House of Commons. He was
taken to Cold Bath Fields and confined there as insane.

Charles Abbot, Lord Colchester, *Diary*, 1824

ENJOYABLE KNIGHTSBRIDGE

This afternoon I enjoyed myself in Brompton Road. First I went to the
International Theatre Exhibition at the Victoria and Albert Museum.
But I was more inclined to look at the human exhibits than the art-
products of Appia and Craig. Then I popped into Brompton Oratory;
the choral Mass seemed the last word in dope. (I noticed the drugged
look in the faces of the audience as they came out.) The choir sung a
bit of Elgar's Apostles very finely. It was a pleasant and interesting
intermezzo, that Catholic celebration. I sat next to a red-haired youth
whose beauty added to the interest of the proceedings.

Siegfried Sassoon, *Diary*, 1922

∼ 12 JUNE ∼

HAM ON HAYMARKET

Going through streets leading out of St James's Market into Haymarket, saw some ham at window in Royal Larder – went in and had some and some porter. NB: I believe this the same person kept house of that name 3 or 4 years ago in Jermyn Street, où many people caught gaming and seemed as if ham (for seemed to have nothing else) only a pretence.

John Baker, *Diary*, 1776

THE GREAT SCALE OF THE METROPOLIS

We proceeded without any event to town, where we arrived by five o'clock next morning. The astonishment of the boys was as is usual with their age on first seeing the great scale of . . . the metropolis. We proceeded in a hackney coach to a lodging I had prepared in Duke Street, Grosvenor Square, and went to bed for three hours. Walked to Westminster to see Mr. Packharris, the boarding-house in Dean's Yard. I think the carriages and horses attracted their notice more than any other circumstance. After making the necessary arrangements at the boarding-house, we set out to see sights, to panoramas, wild beasts, etc., and dined with my friend Colonel Wright. Sunday to church and showed them all the world in Kensington Gardens and the Park.

General William Dyott, *Diary*, 1819

AN ASSASSINATION ATTEMPT

On Wednesday afternoon, as the Queen and Prince Albert were driving in a low carriage up Constitution Hill, about four or five in the afternoon, they were shot at by a lad of eighteen, who fired two pistols at them successively, neither shot taking effect. He was in the Green Park without rails, and he was only a few yards from the carriage, and moreover, very cool and collected, it is marvellous he should have missed his aim. In a few moments the young man was seized, without any attempt on his part to escape or deny the deed, and was carried off to prison.

The Queen, who appeared perfectly cool, and not the least alarmed, instantly drove to the Duchess of Kent's, to anticipate any report that might reach her mother, and having done so, she continued her drive and went to the Park. By this time the attempt upon her life had become generally known, and she was received with the utmost enthusiasm by the immense crowd that was congregated in carriages, on horseback, and on foot. All the equestrians formed themselves into an escort and attended her back to the Palace, cheering vehemently, while she acknowledged, with great appearance of feeling, these loyal manifestations.

Charles Greville, *Journal*, 1840

ATTACKS IN SOHO

Eileen and I last night walked though Soho to see whether the damage to Italian shops etc. was as reported. It seemed to have been exaggerated in the newspapers, but we did see, I think, 3 shops which had had their windows smashed. The majority had hurriedly labelled themselves 'British'. Gennari's, the Italian grocer's, was plastered all over with printed placards saying 'This establishment is entirely British'. The Spaghetti House, a shop specialising in Italian foodstuffs, had renamed itself 'British Food Shop'. Another shop proclaimed itself Swiss, and even a French restaurant had labelled itself British. The interesting thing is that all these placards must evidently have been printed beforehand and kept in readiness . . .

Disgusting though these attacks on harmless Italian shopkeepers are, they are an interesting phenomenon, because English people, i.e. people of a kind who would be likely to loot shops, don't as a rule take a spontaneous interest in foreign politics. I don't think there was anything of this kind during the Abyssinian war, and the Spanish war simply did not touch the mass of the people. Nor was there any popular move against the Germans resident in England until the last month or two. The low-down cold-blooded meanness of Mussolini's declaration of war at that moment must have made an impression even on people who as a rule barely read the newspapers.

George Orwell, *Diary*, 1940

DETESTING THE FESTIVAL

Went to the Festival of Britain fun-fair. Really the last word in squalor and completely ungay. The Giant Dipper was disgraceful, like an old-fashioned switchback.

Noël Coward, *Diaries*, 1951

～ 13 JUNE ～

THE COCKS OF HAY

Went with Lady Georgina Morpeth to George, the silk mercer's, through all the dirtiest streets of London, and round by Covent Garden theatre, of which the immense walls but more immense scaffolding is really curious. After dinner walked with my father and sister to the fields between Paddington and Bayswater. The haymaking, a beautiful warm quiet evening; we sat for some time on the cocks of hay, which I really enjoyed, but in how melancholy a manner, Heaven, who sees within my soul, alone can know!

Mary Berry, *Journal*, 1809

BEAUTIFUL LONDON

We all walked together up Whitehall, Mackintosh in great spirits and London looking still and free from smoke. I never saw it in such beauty. We took leave of John just as we got into a hackney coach, which I was sorry for, as I liked the walk better, and the red eastern sky looked beautiful.

Fanny Allen, Letter to Mrs Josiah Wedgwood, 1824

PROTESTS AT THE LSE

The other thing this week that's in my mind is the developing situation in Vietnam . . .

On Friday night there was the first 'teach-in' at the LSE in London on Vietnam. It was based on the 'teach-ins' that have appeared in the United States and which are an aspect of the non-violent movement. I think they probably will have an influence and I'm told that whenever Harold Wilson's name was mentioned at LSE people booed. It may well be that when the time comes the Labour government will have been held to fail not because it was too radical but because it was not radical enough.

Tony Benn, *Diaries*, 1965

MISPLACING THE PALACE OF WESTMINSTER

After French class, we found Harold and Doris watching a Bernard Shaw play on TV and Mum in the kitchen making yet more tea. She told us they'd been to Westminster on a pleasure-boat, preferring to see the Abbey to St Paul's. 'Don't say anything, will you?' she asked us in an undertone, 'only we thought it was funny when they searched us at the door but I said it was because of terrorists. And when we got inside, they only let us sit in a sort of gallery, very small. And I was surprised to see that it wasn't a bishop speaking but the Prime Minister. And there was all the government behind him and the others facing.' All the same they'd been quite happy, especially when the MP for Bristol North got up to urge the building of a third London airport. But she wasn't sure they quite grasped that they hadn't seen the Abbey.

Peter Nichols, *Diary*, 1973

～ *14 June* ～

A DISGRACEFUL TUMULT

We went to Drury Lane theatre, and anything more offensive, brutal, stupid and disgusting I have not seen. A number of persons, players and fellows connected with the theatres kept up a disgraceful tumult the whole night – at least till ten o'clock, when after suffering much from impatience, disgust, and indignation, we went away. The actors seemed good as far as it was possible to judge. There was a considerable crowd outside the doors.

William Charles Macready, *Diary*, 1848

LONGING FOR LONDON

Have just returned from a fortnight in Penzance. Noisy and trying as life is at City Road it seemed like heaven when compared to the dullness of the country! I longed for London and home and was surprised at myself. I felt so thankful that life for me was not a mere round of pleasure taking. A fortnight of idleness was too much by half. It seemed such a blessed thing to have duties and work, and an appointed sphere, and not to have riches and leisure and 'no occupation'. Even the friction and irritation of daily life is a salutary antagonism that keeps life fresh. Rather for me a garret in London than a palace in the country! I love the hurry, the press of things, the 'must' in my life and am quite impatient of the jog-pace of country life. In the rush of city life I have often sighed for the beauty and stillness of nature. When I had it in its rich abundance it failed to satisfy me.

Helen G. McKenny, *Diary*, 1888

∼ *15 June* ∼

A LITERARY LION

Went to the British Museum, and, having been told that it was a holiday, asked for Panizzi, who was full of kindness, and told me the library should be at all times accessible to me, and that I should also have a room entirely to myself, if I preferred it at any time to the public room. He then told me of a poor Irish labourer now at work about the Museum, who, on hearing the other day that I was also sometimes at work there, said he would give a pot of ale to any one who would show me to him the next time I came. Accordingly, when I was last there, he was brought where he could have a sight of me as I sat reading; and the poor fellow was so pleased, that he doubled the pot of ale to the man who performed the part of showman.

Thomas Moore, *Diary*, 1839

A BUSY DAY OUT

We went to the Royal Academy, not so many nice pictures as usual to my mind, perhaps I am getting too old to enjoy them as I used to. Only three struck me so as to fix themselves in my memory, The Derby Day, Eastward Ho, and Old Holland, the last most beautiful. Tea in the Haymarket, back to Highgate with Papa, by Blackwall, leaving Margaret and Mary to go to the Horse riding in Leicester Square with their brothers.

Louisa Bain, *Diary*, 1845

SPEAKING OF THE CITY

Browning spoke of London, parties, theatres, Sullivan, Gounod etc. 'If I could do exactly as I liked I should often go to a play instead of to a party. I could amuse myself a good deal better. I should always treat myself to a good place.' He spoke of his own poems – would rather write music – longs also to be a sculptor. 'If I could only live six hundred years or have two lives even.'

William Allingham, *Diary*, 1864

WORKHOUSE INMATES

Fulham Road is dotted with the aged, male inmates of the workhouse in their brown coats and corduroy trousers, out on leave. (The clean, soft pinkiness of their gnarled, work-worn hands seems curiously inapposite.) One sees a few of them in every public-house along the street. Strange that the faces of most of them afford no indication of the manner of their downfall to pauperdom. I looked in vain for general traces either of physical excess or of moral weakness.

Arnold Bennett, *Journal*, 1896

∽ 16 JUNE ∽

MEETING DICKENS, ALIAS BOZ

Sent to the theatre about the rehearsal, and after looking at the newspaper to ascertain the state of the King's health – what an absurdity that the natural ailment of an old and ungifted man should cause so much perplexity and annoyance! – went to the Haymarket and rehearsed, with some care, Othello. Acted Othello in some respects very well, but want much attention to it still. Mr. Elton is not good, and is unfair. I was called for, and after long delay went forward. Forster came into my room with a gentleman, whom he introduced as Dickens, alias Boz – I was glad to see him.

William Charles Macready, *Diary*, 1837

PREPARING FOR THE JUBILEE

Never since I first came to London has the West End been so crowded with sightseers, so congested by the business of pleasure: lines of women, gay and perspiring in the hot sun, recklessly ruffling their light thin frocks in scrambles for seats on the tops of buses; straw-hatted and waistcoatless men continually discussing the prices of seats to view the procession,* and the fortunes made and lost thereby; the thoroughfares packed with vehicles six and eight deep, and the drivers in their grey felt hats as imperturbable as ever, save for a stronger tendency to quarrel cynically among themselves for right of way. On all sides the sounds of hammers on wood, and the sight of aproned carpenters working with the leisurely content of men earning eighteenpence an hour. In all the gutters poles springing up, decorated with muslins and streamers and gilt apexes, and here and there patches, daily growing bigger, of red and blue draperies covering the yellow wood of jubilee stands. Everything, taken separately, ugly and crude, yet in combination, by sheer immensity and bold crudity, certain in the end to produce a great spectacular effect.

Arnold Bennett, *Journal*, 1897

* For Queen Victoria's Diamond Jubilee.

INN BOROUGH

With Thelma to the George Inn, Southwark, for a lunch of steak-and-kidney pie, cherry pie and beer. Expected hordes of American tourists but found only English, including three young men with posh accents who went through a repertoire of advert slogans, radio catchphrases and anecdotes about cricket, bloodsports and motors, even calling beer 'ale'. We decided they were the urban counterpart to those yokels the National Trust employs to lean over five-bar gates on its rural properties. Afterwards to Southwark Cathedral crammed between the vegetable market and the overhead railway. Then walked across the partly-built London Bridge (the previous one sold to decorate an American golf course) and turned down the steps to Lower Thames Street and Magnus Martyr Church. Last time I came here was a Sunday morning on my bicycle in the 50s. A woman was replacing flowers and a church cat ran among the pews. I could see what refreshment Eliot must have found in this place during his lunch-break from the City bank.

Peter Nichols, *Diary*, 1971

∼ 17 *June* ∼

MOVING TO UNFASHIONABLE CHELSEA

I know not if you ever were at Chelsea, especially at old Chelsea, of which this is a portion. It stretches from Battersea Bridge (a queer old wooden structure, where they charge you a halfpenny) along the bank of the River, westward a little way; and eastward (which is our side) some quarter of a mile, forming a 'Cheyne Walk' (pronounced Chainie Walk) of really grand old brick mansions, dating perhaps from Charles II's time ('Don Saltero's Coffeehouse' of the Tatler is still fresh and brisk among them), with flagged pavement; carriage way between two rows of stubborn-looking high old pollarded trees; and then the River with its varied small-craft, fast-moving or safe-moored, and the wholesome smell (among the breezes) of sea Tar. Cheyne Row (or Great Cheyne Row, when we wish to be grand) runs up at right angles from this; has some twenty Houses of the same fashion; Upper Cheyne Row (where Hunt lives) turning again at right angles, some stone-cast from this door. Frontwards we have the outlook I have described already (or if we shove out our head, the River is disclosed some hundred paces to the left); backwards, from the ground floor, our own gardenkin (which I with new garden-tools am actually re-trimming every morning), and, from all the other floors, nothing but leafy clumps, and green fields and red high-peaked roofs glimmering thro' them: a most clear, pleasant prospect, in these fresh westerly airs! Of London nothing visible but Westminster Abbey and the topmost dome of St Paul's; other faint ghosts of spires (one other at least) disclose themselves, as the smoke-cloud shifts; but I have not yet made out what they are. At night we are pure and silent, almost as at Puttoch; and the gas-light shimmer of the great Babylon hangs stretched from side to side of our horizon. To Buckingham Gate it is 32 minutes of my walking (Allan Cunningham's door about half way); nearly the very same to Hyde Park Corner, to which latter point we have Omnibuses every quarter of an hour (they say) that carry you to Whitehorse Cellar, or even to Coventry Street, for sixpence; calling for you at the very threshold. Nothing was ever so discrepant in my experience as the Craigenputtoch silence of this House and then the world-hubbub of London and its people into which a few minutes bring you: I feel as if a day spent between the two must be the epitome of a month.

The rent is £35; which really seems £10 cheaper than such a House could be had for in Dumfries or Annan. The secret is our old friend, 'Gigmanity:' Chelsea is unfashionable; it is also reputed unhealthy. The former quality we rather like (for our neighbours still are all polite-living people); the latter we do not in the faintest degree believe in, remembering that Chelsea was once considered the 'London Mont-pelier,' and knowing that in these matters now as formerly the Cockneys 'know nothing,' only rush in masses blindly and sheepwise. Our worst fault is the want of a good free rustic walk, like Kensington Gardens, which are above a mile off: however, we have the 'College' or Hospital Grounds, with their withered old Pensioners; we have open carriage-ways, and lanes, and really a very pretty route to Piccadilly (different from the Omnibus route) thro' the new Grosvenor edifices, Eaton Square, Belgrave Place &c: I have also walked to Westminster Hall by Vauxhall Bridge-end, Millbank &c; but the road is squalid, confused, dusty and detestable, and happily need not be returned to. To conclude, we are here on literary classical ground, as Hunt is continually ready to declare and unfold: not a stone-cast from this House Smollett wrote his Count Fathom (the house is ruined and we happily do not see it); hardly another stone-cast off, old More entertained Erasmus: to say nothing of Bolingbroke St. John, of Paradise Row and the Count de Grammont, for in truth we care almost nothing for them. On the whole we are exceedingly content so far.

Thomas Carlyle, Letter to John A. Carlyle, 1834

A TEAM OF ZEBRAS

I saw a sight this morning which surprised me . . . a pretty and well-turned out team of zebras in Queen's Gate Gardens.

Mountstuart Grant Duff, *Notes from a Diary*, 1896

~ 18 JUNE ~

A DROWNING AT TWICKENHAM

I walked to the ferry at Twickenham with Car and her husband. On approaching the banks of the river, under Lord Dysart's trees, we saw five or six men drawing something out of the water — it was the body of a man who was nearly drowned. Two young ladies who were out walking, seeing the body in the water, had first given the alarm. It was not cold when it was drawn out, but all the efforts which were made to restore him to life were ineffectual. Captain Scott assisted; and the Duc d'Orleans, who was walking in his garden on the other side of the river, was there in ten minutes, bringing with him two or three servants, and directing the means that he wished to try, but in vain. No one knew if it was accidental or on purpose that the unfortunate man was drowned. He was pretty well dressed, and had 3l, in his pockets. This scene was not cheering.

Mary Berry, *Journal*, 1816

MOONLIT NORTH LONDON

What a divine night it is. I have just returned from Kentish Town; a calm twilight pervades the clear sky; the lamp-like moon is hung out in heaven, and the bright west retains the dye of sunset. If such weather would continue, I should write again; the lamp of thought is again illuminated in my heart, and the fire descends from heaven that kindles it.

Mary Shelley, *Diary*, 1824

THE LONDON MOB

Anniversary of the battle of Waterloo. The Duke,* on returning from the Tower this morning on horseback, was assailed in the streets by a mob of ruffians, who hissed and abused him. Their conduct at last became so violent, that a band of the police were obliged to escort him to his house. In the evening he gave the annual banquet at Apsley House to all the field officers who were present at the battle, and it was deemed necessary to have a large armed force of regulars, besides numerous police, in the neighbourhood; but no further riots ensued. To such a pass, then, has popular ferment arrived! I am even glad that the brutes have singled out this very day to exhibit their malicious vengeance; that they may show to all Europe what monsters the Radicals really are. May it be, though I fear too late, a lesson to the desperate Government which has relied on such support! may they learn their own future fate from this disgraceful instance, when the fleeting breath of popularity, which they are now so anxious to court, shall no longer fan their sails! These are indeed signs of the times which he that runs may read.

Thomas Raikes, *Journal*, 1832

* The Duke of Wellington, whose popularity as the victor at Waterloo was compromised by his opposition to the idea of parliamentary reform seventeen years later.

CAPITAL MUSIC IN CRYSTAL PALACE

To the rehearsal of the Handel Festival at Crystal Palace: close upon 20,000 people there; had great difficulty in getting anything to eat, could get no tea but the music capital.

Louisa Bain, *Diary*, 1859

~ *19 June* ~

A MOCK BATTLE AT DEPTFORD

I went to Deptford, being bidden to supper by the lord Clinton, where before supper I saw certain stand upon th' end of a boat without hold of any thing, and run one at another till one was cast into the water . . . After supper was there a fort made upon a great lighter on the Thames, which had three walls and a watch tower in the middle, of which Mr. Winter was captain, with forty or fifty other soldiers in yellow and black. To the fort also appertained a galley of yellow colour, with men and munition in it, for defence of the castle. Wherefore there came 4 pinnaces with their men in white handsomely dressed, which intending to give assault to the castle, first drove away the yellow pinnace, and after with clods, squibs, canes of fire, darts made for the nonce, and bombards, assaulted the castle; and at length came with their pieces, and burst the outer walls of the castle, beating them of the castle into the second ward, who after issued out and drove away the pinnaces, sinking one of them, out of which all the men in it, being more than twenty, leaped out, and swam in the Thames. Then came th' admiral of the navy with three other pinnaces and won the castle by assault, and burst the top of it down, and took the captain and undercaptain. Then the admiral went forth to take the yellow ship, and at length clasped with her, took her, and assaulted also her top, and won it by composition, and so returned home.

Edward VI, *Journal*, 1549

CRICKET IN ISLINGTON

Walked to White Conduit House, to see a great cricket match played; Lords Winchelsea, Easton, and Strathaven, and Sir Peter Burrill, etc.; a very severe headache drove me off the field.

Samuel Curwen, *Journal*, 1783

~ *20 June* ~

THE ARCHITECTS HAVE A NIGHT OUT

To Sir Ch. Wren. Dined with him. Woodrood there. To Hoskins with Sir Ch. Wren. By water with him to the Playhouse. Saw Tempest. Paid 3sh. Home to bed. Drank wine. Slept ill.

Robert Hooke, *Diary*, 1674

HEARTILY SICK OF THE GREAT EXHIBITION

A man who keeps a journal must recollect that he is writing, in a measure, for posterity, as he cannot be sure that his jottings may not some day see the light. It consequently behoves him to be careful not to compromise himself by saying, or admitting, anything calculated to damage him in the estimation of those who come after him. It is therefore with some little hesitation that I venture to put on record, at this period of excitement, that I am heartily sick of the ' Great Exhibition.' Granted, it was a splendid idea that does great credit to the Prince, but it is yet to be proved that it will have the effect desired or contemplated, that of giving a stimulus to manufactures throughout the world, and of so promoting the arts of civilization . . . meanwhile Hyde Park is very much cut up, and London is unbearable. Cousins and uncles and aunts, and other collaterals, who were content to potter away their lives at Torquay, or bask in the sunshine of Grand Ducal favour in some German town, consider that their loyalty and patriotism would be questioned if they did not visit London to see the great show, and, as a necessary consequence, they seek, for their own convenience, to revive all the obsolete sympathies of their childhood, and recall all the memories of

ALL THE WORLD GOING TO SEE THE GREAT EXHIBITION OF 1851.

nearly forgotten relationship, till family affection has become a 'drug', and one is in danger of being hugged by an aunt or embraced by a sister-in-law at every corner.

William Archer Shee, *My Contemporaries*, 1851

TEARS TO THAMESIS

Went to the Tower Pier at six to go on a yacht party up the river. Very grand and enjoyable, particularly coming back and looking at the South Bank, which looks like a dog's dinner, and the North Bank — floodlit — which with St Paul's, Somerset House, The Houses of Parliament, etc., was breathtakingly lovely. Felt tears spring to my eyes when one of the ship's crew nudged me and said, 'How's this for "London Pride", eh?'

Noël Coward, *Diaries*, 1951

~ 21 JUNE ~

VICTORIA'S GOLDEN JUBILEE

Wonderful day for Queen Victoria's Golden Jubilee celebration. I spent most of last night wandering through the streets to observe the decorations and preliminary illuminations. The gas-lit streets looked brilliant. Holborn, which with great enterprise, has electric street lighting, particularly attractive; walked from the Inns of Court Hotel in Holborn at eight o'clock this morning in order to take up my place in the window at the foot of Haymarket, opposite Her Majesty's Opera House, but the crowd was so dense that I could get no further than Waterloo Place, facing my window, and there I was stuck in the heat until long beyond noon after the procession had passed. I climbed up the statue of King George, but could not maintain myself and came down. But I got a good view of most of the procession . . . I drove round London to-night in a curricle with Walter Winans inspecting the fireworks. I have never seen so many people; certainly never so many drunken ones.

R. D. Blumenfeld, *R.D.B.'s Diary*, 1887

THE COUNTRY MOUSE IN TOWN

Stood for some time on the doorstep, drawing in the electrical force of London, and feeling like a mouse in oxygen. It is only we country cousins who really enjoy London, just as it is only Londoners who really enjoy the country, and the enjoyment on both sides may be a good deal due to misunderstanding. A little chap from Seven Dials is said to have called a lark 'a bloomin' cock-sparrow in a fit', and I may be doing even greater injustice to the passers-by when I fancy them pulsing with the high fever of existence.

H. C. Beeching, *Pages from a Private Diary*, 1896

～ *22 JUNE* ～

A MOUNTEBANK IN MOORFIELDS

Through Moorfields came across a mountebank or stage doctor, on an elevated scaffold, covered with a ragged blanket, discoursing to the more dirty-faced ragged mob; demonstrating to their satisfaction, no doubt, the superior excellence of his nostrums to those of the dispensary, and the more safe and secure state of patients under his management than hospitals and common receptacles of sick and wounded poor; whose lives, health, and ease, he said truly, were as dear to them as those of the best gentry or highest nobility in the land; and he farther added, of as much use to the public, which for aught I know is equally true.

Samuel Curwen, *Journal*, 1781

TOOLEY STREET FIRE

A few of the regular omnibuses had got, but hardly, into the station: men were struggling for places on them, offering three & four times the fare for standing room on the roofs, to cross London Bridge. I achieved a box seat on one, and we moved off towards the Bridge, but with the greatest difficulty . . . From my perch I overlooked the whole scene: and what a scene! For near a quarter of a mile, the south bank of the Thames was on fire: a long line of what had been warehouses, their roofs and fronts all gone; and the tall ghastly sidewalls, white with heat, standing, or rather tottering, side by side in the midst of a mountainous desert of red & black ruin, which smouldered & steamed here, & there, sent up sheets of savage intolerable flame a hundred feet high. At intervals a dull thunder was heard through the roar of fire – an explosion of saltpetre in the vaults, which sent up a pulse of flame higher than before. Burning barges lined the shore; burning oil & tallow poured in cascades from the wharfs, and flowed out blazing on the river. A schooner was being cut from her moorings, just in time, as we came up. And all this glowing hell of destruction was backed by enormous volumes of lurid smoke, that rolled sullenly across the river and shut out all beyond. Just above the highest flames stood the full moon in a clear blue sky: but except a pale tint in far off windows, not a gleam nor a shadow of hers could be seen. But the north bank, where she should have shone, was one fairylike panorama of agitating beauty. Every building from the Bridge to the Customhouse was in a glow of ruddiest light: every church tower and high roof shone against the dark, clear in outline, golden in colour: the monument was like a pillar of fire: and every window and roof and tower top and standing space on ground or above, every vessel that hugged the Middlesex shore for fear of being burnt, & every inch of room on London Bridge, was crowded with thousands upon thousands of excited faces, lit up by the heat. The river too, which shone like molten gold except where the deep black shadows were, was covered with little boats full of spectators, rowing up & down in the overwhelming light.

So, through the trampling multitude, shouts and cries & roaring flame and ominous thunder, the air full of sparks and the night in a blaze of light, our omnibus moved slowly on, and in *half an hour* we gained the other end of the Bridge. All along King William St. and Cheapside the people were pouring in to see the fire, and eagerly questioning those who had seen it. And even far away in the dim streets where the houses were all in shade, every church tower that we passed reflected back the light of the conflagration. Bow Church was ruddy bright: the dome of St. Paul's was a pale rose colour on its eastern side . . .

Arthur Munby, *Diary*, 1861

TOO BORED TO GO TO DULWICH

Evelyn and I began to go to Dulwich to see the pictures but got bored waiting for the right bus so went instead to the vicar-general's office and bought a marriage licence. Lunched at Taglioni. Went to Warwick Square to see Harold and show him our licence. With him to Alec where we drank champagne.

Evelyn Waugh, *Diaries*, 1928

∼ *23 June* ∼

A FORETASTE OF HELL

I had my first experience of Hades to-day, and if the real thing is to be like that I shall never again do anything wrong. I got into the Underground railway at Baker Street after leaving Archibald Forbes's house. I wanted to go to Moorgate Street in the City. It was very warm − for London, at least. The compartment in which I sat was filled with passengers who were smoking pipes, as is the British habit, and as the smoke and sulphur from the engine fill the tunnel, all the windows have to be closed. The atmosphere was a mixture of sulphur, coal dust and foul fumes from the oil lamp above; so that by the time we reached Moorgate Street I was near dead of asphyxiation and heat. I should think these Underground railways must soon be discontinued, for they are a menace to health. A few minutes earlier can be no consideration, since hansom cabs and omnibuses, carried by the swiftest horses I have seen anywhere, do the work most satisfactorily.

R. D. Blumenfeld, *R.D.B.'s Diary*, 1887

AN ARRESTING GAME

As A. and I are walking in Regent's Park this evening we stop to watch a baseball game. A police car comes smoothly along the path, keeping parallel with a young black guy who is walking over the grass. The police keep calling to him from the car, but he ignores them and eventually stops right in the middle of the game. A policeman gets out and begins questioning him, but warily and from a distance. The baseball players, unfortunately for the suspect, are all white and they mostly pretend it isn't happening. Some laugh and look at their feet. Others break away and talk among themselves. Only a few unabashedly listen. Someone shouts, 'What's he done?' 'I want you to bear witness,' the man shouts, 'You all bear witness.' For his part the policeman ignores the players, sensing that he is at a disadvantage and that the middle of a game is some sort of sanctuary and too public for the law's liking. It's the sort of refuge Cary Grant might choose in a Hitchcock movie. Meanwhile reinforcements are on the way, and, as a police van speeds over the grass, another policeman gets out of the car and the two of them tackle the suspect. Still one watched, nobody saying anything, those nearest the struggle moving away, their embarrassment now acute. Eventually the police bundle the man into a van and he is driven off. The game is restarted, a little shamefacedly at first, then gathering momentum as we walk on. But the players must have lost heart, because five minutes later the pitcher passes us with his baseball mitt and a young man in a funny hat.

Alan Bennett, *Diary*, 1983

~ 24 JUNE ~

EXCESSIVE EXCHANGE RATES

Midsummer-day. We kept this a holiday, and so went not to the office at all. All the morning at home. At noon my father came to see my house now it is done, which is now very neat. He and I and Dr. Williams (who is come to see my wife, whose soare belly is now grown dangerous as she thinks) to the ordinary over against the Exchange, where we dined and had great wrangling with the master of the house when the reckoning was brought to us, he setting down exceeding high every thing. I home again and to Sir W. Batten's, and there sat a good while.

Samuel Pepys, *Diary*, 1661

BACK TO THE BELL SAVAGE

We all got to London (thank God) safe and well by 3 o'clock this afternoon – to the Swan and 2 Necks in Lad Lane where we had some rum and water. To the last coachman gave 0. 3. 0. After staying some little time in Lad Lane we had a coach and went with our luggage to our old inn the Bell Savage at Ludgate Hill where we supped and slept – and kept by the same people, Burton and his wife. Nancy and her brother walked out in the evening by themselves, giving me the slip, and did not return till supper time, at which I was much displeased and gave it to them smartly, and to make it still worse soon as supper was removed and having ordered a bottle of wine, they left me without drinking a drop and went to bed leaving me by myself – I sat up by myself very uneasy till about 12 and then I went.

James Woodforde, *Diary*, 1786

A GATHERING AT ARNOS GROVE

At one o'clock Miss Cooper, Mrs. B and I set out for Arno's grove in Sir Wm Mayne's chariot which was sent for us. Arrived there in time to dinner. Lady (Sir John) Lindsay, Mrs. Ramsay wife of Mr. Ramsay the painter, and her daughter, were at dinner, but went away soon after. Morning clear and warm – afternoon rainy. Arno's grove a most pleasant place ten miles from town, and two eastward from Finchley common. Here we passed the rest of the day, and staid all night. A great deal of musick and cheerful conversation.

James Beattie, *Diary*, 1773

～ 25 JUNE ～

CIVILIZATION ONE HUNDRED YEARS
BEHIND IN THE BOROUGH

I dined in the Borough with my Friend Parkinson en famille, and in the evening walked thro some Gardens near the Kentish Road at the expense of one halfpenny each. We met and saw a variety of people who had heads on their shoulders and eyes and legs and arms like ourselves, but in every other respect, as different from the race of mortals we meet at the West End of the Town, and in the more polished circles of society, as a native of Bengal from a Laplander. This observation may be applied with great truth in a general way to the whole of the Borough, and all that therein is. Their meat is not so good; their fish is not so good; their vegetables are not so good; their persons are not so cleanly; their dress is not equal to what we meet in the City or in Westminster; — indeed, upon the whole, they are one hundred years behindhand in civilization. I must not, however, omit their hospitality and kindness, which, if measured by Mr. Parkinson's standard, is at least equal to the best in either of the other cities.

George Mackenzie Macaulay,
The War Diary of a London Scot, 1797

AN ORNITHOLOGICAL RETREAT

In the afternoon I made out an excellent place for retreat on a fine day, the island for aquatic birds in St. James's Park. There is a grass walk, hedged by roses, and no risk of intrusion.

George Howard, *Journals*, 1849

A BIG HIT IN COVENT GARDEN

Last night, just after midnight, I was physically attacked by a man for the first time since Kathleen's first husband brought me down with a flying tackle in the driveway of her mother's house ten years ago. We were driving home from a restaurant near Covent Garden (Tennessee [Williams] and Gore [Vidal] were among the other guests) when a lorry stopped in front of us, blocking the road, and two more behind me. The drivers calmly got out and disappeared into late-night cafés. Annoyed as I always am by the way in which the market personnel assume that the whole area around the garden belongs to them after 11 p.m., I honked my horn, hoping either a. to lure the drivers out of their cafés or b. to attract a copper and lodge a complaint. A cop certainly arrived,

but when I explained why I was honking he said he was going to pros-
ecute me for unnecessary use of my horn. The lorry ahead now moved
on and the PC asked me to pull over into a loading bay near the market.
As I did so, a porter sitting with some friends on a pile of crates threw
a piece of metal at the car, hitting the radiator and scratching it. I got
out and told him crisply to fuck off. To my alarm, he rushed at me from
a distance of about ten yards, bashed me in the chest, kneed me in the
stomach and grappled me with all the strength of his twenty-odd years.
The cop watched without interfering until the porter's chums had
pulled him off me, and then finished taking down the number of my
car etc.

Kenneth Tynan, Diaries, 1973

TOO HOT IN TICHFIELD STREET

The boiling sun is relentless: the sort of weather which one loves on a
holiday & loathes in London. I feel actually *angry* as I look at it & know
the damage it's doing to people, to business and to spirits . . . one is
sweating before the day begins & I have one sheet over me on the bed
& it's still uncomfortable. To the theatre thro' sweltering streets . . .
everyone standing *outside* pubs holding beer in their hands . . . In Tich-
field Street they shouted, 'Don't go in tonight, Kenny! They'll be no
bugger there!' and I smiled sickly. In the event, the auditorium had
about two hundred in it, and they were very kind and indulgent.

Kenneth Williams, Diary, 1976

～ 26 JUNE ～

KILBURN MEADOWS

Walked in the evening in my old haunts in the Kilburn meadows, where
I have walked so often with Keats; went on to Hampstead to Well Walk,
and home in a state of musing quiet. The grass, and hay, and setting
sun, and singing birds and humming bees entered into my soul, and I

lay dozing in luxurious remembrances till the evening star began to glitter dimly in the distance.

Benjamin Haydon, *Journals*, 1828

A MUSICAL EVENING

Rose wanted to go to *Les Miserables*. Naturally there were no tickets. However a quick call to James Osborne and a couple of good stalls were whistled up through the show business underground, and I collected them from the major domo at Aspers – who wouldn't take a tip. I'm out of touch with these things. I suppose my humble £20 note was beneath him . . . I haven't been inside a theatre in ages. How evocative is that smell – greasepaint, dust, scenery – that wafts out across the stalls when the curtain goes up. And how very tiresome and ego and generally oopsy-la are most of the audience (though not as bad, I must admit, at the Cambridge as at Covent Garden). On the way back, as we walked down Shaftesbury Avenue, everybody seemed to be staring. Women, in particular, were looking at Rose. Did they think they 'recognised' her? Or was it just prurient curiosity? Strange and unusual.

Alan Clark, *Diaries*, 1987

～ 27 JUNE ～

RIVER SOUNDINGS

We then lay, in the confines of Wapping and Rotherhithe, tasting a delicious mixture of the air of both these sweet places, and enjoying the concord of sweet sounds of seamen, watermen, fish-women, oyster-women, and of all the vociferous inhabitants of both shores, composing altogether a greater variety of harmony than Hogarth's imagination hath brought together in that print of his, which is enough to make a man deaf to look at.

Henry Fielding, *Journal of a Voyage to Lisbon*, 1754

A SAD SCENE OF PUNISHMENT AND SHAME

Called at Forster's, where a note had been left, which I got at 61, Lincoln's Inn Fields, and on its direction proceeded to Dickens's in Doughty Street. Another note directed me, under the guidance of his brother, to Cold-Bath Fields, where I found Dickens, Forster, Cattermole and Brown, the Pickwick artist. I went through this sad scene of punishment and shame, and my heart sank in its hope for the elevation of my kind. From this place we proceeded to Newgate, over which we went, and in the second room into which we were shown I saw a man reading; he turned as we entered – it was Wainewright – with large, heavy moustaches – the wretched man overlaid with crime. Several in solitary cells under sentence, and one to be hanged for rape. He seemed the most cheerful of them all; but in all the pride of our nature seemed eradicated or trodden down – it was a most depressing sight. We proceeded to Dickens's to dinner, where Harley, Mr. Hogarth, and a Mr. Banks (who had married Maclise's sister) joined us. Our evening was very cheerful, and we laughed much at Mr. Harley's theatrical efforts to entertain.

William Charles Macready, *Diary*, 1837

SHOPPING IN THE WEST END

Wednesday morning, David Rice accosted me in Bond St. Hadn't seen him for at least 15 years. He cursed the British tradesmen. So did I. On Thursday morning I went into a swagger West End hosier's to buy a necktie. I said 'Good morning' on entering. Vendeur was a man of 50 at least. Through sheer social clumsiness and heaviness he made no response, didn't even smile. It was not that he meant to be impolite. He thawed before I had bought two neckties, and gloomily saluted me as I went out. Many of the shops in this district are being cleaned and garnished at 10am.

Arnold Bennett, *Journals*, 1913

∼ *28 June* ∼

THE INVISIBLE GIRL

Lady Thomond spoke so warmly of the extraordinary contrivance called 'The Invisible Girl', at an apartment in Leicester Square, I went to see it. Four mouths of Trumpet shapes to any of which persons place their ears & hear as from within a voice like that of a girl, which answers any question, describes your person & dress, sings, plays on a pianoforte, tells you what a Clock it is &c. &c. The Ball is suspended from the Ceiling, and with the Trumpets inclosed within a standing frame. The effect of the voice & the music was surprising, and no conjecture that was made by persons present of the nature of the contrivance seemed satisfactory. One thought that the sound passed from below through Tubes into the mouths of the Trumpets & seemed to the hearer to proceed from the inside of the Ball. The voice spoke English, French & German. The admittance to hear it is 2s. 6d.

Joseph Farington, *Diary*, 1803

AN ASSEMBLAGE OF NICK-NACKS

The Duke took me with him to Sir John Soane's Museum in Lincoln's Inn Fields. It is worth inspection, not only from the works of *vertu* and the curiosities and antiquities it contains, but for the small compass into which they are all compressed. The Duke had sent word that he was coming, and the old gentleman was full dressed, and very garrulous and amusing, though he often did not talk loud enough for the Duke to hear him. He was particularly anxious that the Duke should see the contrivance he had introduced into what is usually (and too often) the smallest apartment in the house: the Duke, laughing heartily, was led into it by the conceited old architect; but I did not think it necessary to follow them, and remained behind looking at the admirable Hogarths, the series of the Rake's Progress, and the Election: to save room on the surface of the walls they were let in, one behind another, in the depth of the walls, very ingeniously, so that when a spectator had done with one picture, he turned it back on hinges, and exposed another and another. Sir John took infinite pains to be facetious and agreeable, and to make the Duke sensible of the value of his assemblage of nick-nacks. He was especially vain of one relic – the walking-cane of Sir Christopher Wren, having a compass at the head, a case of instruments in the handle, and a five-foot rule enclosed in the lower part of the stick. I had never seen the Hogarths before, and they infinitely gratified me: so they did the Duke, who had also never seen the originals.

John Payne Collier,
An Old Man's Diary, 1833

DIVINE INTERVENTION NEAR GOSPEL OAK

Alastair and I spent most of the day at Paddington Station drinking and eating buns and watching trains. We went to the Stoll Cinema and came home to dinner. At about 11 we went for a walk and lost ourselves. A very remarkable thing occurred. God took away Parliament Hill Fields entirely for some time; it was most puzzling. When we came home Alastair cooked an omelette which tasted remarkably and looked like a buttered egg.

Evelyn Waugh, *Diaries*, 1924

∼ *29 June* ∼

NEVER GO IN PIT

Saw Mrs. Siddons take her leave in the character of Lady Macbeth; she made a farewell poetical address written by Horace Twiss; play stopped after her last scene. Pit waved hats. I went into the pit; almost killed getting in. House filled from top to bottom with all the rank of London. Sheridan in the orchestra. Mrs. Siddons affected, but Kemble more so. Never go in pit again.

John Cam Hobhouse, *Diary*, 1812

NEW BUILDINGS AND MONUMENTS

Balloon went up from Cremorne Gardens, Chelsea. Saw it very plain in the Quadrant. Grand Review in Hyde Park this morning, His Grace the Duke of Wellington Commander in Chief.

The weather this month has been extremely warm and dry, things scorched up for the want of rain till the 22nd, since which we have had slight intermediate rains which gives hopes yet of a favourable harvest. Coals sold at Eccleston Wharf this month: 908 tons 6 sacks.

The new carriage and foot road fronting Chelsea Hospital was opened the 16th instant: this is a decided improvement, being before so very narrow, and looking so confined.

St James's Church Piccadilly has a new painted window being put in place of the old one which was very plain, having no stained glass. The present from without, though not finished, looks very showy.

There is now erecting a strong scaffold at the top of the Triumphal Arch, Constitution Hill, opposite Hyde Park Gates, and immediately fronting St George's Hospital, for the purpose of erecting an equestrian statue of the Duke of Wellington, which will be very conspicuous from the Duke's residence, Apsley House. It is expected it will shortly be erected.

This month has been unfortunate to our family for illness, my mother being very bad all the month and at one time not expected to live and still keeping her bed. My Uncle John Shepard has also had a severe attack of the lumbago in his back, which confined him to his bed about a fortnight, but from which he is now fast recovering, though unable to work. Myself have been very indisposed, having a stoppage in my bowels accompanied with a severe headache, which one time I thought would have confined me also, but have managed to keep my work. Granny Shepard has been nearly knocked up with attending on them, her son and daughter. It also fatigued M. Ward very much having his rest broke every night by attending a sick wife, and also attending the bugs, which in their room in warm weather, almost devour them.

Nathaniel Bryceson, *Diary*, 1846

∾ *30 June* ∾

SAILING FROM THE POOL OF LONDON

Nothing worth notice passed till that morning, when my poor wife, after passing a night in the utmost torments of the toothache, resolved to have it drawn. I despatched therefore a servant into Wapping to bring in haste the best tooth-drawer he could find. He soon found out a female of great eminence in the art; but when he brought her to the boat, at the waterside, they were informed that the ship was gone; for indeed she had set out a few minutes after his quitting her; nor did the pilot, who well knew the errand on which I had sent my servant, think fit to wait a moment for his return, or to give me any notice of his setting out, though I had very patiently attended the delays of the captain four days, after many solemn promises of weighing anchor every one of the three last.

The tooth-drawer, who, as I said before, was one of great eminence among her neighbors, refused to follow the ship; so that my man made himself the best of his way, and with some difficulty came up with us before we were got under full sail; for after that, as we had both wind and tide with us, he would have found it impossible to overtake the ship till she was come to an anchor at Gravesend.

The morning was fair and bright, and we had a passage thither, I think, as pleasant as can be conceived: for, take it with all its advantages, particularly the number of fine ships you are always sure of seeing by the way, there is nothing to equal it in all the rivers of the world. The yards of Deptford and of Woolwich are noble sights, and give us a just idea of the great perfection to which we are arrived in building those floating castles, and the figure which we may always make in Europe among the other maritime powers. That of Woolwich, at least, very strongly imprinted this idea on my mind; for there was now on the stocks there the Royal Anne, supposed to be the largest ship ever built, and which contains ten carriage-guns more than had ever yet equipped a first-rate.

Besides the ships in the docks, we saw many on the water: the yachts are sights of great parade, and the king's body yacht is, I believe, unequaled in any country for convenience as well as magnificence; both which are consulted in building and equipping her with the most exquisite art and workmanship.

We saw likewise several Indiamen just returned from their voyage. These are, I believe, the largest and finest vessels which are anywhere employed in commercial affairs. The colliers, likewise, which are very numerous, and even assemble in fleets, are ships of great bulk; and if we descend to those used in the American, African, and European trades, and pass through those which visit our own coasts, to the small craft that lie between Chatham and the Tower, the whole forms a most pleasing object to the eye, as well as highly warming to the heart of an Englishman who has any degree of love for his country, or can recognize any effect of the patriot in his constitution. Lastly, the Royal Hospital at Greenwich, which presents so delightful a front to the water, and doth such honour at once to its builder and the nation, to the great skill and ingenuity of the one, and to the no less sensible gratitude of the other, very properly closes the account of this scene; which may well appear romantic to those who have not themselves seen that, in this one instance, truth and reality are capable, perhaps, of exceeding the power of fiction. When we had passed by Greenwich we saw only two or three gentlemen's houses, all of very moderate account, till we reached Gravesend: these are all on the Kentish shore, which affords a much dryer, wholesomer, and pleasanter situation, than doth that of its opposite, Essex. This circumstance, I own, is somewhat surprising to me, when I reflect on the numerous villas that crowd the river from Chelsea upwards as far as Shepperton, where the narrower channel affords not half so noble a prospect, and where the continual succession of the small craft, like the frequent repetition of all things, which have nothing in them great, beautiful, or admirable, tire the eye, and give us distaste and aversion, instead of pleasure. With some of these situations, such as Barnes, Mortlake, etc., even the shore of Essex might contend, not upon very unequal terms; but on the Kentish borders there are many spots to be chosen by the builder which might justly claim the preference over almost the very finest of those in Middlesex and Surrey.

Henry Fielding, *Journal of a Voyage to Lisbon*, 1754

A BALLOON ON RICHMOND HILL

I have, at last, seen an air-balloon*. . . I was going last night to Lady Onslow at Richmond, and over Mr. Cambridge's field I saw a bundle in the air not bigger than the moon, and she herself could not have descended with more composure if she had expected to find Endymion fast asleep. It seemed to 'light on Richmond-hill; but Mrs. Hobart was going by, and her coiffure prevented my seeing it alight.

Horace Walpole, Letter to the Honourable H. S. Conway, 1784

* Walpole is writing only a year after the Montgolfier brothers in Paris made the first manned balloon flight.

JULY

~ 1 JULY ~

A STRAWBERRY SELLER IN THE PILLORY

The first day of July there was a man and a woman on the pillory in Cheapside; the man sold pots of strawberries, the which the pot was not half full, but filled with fern; the man's name is Grege; sometime he counterfeited himself a profit, for he was taken for it, and set by the pillory in Suwthwark.

Henry Machyn, *Diary*, 1552

FEW SICK IN HOSPITAL

Stayed at home this morning. Went in the evening to show Mr. Arragoni Greenwich Hospital, which now contains 900 seamen, and is designed to contain 1,600. 'Tis remarkable that of the 900 there are now but ten sick.

Earl of Egmont, *Diary*, 1732

THE MOST MAGNIFICENT THING OF THE KIND

At nine I put on my Albanian clothes and went with Byron to the great masquerade given by Wattier's Club in honour of Lord Wellington at Burlington House. I presume the supper in the temporary room, in which 1,700 persons sat at ease, was the most magnificent thing of the kind ever seen. The dress was much admired. Byron as a monk looked very well. Miss Rawdon said to me, 'Does he not look beautiful?' The Duke of Wellington was there in great good humour apparently, and not squeezed to death. Lady C. Lamb played off the most extraordinary tricks — made Skeffington pull off his red guard's coat — walked up into the private rooms. A mask annoyed me much by saying: 'Is that your electioneering dress?' 'Twas one of the Miss Kinnairds. I walked home between six and seven.

John Cam Hobhouse, *Diary*, 1814

SEE HOW YOU LIKE IT

Went in an omnibus to Coutts's Bank to pay my rent. Returned on foot, stopping in Pall Mall to pay the fire insurance. 'How provoking it is,' I said to the man, 'to be paying all this money every year, when one never has anything burnt.' 'Well Mam,' said the Man, 'you can set fire to your house and see how you like it.'

Jane Welsh Carlyle, Journal, 1856

~ 2 JULY ~

FIRE AT SHAKESPEARE'S GLOBE

I will entertain you at the present with what hath happened this week at the Bank's side. The King's players had a new play, called All is true, representing some principal pieces of the reign of Henry VIII, which was set forth with many extraordinary circumstances of pomp and majesty, even to the matting of the stage; the Knights of the Order with their Georges and garters, the Guards with their embroidered coats, and the like: sufficient in truth within a while to make greatness very familiar, if not ridiculous. Now, King Henry making a masque at the Cardinal Wolsey's house, and certain chambers being shot off at his entry, some of the paper, or other stuff, wherewith one of them was stopped, did light on the thatch, where being thought at first but an idle smoke, and their eyes more attentive to the show, it kindled inwardly, and ran round like a train, consuming within less than an hour the whole house to the very grounds. This was the fatal period of that virtuous fabric, wherein yet nothing did perish but wood and straw, and a few forsaken cloaks; only one man had his breeches set on fire, that would perhaps have broiled him, if he had not by the benefit of a provident wit put it out with bottle ale.

Sir Henry Wotton, Letter to Sir Edmund Bacon, 1613

NEW BRIDGES ACROSS THE THAMES

Took a boat at Whitehall Stairs, to see the Strand Bridge,* first by water, and then landed and walked upon the bridge itself. It is already passable for foot passengers, though neither covered nor paved. The nine arches of 120 feet each are beautiful, but I can never reconcile myself to columns upon a bridge, and here they are placed between every arch – two of the Tuscan order, and well-proportioned; but what have they to do there? Went by boat as far as Vauxhall, to see the iron bridge there, which is nearly finished, and, it is said, will be open to the public the 25th of this month. I do not like iron bridges, they can never have that look of solidity which constitutes one of the beauties of a bridge; but it is fine of its kind.

Mary Berry, *Journal*, 1816

* The bridge was soon to be called Waterloo Bridge.

~ 3 JULY ~

A CONSTABLE GOING CHEAP

Mr. Appleton, the tub-maker, of Tottenham Court Road, called to know if I had a damaged picture which I could let him have cheap, as he is fitting up a room up one pair of stairs.

John Constable, *Diary*, 1824

SICKENING SPECTACLE AT THE OPERA

The Opera management of Covent Garden regulates the dress of its male patrons. When is it going to do the same to the women? On Saturday night I went to the Opera. I wore the costume imposed on me by the regulations of the house . . . At 9 o'clock (the Opera began at 8) a lady came in and sat down very conspicuously in my line of sight. She remained there until the beginning of the last act. I do not complain of her coming late and going early; on the contrary, I wish she had come later and gone earlier. For this lady, who had very black hair, had stuck over her right ear the pitiable corpse of a large white bird, which looked exactly if someone had killed it by stamping on the beast, and then nailed it to the lady's temple, which was presumably of sufficient solidity to bear the operation. I am not, I hope, a morbidly squeamish person; but the spectacle sickened me. I presume that if I had presented myself at the doors with a dead snake round my neck, a collection of black beetles pinned to my shirtfront, and a grouse in my hair, I should have been refused admission. Why, then is a woman to be allowed to commit such a public outrage? Had the lady been refused admission, as she should have been, she would have soundly rated the tradesman who imposed the disgusting headdress on her under the false pretence that 'the best people' wear such things, and withdrawn her custom from him; and thus the root of the evil would be struck at; for your fashionable woman generally allows herself to be dressed according to the taste of a person who she would not let sit down in her presence. I once, in Drury Lane Theatre, sat behind a matinee hat decorated with the two wings of a seagull, artificially reddened at the joints so as to produce the illusion of being freshly plucked from a live bird. But even that lady stopped short of a whole seagull. Both ladies were evidently regarded by their neighbours as ridiculous and vulgar; but that is hardly enough when the offence is one which produces a sensation of physical sickness in persons of normal human sensibility. I suggest to the Covent Garden authorities that, if they feel bound to protect their subscribers against the dangers of my shocking them with a blue tie, they are at least equally bound to protect me against the danger of a woman shocking me with a dead bird.

George Bernard Shaw, Letter to *The Times*, 1905

∼ *4 JULY* ∼

GREAT PREPARATIONS

There's great preparations in Smithfield with many great Images Representing Gog & Magog is to be illuminated next 3rd day being the day called Thanksgiving Day on acct. of the peace with France. As also mighty preparations in Lighters to be performed as on the night on the Thames.

Peter Briggins, *Diary*, 1713

PEACE LOVERS IN GROSVENOR SQUARE

[During a reception at the American Embassy] about 30 or 40 anti-American protesters paraded up and down outside the Embassy gates, shouting at the diplomats and other guests as they arrived. There was a large posse of police, so the demonstration never got out of hand. Such was not the case last night in Grosvenor Square, where about 4,000 people gathered to protest against our Vietnam policy and shout abuse in the air. They turned on the police who were guarding the building, and injured six of them. They also tried to burn an American flag in the street. One policeman had his skull cracked and may have been seriously injured. Another was overturned on his motorcycle, and when the petrol spilled out, some peace lover in the mob set fire to it.

David Bruce, *Diary*, 1966

～ *5 JULY* ～

A CHILD'S VIEW OF TOWN

We first went to see the new London Bridge. This bridge is very beautiful, but not yet completed; it is of white stone, and consists of very wide semi-circular arches, thrown across the Thames just above the old bridge, which is a heavy, ugly fabric. We were likewise much pleased with the Thames itself, which is filled with vessels of all kinds. The Monument is very near; it looks immensely tall, but we did not ascend it. I have read of a man getting over the rails at the top, and throwing himself over; he was dashed to pieces. I believe he was insane. I do not much like the Urn at the top of the Monument; it is very ugly. We next went to see St. Paul's Cathedral, which I admire extremely. The exterior

is too immense for me to see correctly enough to describe, but when we entered it, it was most beautiful. The pavement is black and white marble, as well as the whole interior . . . The Dome is immense. Papa took Richard and me up to the Whispering Gallery, which extends round it, and looks down into the church. Everybody in the church looked like dolls or monkeys from it, it was so high up.

Emily Shore, *Journal*, 1831

AN INTOXICATED OCTOPUS

Leaving the Café Royal we linked arms and charged up the narrow staircase leading to the Arts Theatre Club. We were instantly spotted by reception and it was a right turn, down the stairs, and out into St Martin's Lane in five minutes flat. It seems that it is not, 'Ah, here comes Dylan [Thomas], that promising young poet!' but 'Watch out, here comes that crashing old bore Dylan, let's get him out of here quick'.

Just then the air-raid siren went off. We hailed a taxi and persuaded the driver to take us to Ruthven's studio. As soon as I'd sunk into my seat Dylan smothered me in wet beery kisses, his blubbery tongue forcing my lips apart. It was rather like being embraced by an intoxicated octopus. I tried to tell myself that I was being kissed by a great poet but it was a relief when the taxi finally stopped.

Joan Wyndham, *Love Is Blue*, 1943

~ 6 *JULY* ~

SO MUCH FOR THE BRASS PLATE

Called in to see my dear old painting-room, at 41 Great Marlborough Street, where I painted my Dentatus, Macbeth, Solomon, and a part of Jerusalem. Perkins, my dear old landlord (who behaved so nobly through Solomon, and whom I paid off after, but who lost in the end) was dead. The house was bought and undergoing repair; the rooms stripped and desolate; the cupboard, the little room where I slept, and the plaster-room, with all their associations, crowded on me . . . I thought once of putting up a brass plate, 'Here Haydon painted his Solomon, 1813'. For want of engraving, the picture is now forgotten, and the surgeon who has bought the house would perhaps have papered it up. So much for the brass plate.

Benjamin Haydon, *Journals*, 1842

GINGER BEER AND SANDWICHES

The Duke of York was married to Princess May. I never thought I should be well enough to go & see the procession, but as Sir Julian Goldsmid was so good as to let me go to his big house in Piccadilly I was able to see it all. Piccadilly itself was lined with troops & only the wedding guests allowed to drive down. The streets were crammed with hurrying crowds going Eastwards. The Park itself was a perfect sight, omnibuses, cabs, everything which as a rule is most strictly kept out . . . I never saw such a crowd, quite good tempered, but oh so hot. They were sitting about on the pavement or standing about in rows against the wall in the shade eating sandwiches or drinking ginger beer or fanning themselves; poor things.

Mary, Lady Monkswell, *Journal*, 1893

SMUDGY GILT ON CHEAP FRAMES

I sat drinking late last night, after the vote (Roman hot it was at eleven p.m.) with Jonathan Aitken in the garden of his house in Lord North

Street. I remember thinking these houses were a bit poky, blackly crumbling . . . I now see, of course, that they are the choicest thing you can have if you are a Tory MP. Number 8 is bigger than the others; was Brendan Bracken's in the Thirties, and he built on a long drawing room at the back. Furniture not bad, but pictures ridiculous, art dealers' junk. Not even shiny decorative Mallet pieces, but smudgy gilt on cheap frames.

Alan Clark, *Diaries*, 1983

~ 7 JULY ~

A SCHOOL FOR PICKPOCKETS

The same daye my Lord Maior beinge absent . . . we fewe that were there did spend the same daie abowte the searchinge out of sundrye that were receptors of ffelons, where we fownd a greate manye as well in London, Westminster, Sowthwarke, as in all other places abowte the same. Amongst our travells this one matter tumbled owt by the waye, that one Wotton a gentilman borne, and sometyme a marchauntt man of good credyte, who fallinge by tyme into decaye, kepte an Alehowse att Smarts keye neere Byllingesgate, and after, for some mysdemeanor beinge put downe, he reared upp a newe trade of lyffe, and in the same Howse he procured all the Cuttpurses abowt this Cittie to repaire to his said howse. There, was a schole howse sett upp to learne younge boyes to cutt purses. There were hung up two devises, the one was a pockett, the other was a purse. The pockett had in yt certen cownters and was hunge abowte with hawkes bells, and over the toppe did hannge a litle sacring bell; and he that could take owt a cownter without any noyse, was allowed to be a publique ffoyster: and he that could take a peece of silver owt of the purse without the noyse of any of the bells, he was adjudged a judicial Nypper. Nota that a ffoister is a Pick-pockett, and a Nypper is termed a Pickepurse, or a Cutpurse. And as concerninge this matter, I will sett downe noe more in this place.

William Fleetwood, Letter to Lord Burghley, 1585

FLASH MOB

Great mobbing & Fireworks on the Thames & in Smithfield for the Thanksgiving (as they call it) on acct. of the Peace.

Peter Briggins, *Diary*, 1713

THE STINKING THAMES

I traversed this day by steam-boat the space between London and Hungerford Bridges between half-past one and two o'clock; it was low water, and I think the tide must have been near the turn. The appearance and the smell of the water forced themselves at once on my attention. The whole of the river was an opaque pale brown fluid. In order to test the degree of opacity, I tore up some white cards into pieces, moistened them so as to make them sink easily below the surface, and then dropped some of these pieces into the water at every pier the boat came to; before they had sunk an inch below the surface they were indistinguishable, though the sun shone brightly at the time; and when the pieces fell edgeways the lower part was hidden from sight before the upper part was under water. This happened at St. Paul's Wharf, Blackfriars Bridge, Temple Wharf, Southwark Bridge, and Hungerford; and I have no doubt would have occurred further up and down the river. Near the bridges the feculence rolled up in clouds so dense that they were visible at the surface, even in water of this kind.

The smell was very bad, and common to the whole of the water; it was the same as that which now comes up from the gully-holes in the streets; the whole river was for the time a real sewer. Having just returned from out of the country air, I was, perhaps, more affected by it than others; but I do not think I could have gone on to Lambeth or Chelsea, and I was glad to enter the streets for an atmosphere which, except near the sink-holes, I found much sweeter than that on the river. I have thought it a duty to record these facts, that they may be brought to the attention of those who exercise power or have responsibility in relation to the condition of our river; there is nothing figurative in the words I have employed, or any approach to exaggeration; they are the simple truth. If there be sufficient authority to remove a putrescent pond from the neighbourhood of a few simple dwellings, surely the

river which flows for so many miles through London ought not to be allowed to become a fermenting sewer. The condition in which I saw the Thames may perhaps be considered as exceptional, but it ought to be an impossible state, instead of which I fear it is rapidly becoming the general condition. If we neglect this subject, we cannot expect to do so with impunity; nor ought we to be surprised if, ere many years are over, a hot season give us sad proof of the folly of our carelessness.

Michael Faraday, Letter to *The Times*, 1855

BOMBS ON THE UNDERGROUND

After a series of bomb attacks in town, London Transport has been pretty much closed down for the time being (tempting the Dorothy Parker quote about the dead president – 'How can you tell?').

The bombs were initially reported as 'power surges' on the Tube. Later it transpires this was an accidental interpretation rather than a deliberate euphemism, but at the time I assume the latter, and muse if this is the 2005 terrorist equivalent of the theatre fire signal, 'Mr Sands is in dressing room 3.' Anything rather than shouting 'Fire!'

Two pictures on the news take me aback before I turn off. One is a dark, cave-like photo of people walking along Tube tunnels. The other is of splattered bloodstains halfway up the wall of the BMA building in Tavistock Square. The stains are level with the top deck of the exploded bus.

Dickon Edwards, *Diary*, 2005

∼ 8 J ULY ∼

PRODIGIOUSLY BIG CHILDREN

So called on my wife and met Creed by the way, and they two and I to Charing Cross, there to see the great boy and girle that are lately come out of Ireland, the latter eight, the former but four years old, of most prodigious bigness for their age. I tried to weigh them in my arms, and find them twice as heavy as people almost twice their age; and yet I am apt to believe they are very young. Their father a little sorry fellow, and their mother an old Irish woman. They have had four children of this bigness, and four of ordinary growth, whereof two of each are dead. If, as my Lord Ormond certifies, it be true that they are no older, it is very monstrous.

Samuel Pepys, *Diary*, 1667

BLOWN TO ATOMS

Directly I set foot in town I went . . . to the factory of poor Eley,* where I was astonished to see that scarcely any damage had been done beyond the appalling accident that blew him to atoms. His own son was within two yards of him, and people were working in the factory, at the time the explosion took place; but so little was the expansion that, although he blew up 2lb. of fulminating mercury, not even a paper was burnt;

and the walls were no more disfigured than if cold water had been thrown over them. In short, a few panes of glass being broken was all that could be seen in the way of damage. The usual quantity of fulminating mercury that people venture to mix at a time is from ¼ to ½ an ounce; and how so clever a man as Eley could have run the risk of mixing such a quantity was the surprise of everyone.

Colonel Peter Hawker, *Diary*, 1841

* William Eley, one of two brothers who founded a well-known ammunition firm, had blown himself up in an accident at his workshop off Old Bond Street.

THE SWEDISH NIGHTINGALE

I had the wonderful treat of going to S. James Hall with Miss Gladstone, to hear Jenny Lind sing in the 'Allegro' and 'Penseroso'. I suppose her high notes are a little gone, but the matchless expression and *heart-feeling* can never go out of her voice, and there is a ringing purity of tone unlike anything else . . . It was a rare perfection to have words, voice, and airs all so glorious and all glorifying each other.

Lady Frederick Cavendish, *Diary*, 1863

∼ *9 July* ∼

THE SWEAT IN LONDON

At this time came the sweat into London, which was more vehement than the old sweat. For if one took cold he died within 3 hours, and if he escaped it held him but 9 hours, or 10 at the most. Also if he slept the first 6 hours, as he should be very desirous to do, then he raved, and should die raving.

Edward VI, *Journal*, 1551

STILL CHAMPING ACORNS

Went to breakfast with Rogers, and found Luttrell and him going upon the water to follow the Fishmongers' barge, and enjoy the music . . . Luttrell, as usual, very agreeable. We were talking of the beauty of the bridges, and how some persons had opposed the building of the Waterloo Bridge, saying it would spoil the river: 'Gad, sir,' says Luttrell, 'if a few very sensible persons had been attended to, we should still have been champing acorns.'

Thomas Moore, *Diary*, 1819

NO CHAIR FOR PRINCE ALBERT

I took my daughter Charlotte to the Ball at the Guildhall, given to H.M. and the Prince on the occasion of the Great Exhibition. The sight in the streets was splendid indeed. Hundreds of thousands of happy, orderly, loyal people thronged the whole passage from Buckingham Palace to the Guildhall. Inside the Hall the scene was not so satisfactory; the crowd was very great, and not very quiet. The managers of the fete had forgotten to make proper preparations, and even a chair for Prince Albert was forgotten. Corbitt, M.P., handed one across the Queen's knees, for H.R.H. I was on the dais, and stood nearly four hours. The squeezing and the heat were far from agreeable.

John Cam Hobhouse, *Journal*, 1851

～ 10 JULY ～

LADY JANE GREY PROCLAIMED QUEEN

The 10 day of July was received in to the Tower the Queen Jane with a great company of lords and nobles . . . after the queen, and the duchess of Suffolk her mother, bearing her train, with many ladies, and there was a shot of guns and chambers has not been seen oft between 4 and 5 of [the clock]; by 6 of the clock began the proclamation the same afternoon of queen Jane with 2 heralds and a trumpet blowing, that my lady Mary was unlawfully begotten, and so [went through] Cheap to Fleetstreet, proclaiming queen Jane; and there was a young man taken that time for speaking certain words of queen Mary, that she had the right title.

Henry Machyn, *Diary*, 1553

A DEPRESSING EVENING

At five I return 'home' to the Boarding-house and get more desperate. Two old maids sat down to dinner to-night, one German youth (a lascivious, ranting, brainless creature), a lady typist (who takes drugs they say), a dipsomaniac (who has monthly bouts – H— carried him upstairs and put him to bed the other night), two invertebrate violinists who play in the Covent Garden Orchestra, a colonial lady engaged in a bedroom intrigue with a man who sits at my table. What are these people to me? I hate them all. They know it and are offended.

After dinner, put on my cap and rushed out anywhere to escape. Walked to the end of the street, not knowing where I was going or what doing. Stopped and stared with fixed eyes at the traffic in Kensington Road, undetermined what to do with myself and unable to make up my mind (volitional paralysis). Turned round, walked home, and went straight to bed 9 p.m., anxiously looking forward to to-morrow evening when I go to see her again, but at the same time wondering how on earth I am to get through to-morrow's round before the evening comes.

W. N. P. Barbellion, *The Journal of a Disappointed Man*, 1913

～ 11 JULY ～

THE GREAT EXHIBITION

I find I am 'used up' by the Exhibition. I don't say 'there is nothing in it' – there's too much. I have only been twice; so many things bewildered me. I have a natural horror of sights, and the fusion of so many sights in one has not decreased it. I am not sure that I have seen anything but the fountain and perhaps the Amazon. It is a dreadful thing to be obliged to be false, but when anyone says, 'Have you seen — ?' I say, 'Yes,' because if I don't, I know he'll explain it, and I can't bear that. — took all the school one day. The school was composed of a hundred 'infants', who got among the horses' legs in crossing to the main entrance from the Kensington Gate, and came reeling out from between the wheels of coaches undisturbed in mind. They were clinging to horses, I am told, all over the park.

When they were collected and added up by the frantic monitors, they were all right. They were then regaled with cake, etc., and went tottering and staring all over the place; the greater part wetting their forefingers and drawing a wavy pattern on every accessible object. One infant strayed. He was not missed. Ninety and nine were taken home, supposed to be the whole collection, but this particular infant went to Hammersmith. He was found by the police at night, going round and round the turnpike, which he still supposed to be a part of the Exhibition. He had the same opinion of the police, also of Hammersmith workhouse, where he passed the night. When his mother came for him in the morning, he asked when it would be over? It was a great Exhibition, he said, but he thought it long.

Charles Dickens, Letter to Mrs Watson, 1851

AS BAD AS CHICAGO

At 8.30 I went over and had a meal with Peter Shore and Tom Williams* at the Commons. Tom is now engaged in defending one of the gangsters charged with murdering someone at an array in Mr Smith's Club, Catford, and he talked for about an hour on gangsterism in Britain. He said that this particular South London gang was strongly entrenched and almost all the restaurants, dance halls, strip clubs and so on in Central London were paying protection money to the gang. A lot of this money was getting into pirate radio. He said that witnesses to the murder in which his client was involved absolutely refused to give any evidence in court and that one member of the jury had been threatened at midnight. In all he gave the impression that London was in the grip of a gang war quite as serious as that which held Chicago in the 1920s and 30s. His own remedy was virtual abolition of short sentences and the concentration upon serious criminals by means of indeterminate sentences.

Tony Benn, *Diary*, 1966

* Labour MP for Hammersmith South.

HOORAY FOR CHEQUE

Got a lift in Westbourne Grove from Davie Gilmour to Marble Arch where a teacher demonstration was going on. I had to walk through Hyde Park to Denis O'Brien where the cheque was waiting – Hooray.

Ossie Clark, *Diaries*, 1974

～ 12 JULY ～

THE BEST SPORT OF ALL?

The Spanish Ambassador is much delighted in beare baiting; he was the last weeke at Paris garden, where they shewed him all the pleasure they could both with bull beare and horse, besides jackanapes; and then turned a white beare into the Thames, where the dogges baited him swimming, which was the best sport of all.

John Chamberlain, Letter to Dudley Carleton, 1623

A NEW BRIDGE

Proceeded to London Bridge to view the proposed situation for a new bridge and its terminations on the City side at Angel Lane, and on the Borough side at St. Saviour's Church.

Charles Abbot, Lord Colchester, *Diary*, 1800

POOR KEW

Rode, and met G. Lennox and Apsley going to Kew. I joined them; the party was pleasant. Kew is not the least worth seeing. We walked to the Pagoda and back. It was hot, and I rode fast home.

Henry Fox, *Journal*, 1822

BYRON'S REMAINS

Saw the remains of our unrivalled and immortal bard, Lord Byron, removed into the hearse, and moved off in procession for interment.

Colonel Peter Hawker, *Diary*, 1824

~ 13 JULY ~

THE BODIES OF THE HANGED

I saw the bodies of the 2 coleheavers at Schirurgeons Hall, who were hanged on Monday last – Buried a boy at St. Giles's. I bought the pictures of the king and Queen 1/- each – I bought a small stone seal for 3/-.

Reverend John Tyler, *Journal*, 1768

A SIGHT TO SEE

Saw the living skeleton in Pall Mall.

Colonel Peter Hawker, *Diary*, 1825

A MURDER VICTIM IN SHADWELL

I went in the afternoon to Shadwell, thinking it would be a good opportunity of seeing the people of that district turn out in force. For I had seen in the papers that a young Irish prostitute, one Nora Scannell, who was murdered there lately by a Spanish sailor, was to be buried today with professional honours: fourteen of her fellow harlots walking behind the coffin, seven in white and seven in black.

I walked along Ratcliff Highway and the neighbouring streets as far as Rosemary Lane, where the body lay. The streets were all sunny and quiet, and in any other country would have been picturesque: for the roadways and doorsteps and windows were full of loungers – sailors of all countries, and crowds of women, young but hard featured, strolling about in light cotton jackets and gowns, without bonnet or shawl. Near the house where the corpse was, the crowds became more dense and more wide: the report I had heard about the fourteen mourners was true, I was told, and the people were waiting to see them come out. No one seemed to see anything odd or unusual in such a procession. However, a rumour began to spread, and it was confirmed to me privately by the policeman on guard at the house, that the funeral would not be till Tuesday at noon: 'the girls had been disappointed – the dressmakers had not yet sent their mourning things home.' This being so, I came away. I was nearly an hour among these crowds, in and about the notorious Ratcliff Highway; and I did not see a single policeman, except the one I have mentioned, nor see a drunken person, nor hear an evil word.

Arthur Munby, *Diary*, 1862

A PENIS-ENVY JACKET

Spent the day with Mo's help making a black suede cock-feather penis-envy jacket for Ronnie Wood – came out really divine. We are to meet in the King and Queen pub, Marble Arch. Mick (Sidea) took us and we had a few drinks with Roddie Stewart and the roadies until he showed up with Keith Richards and a few other blasts from the past. Lots of hangers on and drug-pushers. Good vibes and a really nice time was had by all especially me. 'Are you from Mars?' asked Cathie Simmons – there with George Harrison so I was able to thank him personally. The music is terrific. They really have been rehearsing and already it's in the can. When it was all over I lost Mo, who had my snake jacket, and I was transferred to Richmond with three ecstatic pop stars.

Ossie Clark, *Diary*, 1974

～ *14 July* ～

A TRIP ON THE RIVER

Called upon by Mr. Boulter; coached it to the Tower; then took boat; coasted by St. Catherine's, Wapping, Shadwell, Radcliff, Limehouse, Poplar, and down to Blackwall, where we had a view of the turn of the river Thames; we called at the Isle of Dogs, to see the skeleton of a whale, forty-eight yards long, and thirty-five round: upon the South-wark side, we had St. Olave, Horsly Down, Redriff, or Rotherhithe, Cuckold's Point, Deptford, and Greenwich, where we landed and viewed first the new church, now building, which is a most noble one, with pillars in the front, like that of Covent Garden but much more stately.

Ralph Thoresby, *Diary*, 1714

A FIRE IN DOWNING STREET

As I came home last night, they told me there was a fire in Downing Street; when I came to Whitehall, I could not get to the end of the street in my chariot, for the crowd; when I got out, the first thing I heard was a man enjoying himself: 'Well! if it lasts two hours longer, Sir Robert Walpole's house will be burnt to the ground!' it was a very comfortable hearing! but I found the fire was on the opposite side of the way, and at a good distance. I stood in the crowd an hour to hear their discourse: one man was relating at how many fires he had happened to be present, and did not think himself at all unlucky in passing by, just at this. What diverted me most, was a servant-maid, who was working, and carrying pails of water, with the strength of half-a-dozen troopers, and swearing the mob out of her way — the soft creature's name was Phillis! When I arrived at our door, I found the house full of goods, beds, women, and children, and three Scotch members of parliament, who lodge in the row, and who had sent in a saddle, a flitch of bacon, and a bottle of ink. There was no wind, and the house was saved, with the loss of only its garret, and the furniture.

Horace Walpole, Letter to Sir Horace Mann, 1742

~ 15 JULY ~

THE FUNERAL OF GEORGE IV

This being the day of the funeral of George IV it was observed in London by the closing of all the shops. The appearance of the town was very singular, and never, I should think, could it have been seen before so completely deserted. The day, with the exception of a very few drops of rain, was fine, and myriads had poured out of town, some to enjoy it in the country, others to witness the solemn pageant at Windsor. The few who were left, being in mourning, except those of the lowest classes, and no holiday attire to be seen, as on Sundays, produced an effect such as I certainly had never before seen in the streets of the Metropolis . . . It requires but trifling exertion on the part of the great to be popular, and nature, in having bestowed a graceful appearance and fine manners on George the Fourth, might have rendered it peculiarly easy to him, but he had latterly neglected all the means to secure the affection and respect of his subjects by living entirely secluded from them. However, he is gone to his account, and it will be well for his memory if no rude hand throws back the curtain which he had drawn so closely round his private life and closing years.

Mary Bagot, *Journal*, 1830

A BACHELOR PARTY IN BELGRAVIA

I arrived early at 115 Ebury Street where he* lived in a flat painted all over in a particularly awful shade of 1940s green. But he did have good pictures by Matthew Smith and Graham Sutherland. It had never crossed my mind what kind of party this was to be but that began rapidly to dawn on me as not a woman appeared and twenty men gradually filled the room. I left as soon as I could decently extricate myself, appalled at the sight, amongst other things, of all those bottles of cosmetics ranked above his dressing-table.

Sir Roy Strong, *Diary*, 1969

* The newspaper columnist Godfrey Winn.

THE LONDON LIBRARY TIME WARP

To St James's Square. Slowly because of the heat. All the flowers around the 'shrine' for the policewoman shot by the Libyans are dried up and dead as I cross the square and into the time-warp that is the London Library. Nervous, bookish, soft-spoken assistants with mad clothing direct you to the various areas of human experience. 'Domestic Servant, next to Dogs.' Takes a while to familiarise myself with the layout, but soon I'm getting into the swim of turning the lights on and off and encountering strange figures in between Ireland and the Gambia.

Michael Palin, *Halfway to Hollywood*, 1986

~ *16 JULY* ~

SUNDRY MENTAL OATHS

I did not know what to do with myself this afternoon so after thinking a little of Ealing, I determined to go to Richmond where Viv. & Clara Fenton are staying, so took a 'bus at Piccadilly, & proceeded to the latter place arriving at Riverdale at about 4 p.m. & asked to go for a walk, & Miss Emmett & Miss Green said they would go too but Clara & (to my vexation) Jane would not go, vowing it was too hot – So we started off, & it being nice & fine, we had a pleasant walk, passing on our way Hamm House, a not imposing red brick building (on the River Bank) there being in front what was originally a paved court yard, with an old stone figure of Father Thames in the centre, the house formerly belonging to the Dysart family was built in 1610. Miss Emmett I think is a nice person, & has any amount of conversation. She discoursed eloquently to me of love, types of beauty &c. Had she been young & pretty I might have made something of it. Returned to the house & sat a long time in the garden, the river looking very jolly & lively. Jane Green looked very pretty but morose, which elicited from me sundry mental oaths. Home by train.

Rafe Neville Leycester, *Diary*, 1865

A STRANGE DREAM

A messy day. In the morning went to the Test Match at Lord's. In the afternoon, in capacity of godfather, to a christening at Westminster Cathedral. The priest having some difficulty finding the right place in his prayer-book, I very nearly asked him the question Jack Worthing put to Dr Chasuble: 'I suppose you do know how to christen all right?' In the evening to *Salome, Where She Danced* at the Leicester Square, an appalling film about Generals Grant and Lee and a Viennese bubble-dancer who was lured to a mining town in California where she sang Der Tannenbaum, accepted the offer of a Rembrandt, and went off in a Chinese junk, the captain of which spoke with a Scottish accent, having been a medical student in Edinburgh. Supper at the Cafe Royal, and read myself to sleep with Dombey and Son. Am writing this in bed at 5 a.m. fearing the repetition of a nightmare in which Paul Dombey, who appears to be me, goes straight from his christening to Lord's, where he bowls out K. R. Miller when he is one short of Hutton's record and is promptly lassoed by a Chinese thug, hauled off the field, and hanged from the clock-tower.

James Agate, *Ego*, 1945

～ *17 July* ～

WITHOUT A RAG TO HER BACK

Late at night I landed at Billingsgate, where my maid Margaret lost every rag of my clothes and a mantua and petticoat I would not have taken thirty pounds for, nor shall I ever be mistress of the like again. But without a rag to my back I came about midnight to my dear sister's the Lady Norton's at her house in Brownlow Street in Drury Lane.

Elizabeth Freke, *Remembrances*, 1696

A MASQUERADE BALL

Rode till very late with Miss Villiers in the park. She is not only clever but very sensible and well-informed. Certainly she is the pleasantest girl in London. Maria Copley deals too much in repartee and punning. Miss Villiers can talk more calmly, and can resist twisting all that is said to her into puns, which is beyond Maria's fortitude. I was too late for my Lady's early dinner, but followed her to the Haymarket, where I saw *Sweethearts and Wives*. Liston and Terry act inimitably. Afterwards to the Masquerade Ball given by the dandies in the Argyll Rooms. On the whole it was pretty, and some characters well sustained. Lords Alvanley, Glengall and Arthur Hill were three admirable old women and tormented poor little M. A. Taylor delightfully. Lord Molyneux was a French postillion, and acted well till he got drunk.

Henry Fox, *Journal*, 1823

PAGANINI IS A QUACK

Went to Drury Lane to see Paganini; foolishly allowed myself to be angry at the doorkeeper's obstinacy, refusing me passage. Dignity is only truly displayed in coolness. Passion is the snare of reason. Saw Paganini; his power over his instrument is surprising; the tones he draws from it might be thought those of the sweetest flageolet and hautboy, and sometimes of the human voice; the expression he gives to a common air is quite charming. His playing of 'Patrick's Day' was the sweetest piece of instrumental music I ever heard, but he is a quack.

William Charles Macready, *Diary*, 1833

～ *18 J*ULY ～

A TRIO OF TURKS IN ST JAMES'S STREET

At the head of St. James's Street I observed three Turks staring about in a strange manner. I spoke a little of English, French, and Latin to them, neither of which they understood a word of. They showed me a pass from a captain of a ship declaring that they were Algerines who had been taken by the Spaniards and made slaves. That they made their escape, got to Lisbon, and from thence were brought to England. I carried them with me to a French house, where I got a man who spoke a little Spanish to one of them, and learnt that they wanted to see the Ambassador from Tripoli, who though not from the same division of territory, is yet under the Grand Signior, as they are. I accordingly went with him to the Ambassador's house, where I found a Turk who could speak English and interpret what they said; and he told me that they had landed that morning and had already been with the Ambassador begging that he would get liberty for them to go in an English ship to their own country; that he was to get them liberty from the Lords of the Admiralty; and that he had ordered them victuals. I gave them half a crown. They were very thankful, and my Turkish friend who spoke English said, 'GOD reward you. The same God make the Turk that make the Christian. But the English have the tender heart. The Turk have not the tender heart.'

I was anxious to have my poor strangers taken care of, and I begged that they might sleep in the house with the Ambassador. The landlady, a hard-hearted shrew, opposed this vehemently. 'Indeed,' said she, 'I would not suffer one of 'em to sleep in my beds. Who knows what vermin and nastiness they may have brought with them? To be sure I may allow them to sleep on the floor, as they do in their own country; but for my beds, Sir, *as I'm a Christian*, I could not let them sleep in a bed of mine.' Her Christian argument was truly conclusive. Abandoned wretch! to make the religion of the Prince of Peace, the religion which so warmly inculcates universal charity, a cloak for thy unfeeling barbarity! However, I was glad to have it fixed that they should sleep under a roof; and I begged my friend to take care that they lay comfortably.

James Boswell, *London Journal*, 1763

DONKEYS ON THE HEATH

In the afternoon, Emma Underwood, her niece Lucy, the two girls, and two boys and myself went to Hampstead Heath, so famous for donkeys. We first hired a donkey-chaise, which I drove – and then rode separately in saddle 'he-haws'; we were delighted with our afternoon sport. Emma is a rare high-spirited woman, Lucy is rather a pretty girl, but seems to have no animation – no life or interest about her.

John Thomas Pocock, *Diary*, 1827

∼ *19 July* ∼

A DEPTFORD DIVING-BELL

We tried our Diving-Bell or Engine in the water-dock at Deptford, in which our Curator continu'd half an hour under water; it was made of cast lead, let down with a strong cable.

John Evelyn, *Diary*, 1661

A BALLAD SELLER IN THE NEW ROAD

I walked up to the New Road,* and had a long talk with the old ballad seller opposite S. Pancras church. A very respectable intelligent man, of some education: said he had been there twenty years and brought up a family of nine children on the proceeds of his stall. The trade, he said, was never so good as now: the public concert rooms have created a large demand for popular songs of the day, and the old fashioned ballads sell well too. Has customers of all classes, but mostly young men, shopmen and artisans, who buy comic songs, tradesmen's daughters, who buy sentimental parlour ditties, and servantmaids. These when they first come to London buy the old ballads they've heard at home in the country; but afterwards they choose rather the songs – from English operas and so on – which they hear young missis a playing upstairs.

Arthur Munby, *Diary*, 1861

* What was then part of the New Road is now Euston Road.

∼ 20 JULY ∼

QUEEN LOOKS LIKE BLOWSY LANDLADY

William Offley at breakfast spoke of the fine display at the Coronation Procession.* He took his seat in the Central Pavilion at an early hour in the morning and had Coffee at 5 o'clock, about half past 6 o'clock the Queen appeared. She had attempted to obtain entrance into the Abbey but had been refused. He saw her cross the Procession platform. Lord Hood and a lady or two were with her. He thought she looked like a blowsy landlady. Her reception was very unfavourable. 'Shame, Shame,' and 'Off, Off,' was the general cry though a few cried 'Queen.' He said she must now be convinced of her unpopularity with the respectable part of the Community, and that she has only the notice of the vulgar mob. The King in proceeding to the Abbey looked pale, but on his return to Westminster Hall had recovered his look and appeared cheerful. He was much applauded.

Joseph Farington, *Diary*, 1821

* The coronation of George IV had taken place the previous day. His estranged wife, Queen Caroline, had not been officially invited and attempted to gatecrash the ceremony. She died three weeks later.

PHILOSOPHY OF A TRAFFIC JAM

At a street-crossing by the Embankment . . . Why do all these motor-cars wait here in this long line? A long line of small huts on wheels with people sitting inside them, silently? Supposing the white hand of the policeman should never move and they should stay here for ever? But the white hand falls. The engines whir, the cars move off, the stream has continued.

George Buchanan, *Passage through the Present*, 1932

~ 21 JULY ~

MORE ANTI-VIETNAM PROTESTERS

Our Embassy expected to be a main object of attack by anti-US Vietnam policy objectors, but the police funnelled them down one side of Grosvenor Square into South Audley Street, where they ran amok against the Hilton Hotel, private houses, automobiles, pedestrians, and anything else obstructing their progress.

David Bruce, *Diary*, 1968

~ 22 JULY ~

A SAILING MATCH ON THE RIVER

Pass Blackfriars Bridge, and set out along the south side of the river to Westminster Bridge.

Arrive there happily in time to witness a grand anniversary sailing match on the river. The prize a silver bowl, run for by six barges with four men in each; the distance from Blackfriars Bridge to Putney Bridge, about eight miles up the river, and back again to opposite Vauxhall. The vast concourse of people on the Bridge and on each side of the river, the vast number of boats and barges with splendid company on board, the rowers keeping time in the most regular harmony, &c., was to me a scene of perfect astonishment. While engaged in the contemplation of this scene, whom do I observe on the bridge beside me but my old school and college-fellow Mr. David Ritchie, deputy-chaplain to the Scotch Brigade. Tap him on the shoulder; he turns about and immediately recognises me. We walk together arm-in-arm up the river on the Westminster side to view the boats on their return from Putney; each bank of the river lined with a crowd of spectators almost impenetrable. Take our station opposite to Vauxhall. About half-past seven the boats return with the returning tide, preceded by a very unusual and extraordinary spectacle; viz.: – A most magnificent barge, constructed somewhat in the form of Neptune's triumphal car, as described by Virgil and the old Roman and Grecian poets.

This elegant, expensive, fanciful machine, it seems, was first designed in honour of Lord Howe's Victory over the French fleet and it has lately been altered a little in honour of the Prince of Wales's marriage. It was accompanied by a thousand other barges with ladies and gentlemen; and as it dropt slow down the river, its wheels seemed to move upon the surface of the water, and it appeared to be drawn along by two large sea-monsters having the necks and manes and heads of horses that proudly arched their necks, and moved their heads, and bit their reins as they moved along the deep. In the Car aloft the torch of Hymen burned, while Cupids fanned the flame. In the mean time the musical band of the Duke of York, that is, the Band of the Horse Guards, being stationed on board this wonderful machine, performed the most sublime pieces of music in the most masterly manner . . .

Soon after this watery procession had stopped past the Park Bridge, the sailing-racers came down the river with vast rapidity, accompanied also by a thousand barges covering the whole surface of the Thames. While the gaining vessel approached to the goal, the guns were fired on each side: and the whole vessels in the evening sailed down towards Westminster Bridge, while the crowds on each side of the river withdrew by slow degrees to the City. Even in the most luxurious times of ancient Rome, never sure could old Father Tiber boast a nobler spectacle.

Reverend William MacRitchie, Diary of a Tour
through Great Britain, 1795

A SHOOTING AT STOCKWELL TUBE

This morning the police chased a man into Stockwell Tube station and shot him dead in front of terrified commuters. According to eye witnesses he was more or less executed. Five bullets in the head. It turns out he was unarmed and is not suspected of having been one of yesterday's bombers.

Chris Mullin, Diary, 2005

～ *23 JULY* ～

A WOMAN IN A KILT

Home to the Temple at 6 and to Mudies. Coming thence along Oxford Street, I saw before me, striding along in company with an Italian organ-grinder, a tall young man in full Highland costume; wearing a Glengarry bonnet, a scarlet jacket, a sporran and a tartan kilt and stockings, his legs bare from the knee to the calf. It was not a man – it was Madeleine Sinclair the street dancer, whom I used to see in a similar dress a year ago. She and her companion turned into a quiet street, and she danced a Highland fling to his music, in the midst of a curious crowd.

For no one could make out whether she was a man or a woman. Her hair and the set of her hips indeed were feminine; but her hard weather-stained face, her large bony hands, and her tall strong figure, became her male dress so well that opinions about equally divided as to her sex. 'It's a man!' said one, confidently. 'I believe that it's a woman,' another doubtfully replied. One man boldly exclaimed, 'Of course it's a man; anybody can see that!' I gave her a sixpence when she came round with her tambourine; and she told me she had been in Paris for five months for pleasure, and was now living on Saffron Hill, and dancing in the streets every day, always wearing her male clothes.

Arthur Munby, *Diary*, 1861

WE MIGHT AS WELL BE FRENCH

I went to a meeting at Stafford House for promoting Saturday half-holydays. Then to see Emma, who was yesterday not at all well, but is all right to-day. The 'populace', poor souls, having been goaded all the summer for not making any demonstration in favour of Reform, wished to hold a big meeting in Hyde Park to-day to express such an opinion. In a most un-English fashion the meeting was forbidden, the gates of the park shut at 5, and all the police had to come out to guard them. There was not the smallest pretext for believing there would have been any riot; but naturally this tyranny produced one among the roughs, who uprooted the rails (probably they were pushed down, being rotten), and remained masters of the field. The Life Guards were called out, which was not done in '48, and which was truly absurd as they did nothing whatever; and the people dispersed in time after some knocks had been exchanged. We might as well be French authorities, screwing down the safety-valve! and very nice and high-minded it will read on the Continent.

Lady Frederick Cavendish, *Diary*, 1866

～ 24 JULY ～

GRIFFITHS THE COWKEEPER

At Griffiths the cowkeepers in Grays Inn Fields the rabble again assembled, and grew very tumultuous, but the train'd bands keeping guard there kept them in some order; however, 'tis said a woman was kill'd there.

Narcissus Luttrell, *Diary*, 1687

LOTIONS FOR THE LEFT TESTICLE

On Saturday last G. Cuerton came down to Putney, & I intended having a pull with him but on that day I was seized with a swelling & severe pain in the left testicle which prevented me from doing anything. On the following day I was so much worse that I went to Dr White and to my disgust learned that he would not be at home till nine or ten at night. I had my invitation to dine with the Hanmers so there I went but it was very unpleasant work to talk & appear at ease when every movement was very painful. However I got through it all right & then went to the doctor who told me I had strained myself in some way. He recommended me to take lodgings somewhere in Town and remain quiet for a few days. So I went to 25 Blomfield St, & was there five days undergoing a course of medicine & lotions.

Rafe Neville Leycester, *Diary*, 1864

PHILOSOPHERS ON PRIMROSE HILL

Walked with George over Primrose Hill. We talked of Plato and Aristotle.

George Eliot, *Journal*, 1861

STRIPPING OFF IN THE HEAT

London in the heat – what an unbuttoning! What a Bacchanalian rout crowds the pavements, wearing brilliant beach shirts, bare legs, sandals, crinolines, jeans. Normally many people wear their clothes rather for the unwritten things they say than because they suit them: whether it is their background (families in the Highlands, social and political values) or to declare their readiness for sex and adventure. But when it's as hot as now they strip off this print, these flags they've been waving, with one idea alone – to be cool and comfortable.

Frances Partridge, *Diary*, 1959

~ 25 JULY ~

LONDON NOT WHAT IT WAS

I have had the loneliest time near 10 weeks, broken by a short apparition of Emma for her holydays, whose departure only deepend the returning solitude, and by 10 days I have past in Town. But Town, with all my native hankering after it, is not what it was. The streets, the shops are left, but all old friends are gone. And in London I was frightfully convinced of this as I past houses and places – empty caskets now. I have ceased to care almost about any body. The bodies I cared for are in graves, or dispersed. My old Clubs, that lived so long and flourish'd so steadily, are crumbled away. When I took leave of our adopted young friend at Charing Cross, 'twas heavy unfeeling rain, and I had no where to go. Home have I none – and not a sympathising house to turn to in the great city. Never did the waters of the heaven pour down on a forlorner head. Yet I tried 10 days at a sort of a friend's house, but it was large and straggling – one of the individuals of my old long knot of friends, card players, pleasant companions – that have tumbled to pieces into dust and other things – and I got home on Thursday, convinced that I was better to get home to my hole at Enfield, and hide like a sick cat in my corner. Less than a month I hope will bring home Mary. She is at Fulham, looking better in her health than ever, but sadly rambling, and scarce showing any pleasure in seeing me, or curiosity when I should come again. But the old feelings will come back again, and we shall drown old sorrows over a game at Picquet again.

Charles Lamb, Letter to Bernard Barton, 1829

A CHARMING YOUNG THING

While sketching under Hammersmith Bridge yesterday, R— heard a whistle, and, looking up, saw a charming 'young thing' leaning over the Bridge parapet smiling like the blessed Damozel out of Heaven.

'Come down,' he cried.

She did, and they discussed pictures while he painted. Later he walked with her to the Broadway, saw her into a 'bus and said 'Good-bye,' without so much as an exchange of names.

'Even if she *were* a whore,' I said, 'it's a pity your curiosity was so sluggish. You should have seen her home, even if you did not go home with her. Young man, you preferred to let go of authentic life at Hammersmith Broadway, so as to return at once to your precious water-colour painting.'

'Perhaps,' replied he enigmatically.

W. N. P. Barbellion, *The Journal of a Disappointed Man*, 1914

～ 26 JULY ～

SOLDIERS IN THE PARK

In the forenoon about 10 o'clock I went to Hide Park to see the soldiers* – horse & foot encampt, & crossed over by the corne fields to Chelsey & took a boat to Wandsworth & dyned there, & crossed the cornefields to Battersey & crossed the Water to Chelsey . . . & walkt in the Garden & so home by Water.

Peter Briggins, *Diary*, 1715

* Soldiers were massing in larger numbers than usual in London because of fears of Jacobite insurrection.

～ 27 JULY ～

CURSING THE KING

Lately, two or three days before the King left Richmond for Hampton Court, a waterman coming down the river, and seeing the King alone on the Terrace, called to him and cursed him with all his Hanover dogs. The King held up his stick at him, but being alone, the rogue could not be pursued.

Earl of Egmont, *Diary*, 1737

A HANGING AT TYBURN

Just after 10 o'clock I saw one Blake hanged at Tiburn in London for firing a pistil at his wife the ball of which graz'd her neck – Miss Green gave me a 100 crow pens* & a stick of sealing wax – I drank tea at Miss Brown's.

The Reverend John Tyler, *Journal*, 1768

* Pens made from the quill feathers of crows.

DICKENS AND A HALFPENNY WORTH OF CHERRIES

I observed a great difference in C. D.'s* appearance and dress; for he had bought a new hat and a very handsome blue cloak, with black velvet facings, the corner of which he threw over his shoulder *à l'Espagnol*. I overtook him in the Adelphi, and we walked together through Hungerford Market, where we followed a coal-heaver, who carried his little rosy but grimy child looking over his shoulder; and C. D. bought a halfpenny worth of cherries, and, as we went along, he gave them one by one to the little fellow without the knowledge of the father. C. D. seemed quite as much pleased as the child. He informed me, as we walked through it, that he knew *Hunger*ford Market well, laying unusual stress on the two first syllables. He did not affect to conceal the difficulties he and his family had had to contend against.

John Payne Collier, *An Old Man's Diary*, 1833

* Charles Dickens, then aged twenty-one and working as a journalist.

MIDNIGHT ON THE TUBE

I returned home at midnight in the tube train. On the platform a tall man, evidently warm inside with drink, sang powerfully. The porters chaffed him. In the train, near where I sat, a man, possibly a barrister, was bent over a huge portfolio, apparently studying some papers very hard. He was asleep. At the next station the seats got filled, and a fair, rather exquisite girl sat next to him. She wore a deep-blue shirt-blouse with a collar and a coat – a man's style taken to show how much a woman she is. The men on the seats opposite were always glancing at her legs, one of which, crossed over the other, was pointed out in front. A man, fresh from the theatre, wearing an opera hat, pulled the ticket from the barrister's hand and said: 'Where's he going?' and then jogged him to waken him. The other started to cough and saliva ran down his chin. He could not stop coughing. The man who wakened him looked alarmed; was he going to be ill? The nice girl turned her head away; her body leaned away, too. The opera hat spoke loudly: 'Where are you going to?' The other suddenly looked at his face, with an expression, transfigured, fixed, intense, as if he had suddenly seen the face of his greatest enemy. Everybody waited, wondering what would happen. But that hostility was only the hostility of the dreamer to awakening. He replied meekly and hurried out of the compartment the minute the train stopped at the next station. He was saying to himself: 'What a fool I was to go to sleep!'

George Buchanan, *Passage through the Present*, 1932

～ 28 JULY ～

TAKING THE AIR IN A CHARIOT

Then visited Mr. Boulter, who desired my company to take the air with him in his chariot; but from Kensington (whither I only designed) the pleasantness of the country, the weather, and way, &c. tempted him to proceed by Acton, Sion-house, and Thistleworth, to his favourite place Richmond, where we walked to view several pleasant prospects and seats of the nobility and gentry, the ancient palace where several of the Royal Family were born, and some died, as Queen Elizabeth, &c. The Duke of Ormond's seat was particularly charming; the house, gardens, avenues, with the park and river adjoining. After dinner, we returned the other road; and from the height of the town had a most noble prospect of the city of London on the one hand, and on the other a most delightful view of the Thames, with islands, woods, corn, meadows, intermixed with the seats of the nobility (the Earl of Rochester's, &c.) and gentry. We returned through a pleasant and populous country, Mortlake, Putney, Wandsworth, Barn Elms, to Lambeth, whence we ferried over to Hungerford Stairs; in the Strand parted with my kind friend.

Ralph Thoresby, *Diary*, 1714

A TEMPLE OF PEACE

At 5 o' clock I walked with H. Hamond to the Green Park and by means of one of the workmen saw the construction of the Temple erected to Peace which is to be illuminated on the day of the Fete, and works which were preparing under the direction of General Sir Willm. Congreve. The contrivance of it was such as to admit of the whole of it being turned round the lower part by wheels turning on a circle of Iron plate; and the upper part by wheels working on an inner circle. – About 50 men were required to turn it when the experiment was made yester-day. The Temple is 100 feet diameter & 130 feet high. Transparent Paintings alluding to Victory and Peace were to be placed in the different fronts of the Temple. – From hence we walked down the Mall & saw the new Chinese Bridge & Pagoda erected over the canal in St. James's Park.

Joseph Farington, *Diary*, 1814

A HERON IN BAKER STREET

This evening I saw a heron flying over Baker Street. But this is not so improbable as the thing I saw a week or two ago, i.e. a kestrel killing a sparrow in the middle of Lord's cricket ground. I suppose it is possible that the war, i.e. the diminution of traffic, tends to increase bird life in inner London.

George Orwell, *Diaries*, 1940

∼ 29 JULY ∼

NAKED MAN CALLS FOR REPENTANCE

To Westminster Hall, where the Hall full of people to see the issue of the day, the King being come to speak to the House to-day. One thing extraordinary was, this day a man, a Quaker, came naked through the Hall, only very civilly tied about the privities to avoid scandal, and with a chafing-dish of fire and brimstone burning upon his head, did pass through the Hall, crying, 'Repent! repent!'

Samuel Pepys, *Diary*, 1667

SHIPS AT WOOLWICH

Went to Woolwich by water through a vast number of shipping. Many ships of war were on the stocks, some ready or almost ready to be launched. I saw the convicts come ashore from the hulks. Their number is between four and five hundred. They work on shore, and eat and lodge on board. They have light irons hoppling their legs, and sentries and guards armed have the custody of them. There are instances of their attempts to escape, in which they have sometimes succeeded. They continue in their vices with little or no reformation, and they look forward to the end of their punishment only to have an opportunity of committing crimes too atrocious for even this kind of chastisement; this is the subject of their frequent conversation.

Peter Van Schaack, *Journal*, 1779

RAMBLING THROUGH SOUTHGATE

Walked on the New Road towards Islington, and about ½ past 3 was taken up by Mr. Alderman Curtis in his phaeton and carried to South-gate, where we dined well *en famille* and in the evening rambled thro' the Village.

George Macaulay, *The War Diary of a London Scot*, 1797

DYING OF CHOLERA

People dying in every direction with this dreadful cholera, and many of them close to my own town residence.

Colonel Peter Hawker, *Diary*, 1832

∼ *30 J*ULY ∼

DRINKING THE WATERS AT ISLINGTON

I see your porter every morning in the grove, as he returns from Islington, where he is drinking the waters; he looks a little better, but not much. They have lent him a horse to ride there, and he says that he finds the air where he is to agree better with him than that of the country.

George Selwyn, Letter to Lord Carlisle, 1774

ARRANGEMENTS FOR HIS SKELETONS

Went to London by the 8 o'clock Stage with Walter and Ellen: sent Walter off by the Tottenham coach from Bishopsgate Street, and accompanied Ellen to Dulwich, where we arrived soon after four. Strolled about that beautiful village, and left my sweet girl at seven; proceeded to Lambeth, and arranged with Flower respecting my skeletons, and drove to Mr Saull in Aldersgate Street, where I slept.

Gideon Mantell, *Journal*, 1834

AND NEVER DIE

I joined Jamesey at Rule's restaurant. We drank quantities of Pimm's and enjoyed ourselves hugely . . . As we talked and laughed in an animated way two very tough-looking men at a neighbouring table were staring at us critically and discussing us. I then realised how we must have struck them, both youngish and out of uniform, both enjoying ourselves, which in their eyes we had no right to do. In truth they had no right to judge us, for James is in the army, and I was.

We walked out of the restaurant into the heat, and down the embankment. We crossed London Bridge to the south side of the river and ambled along Cardinal's Wharf. Jamesey was extolling in the most candid and engaging manner his age – he is twenty-six – his good looks and his successes, saying he did not believe he could ever die.

James Lees-Milne, *Diary*, 1943

～ 31 JULY ～

QUEEN ANNE IS DEAD – OR IS SHE?

In the morning went to the coffee house to inquire about the news & the report was the Q. was dead & it continued till noon the same reported, tho' with some not believed. In the evening it was believed she was a little revived & I hope may recover if God sees it good.

Peter Briggins, *Diary*, 1714

A GIANT BOOKSHOP

Leave the Tower, and direct our course to Finsbury Square and *Lack-ington's Temple of the Muses*. This the largest stationery shop in the world. A rotundo with five stories of books, rising one above another by five flights of stairs, the cupola lighted from the top. From this rotundo rooms extend on each side, with different assortments of books, and different offices for different purposes, &c. The building itself is like a palace. The cheapest books here in Europe.

Reverend William MacRitchie, *Diary of a Tour through Great Britain*, 1795

'EARTH HAS NOT ANYTHING TO SHOW MORE FAIR'

After various troubles and disasters, we left London on Saturday morning at half-past five or six, the 31st of July. We mounted the Dover coach at Charing Cross. It was a beautiful morning. The city, St. Paul's, with the river, and a multitude of little boats, made a most beautiful sight as we crossed Westminster Bridge. The houses were not overhung by their cloud of smoke, and they were spread out endlessly, yet the sun shone so brightly, with such a fierce light, that there was even something like the purity of one of nature's own grand spectacles.*

Dorothy Wordsworth, *Journal*, 1802

* This short description can be compared with the poem 'Composed Upon Westminster Bridge' by Dorothy's brother William, written in the same year and clearly inspired by the same experience.

REMOTE FROM CIVILIZATION

I am living at present in Lambeth, doing my best to get at the meaning of that strange world, so remote from our civilization . . .

George Gissing, Letter to his sister Margaret, 1886

STILL REMOTE

I am again day after day in Lambeth; this morning I got home only at 2 o'clock. Ah, but you will see the result, I have a book in my head which no one else can write, a book which will contain the very spirit of London working-class life. Little by little it is growing . . .*

George Gissing, Letter to his sister Ellen, 1886

* The book proved to be *Thyrza* (1887).

AUGUST

～ 1 AUGUST ～

QUEEN ANNE IS DEFINITELY DEAD

This morning about 40 minutes past 7 it's said Q. Ann died & abt 2, the
Elector K. George was proclaimed King at Charing X & Temple Bar at
3 & at the Exchange abt 5, the guns going off & I saw the flag out at
the Tower, all things very still.

Peter Briggins, *Diary*, 1714

SHIPS ON THE SERPENTINE

Went to London to see the Grand Jubilee. I saw by the placards that the
public was *respectfully* informed that the Parks were shut up. I dined
at Cuthbert's, and went with him, Miss Doyle, Lady L., and Lord P.
Bentinck, to the Hyde Park, where the ships fought, on the Serpentine,
coming on stern foremost and firing one pop-gun at a time. Afterwards
I went to Burdett's house, and sat in a room there with a large party
until past one to see the fireworks from the Castle in the Green Park,
which were very brilliant but very tiresome. The whole room was
asleep. I rode off to Whitton, tired to death. The pagoda in St. James's
Park was burnt down accidentally, and two men killed.

John Cam Hobhouse, *Diary*, 1814

A BIBLIOPHILE MISSES A BARGAIN

I met with a vexatious disappointment to-day. I was passing through
Turnstile to Lincoln's-inn-Fields, and so to Somerset House, when I cast
my eyes upon some shelves with books, outside a shop kept by a man
of the historical name of Cornish. I saw one book that I much desired
to possess, viz., the Kilmarnock edition of the Poems of Burns, dated
1786. As I was going farther, and intended to return directly, I put it
back on the shelf, making up my mind to purchase it on my way home:
the price was only 1s 6d., but I knew that it would not be dear at a
guinea; and when I returned by the same way, I did not for a moment

forget my book – for I already considered it mine. My mortification, therefore, was not a little when, as I passed the place again, I found it gone – sold for 1s. 6d. to somebody else. I resolved from that time never to run such a risk again. It was uncut, and in the original boards: I have never seen any such copy.

John Payne Collier, *An Old Man's Diary*, 1832

A LOVELY BANK HOLIDAY

Charles, I can't tell you how lovely London is looking. It's completely knocked me flat – I've fallen in love with it all over again! Glittering fresh paint, of every possible pretty colour, endless striped awnings, trees everywhere (I had forgotten how many trees!) and most of all FLOWERS, liberally all over the place – in window-boxes, along in front of the houses. And the whole place looks as clean as a new pin, and as fresh as the month of May – not, as I'd expected, the frowstiness of August. I speak chiefly, of course, of SW3, which so far I've barely been outside of. In the evenings I walk about the roads and streets in a dream, dining at one or another small restaurant – there are now masses of them all along Kings Rd and Fulham Rd, quite a number of them quite elegant – charming on these warm evenings, with the doors standing open. I'm surprised how many people there are 'in town' – I mean considering this is the August Bank Holiday. I cannot imagine a lovelier place for you and me to be. Imagine if we had this house all to ourselves – you and me, sitting in this garden and walking in these pretty streets, past these enviable and fleuries little houses, in the evening.

What's come over London (in the favourable sense!) I can't imagine. I suppose actually this change for the better's been going on for a long time. Really, now it's very much more attractive, pretty, stylish and gay-feeling than ever it was before the war (I mean in the 1930s). And really a lot of nice-looking people around. Sooner, or later, do you know, I would awfully like to come back and again live here. It's being so different from what it was would make living here like starting life all over again – Oh it would, now, be such a perfect city for you and me . . .

Elizabeth Bowen, Letter to Charles Ritchie, 1959

AN ANIMAL MARKET IN BETHNAL GREEN

To Club Row animal market in Bethnal Green. Amazing, the East End on Sunday morning, a Jewish Saturday atmosphere, despite there being far fewer Jews than when I came as a child with Aunt Lil to Petticoat Lane.

''Ere yar, Alsatians arf-price!' shouted a bored woman over a box of struggling puppies.

'Labradors 'ere guaranteed,' said another.

Parrots, mynah-birds, canaries, budgies, white doves and finches perched in cages; minuscule and multi-coloured tropical fish swam in plastic bags. Tubby Isaacs sold eels, dead and jellied, under the sign: 'We lead, others follow.'

'We're out of Malayan Angelfish,' said an assistant in the only shop in a permanent structure around which the other stalls cluster. The people look savage with each other, tender with their pets.

Peter Nichols, *Diaries*, 1970

∽ 2 *AUGUST* ∽

A PRODIGY OF NATURE

Walk up to Kew. The Gardens not being open, go into the Pleasure-Ground. See here a prodigy of nature, the Kangaroo from Botany Bay. This animal, like the Opossum, carries and defends its young in a pouch under its belly. It hops with amazing agility on its two hinder legs, which are exceedingly long and strong compared with its fore legs, which are short and weak. Its tail, which is also very long, seems to serve the animal both as a balance and as a rudder. It is fearful as the roe, and

about the size of a fawn. It seems to belong to the rat-kind. There are
seven of them here, and they have propagated since they were brought
home.

Reverend William MacRitchie, *Diary of a Tour
through Great Britain*, 1795

SHELTERING FROM THE RAIN IN
THE HOUSE OF LORDS

To-day, as I drove down to dine at Greenwich with Alvanley, Foley, and
the Duke of Argyll, we were overtaken near Westminster Bridge by a
violent thunder-storm, and went into the House of Lords for shelter.
We passed the time in the library, where the librarian showed us various
curiosities; among others, the original Warrant for the execution of
Charles I signed by Cromwell and the other parliamentary leaders. It
was found after the Restoration in the possession of an old lady in Berkshire, and formed the ground of the prosecution against the regicides.
It is newly framed and glazed, and preserved in the library of the Lords
as a most curious document.

Thomas Raikes, *Journal*, 1832

AN ACCIDENT IN THE STREET

I was returning from Islington . . . The Islington omnibus put me down
within some eighth part of a mile of my own house. I had one rather
dark street to pass through first – taking the shortest way – and it was
near eleven o'clock at night. I didn't care for being alone so late; but I
didn't want to be seen by any of the low people of that street alone. So
I stepped off the pavement to avoid passing close to a small group standing talking at a door; when I had cleared these only people to be seen
in the whole street, I was stepping back on to the pavement, when, the
curbstone being higher than I noticed in the shadow, I struck the side
of my right foot violently against it and was tripped over, and fell smack
down, full length on the pavement.

Considering how easily I might have broken my ribs, it is wonderful
that the fall did me no harm. I scrambled up directly; but the foot I had

struck on the curbstone before falling was dreadfully sore, and it was made worse, you may believe, by having to use it, after a sort, to get myself home. How I got home at all, even in holding on to walls and railings, I can't think. But once at home on a chair, I couldn't touch the ground with it on any account.

Mr. C. had to carry me to bed, at the imminent risk of knocking my head off against the lintels. So I wouldn't be carried by him any more, my head being of more consequence to me than my foot.

Jane Welsh Carlyle, Letter to Mrs Russell, 1862

A BRAHMIN IN PRISON

An old Brahmin who speaks no word of English is remanded for causing a disturbance by objecting to the annoyance of street-boys. His caste overcomes his hunger, and he will not take any food from us except milk, which he pours into his hands and drinks. I write to the Asiatic Home in Limehouse, and find he has strayed from thence and will be taken care of there on discharge.

J. W. Horsley, *Jottings from Jail*, 1886

∼ 3 AUGUST ∼

ILLICIT LOVE WRONG BUT FUN

I should have mentioned that on Monday night, coming up the Strand, I was tapped on the shoulder by a fine fresh lass. I went home with her. She was an officer's daughter, and born at Gibraltar. I could not resist indulging myself with the enjoyment of her. Surely, in such a situation, when the woman is already abandoned, the crime must be alleviated, though in strict morality, illicit love is always wrong. I last night sat up again, but I shall do so no more, for I was very stupid today and had a kind of feverish headache. At night Mr Johnson and I supped at the Turk's Head. He talked much for restoring the Convocation of the Church of England to its full powers, and said that religion was much assisted and impressed on the mind by external pomp. My want of sleep sat heavy upon me, and made me like to nod, even in Mr Johnson's company. Such must be the case while we are united with flesh and blood.

James Boswell, *London Journal*, 1763

THE WARDROBE OF AN ODIOUS KING

I went yesterday to the sale of the late King's wardrobe, which was numerous enough to fill Monmouth Street, and sufficiently various and splendid for the wardrobe of Drury Lane. He hardly ever gave away anything except his linen, which was distributed every year. These clothes are the perquisite of his pages, and will fetch a pretty sum. There are all the coats he has ever had for fifty years, 300 whips, canes without number, every sort of uniform, the costumes of all the orders in Europe, splendid furs, pelisses, hunting-coats and breeches, and among other things a dozen pair of corduroy breeches he had made to hunt in when Don Miguel was here. His profusion in these articles was unbounded, because he never paid for them, and his memory was so accurate that one of his pages told me he recollected every article of dress, no matter how old, and that they were always liable to be called on to produce some particular coat or other article of apparel of years gone by. It is difficult to say whether in great or little things that man was most odious and contemptible.

Charles Greville, *Diary*, 1830

PRETENDING TO BE BLIND

Went to the London Library with Alix after breakfast this morning. Found a brilliant new game, completely shutting my eyes and being a blind girl led by Alix. I did it without opening them once from Piccadilly to the Library, amid the most sympathetic of glances of the onlookers! But the rest. Do you know one could live 15 more years if one never had to look at vehicles, and faces, and bad architecture.

Dora Carrington, Letter to Lytton Strachey, 1917

∼ 4 *August* ∼

BYRON AT THE WICKET AND AFTERWARDS

We have played the Eton and were most confoundedly beat;* however it was some comfort to me that I got 11 notches the 1st Innings and 7 the 2nd, which was more than any of our side except Brockman & Ipswich could contrive to hit. After the match we dined together, and were extremely friendly, not a single discordant word was uttered by either party. To be sure, we were most of us rather drunk and went together to the Haymarket Theatre, where we kicked up a row, as you may suppose, when so many Harrovians & Etonians met at one place; I was one of seven in a single hackney, 4 Eton and 3 Harrow, and then we all got into the same box, and the consequence was that such a devil of a noise arose that none of our neighbours could hear a word of the drama, at which, not being *highly delighted*, they began to quarrel with us, and we nearly came to a *battle royal*. How I got home after the play God knows. I hardly recollect, as my brain was so much confused by the heat, the row, and the wine I drank, that I could not remember in the morning how I found my way to bed.

Lord Byron, Letter to Charles O. Gordon, 1805

* The annual Eton v. Harrow cricket match. In 1805, it was played on the original Lord's Cricket Ground at Dorset Square, Marylebone.

WAR DECLARED

Tuesday, midnight. War declared against Germany. Great crowds waited at night in Downing Street, and as soon as they learnt that the die was cast, they marched to Buckingham Palace, remaining outside the railings, cheering for the King, who with the Queen and the Prince of Wales came to the balcony to acknowledge the cheers. For two or three days there had been enthusiastic cheering at the Palace.

William Mansfield, Viscount Sandhurst, *From Day to Day*, 1914

～ 5 *A U G U S T* ～

THE DAY AFTER WAR BROKE OUT

It was a strange London on Sunday: crowded with excursionists to London and balked would-be travellers to the Continent, all in a state of suppressed uneasiness and excitement. We sauntered through the crowd to Trafalgar Square, where Labour, socialist and pacifist demonstrators, with a few trade union flags, were gesticulating from the steps of the monument to a mixed crowd of admirers, hooligan warmongers and merely curious holiday-makers. It was an undignified and futile exhibition, this singing of the 'Red Flag' and passing of well-worn radical resolutions in favour of universal peace. We turned into the National Liberal Club: the lobby was crowded with men, all silent and perturbed . . . Even staunch Liberals agree we had to stand by Belgium. But there is no enthusiasm about the war: at present it is, on the part of England, a passionless war; a terrible nightmare sweeping over all classes – no one able to realise how the disaster came about.

The closing of the Bank for four days and the paralysis of business (no one seems to know whether the closing is limited to banks and many businesses have stopped because there is no money to pay wages) gives the business quarters of London a dispirited air. Every train that steams out of London, every cart in the street, is assumed to be commandeered by the Government for the purposes of war. Omnibuses and taxi-cabs are getting sparse. There is strained solemnity on every face – no one has the remotest idea of what is going to happen now that we are actually at war with Germany.

Beatrice Webb, *Diary*, 1914

VISITING COLERIDGE'S GRAVE

To Kentish Town and walk to Highgate Cemetery, terrace, catacombs, yews, view of London. Out to churchyard to find Coleridge's grave, locked; inquire for sexton's house, he is 'at church'; so I have to peep through gate at what a man tells me is the railing round C's grave, under an ivied wall. Look then at the house where he lived with Dr. Gilman (now Surgeon Brendon's), plain corner house of last century with dormer windows and large window in gable, shaded by a mimosa. Some fine elms and beeches are ranged in front, and tall trees rise behind. Out of one window looks a black cat, perhaps belonging to the Witch of Christabel. Splendid evening, sun-lighted road, down Highgate Hill on omnibus. Fleet Street. Chop at 'The Cock'.

William Allingham, *A Diary*, 1849

～ 6 *August* ～

A TULIP TREE AS TALL AS AN OAK

The hour being about 10, went into the coach where the Alderman took with him Dr. Desaguliers, a young gentleman and I. We proceeded through the town . . . We came safe as far as Vauxhall without any sort of accident, where we took boat separately, the Dr. and his young gentleman and the Alderman and I. We landed at the nearest stairs to Exchange Alley, went directly to the Swan, when the Alderman gave me a very good dinner, some of his own small beer and burgundy. Sent away a message to my friend Mr. Deard, who answer'd the same by appointing me to meet him at Salisbury Stairs. Accordingly, between 4 & 5, took coach and went directly to Salisbury Court where I had the good luck to meet Mr. Deard, who brought me into a house where the company assembled, and as soon as we were all come we took boat and went up as far as the new bridge, then return'd and walk'd in some gardens belonging to Lord Mordaunt. They were very pleasant, in which there was a tree as tall as an old oak as bore tulips as I was inform'd. The whole was very pleasant and had no fault in my eye except not being my own . . . From thence we took boat and landed at Temple Stairs, then proceeded to the Devil Tavern where my friend gave me an elegant supper . . . There was in company my good friend Sir Robert Montgomery, Mr. Deard, two ladies and two other gentlemen. 'Twas four before we parted and about five got to my old quarters in the Borough and so went directly to bed.

John Baptist Grano, *Diary*, 1729

A VERY SHABBY BOWER

To the Zoological Gardens in Regent's Park in the afternoon. The 'Reptile House' recently erected, contains many highly interesting specimens. The Rattle Snakes are thriving: a healthy looking Cyclara — Beautiful Lacertae and Hylaeviridae. The bower birds of Australia have begun a bower — but a very shabby one.

Gideon Mantell, *Journal*, 1849

～ 7 *August* ～

A CHELSEA GARDEN

I went to see Mr. Watts, keeper of the Apothecaries' garden of simples at Chelsea, where there is a collection of innumerable rarities of that sort; particularly, besides many rare annuals, the tree bearing Jesuits' bark, which has done such wonders in quartan agues. What was very ingenious was the subterraneous heat, conveyed by a stove under the conservatory, all vaulted with brick, so as he has the doors and windows open in the hardest frosts, secluding only the snow.

John Evelyn, *Diary*, 1685

SO LITTLE THRONGED

We went along Piccadilly as far as the Egyptian Hall. It is quite remarkable how comparatively quiet the town has become, now that the season is over. One can see the difference in all the region west of Temple Bar; and, indeed, either the hot weather or some other cause seems to have operated in assuaging the turmoil in the city itself. I never saw London Bridge so little thronged as yesterday.

Nathaniel Hawthorne, *English Notebooks*, 1856

WHAT CAN BE DONE?

A young man, crippled and with only one hand, a friendless clerk, is helped and taken in by Mr. Wheatley, of the St Giles's Christian Mission. Trusted on an errand with a cheque he absconds. Eventually he gets work at Westminster, and plays his employer the same trick. When no spark of honesty or of gratitude is discoverable, what can be done?

J. W. Horsley, *Jottings from Jail*, 1886

～ *8 August* ～

'I SHALL ALWAYS LOVE LITTLE KEW'

An exceedingly pretty scene was exhibited to-day to their majesties. We came, as usual on every alternate Tuesday, to Kew. The queen's Lodge is at the end of a long meadow, surrounded with houses, which is called Kew green; and this was quite filled with all the inhabitants of the place – the lame, old, blind, sick, and infants, who all assembled, dressed in their Sunday garb, to line the sides of the roads through which their majesties passed, attended by a band of musicians, arranged in the front, who began 'God save the King!' the moment they came upon the green, and finished it with loud huzzas. This was a compliment at the expense of the better inhabitants, who paid the musicians themselves, and mixed in with the group, which indeed left not a soul, I am told, in any house in the place. This testimony of loyal satisfaction in the king's safe return, after the attempted assassination,* affected the queen to tears: nor were they shed alone; for almost everybody's flowed that witnessed the scene. The queen, speaking of it afterwards, said, 'O! I shall always love little Kew for this!'

Fanny Burney, *Diary*, 1786

* A few days earlier, a madwoman named Margaret Nicholson had made a very half-hearted attempt to stab George III as he alighted from a coach outside St James's Palace.

LOOKING FOR ADVENTURE AT
THE BLACKWALL TUNNEL

I felt that I must have some adventure. It was a very nice afternoon, with threatening clouds. I hurried out and taxied to St Paul's. Immense flock of tame pigeons on the piazza, being fed. A congregation (sparse) assembled inside for a service. I then took a bus for Hackney Wick. I thought that would do as well as anywhere. But before I got to the Wick I saw buses going in the opposite direction to Blackwall Tunnel, which I had never seen. So I got off, and took one of these latter, and went all down the Burdett Road into East India Dock Road to Poplar, and I saw big steamers and even a fine 3-master, and a huge home or hostel for sailors. Incidentally the top of the slope leading to the tunnel: the thoroughfares are superb in width and very clean, and I noted lots of very interesting things. The East End keeps on till you get to Aldgate when it stops all of a sudden, and you begin to see Theatre Ticket Agencies.

Arnold Bennett, *Journal*, 1926

~ 9 *AUGUST* ~

UP TO OLD TRICKS

Rose at 6 o'clock, went to Westminster Baths, Charles Street, Oakley Street, Westminster Bridge Road, for first time this season. Home to breakfast half past eight and after ditto went to St Margaret's Westminster. Very well amused with monuments etc therein; sat on free seats north side. After dinner took walk up Holborn to see the late smash of two houses falling down, 22 and 23 Middle Row, directly opposite Grays Inn Lane. Such a sight I never before saw. The ruins have not been disturbed since they fell (one day last week – Sunday last, 2nd instant), and they falling straight have carried all the furniture with them, completely burying greatest part, but some few articles may be seen sticking out, of which I noticed a chest of drawers and a chair, and against the wall I saw a print or two hanging, with two looking glasses, presenting a novel sight. One flight of stairs was still hanging. This event had likely to have caused a great loss of life, but they providentially escaped, having just quitted the crumbling fabric. Walked on through the City and returned by Clerkenwell, noticing the damage done by the late storm and the fast increase of buildings in the new street in continuation with Farringdon Street. *After tea had Ann Fox up. After looking through prints got to our old tricks in which I got a little further than ever by just catching a glimpse of the hairs covering her c—t. She wore a new straw bonnet for the first time. Hope to get on better hereafter in matters of secrecy.** Saw two persons of whom I have not seen a long time, Benjamin Smart and Henry Kitchingman – the former in Fore Street, Cripplegate, the latter in Dean Street, Soho – neither of whom spoke to me, not liking my appearance, being too ancient. At home the rest of evening.

Nathaniel Bryceson, *Diary*, 1846

* The passage in italics was written in Pitman's shorthand. Other entries in Bryceson's diary, particularly those describing his relationship with Ann Fox, are also written in shorthand.

A NONAGENARIAN IN CLIFFORD'S INN

My first call was on Mrs. Dyer . . . who attained her ninety-ninth year on the 7th December. If cleanliness be next to godliness, it must be acknowledged she is far off from being a good woman; yet what strength of constitution! She was in an arm-chair. The apartment at the top of Clifford's Inn small, and seemingly full of inhabitants; a child was playing about – her great-grandchild. It fell out of a window thirty-six feet from the ground, and was uninjured by the fall.

Henry Crabb Robinson, *Diary*, 1860

～ 10 AUGUST ～

A ROBBERY NEAR WOODFORD BRIDGE

Left London; the camps of Hyde park* broke up; stopt and staid at Mr. Grosvenor's at Walthamstow; in the morning saw Wanstead house; in the evening went to Ray house; Sir James Wright rob'd near Woodford bridge two nights before by a man on a grey horse marked with the small pox, suspected to be one who had been a servant of Sir J. G. G. living near his gate.

William Hervey, *Journals*, 1780

* Hervey was a soldier and the camps were military camps.

AN EXCURSION ON THE RIVER

Yesterday I had a note from V. Fenton asking me to join them in a Boat excursion up the River, & to be at Kew at 4 p.m., so I made all haste to Sloane St & took a Kew bus and after many delays got to the bridge at 4.35 passing on the way the P. of Wales who was driving the Princess. I thought I was too late but wasn't so we took a boat (the *P. of Wales*) and quietly pulled up to Richmond. The Party consisted of Clara Dally & Viv Fenton, Agnes Brooks, Tupholme the Parson & myself. We landed at Richmond & went to Riverdale where some of us played at Croquet.

At 6 o'clock we were joined by Mr Fenton & a Miss Emmett, and we then pulled up to Teddington thro' the lock, to Kingston Br and returned to R.mond at 10 p.m. some of the girls having taken part in rowing. Miss Brooks is a very jolly sort of girl, and as she pulled bow oar I sat behind her, & instructed her in the novel art and talked & chaffed with her to my satisfaction. When landed we went round to Riverdale leaving Viv in the boat to take her round to some steps, we were in hopes of getting something to eat having dined at 6 o'clock, but there was none to be had, so we returned to the bank and found both Viv & his boat gone in a most mysterious manner, we shouted & hunted about for him without result, and Mr Fenton began to get nervous, however the boat soon turned up in charge of a waterman who said Viv had gone up to the house – and at last he returned. We then pulled back to Kew, & after a slight altercation with the Waterman, tried to get a cab without success, so walked over to Ealing, where Mr Fenton offered me a sofa & some supper to my great joy. I went into the Beer & Bread & cheese with great effect, and then apples & pears, and as I had a slight touch of Diarrhoea was completely upset thereby.

Rafe Neville Leycester, *Diary*, 1864

~ 11 August ~

A MYSTERIOUS FIRE

There are various reports how the late fire in Thames street began: some say by carelessnesse; others, by a sky rocket falling amongst hay; and some suspect treachery, for that 'tis said a tradesmans apprentice in Pater Noster rowe hath writt a letter intimating as if he had done it, and that he is in custody about it; time will shew.

Narcissus Luttrell, *Diary*, 1688

THE DANGERS OF LIME

In the morn went to see the fier at Somerset House. It burnt down 2 or 3 stables. It came, they say, by unslacked lyme being laid near one of the Doors & by a shower of Raine it kindled the fier, the wind being very high.

Peter Briggins, *Diary*, 1705

A POET SWIMS IN THE THAMES

Last week I swam in the Thames from Lambeth through the two bridges, Westminster and Blackfriars, a distance, including the different turns and tracks made on the way, of three miles! You see I am in excellent training in case of a *squall* at sea.

Lord Byron, Letter to Elizabeth Pigot, 1807

～ 12 *AUGUST* ～

A MAD DOG IN RICHMOND

I have in my last fright forgot one where there were better grounds for it. The day I wrote to you last, as you know, I was at Isleworth. Coming from thence, and when I landed,* the first thing I heard was that people with guns were in pursuit of a mad dog, that he had run into the Duke's garden. Mie Mie came the first naturally into my thoughts; she is there sometimes by herself reading. My impatience to get home, and uneasiness till I found that she was safe and in her room, *n'est pas a concevoir*. The dog bit several other dogs, a blue-coat boy, and two children, before he was destroyed. John St. John, who dined with me, had met him in a narrow lane, near Mrs. Boverie's, him and his pursuers. John had for his defence a stick, with a heavy handle. He struck him with this, and for the moment got clear of him . . . It is really dreadful; for ten days to come we shall be in a terror, not knowing what dogs may have been bitten.

George Selwyn, Letter to Lady Carlisle, 1790

* At Richmond, on the other bank of the Thames, where Selwyn had a house.

LIVING IN UTTER SOLITUDE

London is deserted; only some three million and a half people remain to await the coming of next season. All the houses round Regent's Park are shut up, and the sight of the darkened windows does not make one cheerful. I myself live in utter solitude, it is more than three weeks since I opened my lips to speak to anyone but the servant.

George Gissing, Letter to his sister Margaret, 1884

A HAPPY FAMILY?

I wonder if this flower-girl, aged 18, used to sing the popular song, 'We are a happy family'. She is in for assaulting her mother with a poker, and has twice previously been in for drunkenness: the mother is living apart from her husband, and has spent ten months out of twelve in Millbank doing short terms for drunkenness: a younger brother and sister have been sent to Industrial Schools. Yet the wonder is that any members of some families do right, and not that many do wrong. On what a pinnacle of virtue, inaccessible to a countess, is the daughter of a convict father and gindrinking mother who keeps straight!

J. W. Horsley, *Jottings from Jail*, 1886

～ *13 August* ～

A NIGHT OF FIRSTS

Yesterday was my first night out in Soho, my first dinner date, my first visit to the Cafe Royal and the second time I ever got drunk – quite a night to remember!

Rupert and I set out about seven and sat on top of the number 14 bus to Piccadilly. I was wearing my blue cotton dress with orange sash, and was determined to get good and tight.

'The vast metropolis unrolls before us!' Rupert cried.

So there we were at Bertorelli's, a lovely old-fashioned Italian place with oak panelling. We'd got a corner table and it was minestrone first, and then veal with spaghetti.

Rupert doesn't know one wine from another but I was very impressed by the *au fait* manner with which he ordered the Médoc. He even poured a little out and sniffed it, when the fat woman in black brought it over.

'I don't know what it is,' he said to me afterwards, 'but it's the cheapest.'

'You sounded as if you knew all about it!'

'Oh, I can always carry it off when cornered.'

We finished the bottle and I felt fine, but when I got to the ladies I was mildly surprised to see the door of the cloakroom retreating from my outstretched hand at a fast rate. 'This won't do,' I muttered, and clamping my cigarette between my teeth I attacked it with both hands, captured it and managed to get it open. 'Gee,' I remarked to the lavatory seat, 'I'm really good and plastered!'

My return journey was more successful. I threaded the tables with swan-like undulations, and only clutched at the woodwork once.

'Nice work,' Rupert said, as I sank gratefully into my chair. We counted up our joint resources and decided we could just manage the Cafe Royal. Rupert was pretty tight too and on the way there we had one or two unfortunate encounters with sandbags.

'You can take it from me, Rooples,' I crooned happily, 'my head will be resting on your shoulder before the evening's out.'

'I don't doubt it,' said R suavely. 'Look out, here comes a kerb.'

We reached the Cafe Royal and went in through a back entrance with heavy velvety curtains. It was like making a stage entry. You pushed open the curtains in the darkness and there you were in the dazzling light and red plush. It was a lovely place, crystal chandeliers and Napoleon's arms, and plush and gilt and yellow glaring lights, and lots of very dull people who had come to see everyone else, only there wasn't anyone much to see. Everyone thought Rupert was a celebrity because he had a beard. We sat in the middle at a marble table and ordered lager, thinking of Oscar Wilde and Shaw and all the great geniuses who had sat there before us . . .

Joan Wyndham, *Love Lessons: A Wartime Diary*, 1940

~ *14 August* ~

BAITING THE BULL

So home and dined, and after dinner, with my wife and Mercer to the Beare-garden, where I have not been, I think, of many years, and saw some good sport of the bull's tossing of the dogs: one into the very boxes. But it is a very rude and nasty pleasure. We had a great many hectors in the same box with us (and one very fine went into the pit, and played his dog for a wager, which was a strange sport for a gentleman), where they drank wine, and drank Mercer's health first, which I pledged with my hat off; and who should be in the house but Mr. Pierce the surgeon, who saw us and spoke to us. Thence home, well enough satisfied, however, with the variety of this afternoon's exercise; and so I to my chamber, till in the evening our company come to supper.

Samuel Pepys, *Diary*, 1666

A DUKE'S DAY

The Duke of Devonshire's manner of living while he is in London is singular. He seldom rises before three o'clock in the afternoon; breakfasts, & then rides out, dines, and at night goes to Brookes's; where he remains till two or three o'clock in the morning. Mr Trebeck, the vicar of Chiswick, having prevailed upon the Duke to engage to vote on some occasion at St. Georges, Hanover square, the Duke was startled on being informed he must attend at two o'clock in the day.

Joseph Farington, *Diary*, 1796

THE STORMING OF SEBASTOPOL

I am stiff to-day. I had to walk to St Paul's last night, after all my walking, before I got an omnibus, and then from Alsop's home. And last night the results of Cremorne in the King's Road* were — what shall I say? strange, upon my honour! First I heard a measured tread; and then, out of the darkness, advanced on me eight soldiers carrying, high over their heads, a bier on which lay a figure covered with a black cloth, all but the white, white face! And before I had recovered from the shock of that, some twenty yards farther on, behold, precisely the same thing over again. I asked a working man what had happened. 'It was a great night at Cremorne, storming of Sebastopol; thirty or forty soldiers were storming, when the scaffolding broke, and they all fell in on their own bayonets. The two who had passed were killed, they said, and all the others hurt.' But a sergeant, whom I accosted after, told me there were none killed and only three hurt badly.

Jane Welsh Carlyle, Letter to Thomas Carlyle, 1855

* A reconstruction of the recent storming of Sebastopol in the Crimean War took place at Cremorne Gardens in Chelsea. The staging gave way and many soldiers were injured.

∼ 15 AUGUST ∼

MEETING A PLAGUE VICTIM

It was dark before I could get home, and so land at Church-yard stairs, where, to my great trouble, I met a dead corpse of the plague, in the narrow alley just bringing down a little pair of stairs. But I thank God I was not much disturbed at it.

Samuel Pepys, *Diary*, 1665

∼ 16 AUGUST ∼

HEADS ON TEMPLE BAR

I have been this morning at the Tower, and passed under the new heads at Temple Bar,* where people make a trade of letting spying-glasses at a halfpenny a look.

Horace Walpole, Letter to George Montagu, 1746

* The heads of Scotsmen executed after the Jacobite Rebellion of 1745.

VAUXHALL GARDENS

After a long and fatiguing day's business I accompanied Mrs Dalby to Vauxhall Gardens, where a great number of people were assembled, it being a Gala Night on account of the Duke of York's birthday. We first noticed the orchestra, which is erected amidst trees, and ornamented by coloured lamps in various forms and devices. A band of music and some of the first singers in town occupied it, and at the time we entered Mrs Bland was singing. In a short time they left the orchestra for a little repose, and it was occupied by the Duke of York's military band which played several martial spirit-stirring airs. 10 o'clock arrived and suddenly a bell rang which announced an exhibition of waterworks, after which the restless auditors and spectators again flocked to the orchestra, which was again the theatre of singing til 12 o'clock, when they finally concluded, and the fireworks commenced. After this spectacle the gardens are generally a scene of merriment and jollity. The Pandeans, German, Turkish and military bands are stationed in various parts of the place, and some of them are continually playing, while parties of joyful visitors 'trip it on the light fantastic toe'. Here might be seen fat clumsy boors dancing with the taper, light London Miss, a jumble of oddity and levity truly ridiculous. Long covered promenades (with little cells in which were spread a profusion of refreshments) served to protect the votary of pleasure from dire effects of the midnight air, which many, more ardent, braved in the dark green alleys, whose cool and kindly shade afforded a charming retreat to the lovers of darkness. Should the pitiless rain intrude its unwelcome patter, all take refuge in a large room which is elegantly fitted up with various patriotic and emblematic devices, where the walk, the dance, the music, and the supper, continually offer themselves to the senses. The lights, the transparencies, the trees, the magic-resembling, fairy-like whole, formed for me a truly new scene. Mrs D and I retired 2 hours before the usual time it closes, which is 4 o'clock.

Thomas Asline Ward, *Diary*, 1804

～ 17 *August* ～

JUDGE ORDERS WINDOWS SMASHED
AT THE OLD BAILEY

To the Old Bailey, where Smethurst was being tried for the murder of his wife before the Chief Baron. Towards the end of the sitting an incident occurred which strongly illustrated the tendency to laugh which always exists in a court of justice, however solemn and serious the occasion may be. It was a very hot and close day, and my father had made repeated demands for more fresh air to be admitted. At last the sheriffs told him that they had come to the end of their means of ventilation and could do no more. 'Then,' said my father, 'open the windows.' 'The windows will not open, my lord,' said the sheriff. 'Then break them,' said the judge. Upon which one of the ushers, armed with his long white wand, went into the jury-box and, mounted upon the back of another, began thrashing away at the panes of glass in the large window above the jury-box. Another usher, similarly provided, and leaning as far forward as he could from the gallery, while a second man held him to prevent him from falling over, began to attack the upper part of the window, and the two men belaboured it as if they were beating a walnut tree to bring down the walnuts. The effect was irresistibly droll, and for five minutes every one in court, including the judge and the prisoner at the bar, was convulsed with laughter. At last enough glass was smashed to let in the desired amount of fresh air, gravity was resumed, and the case was proceeded with as if nothing had happened.

Sir Frederick Pollock, *Diary*, 1859

'ALL MY GENTLEMEN HAVE LEFT TOWN'

In Oxford Street a fashionable prostitute accosted me who once before had begged me to go home with her; & she now explained her importunity by saying, 'All my gentlemen have left town, and I really am so hard up – I shall have to give up my lodgings!' 'Then why not go out of town too?' 'I've nowhere to go to!' This spoken by a girl who though not interesting was elegant & well-dressed, gives one a sad sense of the loneliness of such a life – and a glimpse also of the embarrassment which besets these London butterflies when the season is over. She was a farmer's daughter from near Chesterfield; & came to town, nominally to be a draper's assistant, but really to become of her own accord what she is. N. B. *After nine months*, her family still think she is at the shop.

Arthur Munby, *Diary*, 1860

YOUR FEET'S TOO BIG

Went to see two ex-prisoners now in Great College Street Female Refuge. Temper has caused both of them to leave several good Homes. One gravely tells me that the reason for her fury and leaving was that another girl told her that among some new slippers she thought there would not be a pair small enough for her.

J. W. Horsley, *Jottings from Jail*, 1886

～ 18 *August* ～

MAIDS WITH PINS AND HORSES WITH STAGGERS

After dinner comes Mr. Pelling the Potticary, whom I had sent for to dine with me, but he was engaged. After sitting an hour to talk we broke up, all leaving Pelling to talk with my wife, and I walked towards White Hall, but, being wearied, turned into St. Dunstan's Church, where I heard an able sermon of the minister of the place; and stood by a pretty, modest maid, whom I did labour to take by the hand and the body; but she would not, but got further and further from me; and, at last, I could perceive her to take pins out of her pocket to prick me if I should touch her again – which seeing I did forbear, and was glad I did spy her design. And then I fell to gaze upon another pretty maid in a pew close to me, and she on me; and I did go about to take her by the hand, which she suffered a little and then withdrew. So the sermon ended, and the church broke up, and my amours ended also, and so took coach and home, and there took up my wife, and to Islington with her, our old road, but before we got to Islington, between that and Kingsland, there happened an odd adventure: one of our coach-horses fell sick of the staggers, so as he was ready to fall down. The coachman was fain to 'light, and hold him up, and cut his tongue to make him bleed, and his tail. The horse continued shaking every part of him, as if he had been in an ague, a good while, and his blood settled in his tongue, and the coachman thought and believed he would presently drop down dead; then he blew some tobacco in his nose, upon which the horse sneezed, and, by and by, grows well, and draws us the rest of our way, as well as ever he did; which was one of the strangest things of a horse I ever observed, but he says it is usual. It is the staggers. Staid and eat and drank at Islington, at the old house, and so home, and to my chamber to read, and then to supper and to bed.

Samuel Pepys, *Diary*, 1667

LIKE THE DAY OF JUDGEMENT

We came to Hampstead Heath, and looked past a foreground of fir-trees over a wide undulating prospect tufted with trees, and richly cultivated, a lake shining in the distance under the evening sky. On the other side huge London lying sombre and silent. We were just in time to see the effect of the lighting of the lamps. The dusky mass awoke, and here and there, and soon all over, glowed with multitudinous sparks, – 'like,' said Patmore, 'the volcanic crust of the earth not yet cooled' – or like the advancing judgment of the Last Day: no ark avails against that fiery deluge. The evening was growing cold as we returned to Highgate and descended the hill, P. showing me on the way the house, in a sort of crescent with trees before it, where he formerly lived, and where Emerson and Tennyson sat at his table and liked each other.

William Allingham, *A Diary*, 1849

∼ 19 *August* ∼

THE ADVANTAGES OF LONDON

But you must not think I am a discontented person and grumble all day long at being in London. *There are many advantages here*, as I say to myself whenever it is particularly disagreeable; and if we can't see even a leaf or a sparrow without soot on it, there are the parrots at the Zoological Gardens and the pictures at the Royal Academy; and real live poets above all, with their heads full of the trees and birds and sunshine of paradise.

Elizabeth Barrett Browning, Letter to Miss Commeline, 1837

A STUPID AUDIENCE

Looked out my clothes at my lodgings; went to rehearsal at the Haymarket. Acted Othello, in part well, in part languidly. The audience did not seem to be of the same quality of intellect as I had been used to at Covent Garden. But let us hope.

William Charles Macready, *Diaries*, 1839

LOOKING VERY CONTINENTAL

I went up to Hampstead yesterday afternoon to see Elizabeth Jenkins . . . She was looking well and pretty, and has painted her house pale pink outside . . . All that part of St John's Wood on the Finchley Road route to Hampstead is completely gone – rather elegant pale yellow brick blocks of flats rising out of the gardens of what used to be those Gothic cottages ornés. In fact all of that NW part of London, beyond Lord's Cricket Ground, now looks very continental. I wondered if I would like to live there, but I don't think so – I'd rather have a stab at SW, next time.

Elizabeth Bowen, Letter to Charles Ritchie, 1959

~ 20 AUGUST ~

A TOURIST FROM SHEFFIELD

Mr Dalby and I walked to Hungerford Stairs, where we took a boat, and landed near Billingsgate. Having inspected this famous fishmarket, we walked to the Tower, where we saw wild beasts kept there, the regalia and the armouries. The ancient armour is interesting, and the modern is beautiful; for the swords, pistols, musquets, etc. quite clean and ready for service, are ranged in the most perfect order, and with the nicest art are placed so as to imitate columns, stars, and other devices.

After seeing the curiosities of the Tower, we sailed to the new docks, appropriated for the vessels in the West India trade, of which 300 homeward bound may lie in the basin at one time, and a dock for those outward bound is making. The fleet was arrived only 2 or 3 days, and we saw an immense crowd of them pressing towards the yards to discharge their lading. The buildings are of stone, 7 stories high, built very strong to contain the heavy stores which are frequently put in them. A moat, wall, and palisade surround the whole, and sentinels are placed to prevent depredations.

Thomas Asline Ward, *Diary*, 1804

DISPLEASED BY ALTERATIONS

Old Walker, proprietor of the hotel, 33 Dean Street, Soho, corner of Queen Street, has had his house lately pointed down and painted, and has this day had a square lamp fixed, lit with gas, which till now has been a round one with tin top and lit with oil, and which was no doubt the original one put up when the house was built, which is about 160 years. This is an alteration which I am both surprised and displeased at as the house preserved its ancient look so like hotel and tavern of the 17th century. The proprietor thereof is very old both in years and fashion, wearing at all times a black suit with breeches and black stockings, and as I have heard saw Margaret Nicholson attempt to stab George III.

Nathaniel Bryceson, *Diary*, 1846

∼ 21 *AUGUST* ∼

NAILED BY THE EAR

John Daye, parson of St Alborow within Bishopsgate, was set on the pillory in Cheape, and had one of his ears nailed, for seditious words speaking of the Queen's Highness. And also a surgeon by Paul's was likewise set on the pillory with him, and had one of his ears nailed also for seditious words speaking of the preacher at the sermon at Paul's Cross on Sunday the 13 of August. And when they had stood on the pillory 3 houres the nails were pulled out with a pair of pincers, and they were had to prison again.

Charles Wriothesley, *Chronicle*, 1553

CENTRE OF GOOD AND EVIL

And now, London, I must bid thee 'Farewell.' Thou art the centre of Good and Evil, of Virtue and Vice! How many and how various are the characters which inhabit thy walls! How magnificent thy palaces! How

mean thy cottages! How miserable some, how happy others! Some fatten on the spoils of poverty, others starve in the midst of plenty. How many thousands are insufficient to supply the luxury of some, while others want a crust of bread to satiate the calls of hunger!

Thomas Asline Ward, *Diary*, 1804

~ 22 AUGUST ~

A MUTTON THIEF

So I home, and took London-bridge in my way; walking down Fish Street and Gracious Street, to see how very fine a descent they have now made down the hill, that it is become very easy and pleasant, and going through Leaden-Hall, it being market-day, I did see a woman catched, that had stolen a shoulder of mutton off of a butcher's stall, and carrying it wrapt up in a cloth, in a basket. The jade was surprised, and did not deny it, and the woman so silly, as to let her go that took it, only taking the meat.

Samuel Pepys, *Diary*, 1668

JOHN WESLEY'S HORSES GIVE HIM TROUBLE

After a few of us had joined in prayer, about four I set out, and rode softly to Snow Hill; where, the saddle slipping quite upon my mare's neck, I fell over her head, and she ran back into Smithfield. Some boys caught her and brought her to me again, cursing and swearing all the way. I spoke plainly to them, and they promised to amend. I was setting forward when a man cried, 'Sir, you have lost your saddle-cloth.' Two or three more would needs help me to put it on; but these, too, swore at almost every word. I turned to one and another and spoke in love. They all took it well and thanked me much. I gave them two or three little books, which they promised to read over carefully. Before I reached Kensington, I found my mare had lost a shoe. This gave me an opportunity of talking closely, for nearly half an hour, both to the smith and his servant. I mention these little circumstances to show how easy it is to redeem every fragment of time (if I may so speak), when we feel any love to those souls for which Christ died.

John Wesley, *Journal*, 1743

LONDON IS THE PLACE FOR ME

Poets may talk of the beauties of nature, the enjoyments of a country life, and rural innocence; but there is another kind of life which, though unsung by bards, is yet to me infinitely superior to the dull uniformity of country life. London is the place for me. Its smoky atmosphere, and its muddy river, charm me more than the pure air of Hertfordshire, and the crystal currents of the river Rib. Nothing is equal to the splendid varieties of London life, 'the fine flow of London talk,' and the dazzling brilliancy of London spectacles. Such are my sentiments, and, if ever I publish poetry, it shall not be pastoral.

Thomas Macaulay, Letter to a friend, 1815

MARCHIONESS DISASTER

Many drowned in the Thames when, in the early hours of Sunday morning, a dredger runs down a pleasure boat. The circumstances are bad enough – the party in full swing, the huge black dredger tipping the boat on its side before running it down, but this doesn't stop the reportage making it worse. 'Revellers,' says ITN, 'were tipped into the freezing waters.' 'Left struggling in the icy waters of the Thames' is another report. It was actually one of the hottest nights of the year, and one of the rescued says that the water was warm, only very dirty. One sane girl, whose Italian boyfriend is missing, refuses to give her name to reporters because 'she doesn't want to become a news item'. Undeterred by becoming a news item, Mrs Thatcher, in her capacity as Mother of Her People, circles the spot in a police launch and is filmed bending caringly over a computer screen in the incident room.

Alan Bennett, *Diary*, 1989

～ 23 *August* ～

THE MOST MAGNIFICENT TRIUMPH

I was spectator of the most magnificent triumph that ever floated on the Thames; considering the innumerable boats and vessels, dressed and adorned with all imaginable pomp, but above all the thrones, arches, pageants and other representations, stately barges of the Lord Mayor and Companies, with various inventions, music and peals of ordnance both from the vessels and the shore, going to meet and conduct the new Queen* from Hampton Court to Whitehall, at the first time of her coming to town. In my opinion, it far exceeded all the Venetian Bucentoras etc on the Ascension, when they go to espouse the Adriatic. His Majesty and the Queen came in an antique-shaped open vessel, covered with a state or canopy of cloth of gold, made in form of a cupola, supported with high Corinthian pillars, wreathed with flowers, festoons and garlands. I was in our new-built vessel, sailing amongst them.

John Evelyn, *Diary*, 1662

* Catherine of Braganza, Charles II's new wife.

PROCLAIMING BARTHOLOMEW FAIR

Went to Guildhall, and thence to Smithfield to proclaim Bartholomew Fair. We stopt under Newgate, where the Keeper presented me with a cold tankard, according to custom. The Proclamation was read by the Attorney of the Mayor's Court in waiting (who sate in the Coach with me) in Cloth Fair, and repeated by one of the Sheriff's Officers. From thence we returned home by way of Bartholomew Close.

Micajah Perry, *Lord Mayor Perry's Diary*, 1739

～ 24 *August* ～

NAPOLEON'S COACH ATTRACTS THE CROWDS

Bullocks Museum I went to, & saw Buonaparte's carriage, – his coachman, and two of his horses. This was the last day of exhibiting it in
London. It is to be taken first to Bristol, from thence to Dublin; and
afterwards to Edinburgh. – The coachman is a well-looking young man.
He was much wounded at the Battle of Waterloo, and in consequence
his right arm was amputated. – Such has been the public curiosity in
London to see this carriage that upwards of 220,000 persons have paid
to be admitted to see it.

Joseph Farington, *Diary*, 1816

MONUMENTS IN WESTMINSTER ABBEY

I lunched and corrected proofs in the train. Then walked straight to the
House of Lords through tortuous streets, ending up with the Abbey.
What a funny place the Abbey is! It is very noble, in its darkness and
mistiness, but spoilt for me, I confess, by the crowds. The monuments
fill me with delight – the more absurd they are the more I love them
. . . The statue of Wilberforce interests me; if it were of the wickedest
man that ever lived, a man satanically cynical, it would be said to be
characteristic. Then some of the recent burials; a president of the Institute of Civil Engineers – I had never heard of him – has a huge brass
on the floor, where he appears in frock-coat and trousers. Street, the
architect, is buried there; he kneels by a crucifix in an Inverness cape.
And yet the Dean won't allow the smallest memorial to Mrs Browning!
It is the rooted distrust in the English mind of an artist – you must do
something else as well . . . The Abbey is so interesting because it reveals
the topsy-turveydom of the English mind so completely – the worship,
not of the people who will last, or whom others will hold to be our ornaments, but the man of the hour, the representative of privilege and
rank.

A. C. Benson, *Diary*, 1907

∼ 25 AUGUST ∼

GOING TO SEE A BRIDGE

On Sunday we are going to see Southwark Bridge. My diary, why do I record this event? Nothing in going to see a bridge. But this is the newest bridge over the Thames and has been opened ONE YEAR. It cost 360,000 pounds to build. And now it's going to be, or is now being torn up entirely to lay down electric cables and other things. I do not understand why they didn't put down the cables and other things when they were BUILDING the bridge . . . and not destroy a perfectly new bridge at a further cost of ten thousand pounds. But we are going to see it on Sunday in case it gets all pulled down to rebuild the bridge.

Fred Bason, *Diary*, 1922

∼ 26 AUGUST ∼

A FIGHT IN ST JAMES'S PARK

Mr Freke . . . coming over St. James Parke about 12 a clock att night, challenged my lord of Roscomon either to fight him in St. James Parke presently or to pay him downe a thousand pounds my lord had long owed Mr Freke. Butt . . . att three a clock in the morning ten men of the lifegard came and fetched Mr Freke outt of his bed from me and immediately hurryed him to Whit Hall before Secetary Coventry, I nott knowing whatt itt was for more then words spoken. This was the beginning of my troubles . . .

Elizabeth Freke, *Remembrances*, 1672

IN LOW HANDS

I drank tea with Dance & afterwards went to see the St. Pancrass Volunteers collected. This evening 7 Candidates for the Rank of Captain were nominated – a Mr. Le June is appointed Major. He is a Stock Broker.

The whole of the military business of this Parish appears to be in low hands.

Joseph Farington, Diary, 1803

AN ARTIST MOVES TO HAMPSTEAD

We are at length fixed in our comfortable little house in Well Walk, Hampstead, and are once more enjoying our own furniture, and sleeping in our own beds. My plans in search of health for my family have been ruinous; but I hope now that our moveable camp no longer exists, and that I am settled for life. So hateful is moving about to me, that I could gladly exclaim, 'Here let me take my everlasting rest!' The rent of this house is fifty-two pounds per annum, taxes, twenty-five, and what I have spent on it, ten or fifteen. I have let Charlotte Street at eighty-two pounds, retaining my two parlours, large front attic, painting room, gallery, &c. This house is to my wife's heart's content; it is situated on an eminence at the back of the spot in which you saw us, and our little drawing room commands a view unsurpassed in Europe, from Westminster Abbey to Gravesend. The dome of St. Paul's in the air seems to realize Michael Angelo's words on seeing the Pantheon: 'I will build such a thing in the sky.' We see the woods and lofty grounds of the East Saxons to the north-east.

John Constable, Letter to John Fisher, 1827

～ 27 August ～

A FAMILY VISITS
VAUXHALL GARDENS

I know a man who delights to make every one he can happy – that same man treated some honest girls with expenses for a Vauxhall evening. If you should happen to know him, you may tell him from me – that last night – three great girls – a boy – and a fat old fellow – were as happy and pleas'd as a fine evening – fine place – good songs – much

company — and good music could make them. — Heaven and Earth! — how happy, how delighted were the girls! — Oh! the pleasures of novelty to youth! — We went by water — had a coach home — were gazed at — followed, &c. &c. — but not much abused.

Ignatius Sancho, Letter to a friend, 1777

∼ 28 *August* ∼

PAINTING THE DOME OF ST PAUL'S

I went to Paul's to view the City from the top of it. It was a fine sight, but I had a great curiosity to see the inside of the scaffolding of the Dome upon which Mr. Thornhill is painting and the man that keeps the keys of the whispering gallery told me that nobody ever went up there. Mr. Thornhill would not admit of it. However, I desired him to show me the door into it, which he did, and told me if I would ring the bell and ask for Mr. Thornhill they would admit me up and I must then make my excuse to Mr. Thornhill. This shocked me a little at first. However, I thought it could be no such great crime to beg the favour of seeing his painting and design. Accordingly I ventured and was admitted up by his servant. When I came I made my bow to Mr. Thornhill and told him I had a great curiosity to see so extraordinary a piece of painting, as that of the Dome of St. Paul's, and begged the favour of being allowed the liberty to view what was done of it. He told me this was a liberty he did not usually allow to anybody, because if it was people would come in so great crowds that they would interrupt him in his study and painting. However, since I was come, I might go about it and view any part of it. I thanked him for the liberty and began to look about me, and then told him we should now be able to vie at least with Paris for history painting which we have been so deficient in before. He told me he had been about this a year already and expected to finish it in a year more.

Dudley Ryder, *Diary*, 1716

AN UNFLIRTATIOUS UMBRELLA

After tea, we all three walked in Kensington Gardens and sat on a seat by the Round Pond. My umbrella fell to the ground, and I left it there with its nose poking up in a cynical manner, as She remarked.

'It's not cynical,' I said, 'only a little knowing. Won't you let yours fall down to keep it company? Yours is a lady umbrella and a good-looking one – they might flirt together.'

'Mine doesn't want to flirt,' she answered stiffly.

W. N. P. Barbellion, *The Journal of a Disappointed Man*, 1912

～ 29 AUGUST ～

COLLISION IN THE TUBE

Coming home by the underground Railway, our train got into a collision with the one ahead of us, in the tunnel between Gloucester Road and High St Kensington stations. There was a violent clap, the gas was suddenly extinguished, I was jerked on to the seat in front of me, losing my hat only. We heard no noise, except that of a lad in the same carriage bellowing in the utter darkness to be let out. He was quieted by some of the other passengers, and at last a man with a lantern came along the tunnel by our side and said the doors would be opened presently. They were so, and we walked along the tunnel a couple of hundred yards to High Street station, where we found one or two persons being carried pigaback by others. One of them carried with a slight stream of blood trickling down his cheek, but apparently not very much damaged. Never heard the cause of the accident.

Alfred Domett, *Diary*, 1873

OFFENSIVE ST PAUL'S

At about 5.15 Dorothy and I went out for a City excursion. We drove to St Paul's Cathedral first, of which the front was in the usual Sunday mess; a fearful litter of paper, and kids feeding the birds, and hawkers; all extremely untidy, slatternly etc. Even offensive . . .

Arnold Bennett, *Journal*, 1926

HOUSE PRICES IN HAMPSTEAD

I don't really know where I want to live – in London or abroad or in the country. Nor, at present prices, do I feel happy about the financial side. The cheapest houses, all in tatty areas, are about £10,000. Nothing under £15,000 in Hampstead. We'd have to borrow at least half the purchase price. And I think about all those writers who lived all their lives in a miserable state of debt.

John Fowles, *Journals*, 1963

~ 30 AUGUST ~

A WALK IN CHISWICK

Helen and I walk on past A. P. Herbert's house until we come to Lord Burlington's villa at Chiswick. An old Italian looking exactly like an English Cockney is selling ice creams at the gate. Helen insists on having one. 'No pies, no pies,' he says, 'only corny-eets, only corny-eets!' Said like this with the long 'e' and suggestion of 'y' the word is so pretty and strange. I must remember that before we got to the villa we passed through the churchyard. The service was on, we could hear the intoning, and as we passed the open door, to reach Hogarth's tomb, a breath of incense came out and surrounded us. The hot sun melted the resinous smell, it floated away through the dry grass, and Helen and I stood reading David Garrick's epitaph aloud, but in a whisper because of the service. And so on to the gates of the villa. When at last we came in sight of the building we saw that it was defaced by everything from posters to dances, firemen's hoses, sandbags, firemen in shirt-sleeves (one had his shirt open to his belt showing a froth of black hair on his chest and a little, bright red identity disc on a greasy string winking through) to sheer neglect. We skirted the building, hating its degradation, wondering why no one cared for its beauty. When we reached the other side we saw spreading in front of us a vista of old cedars, urns and sphinxes, with a semicircle of philosophers guarded by two lions at the end. Everything was coarsened, neglected. But there was a mournful, sinister beauty about the whole wide garden which I think must have been intended. I thought that it was not the place to have been used for a lunatic asylum. Winking through the evergreen oaks and other lovely trees were exquisite classical monuments; a tiny temple with an obelisk set in the middle of a lily pond, a terribly neglected bridge, delicate as ivory-work, a column with something set on the top that I could not distinguish. I thought that this lovely romantic patch could be made into the most beautiful garden in all England, but instead of that it is allowed to go to ruin, while the town worthies spend all their money on silly, gaudy 'beds' and gaunt greenhouses.

The house is the least thought of thing of all.

Denton Welch, *Journals*, 1942

～ 31 *August* ～

SHOPPING AT WEDGWOOD'S

In the morning we went to London a-shopping, and at Wedgwood's,* as usual, were highly entertain'd, as I think no shop affords so great a variety. I there, among other things, purchased one of the new invented *petit soupée* trays, which I think equally clever, elegant, and convenient when alone or a small party, as so much less trouble to ourselves and servants.

Mrs Philip Lybbe Powys, *Diary*, 1798

* The Wedgwood showrooms were then in St James's Square.

IGNORING THE WARNINGS

Air-raid warnings, of which there are now half a dozen or thereabouts every 24 hours, becoming a great bore. Opinion spreading rapidly that one ought simply to disregard the raids except when they are known to be big-scale ones and in one's own area. Of the people strolling in Regent's Park, I should say at least half pay no attention to a raid-warning . . . Last night just as we were going to bed, a pretty heavy explosion. Later in the night woken up by a tremendous crash, said to be caused by a bomb in Maida Vale. E. and I merely remarked on the loudness and fell asleep again.

George Orwell, *Diaries*, 1940

SEPTEMBER

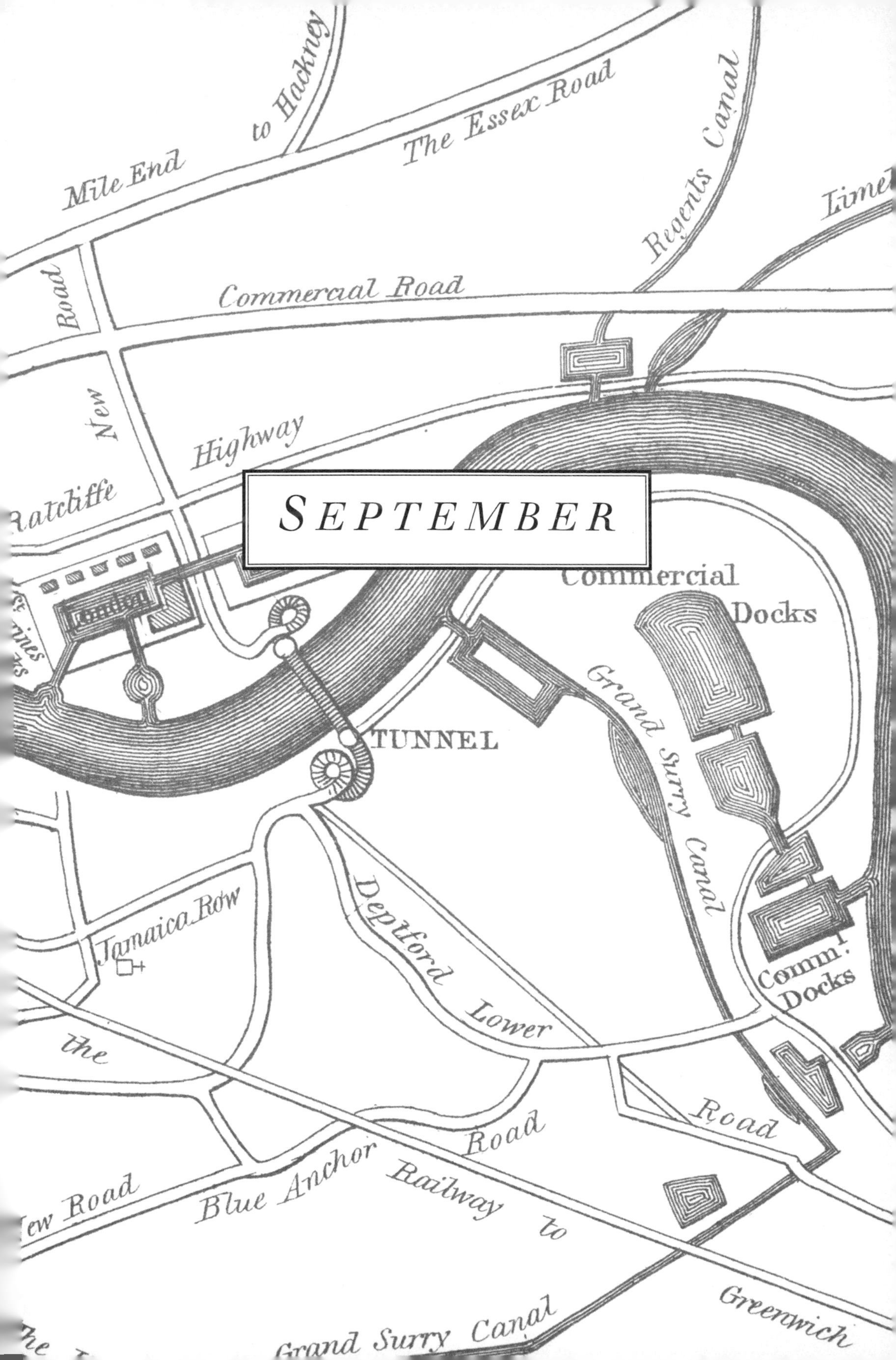
to Hackney
Mile End
The Essex Road
Regents Canal
Road
Commercial Road
New
Highway
Ratcliffe
London
Commercial
Docks
Grand Surry Canal
TUNNEL
Deptford
Lower
Road
Jamaica Row
Comm:
Docks
the
Road
Blue Anchor
Railway
to
Greenwich
Grand Surry Canal

～ 1 SEPTEMBER ～

A HANGMAN HANGED

At Clerkenwell, where the wrestlinge is kept, after the wrestlinge was done, there was hanged on a payre of gallowes, newe made, in the same place, the hangman of London and two more for robbinge a bouth in Bartlemewe fayre, which sayd hangman had done execution in London since the Holy Mayde of Kent was hanged, and was a conninge butcher in quarteringe of men.

Charles Wriothesley, *Chronicle*, 1538

CLUBBED TO DEATH

They have put in the papers a good story made on White's:* a man dropped down dead at the door, was carried in: the club immediately made bets whether he was dead or not, and when they were going to bleed him, the wagerers for his death interposed, and said it would affect the fairness of the bet.

Horace Walpole, Letter to Sir Horace Mann, 1750

* The gentlemen's club, then at Chesterfield Street, now in St James's Street.

BY NO MEANS THE WORST

The Surrey side is by no means the worst part of London. The streets are, in general, very wide and pretty regular, and the houses not mean. We stopped a little while near the Elephant and Castle, and saw close to us, at the corner of two very broad streets, the Rockingham Arms, one of those pestilential gin-shops. It is a very fine large building, handsomely adorned with pilasters. Two ragged and sickly wretches, a man and woman, skulked out at a little door while I was looking. I make no doubt there was a pawnbroker's shop close by.

Emily Shore, *Journal*, 1836

∽ *2 September* ∽

BARTHOLOMEW FAIR

Circuited to Smithfield, in order to see the ceremony of opening Bartholomew Fair by the Lord Mayor – just finished. The whole is a mere rabble rout, relishable only by mene peuple; conducted by men, women, and children, in painted masks and merry-andrew tawdry dresses. The amusements consist in jumping, dancing, riding on round-about horses with legs, speech-making, etc., performed on scaffolds; together with sleight-of-hand tricks, in front rooms hired for that purpose; the ascent whereto is by a kind of rough ladder-stairs, actors and performers inviting in by a thousand antic postures and gestures. Passages round, lined with booths and tents, crammed with ginger-bread, pastry, and all kinds and varieties of baubles.

Samuel Curwen, *Journal*, 1780

A NEW HOME BY THE NEW RIVER

What will you not say to my not writing? You cannot say I do not write now. Hessey has not used your kind sonnet, nor have I seen it. Pray send me a copy. Neither have I heard any more of your friend's MS., which I will reclaim whenever you please. When you come Londonward, you will find me no longer in Covent Garden: I have a cottage in Colebrook Row, Islington, – a cottage, for it is detached; a white house, with six good rooms, The New River (rather elderly by this time) runs (if a moderate walking pace can be so termed) close to the foot of the house; and behind is a spacious garden with vines (I assure you), pears, strawberries, parsnips, leeks, carrots, cabbages, to delight the heart of old Alcinous. You enter without passage into a cheerful dining-room, all studded over and rough with old books; and above is a lightsome drawing-room, three windows, full of choice prints. I feel like a great lord, never having had a house before.

Charles Lamb, Letter to Bernard Barton, 1823

～ *3 September* ～

THE GREAT FIRE

The fire continuing, after dinner I took coach with my wife and son and went to the Bank side in Southwark, where we beheld that dismal spectacle, the whole city in flames near the water side; all the houses from the Bridge, all Thames street, and upwards towards Cheapside, down to the Three Cranes, were now consumed: and so returned exceeding astonished what would become of the rest. The fire having continued all this night (if I may call that night which was light as day for 10 miles round about, after a dreadful manner) when conspiring with a fierce eastern wind in a very dry season; I went on foot to the same place, and saw the whole south part of the city burning from Cheapside to the Thames, and all along Cornhill, (for it likewise kindled back against the wind as well as forward), Tower street, Fenchurch street, Gracious street, and so along to Bainard's Castle, and was now taking hold of St. Paul's church, to which the scaffolds contributed exceedingly. The conflagration was so universal, and the people so astonished, that from the beginning, I know not by what despondency or fate, but crying out and lamentation, running about like distracted creatures without at all attempting to save even their goods; such a strange consternation there was among them, so as it burned both in breadth and length, the churches, public halls, Exchange, hospitals, monuments, and ornaments, leaping after a prodigious manner, from house to house and street to street, at great distances from one the other; for the heat with a long set of fair and warm weather had even ignited the air and prepared the materials to conceive the fire, which devoured after an incredible manner houses, furniture, and everything. Here we saw the Thames covered with goods floating, all the barges and boats laden with what some had time and courage to save, as, on the other, the carts, &c. carrying out to the fields, which for many miles were strewed with moveables of all sorts, and tents erecting to shelter both people and what goods they could get away. Oh the miserable and calamitous spectacle! such as haply the world had not seen since the foundation of it, nor be outdone till the universal conflagration thereof. All the sky was of a fiery aspect, like the top of a burning oven, and the light seen above 40 miles round about for many nights. God grant mine eyes may never behold the like, who now saw above 10,000 houses all in one flame; the noise and cracking and thunder of people, the fall of towers, houses, and churches, was like an hideous storm, and the air all about so hot and inflamed that at last one was not able to approach it, so that they were forced to stand still and let the flames burn on, which they did for near two miles in length and one in breadth. The clouds also of smoke were dismal and reached upon computation near 50 miles in length. Thus I left it this afternoon burning, a resemblance of Sodom, or the last day. It forcibly called to my mind that passage – *non enim hic habemus stabilem civitatum:* the ruins resembling the picture of Troy. London was, but is no more!

John Evelyn, *Diary*, 1666

THE OUTBREAK OF THE SECOND WORLD WAR

The Prime Minister's speech in the House last night was accompanied by tremendous lightning, but hardly any thunder. It was more like stage lightning than the real thing. I watched the storm from the Savage Club. One moment complete darkness; the next a sheet of vivid green showing Westminster cut out in cardboard like the scenery in a toy theatre. The flashes last so long you could count the buildings.

At ten o clock to-day Hibberd, the chief announcer [on the BBC], told us that the Prime Minister would broadcast at eleven o clock . . . at

11.15 precisely ... speaking in an intensely English accent, Chamberlain told us that, since Germany had not replied to the ultimatum, England was now at war. At half-past eleven the first air-raid warning goes. Orderly retreat to dug-out. Nothing happens, 'All clear' after half an hour. We go into the street, and I see a man look at his watch and hear him say, 'They're open!'

Presently Jock comes round in search of his gas-mask ... this morning's air-raid sirens caught him at breakfast in the Strand Corner House, and drove him into the basement. He adjured me to say that his first and chief emotion took the form of the angry exclamation, 'What a very unattractive crowd of people to have to die with!'

So far as I can judge in my suburb, which I have not left to-day, people are taking the war with extraordinary calmness. In one matter I confess that I have been utterly wrong. I expected every road leading out of London to be cluttered and impassable. Actually not only has there been no exodus, but the traffic has been less than on an ordinary Sunday.

James Agate, *Journals*, 1939

CIVIL DEFENCES

It began by being a perfect autumn day and E. and I had planned to go to Kew. When E. came we went for a walk in Hyde Park. It blew from the east and she had to hold her hat on with one hand while we walked past the AA guns to the river and by the cylindrical tin huts behind their barbed wire where the soldiers have made neat little streets and gardens like a fairy tale illustration.

Charles Ritchie, *Diary*, 1942

～ 4 SEPTEMBER ～

HOUNDED OUT OF THE CITY

In London there is a more cruel campaign* than that waged by the Russians: the streets are a very picture of the murder of the innocents –

one drives over nothing but poor dead dogs! The dear, good-natured, honest, sensible creatures! Christ! how can anybody hurt them? Nobody could but those Cherokees the English, who desire no better than to be halloo'd to blood.

Horace Walpole, Letter to the Earl of Strafford, 1760

* Because of a fear of rabid dogs in the summer of 1760, an order had been issued that all strays in the streets should be killed.

INDUBITABLE PROOF OF GENIUS

I did not find my husband at the 'Swan with Two Necks'; for we were in a quarter of an hour before the appointed time. So I had my luggage put on the backs of two porters, and walked on to Cheapside, where I presently found a Chelsea omnibus. By and by, however, the omnibus stopped, and amid cries of 'No room, sir,' 'Can't get in,' Carlyle's face, beautifully set off by a broad-brimmed white hat, gazed in at the door, like the Peri, who, 'at the Gate of Heaven, stood disconsolate.' In hurrying along the Strand, pretty sure of being too late, amidst all the imaginable and unimaginable phenomena which the immense thoroughfare of a street presents, his eye (Heaven bless the mark) had lighted on my trunk perched on the top of the omnibus, and had recognised it. This seems to me one of the most indubitable proofs of genius which he ever manifested.

Jane Welsh Carlyle, Letter to Mary Welsh, 1836

NO WOMEN IN A RESPECTABLE HOTEL

Afterwards to the Café Royal, where at the next table sat two young American airmen arrived in England the same day. One of them leaned over to me and said, 'Say, buddy, d'ya think we could take a coupla women to our hotel?' I asked what hotel they were staying at, and he mentioned one of the most respectable hostelries in London. I told him they could not possibly do such a thing. 'Aw,' says airman No. 2, 'don't get us wrong. We don't mean a coupla women each!'

James Agate, *Journals*, 1942

∼ *5 September* ∼

A ROBBING PARSON

In walking through Parliament-street and seeing crowds running through Scotland-yard, joined them, and on inquiry found they were accompanying Parson Lloyd, a clergyman, returned from Bow-street Justices' examination to Westminster Bridewell, from whence he was taken this morning on a complaint of highway robbery; and it is said he is identified. He seemed hardened, and of a rough, bold cast, and begged with a careless boldness money of every well-dressed person that passed as he was being conducted to prison in irons; his right hand being also chained to an officer's, or one of the justice's men.

Samuel Curwen, *Journal*, 1782

CARTING ONE'S PICTURES ACROSS TOWN

Packed my five pictures in a cart, and at 10 a.m. started on my way to London, down the new Finchley Road – I driving, because it was too heavy to sit both of us in front, and perched up behind was anything but comfort. However, the pony, being a mettlesome beast, had no idea of going unless his own master thrashed him, and seemed to despise my attempts in that line; so we had to change seats. It is Barnet fair, and we were taken for return showmen on the road. As I got to the door in Percy Street, old White was knocking there. He looked at the picture for about one hour, and was most warm in his eulogium. I said last figure was £200 with copyright, or £150 without. I think he did not intend to buy when he came, but he seemed loth to leave it. At last he said: 'I want you to give me copyright in, and will give you a bill at six months, for £150.' So I said, as it was him, I would take it; indeed, I would not have done so otherwise. Then he took the pencil-drawing for £7. He promises speedy fortune, and that in two years more I shall no longer sell my pictures to him, but command the highest prices in the art-market, and only give him a picture for remembrance of old times. Amen! say I.

Ford Madox Brown, *Diary*, 1855

WARTIME WEDDING BELLS

The Camden Town jeweller from whom I bought a cheap wrist-watch told me that he had sold thirty wedding-rings in two days, as against the normal three or four. A poor woman coming in to buy a modest signet ring and asking to have 'From your Loving Wife' engraved on it was told that no engravers were available ... One of the most depressed men in London to-day was the shopkeeper at Chalk Farm whose line is flares, beacons and material for bonfires.

James Agate, *Journals*, 1939

～ *6 SEPTEMBER* ～

BARTHOLOMEW FAIR

At Aldgate I took my wife into our coach, and so to Bartholomew fair, and there, it being very dirty, and now night, we saw a poor fellow, whose legs were tied behind his back, dance upon his hands with his arse above his head, and also dance upon his crutches, without any legs upon the ground to help him, which he did with that pain that I was sorry to see it, and did pity him and give him money after he had done. Then we to see a piece of clocke-work made by an Englishman – indeed, very good, wherein all the several states of man's age, to 100 years old, is shewn very pretty and solemne; and several other things more cheerful, and so we ended, and took a link, the women resolving to be dirty, and walked up and down to get a coach.

Samuel Pepys, *Diary*, 1667

RIDICULOUS EXHIBITION

Went to Bartholomew Fair, a scene of every species of folly and ridiculous exhibition. Bartholomew Hospital is indeed a noble building. It was founded in 1105, and repaired and improved in the reign of Henry VIII.

Peter Van Schaack, *Journal*, 1779

BLACKBERRYING IN HENDON

Started quarter before 8 o'clock for Hendon by Primrose Hill and Hampstead. Had lift in carriage box above a mile beyond Hampstead Heath by offer of the coachman. Got to Hendon Church half past 10 o'clock. Picked and ate a quantity of blackberries in the lanes there, and took down some inscriptions from the tablets and tombs within and without the church. Interfered with by a policeman for not keeping the footpath and annoying the congregation by walking about the grounds. Dined at the 'Greyhound' Public House close to burial ground. Commenced cutting my initials and date on burial ground gate, but only completed 'N B 1' when I was interrupted by the sight of two policemen approaching, upon which I made off, leaving my job unfinished. Left Hendon Church about half past three and dawdled away an hour eating blackberries, when I made for home at a smartish pace, arriving thither soon after six, walking four miles per hour. I tried to paw up Ann but she evaded me somehow, but I saw her comfortably seated in Tottenham Court Chapel where I let her remain unmolested, for which I am not sorry. Very warm, distant thunder throughout the afternoon accompanied with a few large drops of rain. Had tea in coffee shop in Dean Street, opposite Little Dean Street.

Nathaniel Bryceson, *Diary*, 1846

∼ 7 SEPTEMBER ∼

AN ECLIPSE

Great eclipse of the sun – a fine day to see it. When at the greatest obscuration, a little after two p.m., I observed that the streets of London looked as if in moonlight. There will not be so considerable an eclipse again until 1847. If I should live so long, how shall I look back upon the days of this eclipse? . . . Saw every one looking into pails of water and through burnt glasses.

John Cam Hobhouse, *Diary*, 1820

AN AMERICAN'S IMPRESSIONS OF LONDON

I walked forth, for the first time, in London. Our lodgings are in George Street, Hanover Square, No. 21; and St. George's Church, where so many marriages in romance and in fashionable life have been celebrated, is a short distance below our house, in the same street. The edifice seems to be of white marble, now much blackened with London smoke, and has a Grecian pillared portico. In the square, just above us, is a statue of William Pitt. We went down Bond Street, and part of Regent Street, just estraying a little way from our temporary nest, and taking good account of landmarks and corners, so as to find our way readily back again. It is long since I have had such a childish feeling; but all that I had heard and felt about the vastness of London made it seem like swimming in a boundless ocean, to venture one step beyond the only spot I knew. My first actual impression of London was of stately and spacious streets, and by no means so dusky and grimy as I had expected, – not merely in the streets about this quarter of the town, which is the aristocratic quarter, but in all the streets through which we had passed from the railway station.

Nathaniel Hawthorne, *English Notebooks*, 1855

UNDER ATTACK

The biggest air attack launched on London to date started this afternoon and has been going on ever since, the time of writing being 2 a.m. From the roof of the Cafe Royal got a fine view of the blaze, the Tower Bridge being cut out like fretwork. In one corner of the foreground a large flag fluttered, making the whole thing look like one of those old posters of A Royal Divorce, Napoleon's cavalry against a background of red ruin.

James Agate, *Journals*, 1940

SWINGING LONDON

Tonight I took [the actress] Georgina Forbes to the Playboy (Bunny) Club, near the Hilton Hotel, for dinner. We dined about nine o' clock in a large gloomy, candle-lit place called the VIP room. A bunny came up and introduced herself as our waitress. She was not topless, nor were any of the other girls, but each wore on her stern an enormous white ruff, an exaggeration of a rabbit's tail. This most prominent portion of their costume is in constant display, for as the dishes are served they approach tables backwards, and it is quite a contortionary feat to handle plates in this manner. The room was crowded, the food good. On other floors gambling was in full swing, with Bunnies acting as croupiers. Since Georgina had never been to Annabel's, we went on there before midnight. Things were in full swing, and there was hardly room to put a foot down. To me, it was an enjoyable evening, for my companion was not only intelligent and lovely, but interesting as well. She hopes to continue indefinitely with her movie and stage career.

David Bruce, *Diary*, 1967

~ 8 SEPTEMBER ~

AN EARLY DIVING SUIT

The duke of Leinsters engine for working of wrecks was experimented on the Thames, where one Bradley, a waterman, walkt at bottom under water till he came to Somersethouse, and discours'd by the way out of a leather pipe, and a boat went before to blow air to him: he had a tin case fastned about his neck with 2 leather pipes.

Narcissus Luttrell, *Diary*, 1692

THE ORIGINS OF THE NATURAL HISTORY MUSEUM

I walked in the afternoon with Evelyn, across Richmond Park, to call on Professor Owen, who arrived just as we did, coming down from London, where he is engaged in transferring his collection to its new home at South Kensington, and is very happy over a fossil monster from Queensland, who had no less than nine horns upon his tail.

Mountstuart Grant Duff, *Notes from a Diary*, 1880

IMPENDING INVASION

Heavy bombing of London throughout the night, the whole sky being lit up by the glow of fires in London docks. Went to the office in the morning where I found further indications of impending invasion. Everything pointing to Kent and E. Anglia as the two main threatened points.

Lord Alanbrooke, *Diary*, 1940

～ 9 SEPTEMBER ～

PLEASURE BOATS ON THE THAMES

This latter river makes the delight of the cockneys of London; and, on Sunday particularly, the number of pleasure-boats plying between Richmond and the capital is prodigious; they are generally covered with an awning, and decorated with flags and streamers. The custom of stopping on the lawns along the river, and making a *repas champêtre* with provisions brought in the boat, proves, I suppose, a great nuisance to the refined proprietors of these favourite spots; for I have observed on several of them boards put up, with writing, forbidding such trespasses and vulgar sports on their premises. The Bishop of London, wanting to put a stop to this profanation of the Sabbath, thought it necessary to ascertain first the extent of the evil; and to that end had the number of boats passing under the bridge in the course of one Sunday taken down, – but finding it to exceed 4000, he gave it up in despair. Although it should seem difficult to be drowned in so inconsiderable a river as the Thames above London, yet accidents are frequent, from the imprudence of the city navigators, who carry sail in these small boats, flat, and without ballast. I have seen some of them sitting or lying over the awning, with the true temerity of inexperience.

Louis Simond, *Journal of a Tour and Residence in Great Britain, During the Years 1810 and 1811*, 1811

A LONDON CORNER

I am so glad you did enjoy Glen Prosen; I had similar fears to yours about the experiment, but in a day to two I knew it was to be one of the happiest holidays of my life, and so without any doubt it prove. Fain would I have lingered. For the first time perhaps I was 'sweir' to return to the London that eternally thrills me and has been to me all that bright wishes of my youth conceived. I have often felt a wish that Branwell Bronte who yearned for it so much and never reached it had been plunged in as I was. In being able to live in London by my pen I achieved my one literary ambition; I never sought the popularity that is mostly fluke, I would have been as satisfied though I had remained in the nice two-pair-back-to-end, quite unknown round the corner so long as it was a London corner.

J. M. Barrie, Letter to Lady Cynthia Asquith, 1933

SHOT IN NEW BOND STREET

Yesterday the importunance of my mother induced me to suffer the degrading ordeal of being photographed. A place in New Bond Street called Swaine had offered to do it for free. I think it must be the worst shop in London. I waited half an hour in a drawing-room furnished with enormous photographs of the Royal Family. Then I was taken up to the 'studio' where a repulsive little man attempted to be genial while two other men worked a camera. I am confident it will be an abominable photograph.

Evelyn Waugh, *Diaries*, 1924

~ 10 SEPTEMBER ~

BLOOMSBURY IN RUINS

Back from half a day in London, perhaps our strangest visit. When we got to Gower Street a barrier with diversions on it. No sign of damage. But coming to Doughty Street a crowd . . . Wardens there. Not allowed in. The house about 30 yards from ours struck at one this morning by a bomb. Completely ruined. Another bomb in the square still unexploded. We walked around the back. Stood by Jane Harrison's house. The house was still smouldering. That is a great pile of bricks. Underneath people who had gone down to their shelter. Scraps of cloth hanging to bare walls at the side still standing. A looking glass I think swinging. Like a tooth knocked out – a clean cut. Our house undamaged. No windows yet broken perhaps the bomb has now broken them. We saw Bernal with an armband jumping on top of the bricks. Who lived there? I suppose the casual young men and women I used to see from my window; the flat dwellers who used to have flower pots and sit on the balcony. All now blown to bits . . .

Virginia Woolf, *Diary*, 1940

A CHIC NEIGHBOURHOOD

I am getting so fond of this part of London – more and more do I think I'd like to 'settle' somewhere in this neighbourhood, when, about one and a half years hence or so, I do have a flat. Funny how from having been so dowdy Kensington's now getting so chic and streamlined: in fact parts of it are now as pretty as a picture; and of course a great charm are all these bowery trees.

Elizabeth Bowen, Letter to Charles Ritchie, 1959

～ 11 SEPTEMBER ～

LOVELY OXFORD STREET?

We strolled up and down lovely Oxford Street this evening, for some goods look more attractive by artificial light. Just imagine, dear children, a street taking half an hour to cover from end to end, with double rows of brightly shining lamps, in the middle of which stands an equally long row of beautifully lacquered coaches, and on either side of these there is room for two coaches to pass one another; and the pavement inlaid with flagstones, can stand six people deep and allows one to gaze at the splendidly lit shop fronts in comfort. First one passes a watchmaker's, then a silk or fan store, now a silversmiths, a china or glass shop. The spirit booths are particularly tempting, for the English are in any case fond of strong drink. Here crystal flasks of every shape and form are exhibited: each one has a light behind it which makes all the different coloured spirits sparkle. Just as alluring are the confectioners and fruiterers, where, behind the handsome glass windows, pyramids of pineapples, figs, grapes, oranges and all manner of fruits are on show . . . Up to eleven o'clock at night there are as many people along this street as at Frankfurt during the fair, not to mention the eternal stream of coaches. The arrangement of the shops in good perspective, with their adjoining living rooms, makes a very pleasant sight. For right through the excellently illuminated shop one can see many a charming family scene enacted: some are still at work, others drinking tea, a third party is entertaining a friendly visitor; in a fourth parents are joking and playing with their children. Such a series of tableaux of domestic and busy life is hardly to be met with in an hour as I witnessed here.

Sophie von La Roche, *Diary*, 1786

A BIT RICH

Before the play I'd parked the car in Kemble Street or one of the others named after actors, opposite the dosshouse where various vagrants were claiming their bed for the night. I gave a tramp two bob, the same as I'd spent on the programme. Thelma had gone in first and bought me a Scotch and herself a gin in the theatre bar. 'Enjoy it,' she said, 'it cost a pound.' As we sat afterwards putting on our seat-belts, a tramp on the pavement asked me for a hand-out. 'Drive on,' said Thelma, always afraid of drunks. But I couldn't and rummaged in my pockets for change. Finding none, I turned to her. 'I haven't any either,' she said. 'I'm sorry,' I mimed to the man through the closed window, 'we've nothing to give you. Well only these few pence.' Sitting there in an automatic Renault and a Simpson's blazer. 'Thanks very much,' he said and made off. 'I only had a fiver', she said, 'I knew you wouldn't want to give him that.' She was right. But why? Our deposit account stands at £20,000. I *wasn't* meant to be rich. Was anyone?

Peter Nichols, *Diary*, 1972

NIGHT BUS NIGHTMARE

Night buses are starting to prove such hard *work* for me, particularly at the weekend. It's the noise – teenagers carrying on their parties on the bus. Nothing new, so it must be me who's changed. No escape. The bus stops at every possible stop, crawls, stops. Crawls, stops. Interminably.

On a recent night bus trip, I had two girls sitting next to me, one on the other's lap, while they exchanged drunken banter with their red-cheeked male counterparts, drinking but not yet shaving. After a while, the girls grew tired of their seating arrangement and both decided to squeeze themselves on to my seat, pushing me up against the glass. Not even asking me if I minded. I didn't say anything, but I was in hell. At least on tube journeys one can switch to a different carriage. With night buses, I increasingly feel one is at the mercy of the less meek and the more drunk. It's a terrifying combination for a fragile fop old enough to be their slightly peculiar uncle.

Dickon Edwards, *Diary*, 2004

∼ *12 SEPTEMBER* ∼

GETTING STONED IN WHITECHAPEL

I was desired to preach in an open place, commonly called the Great Gardens, lying between Whitechapel and Coverlet Fields, where I found a vast multitude gathered together. Taking knowledge that a great part of them were little acquainted with the things of God, I called upon them in the words of our Lord, 'Repent ye, and believe the gospel.' Many of the beasts of the people laboured much to disturb those who were of a better mind. They endeavoured to drive in a herd of cows among them; but the brutes were wiser than their masters. They then threw whole showers of stones, one of which struck me just between the eyes: but I felt no pain at all; and when I had wiped away the blood, went on testifying with a loud voice that God hath given to them that believe 'not the spirit of fear, but power, and of love, and of a sound mind.' And, by the spirit which now appeared through the whole congregation, I plainly saw what a blessing it is when it is given us, even in the lowest degree, to suffer for His name's sake.

John Wesley, *Journal*, 1742

NOT A LONG WALK

A delightful day. The pleasantest walk by far I have had this summer. The very rising from one's bed at Hamond's house is an enjoyment worth going to Hampstead overnight to partake of. The morning scene from his back-room is exceedingly beautiful. We breakfasted at seven.

He and his sisters accompanied me beyond The Spaniards, and down some fields opposite Kenwood. The wet grass sent them back, and I went on (rather out of my way) till I entered the Barnet road just before the west end of Finchley Common, I crossed the common obliquely, and, missing the shortest way, came to a good turnpike road at Colney Hatch. On the heath I was amused by the novel sight of gipsies. The road from Colney Hatch to Southgate very pleasing indeed. Southgate a delightful village. No distant prospect from the green, but there are fine trees admirably grouped, and neat and happy houses scattered in picturesque corners and lanes . . . I then followed a path to Winchmore Hill, and another to Enfield: the last through some of the richest verdure I ever saw. The hills exquisitely undulating. Very fine clumps of oak-trees, Enfield town, the large white church, the serpentine New River, Mr. Mellish's house, with its woody appendages, form a singularly beautiful picture. I reached Enfield at about half-past ten, and found Anthony Robinson happy with his family . . . A little after five I set out on my walk homeward, through Hornsey and Islington . . . I reached my chambers about nine. Rather fatigued, though my walk was not a long one – only eighteen or twenty miles.

Henry Crabb Robinson, *Diary*, 1812

DEAD RINGERS

Wrote to the telephone manager in Gerrard Street yesterday to inform him that the war is now over and I am tired of wasting one hour a day owing to his blasted telephone not working. Threaten a letter to *The Times* giving an hour-by-hour account of one day's attempt to avail myself of a service for which I pay a half-yearly bill of over twenty pounds. Result: the 'phone has been completely dead.

I cannot understand why the little Carlton Theatre in the Tottenham Court Road is not full to overflowing. The custom there is to have one French film and one British one; by telephoning beforehand one can always find out when the British rubbish has exhausted itself. The French films are invariably entrancing. At least they are entrancing to me.

James Agate, *Journals*, 1945

∼ *13 September* ∼

SHAKESPEARE IN THE PARK

Longest drought for thirty-odd years ended to-day, and appropriately enough Sydney Carroll produced The Tempest in the open air at Regent's Park.

James Agate, *Journals*, 1933

BOMB DAMAGE IN DULWICH

Today I am in bed ill, but yesterday Eric took me to Dulwich Village to see the picture gallery hit by a flying bomb. And we walked down the road by green fields which was the way to his first school, now with all the windows blown-out and derelict. He told me of the singing master who reeked of beer; and told me of his rackerty friend Jack who got drunk and strapped a screwdriver to his shin and said he was going to break into a club, and would Eric come too. It all came to nothing.

We sat on a seat looking on the grounds of Dulwich College and we both smoked the same pipe and then walked back down the road where Eric's house of all his childhood used to be. Now utterly destroyed by a 1941 land mine.

It was nearly dark. We walked over the ruins of the house, almost flat, and down the garden path with the vegetables of someone's allotment growing on what was once the lawn. And in a curious pine tree I saw a beam and two hooks and I said, 'That was your swing?' and Eric nodded.

At the bottom of the garden was still the little tool hut which had been Eric's where he had played and peed out of the door to save going back to the house. And in the evening light the poignancy of this garden of his childhood transformed it.

How tired I was trudging back thinking of myself and him and childhood and age and everything decaying.

The whole city falling to bits, gradually obtruding its skeleton. The war had made the city and everything grow older with a rush.

Denton Welch, *Journals*, 1944

LOSING A FRIEND AT THE
GREAT EASTERN HOTEL

Dear Sir, I went into the Great Eastern Hotel yesterday at lunchtime and I had not been there for more than a year. I was very sad to hear from the Head Waiter and his second-in-command and the wine waiter that Mr Stokes [Arthur Stokes, head waiter in the main dining room for many years] had died. They each came to me with the sad news, for they all regretted him deeply as I do. I can imagine how sad you must feel without him and I told them that in losing him I felt I had lost a friend. There is some consolation in the thought of his having spent his life and having endeared himself to so many. He was the right man for the right job and that does not often happen. Please accept my condolences and sympathy. My long absence from the Great Eastern was because I left the City and came to live in Chelsea which is not so nice.

John Betjeman, Letter to The Manager,
Great Eastern Hotel, Liverpool Street, 1974

~ *14 September* ~

AN UNCHASTE LADY

When we were tired with walking, we stepped into some barges, and rowed down the river Thames, on the banks of which are situated more than twenty fine palaces. In the afternoon a tragic play was acted about Samson and the half tribe of Benjamin. On our way to the theatre, we saw a woman sitting in a little shed made of wood. She had betrayed herself by unchaste conduct, and towards evening was to be taken to the female penitentiary. We were told that in such cases things are managed as follows. If persons are found in illicit cohabitation they are both arrested. The men are taken to a separate prison, and there well whipped with rods secretly, but after that they are at once set at liberty. The women are taken to a house especially appointed for the purpose, and are kept there sometimes for more than half a year, and twice a week they may expect to get a good whipping, but by paying 2 thalers and a half each time, they may escape these. Meanwhile, they earn their living by some handicraft; those that have not learnt anything must indeed be badly off. When at last they have been sufficiently punished, or their friends intercede for them, they are set at liberty on bail, and it has been asserted to us as a truth, that many a husband has taken his wife back from a house of this kind.

Frederic Gershow, 'Diary of the Duke of Stettin's
Journey through England', 1602

THE PLAGUE IN LONDON

Death stares us continually in the face in every infected person that passeth by us; in every coffin which is daily and hourly carried along the streets. The bells never cease to put us in mind of our mortality. The custom was, in the beginning, to bury the dead in the night only; now, both night and day will hardly be time enough to do it. For the last week, mortality did too apparently evidence that, that the dead was piled in heaps above ground for some hours together, before either time could be gained or place to bury them in. The Quakers (as we are informed) have buried in their piece of ground a thousand for some weeks together last past. Many are dead in Ludgate, Newgatt and Christ Church Hospital, and many other places about the town which are not included in the bill of mortality.

John Tillison, Letter to
Dr Sancroft, 1665

The Manner of Burying the Dead at Holy Well Mount near London during the dreadful PLAGUE in the reign of CHARLES II. 1665. By which upwards of One hundred Thousand Lives were swept away.

A BLOCKBUSTER EXHIBITION IN SOUTHWARK

After dinner with Mr. Gale; walked into Southwark to see the Italian
gentleman with two heads; that growing out of his side has long black
hair . . . I bought his picture, which is with the printed ticket.

Ralph Thoresby, *Diary*, 1714

BIG CITY, SMALL CHANGE

Tumblers, hand-organists, puppet-showmen, bagpipers, and all such
vagrant mirth-makers, are very numerous in the streets of London. The
other day, passing through Fleet Street, I saw a crowd filling up a narrow
court, and high above their heads a tumbler, standing on his head, on
the top of a pole, that reached as high as the third story of the neigh-
boring Houses. Sliding down the pole head foremost, he disappeared
out of my sight. A multitude of Punches go the rounds continually. Two
have passed through Hanover Street, where we reside, this morning.
The first asked two shillings for his performance; so we sent him away.
The second demanded, in the first place, half a crown; but finally
consented to take a shilling, and gave us the show at that price, though
much maimed in its proportions. Besides the spectators in our windows,
he had a little crowd on the sidewalk, to whom he went round for contributions, but I did not observe that anybody gave him so much as a halfpenny. It is strange to see how many people are aiming at the small
change in your pocket. In every square a beggar-woman meets you, and
turns back to follow your steps with her miserable murmur. At the
street-crossings there are old men or little girls with their brooms;
urchins propose to brush your boots; and if you get into a cab, a man
runs to open the door for you, and touches his hat for a fee, as he closes
it again.

Nathaniel Hawthorne, *English Notebooks*, 1855

∼ 15 SEPTEMBER ∼

A ROPE DANCER AND A HAIRY WOMAN

Going to London with some company, we stepped in to see a famous rope-dancer, called The Turk. I saw even to astonishment the agility with which he performed. He walked barefooted, taking hold by his toes only of a rope almost perpendicular, and without so much as touching it with his hands; he danced blind-fold on the high rope, and with a boy of twelve years old tied to one of his feet about twenty feet beneath him, dangling as he danced, yet he moved as nimbly as if it had been but a feather. Lastly, he stood on his head, on the top of a very high mast, danced on a small rope that was very slack, and finally flew down the perpendicular, on his breast, his head foremost, his legs and arms extended, with divers other activities. – I saw the hairy woman, twenty years old, whom I had before seen when a child. She was born at Augsburg, in Germany. Her very eyebrows were combed upward, and all her forehead as thick and even as grows on any woman's head, neatly dressed; a very long lock of hair out of each ear; she had also a most prolix beard, and moustachios, with long locks growing on the middle of her nose, like an Iceland dog exactly, the color of a bright brown, fine as well-dressed flax. She was now married, and told me she had one child that was not hairy, nor were any of her parents, or relations. She was very well shaped, and played well on the harpsichord.

John Evelyn, *Diary*, 1657

THE GUILDHALL LOTTERY

To-day Mr. Addison, Colonel Freind, and I, went to see the million lottery drawn at Guildhall. The jackanapes of bluecoat boys gave themselves such airs in pulling out the tickets, and showed white hands open to the company, to let us see there was no cheat. We dined at a country-house near Chelsea, where Mr. Addison often retires . . .

Jonathan Swift, *The Journal to Stella*, 1710

~ *16 September* ~

ARMOUR AT THE TOWER

On the morning of the 16th, his princely Grace, having obtained permission, visited the Tower of London, an old but strong castle built by Julius Caesar, where they keep the prisoners. At first we were led into a long hall, full of harness, maybe for a hundred thousand men, as one might say; but this armour was not properly arranged, nor kept clean.

Frederic Gershow, 'Diary of the Duke of Stettin's
Journey through England', 1602

THE CHAPEL ON THE HILL

Walked on a very fine morning, which made even Kensington Gardens look fresh and sylvan, to Hanbury Chapel, Notting Hill, a handsome Independent place of worship just opened, to hear Dr Vaughan preach.

George Howard, *Journals*, 1849

ZEPPELINS OVER LONDON

If you had been with me last Wednesday you could have watched the Zeppelins and the guns firing at it – as if from a private box. It was a dark night with a few stars, and the Zeppelins stood out very clearly in the searchlights. The firing went on for 20 minutes or so – many guns to the minute, mostly falling short but a few very close, and gradually it got out of range. London seemed very still, a dog could be heard barking far away; it was eerie waiting. What it must have been like to be up there! I went into the streets after; there was no panic but rather a crowding to see a wonderful sight. It was about a mile from here that the damage was done, a good few houses largely destroyed and 20 people killed and twice that badly hurt. The figures published of killed and wounded on these occasions have always been the truth (despite rumours) and it is remarkable that they are so small. That night one bomb dropped in the middle of Queen Square in Bloomsbury (the nicest old square there) smashed about 2000 windows, yet not one person damaged there. The windows just fell in or out – the effect of the bombs on the air I suppose.

J. M. Barrie, Letter to Charles Scribner, 1915

SHELTER IN THE UNDERGROUND

A friend who joined us had come back from his office by Tube; he told us that the sights in the Tube were the most extraordinary imaginable. People were there in all sorts of queer clothes. Some had rushed from their beds to the nearest Tube, carrying their wraps and even their boots in their hands; and the poor sleepy little children were wrapped up in the blankets off their beds, and were sleeping peacefully through it all. Women were dressing on the platforms, and pulling on their stockings. Babies were being given their bottles, and mothers nursing them. The staircases and platforms of the Tube Station were like a huge bedroom and 'night nursery' on that awful night. These Tube scenes take place whenever there is a raid.

Hallie Eustace Miles, *Diary*, 1916

∼ *17 SEPTEMBER* ∼

A CHELSEA CONVERSATION

Lunch with Prudey at the Continental, and she poured out her soul to me, saying I am the only intelligent girl she knows in Chelsea because I can talk of something else besides cocks and poking.

'Now you're a sensible girl,' says Prudey. 'You're the only girl I've met in Chelsea whom I really like!' I returned the compliment and we settled down to talk poking ourselves.

Prudey thinks Rupert and I ought to get married – she says we'd make a lovely couple. She had seen us going out to buy our supper the other night.

'You both looked so nice and happy, you both wore trousers and had long legs and walked in a loose floppy way. You reminded me of two fauns trotting off into the woods to play.'

'That was the day I got poked.'

'Well, no wonder you looked so nice!'

I said, 'But what about Squirrel?'

'Oh, Rupert's very bored with her, she's gone on too long. But she's very good in bed because she's half-coloured.'

Prudey likes Squirrel because she is so beautiful, and Prudey is an imitation lesbian. She likes women to look at and men for their conversation rather than the size of their cocks, that's why she likes Baron because he is so intense.

'Compared with Rupert,' she says, 'the Baron is like going up to the drawing-room after nursery tea. If you ask him an intelligent question you get an adult comeback, but if you ask Rupert he just looks at you gloomily and says "hornswaggle" or something equally unhelpful.'

After lunch, Prudey left in a taxi to go back to Oxford, with Henry Miller in a cat-box.

Half an hour later, return of Prudey and cat-box, Marylebone having been razed to the ground.

Joan Wyndham, *Diary*, 1940

THE CITY REDUCED TO RUBBLE

To get to Paddington, we ordered a taxi; it was a nightmare journey like one of Wells's terrible fantasies. Went along Mile End Road, then through City. Dislocation appalling everywhere; yawning gaps where buildings had been; immense detours, huge traffic blocks, piles of rubble, craters in street. Made me feel too sick for words.

Vera Brittain, *Diary*, 1940

A CND RALLY IN TRAFALGAR SQUARE

It rained all day, till about 3 o'c. Met John Hussey, and we went to Trafalgar Square – or as near as we could get, which was St Martin's in the Fields. The police had blocked all entrances to the sq. where the beleaguered committee was sitting it out. The Police used filthy methods of removing limp, passive people – a man dragged by one arm with his head on the ground ... a woman thrown bodily against a wall ... a police insp. saying 'if our lads have any more leave stopped, they'll be getting tougher ...' One saw the fascist, and the savagery in them start to emerge. The entire crowd that I was in was anti-Police – I didn't hear, for 2 hours, one dissident voice. One thing became abundantly clear. They hated the bomb, and they hated the uniformed bullies that enforce an unjust law. Leaders arrested were John Osborne, Shelagh Delaney and Vanessa Redgrave. All I seem to be able to do is send my miserable donations and pray for them all. Number of arrests today were 800 odd.

Kenneth Williams, *Diary*, 1961

～ 18 SEPTEMBER ～

DEER IN THE PARKS

We went into St. James's and Hyde Parks, where we saw a number of deer, which were grazing among the tame cattle close to the passers-by. In fine weather you meet a number of people on foot, especially in St. James's Park, which is the usual promenade of all who live in this part of the town.

Count Frederick Kielmansegge,
Diary of a Journey to England, 1761

DEPRESSING LONDON

After breakfast left Taplow & returned to London with Lawrence. As we approached the town, Lawrence observed, that He never returned to London from the country without feeling a depression of spirits, arising from an apprehension of finding something unpleasant, and a sense of returning from quiet to the hurry and struggles of life. I told him I had heard other persons make a similar declaration.

Joseph Farington, *Diary*, 1804

FLAMING SOUTHWARK

Took walk in evening with Ann Fox through Holywell and Wych Street, Strand; returned homeward through Soho Square where I believed the sky to be illuminated with a red light over the south east corner thereof, as also Leicester Square, which I saw was from some fire which I ascertained since to be the Oil Mustard and Saw Mills in the Grove, Guildford Street, Southwark, which totally destroyed the stock in trade.

Nathaniel Bryceson, *Diary*, 1846

ASKING A BIT MUCH

To Chelsea by cab to be witnesses at Richard and Felice's nuptials. The Chelsea Register Office is decorated rather like one of those 'no questions asked' hotels where you go when you're not married. There's a lot of Indian restaurant flock wallpaper and cheap chandeliers. As far as I can see there are no fresh flowers. You probably have to order those yourself. The short speech from the Registrar binds Richard and Felice to eternal faithfulness, which Richard thinks is 'a bit much'.

Michael Palin, *Diaries*, 1985

~ *19 SEPTEMBER* ~

INTOXICATING LONDON

Chris returned. Claud, Alastair and I spent several hours at Victoria meeting various boat trains before at last he arrived – quite unchanged except for the accretion of rather more dirt. He was wearing a Mexican ready-made suit and brought with him some books wrapped in a dirty towel and two halves of a suitcase. We went to Golders Green and drank a little beer and then went to meet my brother at the long bar at the Trocadero. We went to the Florence for dinner where we drank a lot and Chris discovered he had no money so Baldhead and Alastair had to pay for practically everything all evening. We went to the Savile and drank good port and then to the Cafe Royal and then to Oddenino's. At the Cafe Royal we found two men, one of whom Chris appeared to have met in America. We took them to drink with us at Oddenino's. Baldhead threw plates on the floor. We went to Baldhead's flat and drank more. One of the Americans turned out to be the man who had played the monster in a film called *Merry-Go-Round*. We left Baldhead and drank at a place called the Engineer's Club and then to the Savoy where the mummer was staying. I got into his bed and Claud sat on the lavatory and worked the plug with his foot for hours. The monster carried round packets of tooth-powder which he said was heroin and everyone took. We returned home at about 4 and cooked sausages – all very drunk.

Evelyn Waugh, *Diaries*, 1925

~ 20 SEPTEMBER ~

BEEFEATERS AT THE THEATRE

In the evening went to the Haymarket to see Foote . . . Their majesties were there. The King entered first, and the plaudit was universal: the Queen entered some time after. His majesty is a very good figure of a man. He seemed to be much dejected. Her majesty appears to be a small woman; her countenance carries such a sweetness, as attracts the esteem of all. She was dressed in white, with a diamond stomacher; a black cap with lustres of diamonds. A maid of honour stood behind her chair the whole time, as well as a Lord behind his majesty. I observed the King & Queen conversed as familiarly together, as we in general do in public company. Two beefeaters stood on each side of their majesties the whole of the play.

Edward Oxnard, *Diary*, 1775

ELOQUENT WATERMAN

Came to town in the morning, I think, by water; with the waterman, whose phraseology I noticed as a specimen of natural eloquence.

William Windham, *Diary*, 1784

∿ *21 September* ∿

A NERVOUS BUS DRIVER

Rehearsed Kingsway 10.30. Got the No. 1 bus home. I sat behind the driver and saw that he was young, handsome and incredibly blonde: I particularly noticed it: then at Warren Street I realised he wasn't using the indicator to turn left, so I banged on the glass & signalled the direction. He turned round, acknowledged it with a nod, and did as I bid. After, the conductress said, 'That was good of you, love, to keep your eye on him – I was upstairs getting the fares you see & he doesn't know this route at all – he's been switched from Catford, you know – only country buses – and he's not used to the West End at all – all this traffic makes him nervous.'

Kenneth Williams, *Diary*, 1965

∿ *22 September* ∿

I DON'T WANT TO GO TO CHELSEA

On Saturday night I squeezed into the gallery at the Lyceum to see Irving in 'The Bells', a melodrama which exhibits some of his most powerful acting. It was his first appearance in London since his return from the Mediterranean. The play was fearful, a perfectly horrible story. He is going to play Shylock for the first time soon. We must certainly try to go . . . I have promised to give an evening of readings and recitations at a Club in Chelsea, at Mercier's request. I hope it won't come off just yet. I *must* finish my novel.

George Gissing, Letter to his brother, 1879

SLUMMING IT IN BOOKS

I went for the first time ever to the Bermondsey Bookshop where they try so hard to hold up the flag for literature in the slums. All were very nice to me. H. W. Nevinson was charming. A lovely small company of real booklovers. I felt so very much at home.

Fred Bason, *Diary*, 1930

UNISEX LONDON

I dropped Diana [Phipps] and Gore [Vidal] at the Melchetts', who were throwing a party. From there, they intended to go on to another blow out. Night life for the young in London must be animated; there seem to be dozens of informal dinners and gatherings every week for a large circle of gay people. The youths are impatient with conventional dress, and make mock of long-established tailors, patronizing producers of novel cuts and fashions. Hair, male and female, is often worn down to the shoulders; many girls ape the boys' costumes, making it difficult to determine which is which.

David Bruce, *Diary*, 1965

~ 23 SEPTEMBER ~

PARADISE CITY

I went to see Paradise, a room in Hatton Garden furnished with a representation of all sorts of animals handsomely painted on boards or cloth, and so cut out and made to stand, move, fly, crawl, roar, and make their several cries. The man who showed it, made us laugh heartily at his formal poetry.

John Evelyn, *Diary*, 1673

GREEN-FINGERED FULHAM

Fulham. Driven by shower into grocer's shop, and amused by the wit of gardeners. Set off on foot to town, but taken up by Lord Spencer. Called on Mrs. Siddons, her mother, and Miss E. Kemble there.

William Windham, *Diary*, 1784

~ 24 SEPTEMBER ~

A HYMN ON A TIN WHISTLE

Coming out of the Café Royal into the pitch darkness of Piccadilly Circus, I heard a man playing on a tin whistle the old hymn: 'How sweet the name of Jesus sounds.' This had a half-eerie, half-emotional effect on the crowd, which was standing still to listen.

James Agate, *Journals*, 1939

REDEVELOPING GREENWICH

Turned up at Town Hall to hear the last day of Greenwich Society's objections to the Greater London Development Scheme, a bureaucratic name for a ruinous network of ringroads. The participants included the GLC party, local witnesses, the panel of inspectors with their chairman, a suave QC, and Colin Buchanan with two hats on – one of a witness for the local interests and other as the advisory planning expert for the council. They all muttered into microphones which just broadcast their proceedings to 'the floor', an audience of about twenty-five sitting on tubular steel chairs. I hadn't read Buchanan's report and had a hard time grasping the planning jargon of 'hierarchies of roads' or 'coarsening the secondary network'. Some startling figures still emerged from this ritual contest, such as that 40,000 vehicles a day pass through Greenwich between Inigo Jones's Queen's House and Wren's Naval College. This massive problem is dealt with, as always in the common-sensible way of all government inquiries. Nobody cares or believes. They have their beliefs and strategies and steer a course between partial interests. After lunch an audience of three came back to hear some residential group's objections. Boring beyond belief, mostly because of the way it was read . . . I didn't speak, though I felt like shouting. I left and walked about the small square of streets that people think of as Greenwich. The appalling din and stench made those figures seem conservative. I saw too the smug bastard who had read out a local woman's letter in a facetious voice, discrediting all she has said by his manner. He looked content with his day's work. We're wrong to leave our lives to men of affairs. Blackheath too is crossed by a cobweb of roads that are never quiet. We've having double-glazing fitted to our bedroom. So everyone who can afford it has to go into retreat against the horrors of modern life. While I've been writing the last paragraph, four jet-liners have gone over, their noise easily penetrating my study's double-windows. As one makes its approach to Heathrow over one of Europe's most densely peopled areas, another queues up behind . . .

Peter Nichols, *Diary*, 1971

～ 25 SEPTEMBER ～

FAILING TO FEED THE FOUR THOUSAND

We remained at home alone on the 25th until evening, as my brother was not quite well; we then drove to Ranelagh, where some fine fireworks were let off in the garden, in honour of the coronation. This gave us another opportunity for witnessing the crowd of people, which, before and after the fireworks, filled both the lower and upper boxes as well as the hall, which also was so crammed that it was difficult to get through the crowd, although many people remained in the garden. After the fireworks, from nine to ten, there was no tea, sugar, bread and butter, or hot water to be had, the caterers apologizing, on the ground that they had only expected two thousand people instead of the four thousand who were present.

Count Frederick Kielmansegge,
Diary of a Journey to England, 1761

THE HANDSOMEST WOMEN IN ENGLAND

Went with Messrs. Willard & Danforth to see the Park Guns fired, it being the seventeenth anniversary of the king's accession to the throne: from thence to the Guard room of St. James Palace to see the Company go to the Levee, where were the handsomest women I have seen in England, remained about an hour, & then set out for home.

Edward Oxnard, *Diary*, 1776

BUMPS AND CRUMPS

Rather a worse night of 'bumps and crumps' than usual, with several unpleasantly close. The Savile Row, Burlington Gardens area was again receiving much attention. Spent a day in the office . . . After tea went round to Huntsman to order a new uniform jacket for the winter and found most of Savile Row in ruins. Also saw bad holes in Bond St including my beloved Dollond and Aitchison who have evacuated their premises.

Lord Alanbrooke, *Diary*, 1940

⌁ 26 SEPTEMBER ⌁

COCKNEY SPARROWS

In the public footroad by Holland Park, I had accustomed the sparrows to come down pretty close to me for crumbs or pellets of bread, as I carried a piece with me when walking there every morning regularly before breakfast. Though I had been out of town nearly 4 weeks, they came down as usual this morning the moment they caught sight of me. A proof how well they know and remember individuals – I have ascertained this in the same way since living in Kensington. Moreover, whatever change I made in dress, with a cloak or without one, in a black hat or white one, seemed to make no difference in their readiness of recognition. I believe they keep as a rule to the localities they were hatched in during lifetime – and not only when pairing, incubation &c. is going on.

Alfred Domett, *Diary*, 1875

A POOR VOICE

3 p.m. today, in Bloomsbury Square, passed a street-piano on a handcart, and a lady turning the handle. Thickly veiled, but thoroughly ladylike in dress & air and manner. Placard on instrument, 'I am a lady by birth, but have lost all my property through no fault of my own.' 'Thank you very much,' she said in soft ladylike voice.

Arthur Munby, *Diary*, 1889

LONDON FICTIONS

The Illustrated London News of to-day, in an article called 'London in Fiction', has this passage: 'In such a book no inconsiderable part would be played by the Temple, which has been the happy hunting ground of so many of our novelists, from Sir Walter Scott to Mr. George Gissing.' The mention is good, but I have never made use of the Temple.

George Gissing, *Diary*, 1891

MEETING OLD FRIENDS

To London for the day. A lovely day of golden sun. I walked to M's flat and drank coffee with him. We discussed whether to remove certain passages in my diaries which may embarrass my friends. His view is that I have already caused so much offence in the first three volumes that I might as well continue in the fourth. Walked to Heraldry Today in Beauchamp Place to collect Ruvigny's European Peerage which costs £40 and weighs a ton. Then to Brooks's where Eardley was waiting for me. We lunched upstairs and although we both expressed pleasure at seeing one another our meeting was not a success. I suppose old friends get bored with one another if they do not meet often. Then I walked to Westminster Hospital to see Norah Smallwood in her ward. Very distressing. She lay with her eyes closed, mind wandering, holding my hand throughout visit. Is maddened by the noise of the ward, lies awake at night in great torment and misery. I left her feeling wretched.

James Lees-Milne, *Diary*, 1984

∼ 27 SEPTEMBER ∼

THE TUBE IN WARTIME

Dined with M. at Waldorf. To get there strange journeys in Tube. Very wet. Very poor women and children sitting on stairs (fear of raid). Also travelling in lift and liftman grumbling at them because no fear of raids, and they answering him back, and middle-class women saying to each other that if the poor couldn't keep to the regulations they ought to be forbidden the Tube as a shelter from raid. S. said he had seen dreadful sights of very poor with babies on Tube on Monday. One young woman was in labour. He asked her if she was and she said she was, and that she had got up because she was told to go with the rest. He got her taken on a stretcher to a hospital.

Arnold Bennett, *Journal*, 1917

TALKING PICTURES COME TO PICCADILLY

Tonight I went to the Piccadilly Theatre (just off Piccadilly Circus) and I saw *The Jazz Singer* which is a talking film. As you *see* the man singing you *hear* the man singing. If it wasn't that the noise sort of blares forth like 20 gramophones at once or six strong voices singing at once it would be a *miracle*. I supposed it *is* a miracle. I had front row and I got a bad headache through looking up at the screen. If this had been a real live show my seat would have been 'best in the house'. As it was talking cinema, it was *worst* in the *cinema*. Still, I ought not to say nothing, because Edgar Wallace (of all people) gave me this ticket. He said, 'Perhaps you can use this?' Ever so calm he said it. When I saw what this was I was flabbergasted with joy. All stars was there. I got eleven autographs – plus an ache in my neck and a real sickening headache. Al Jolson is the Jazz Singer. I dont like him: Sings Awfull.

Fred Bason, *Diary*, 1928

～ *28 September* ～

SOUTH LONDON PEREGRINATIONS

Inclined to rain. In the morning walked through Camberwell to New Cross, and thence all along Old Kent Road. – Evening thought over book. – Wrote to John Davidson, in praise of his [Fleet Street] 'Ecologues'. Note from Roberts.

George Gissing, *Diary*, 1893

AN AIR RAID ON LONDON

We have now had our 'first baptism of fire', for we were actually in the great Zeppelin raid.

E. F. Benson had been dining with us, and of course we had been talking about the raids. I described to him all my preparations for a Zeppelin raid: bags; dressing-case; long coat; Eustace's 'Zeppelin trousers'; and my 'Zeppelin hat', all at the door of our bedroom, ready to snatch up on our way out to the 'basement' of our flat. I showed him the photograph of our basement which appeared in the 'Daily Graphic'. He was very amused at it all, and begged to be allowed to see these grand preparations, including the 'alarm trousers'. So I showed him all the little piles at our bedroom door. He thought it very funny, and said, 'I'm afraid you will be disappointed, and that you won't have any use for all these things,' to which I replied, 'Perhaps you will have a surprise when you get home!' This was prophetic!

He left us about 10.45 p.m. and hardly had he closed the front door when there was the most awful bang, crash and explosion, close to our flat. How I flew out of the drawing-room down the passage to Eustace! The poor servants were standing at their bedroom door, trembling with horror. I told them to put on their warmest coats and thick shoes and stockings as quickly as possible and see to their money. Then we collected all the 'preparations', dressed in our Zeppelin clothes, gathered up the bags, and got the basement keys. Then with the bombs crashing to earth close to our flat, and the guns roaring all round, we began our solemn journey down to the basement in safety. When we got there we found

that someone had used all the matches and candles, and had not replaced them, and my electric torch, for the first time, refused to act. However, I remembered a secret store of candles and matches that I had hidden in a box when I prepared the basement many months ago, and I groped my way in the darkness and found them. I then lit the little lamp, which was trimmed all ready; and there we stood, wondering what would happen next. The servants were a bit hysterical, but very good, and Eustace was very calm. I think I was quite brave too. My heart beat dreadfully, but I wasn't faint at all. I felt I had all the responsibility of seeing to everything, and was the captain of our little flock, and of course this helped me not to break down. I could not exactly describe what I felt. It was such an absolutely new experience. It was frightfully solemn, too, as if the War and the Germans were at our very doors. It was so strange, on our way down the long flights of stairs, to see all the flat doors standing wide open, left so by people in their hurried flights to the lower regions. No one had even time to turn out the lights. Even I had left ours full on! Our lift porter was simply wonderful. He cheered and encouraged us all, and filled his own basement kitchen with the frightened servants.

At last the awful roar of the bombs and guns grew less, and we heard the sound of the Zeppelins going further and further away. So we ventured out of the basement and started home again. I shall never forget what we felt when we reached our flat, looking so bright and homely with all the lights on. What a tale it told, and what a lifetime it seemed since the first great bomb crashed about five minutes from our flat. Eustace hung out of the open window directly after the first bomb fell, and saw the wicked Zeppelin in the sky, like a long grey lighted train, and he saw the bombs dropping. He could not bear leaving the open window to go down to the cellar!

When we looked out of our bedroom windows after our return to the flat, the sky simply looked on fire. This was from the reflection of the fires that had been started.

Hallie Eustace Miles, *Diary*, 1915

～ 29 SEPTEMBER ～

SIN IN THE CITY

As I was walking in Holborn, observed a throng of ordinary people crowding round a chaise filled with young children of about seven years of age; inquiring the reason, was informed they were young sinners who were accustomed to go about in the evening, purloining whatever they could lay their hands on, and were going to be consigned into the hands of justice. Great pity that so many children, capable of being trained to useful employments and become blessings to society, should be thus early initiated, by the wicked unthinking parents of the lower classes in this huge over-grown metropolis, in those pernicious practices of every species of vice the human heart can be tainted with, which renders them common pests, and most commonly brings them to the halter.

Samuel Curwen,
Journal, 1780

THE DUKE OF WELLINGTON'S STATUE

Arrival of the Duke of Wellington's statue at the Triumphal Arch opposite St George's Hospital.* At half past 12 o'clock I went to the top of Grosvenor Place to see if the Duke of Wellington's statue had arrived, but it had not; but Piccadilly was lined with persons to witness its arrival, but I was obliged to get back to business in my hour. It arrived between 1 and 2 o'clock. The carriage was drawn by Goding the brewer's horses; it was said there would be 40, but an eye witness (R. Latham) counted but 29, with a man to each horse. The weight of the carriage was stated to be about 20 tons, and of the statue about 40, and to the top of his head 40 feet. On the roof of Apsley House, the Duke's residence, many persons were assembled which I suppose was the servants and their acquaintances. Coming home I peeped between the board enclosure and caught a glimpse of the horse's hind quarters by moonlight.

Nathaniel Bryceson, Diary, 1846

* The statue was removed in 1883 when the arch was moved to a new position. It is now in Aldershot, Hampshire.

LOVE IN LIVERPOOL STREET

Diana came back from Scotland in the morning. We went to a cine-matograph in the afternoon and I took her to Liverpool Street Station when she went to Newmarket. She was charming. While we were waiting for the train at Liverpool Street we drank port and ate sausage rolls in the refreshment room. I don't know whether I'm in love with her or not, I fancy not, but I have far more fun with her anyway.

Duff Cooper, *Diary*, 1915

REMEMBERING THE BLOOMSBURY SET

In the rainy morning I had gone into the Griffin in Villiers St, near to Charing Cross Station to meet E. It is perhaps to become our London equivalent of the Plaza Bar. We sat drinking, talking and eating cold beef sandwiches. She looked and was extraordinarily young. She began to talk about the figures of Bloomsbury she had known in her youth. Virginia Woolf, the Stracheys, Duncan Grant. It was a sudden outbreak of her odd, brilliant, visual talk which has been muted lately; and it exhilarates. She made me see the ingrowingness of that little Blooms-bury world; their appalling habit of writing endless letters to each other, of analysing, betraying, mocking, envying each other. She thinks that kind of intellectual, professional upper-middle-class of the Stracheys tends more to corruption than any other.

Charles Ritchie, *Diary*, 1967

～ *30 September* ～

HOGARTH'S LONDON

In the morning I drew so entirely to my satisfaction that I decided not to return in the afternoon. Instead I went to Soane's Museum in Lincoln's Inn Fields where I saw much to amuse me. The pride of the curator would appear to be a sarcophagus of great antiquity in the base-ment, but this caused me far less pleasure than the arrangements of the lighting in the rooms and such preposterous things as Shakespeare's Shrine halfway upstairs and the Bank of England Shrine in the study. They have several original Turners and Hogarths – *The Rake's Progress* and the *Election* set exquisitely composed but very ill painted.

Evelyn Waugh, *Diaries*, 1924

INSPIRED BY A BRICK STREET GENTS

I believe I have a book coming . . . Tonight I had a solitary good dinner where I usually go with My Girl & afterwards felt vaguely restless (not sexually, just restless). So I walked to the Cafe Royal & sat & read The Aran Islands (by J. M. Synge) & drank beer till about 10 & then I still felt restless, so I walked up to Piccadilly and back, went back in a gents' in Brick Street, & suddenly in the gents', I saw the three characters, the beginning, the middle & the end, & in some ways all the ideas I had.

Graham Greene, Letter to Catherine Walston, 1947

CHELSEA BOOTS

Tube to Piccadilly Circus, my sudden yen for a pair of brown Chelsea boots must go unsatisfied: none at Simpsons, and in Bond Street am told that the firm has gone out of business. Hatchard's and buy Bill Brandt's book, and an historical gossip book, *The Mistresses*, which I send to Mum at the Old Hall.

Lindsay Anderson, *Diaries*, 1966

OCTOBER

∼ 1 OCTOBER ∼

CUT-THROAT LONDON

Mr Dietrichsen, proprietor of the Royal Almanac, committed suicide by cutting his throat at his residence of the firm of Hannay and Dietrichsen, medicine warehouse, 63 Oxford Street. He was aged about 40 years.

Nathaniel Bryceson, *Diary*, 1846

AN APPALLING SPECTACLE

I saw last night what is probably the most appalling spectacle associated with the war which London is likely to provide – the bringing down in flames of a raiding Zeppelin. I was late at the office, and leaving it just before midnight was crossing to Blackfriars Bridge to get a tramcar home, when my attention was attracted by frenzied cries of 'Oh! Oh! She's hit!' from some wayfarers who were standing in the middle of the road gazing at the sky in a northern direction. Looking up the clear run of New Bridge Street and Farringdon Road I saw high in the sky a concentrated blaze of searchlights, and in its centre a ruddy glow which rapidly spread into the outline of a blazing airship. Then the searchlights were turned off and the Zeppelin drifted perpendicularly in the darkened sky, a gigantic pyramid of flames, red and orange, like a ruined star falling slowly to earth. Its glare lit up the streets and gave a ruddy tint even to the waters of the Thames. The spectacle lasted two or three minutes. It was so horribly fascinating that I felt spellbound – almost suffocated with emotion, ready hysterically to laugh or cry. When at last the doomed airship vanished from sight there arose a shout the like of which I never heard in London before – a hoarse shout of mingled execration, triumph and joy; a swelling shout that appeared to be rising from all parts of the metropolis, ever increasing in force and intensity. It was London's Te Deum for another crowning deliverance. Four Zeppelins destroyed in a month!

Michael MacDonagh, *Diary*, 1916

⁓ 2 OCTOBER ⁓

AN EXPLODING BARGE

This morning a little after five I was awakened by a strange feeling that something very heavy had fallen down. In the course of the day we heard that an explosion had taken place in a barge laden with gunpowder on the Canal in Regents Park, and great damage done to the houses in the neighbourhood. The men in charge were blown to atoms, but we have heard no particulars as yet, and no newspapers can be got.

Louisa Bain, *Diary*, 1874

THE LONDON BLACKOUT

Last night was the first night of the increased darkness of London. They say that London has not been so dark since the days of George the First. The blackness is very weird and terrifying.

Hallie Eustace Miles, *Diary*, 1915

⁓ 3 OCTOBER ⁓

WHY I LIKE LONDON

Would you know why I like London so much? Why if the world must consist of so many fools as it does, I choose to take them in the gross, and not made into separate pills, as they are prepared in the country. Besides, there is no being alone but in a metropolis: the worst place in the world to find solitude is in the country: questions grow there, and that unpleasant Christian commodity, neighbours.

Horace Walpole, Letter to Sir Horace Mann, 1743

MONEY MATTERS

People are complaining that the markets are overcharging. I went into Smithfield this morning. They were asking four shillings for long-tailed pheasants, which is sixpence more than a year ago, but the market people say there are reasons. No doubt. We also hear of higher rents. Digby, the house-agent, told me that there is a good demand for seven-roomed flats at Ravenscourt Park, electric light, all improvements, tennis, no taxes, at 50 to 80 a year. He showed me a sketch of a well-appointed six-room villa at Edmonton at ten shillings a week. I call that reasonable.

I had a whole hour with old Sir Hiram Maxim at lunch to-day at the Cafe Royal. The old man drank water and ate some sort of fancy bread that he had in a paper bag. Every now and then he would suck away at a glass contraption which he called his anti-asthma pipe. He said he had spent £17,000 in trying to make a flying machine, but the thing no sooner rose from the ground than it fell down. As for navigable balloons, he agrees with the late Duke of Argyll that man can never overcome the natural laws that condemn all buoyant bodies to an inertia that makes them useless.

R. D. Blumenfeld, *R.D.B.'s Diary*, 1900

∼ 4 *October* ∼

A TIMELESS HEIRLOOM

Overheard in the Strand: 'And then she died, the clock came into our family, and hasn't lost a bleeding second since.'

James Agate, *Journals*, 1937

~ 5 OCTOBER ~

VISITING ST PAUL'S AND SEVEN DIALS

I went to St. Paul's to see the choir, now finished as to the stone work, and the scaffold struck both without and within, in that part. Some exceptions might perhaps be taken as to the placing columns on pilasters at the east tribunal. As to the rest it is a piece of architecture without reproach. The pulling out the forms, like drawers, from under the stalls, is ingenious. I went also to see the building beginning near St. Giles's, where seven streets make a star from a Doric pillar placed in the middle of a circular area; said to be built by Mr. Neale, introducer of the late lotteries, in imitation of those at Venice, now set up here, for himself twice, and now one for the State.

John Evelyn, *Diary*, 1694

THE GREAT ROTHERHITHE PUDDING

Received the last sheet of the first volume of Mr. Hayward's *British Muse*; with him heard at his house the account of Austin, the ink powder man, noted for his fireworks; also the great pudding he made for his customers; but more especially the pudding which about twelve or thirteen years since he baked ten feet deep in the Thames near Rotherhithe for a wager, by enclosing it in a great tin pan, and that in a great sack of lime; and after in about two hours and a half it was taken up, and eaten with much liking, being only a little overbaked. There was above an 100l. won upon this experiment.

William Oldys, *Diary*, 1737

FLAT OUT IN BLOOMSBURY

On Tuesday we look at a flat we've been offered in King's Bench Walk – very nice – but not so near you as one which we saw in Taviton Street – or another in Tavistock Place. But that had been let already when we got there. King's Bench Walk is very romantic though, – panelled, – and absurdly cheap – with plane-trees and pigeons outside. I shall spend all January and February in London at any rate – perhaps longer – with weekends here [Sevenoaks]. Will that be nice, do you think? Will I see you? will we go on more London expeditions?

Vita Sackville-West, Letter to Virginia Woolf, 1929

A JAMES BOND FILM PREMIERE

We went to Flemings at 7:45 for drinks and sandwiches. There was a galaxy of well-known people, including the spry 88-year-old Somerset Maugham, whose current memoirs in the Sunday Express are shocking and titillating readers. By 8:45 we were all seated at the London Pavilion, on Piccadilly Circus, for the premiere of the picture done from Ian Fleming's 'Dr No'. It was a tribute to Ian and Ann that the house was packed with celebrities from the artistic, political, social and other of the numerous worlds in London. I thought the first half of it excellent, with a series of fast, accomplished murders, as well as the spectacle of a live tarantula walking over James Bond's naked body. Fleming said the hire of this tarantula cost the producers 30 pounds. The second half of the movie took great liberties with the text of the book.

David Bruce, *Diary*, 1962

～ 6 OCTOBER ～

A PICTURE POSTCARD SCENE

This morning, as I walked through the Green Park in an October mist, it occurred to me that the sheep grazing there, and the soldiers practising flag-signals, would, if seen by me in an unfamiliar city, have constituted for me a memorable picture of pure quaintness. Then, walking in the Strand as the sun overpowered the fog, what mellow picturesqueness was there in the vista of churches, backed by the roofs of the Law Courts and further away a tower for all the world like the Beffroi at Bruges. Observed five hundred miles away, a scene less striking than this would be one to talk about and grow enthusiastic over, one to buy photographs of . . . But it happens to be in London.

Arnold Bennett, *Journals*, 1897

GOING UNDERGROUND

Yerkes, the projector of the new Charing Cross, Euston, and Hampstead electric underground, said to me that in spite of the opposition which he meets at every turn he proposes to go through with it. He has secured the backing of some large American financiers to the extent of £30,000,000, and he predicted to me that a generation hence London will be completely transformed; that people will think nothing of living twenty or more miles from town, owing to electrified trains. He also thinks that the horse omnibus is doomed. Twenty years hence, he says, there will be no horse omnibuses in London. Although he is a very shrewd man, I think he is a good deal of a dreamer.

R. D. Blumenfeld, *R.D.B.'s Diary*, 1900

GREENWICH PARK SEX PESTS

Thelma went walking on her own while I mowed the front lawn. When she came back, I was clipping the hedges. 'Where did you go?' 'Greenwich Park. I got picked up by the usual sexual maniac.' 'Good. Who's he?' 'What d'you mean?' 'The usual sexual maniac.' 'I don't mean always the same one. I mean there always *is* one.' He'd told her about the Argentine ship moored at Greenwich Reach and the sailors looking for girls, but he wasn't interested in that for its own sake, only taking pictures of them. He'd been busy at The Mall too, taking photos of the state visit of Emperor Hirohito, but no, he wasn't interested in him as such, more the Girls – what d'you call them? He'd forgot but they did things for men. Geisha Girls, that's it, yes. He enjoyed photographing girls. Hirohito's visit has aroused some dormant jingoism. The tree he planted in Kew was torn up by the next day and a note left: 'They did not die in vain.' Our neighbour heard a man on a train: 'I reckon there's them that died is turning in their flipping graves.'

Peter Nichols, *Diary*, 1971

～ 7 OCTOBER ～

SAUCE FOR THE GOOSE

All this time my Lord was in London where he had all and infinite great resort coming to him. He went much abroad to Cocking and Bowling Alleys to plays and horse races and commended by all the world. I stayed in the country having many times a sorrowful and heavy heart and being condemned by most folks because I would not consent to the agreement so as I may truly say like an owl in the desert.

Lady Anne Clifford, Countess of Dorset, afterwards
Countess of Pembroke, *Diary*, 1617

CURIOUS DETAILS ABOUT THE CHOLERA

Walked into London. Raised £11; bought Lucy some things, and self a pair of shoes. Called on Thomas. Heard from him some curious details of the cholera, which raged furiously round his two streets, but did not molest them. Bodies taken from Middlesex Hospital in vans. In the pest-stricken streets groups of women and children frantic for their relations taken off. Police and others with stretchers running about. Undertakers as common as other people in the streets running about with coffins, like lamplighters. Hearses with coffins outside as well as in; people following in cabs. One funeral consisted of a cab, with coffin atop, and people inside. Thomas and family all well . . .

Ford Madox Brown, *Diary*, 1854

BLACK POWER IN NORTH KENSINGTON

In the evening I went to a North Kensington Labour Party meeting, the first one held there, I think, since the '66 election, and some Black Power people were there. They just laughed at the speaker before me. When I got up they began shouting. So I said, 'Look, I don't want to make a speech. I make about three a week and I would much rather listen to you.' So they came forward and sat in the front, a Black Power man abused me and said I was a lord and the British working movement was bourgeois and so on, and it became interesting after that.

Tony Benn, *Diary*, 1968

~ 8 OCTOBER ~

SHAKESPEARE AND HIS FELLOW ACTORS PROMISE TO BE GOOD NEIGHBOURS

Where my now company of players have been accustomed for the better exercise of their quality, and for the service of her majesty if need require, to play this winter time within the city at the Cross Keys in Gracious [Gracechurch] Street; these are to require and pray your lordship (the time being such as, thanks be to God, there is now no danger of the sickness) to permit and suffer them so to do. The which I pray you rather to do for that they have undertaken to me that, where heretofore they began not their plays till towards four o'clock, they will now begin at two and have done between four and five and will not use any drums or trumpets at all for the calling of people together and shall be contributories to the poor of the parish where they play, according to their abilities.

Henry Carey, 1st Baron Hunsdon, Letter
to the Lord Mayor of London, 1594

VAN GOGH ON LONDON SUBURBS

The suburbs of London have a peculiar beauty; between the small houses and gardens there are open places covered with grass and usually with a church or school or poorhouse between the trees and shrubbery in the middle, and it can be so beautiful there when the sun goes down red in the light evening mist. It was like that yesterday evening, and later I did so wish that you had seen the streets of London when it began to grow dark and the street-lamps were lit and everyone was going home, it was obvious from everything that it was Saturday evening, and in all that hustle and bustle there was peace, one felt, as it were, the need for and joy at the approach of Sunday. Oh those Sundays and how much is done and striven for on those Sundays, it's such a relief to those poor neighbourhoods and busy streets. It was dark in the City, but it

. . .Van Gogh once lived in Hackford Road Brixton . . .

was a lovely walk past all those churches along the way. Close to the Strand I found an omnibus that brought me a long way, it was already rather late. I rode past Mr. Jones's little church and saw another in the distance where light was still burning so late. I headed for it and found it to be a very beautiful little Roman Catholic church in which a couple of women were praying. Then I came to that dark park I already wrote to you about, and from there I saw in the distance the lights of Isleworth and the church with the ivy and the cemetery with the weeping willows on the banks of the Thames.

Vincent Van Gogh, Letter to his brother Theo, 1876

AWFUL, BLINKING, HYPNOTISING VIDEO

A depressing foray to Tottenham Court Road/Oxford Street to buy a new 8 mill film to show at Tom's party. Depressing because of the domination in that corner of London of the awful, blinking, hypnotising spell of video . . . There is video equipment everywhere – video films, video games – and it's like a giant amusement arcade providing a sort of temporary electronic alternative to listlessness. Lights flash and disembodied voices bark out of electronic chess games and football games. There doesn't seem to be much joy around here.

Michael Palin, *Diaries*, 1980

～ *9 OCTOBER* ～

EVELYN TAKES A TUMBLE

I went with Mrs. Godolphin and my wife to Blackwall, to see some Indian curiosities; the streets being slippery, I fell against a piece of timber with such violence that I could not speak nor fetch my breath for some space: being carried into a house and let blood, I was removed to the water-side and so home, where, after a day's rest, I recovered. This being one of my greatest deliverances, the Lord Jesus make me ever mindful and thankful!

John Evelyn, *Diary*, 1676

READING THE RENT ACT

On our way to Lady Rawson's, in passing through George St. Portman Square, I pointed out to Russell, as I had done once before to Tom, the house, No. 44, where I first lodged when I came to London. Seeing a bill on the house of lodgings to let, I took advantage of it to have a peep at my own old two-pair-of-stair quarters, and found that the two rooms were to be let for sixteen shillings a week, which shows they have not gone down in the world since I occupied them, as I paid for the two but half a guinea a week, having for some time inhabited the front room alone at seven shillings a week, and it was in that room that the first proof sheet I ever received (i.e. of my Anacreon*) was put into my hands by Tom Hume.

Thomas Moore, *Journal*, 1836

* Moore's first published work, a translation of the Greek poet Anacreon.

ACTORS WORSHIP

From the zoo down to Covent Garden. Take them into St Paul's – the actors' church. There on the wall of the church is an elegantly simple plaque to Noël Coward – and this the day after I read in his diaries his version of the Bible story – 'A monumental balls-up'.

Michael Palin, *Diaries*, 1983

∼ 10 OCTOBER ∼

A VISIT TO A PRISON

With Shortgrave to Bridewell. Many wenches punisht.

Robert Hooke, *Diary*, 1673

PAY FOR PEELERS

Thanks for your suggestions in regard to the Metropolitan Police. When I fixed the present rate of pay, I fixed it under an impression that it might be necessary to raise it, but I felt quite sure that it would be much easier to raise than reduce the rates of pay. I cannot say that the short experience I have hitherto had has confirmed my first impression. I will not as yet speak decidedly on the point, but I am far from being prepared to admit that the improvement of the situation of a common police constable by giving him more money, would increase the efficiency of the establishment.

Sir Robert Peel, Letter to John Wilson Croker, 1829

CHOLERA IN LAMBETH

I went over some of my former beat in Lambeth, and was glad to find two cholera patients I had seen before were recovered.

George Howard, *Journals*, 1849

AN UNUSUAL AUCTION IN NW3

Viewed a sale of stuffed animals in Hampstead Town Hall. An odd sight, this immobile menagerie, the dogs especially looking as though they were only bluffing, like the attendants at Madame Tussaud's, and would any moment bound off their stands and create havoc. The range was from assassin bugs to elephant heads by way of pangolins, a duck-billed platypus and what the auctioneer called in error 'a stimulated dodo'. Next day I bought a case of storks and egrets (too much at £450), a swan and a brace of cock pheasants. The bidders were as funny as the lots, fringey dealers, half-and-half arty and downmarket commercial, with long hair, outdated clothes and greedy expressions. One man, in green trousers and a yellow sombrero, was as colourful as the bird of paradise he bought. The keenest bidders were a Highlander in a kilt and the rest of that hideous rig, and a lepidopterist who wore two pairs of glasses at a time.

Peter Nichols, *Diary*, 1972

～ 11 OCTOBER ～

LOST ON REGENT'S STREET

'Are you lost or eternally saved?' This was on a sandwich board being carried out in Regent's Street by a young man. I frowned at it, because it isn't really right to ask such intimate questions in public. The young man smiled. 'It's all right,' he said. 'It ain't meant for you.'

J. R. Ackerley, *Diary*, 1950

HOUSEHUNTING IN CANONBURY

I am hardening towards a house in the country, mainly because at least one has space there. Eliz fancied a house in Canonbury – 15 Canonbury Road – fine in itself, but the road is used by long-distance lorries and it seems insane to me, to choose such a position when one will be at home all day trying to write.

John Fowles, *Journals*, 1963

TWO WHEELS GOOD, FREE WHEELING BETTER

Beautiful soft peach evening, freewheeled all the way home, right down Portobello. The pleasure of cycling.

Brian Eno, *Diary*, 1995

～ *12 OCTOBER* ～

THE BLITZ SPIRIT

James [Pope-Hennessy] is writing a book called History Under Fire for which I am doing the photographs. Besides the vandalistic damage, we must show the tenacity and courage of the people, and we do not have to look far. Signs are posted: 'We have no glass, but business continues.' As soon as the rubbish is cleared away, the notice appears 'Open as usual.'

Londoners have had one month so far, and they must look forward to a whole winter of it. The planes come each night at dusk. One hears the drone, then bangs, crunch, zumphs of the bombs. The AA gunfire, which is gay and heartening, is like a firework fiesta: and then an interval. During the lull one tries to read a book, but one's thoughts wander, and soon the hum of more approaching planes is heard. The zumphs come perilously near, and one leaves the chair for a vantage point under the lintel of a door. The restless night continues.

By degrees many people have grown accustomed to being frightened. For myself, most evenings I have beetled off to the Dorchester. There the noise outside is drowned with wine, music and company – and what a mixed brew we are! Cabinet ministers and their self-consciously respectable wives; hatchet-jawed, iron-grey brigadiers; calf-like airmen off duty; tarts on duty, actresses (also), déclassé society people, cheap musicians and motor-car agents. It could not be more ugly and vile, and yet I have not the strength of character to remain, like Harold Acton, with a book.

In the infernos of the underground the poor wretches take up their positions for the night's sleep at four o'clock in the afternoon. The winter must surely bring epidemics of flu, even typhoid. The prospect is not cheery, and Churchill makes no bones about the ardours of the future. The electric trains are out of order and hardly a clock has its face intact. Yet the life of the city manages, more or less, to continue as if in normal times. Nothing can really dash the spirits of the English people, who love to grumble, and who, in spite of their complaints, are deeply confident of victory.

Cecil Beaton, Diary, 1940

NOTHING SURPRISES ME ANY MORE

Reports of the Paddington rail disaster include surreal accounts of rescue workers deafened by a cacophony of abandoned mobile phones ringing like mad: the inappropriate racket of novelty arpeggio trills and vain personalized 'amusing' melody chimes among the carnage and flames giving the tragedy a gut-wrenchingly modern pathos. A sick new homage to The Unknown Commuter: They Couldn't Get A Good Signal. The real tragedy is, of course, Jilly Cooper escaping unscathed. On the platform at Highgate Tube station, the woman standing in front of me tries to throw herself into the path of the incoming train.

The guard who gently leads her away by the arm does so with such nonchalance and sighs of resignation that everyone else on the platform assumes she must be a regular at this sort of thing. Then goes back to talking about how great it is that both escalators are working again.

Nothing surprises me any more.

Dickon Edwards, Diary, 1999

～ *13 October* ～

HIGH WATERS AT KEW

The fote bote for the ferry at Kew was drowned and six persons, by the negligens of the ferryman overwhelming the boat uppon the roap set there to help, by reason of the vehement and high waters.

John Dee, *Diary*, 1579

HANGED, DRAWN AND QUARTERED IN CHARING CROSS

To my Lord's in the morning, where I met with Captain Cuttance but my Lord not being up I went out to Charing Cross, to see Major-general Harrison hanged, drawn, and quartered; which was done there, he looking as cheerful as any man could do in that condition. He was presently cut down, and his head and heart shown to the people, at which there was great shouts of joy. It is said, that he said that he was sure to come shortly at the right hand of Christ to judge them that now had judged him; and that his wife do expect his coming again. Thus it was my chance to see the King beheaded at White Hall, and to see the first blood shed in revenge for the blood of the King at Charing Cross.

Samuel Pepys, *Diary*, 1660

SHELLEY DISPLEASED

Alarm. Determine to quit London; send for £5 from Hookham. Change our resolution. Go to the play. The extreme depravity and disgusting nature of the scene; the inefficacy of acting to encourage or maintain the delusion. The loathsome sight of men personating characters which do not and cannot belong to them. Shelley displeased with what he saw of Kean. Return. Alarm. We sleep at the Stratford Hotel.

Mary Shelley, *Journal*, 1814

~ *14 October* ~

A GREAT WILD FIRE

Bought eight prints (portraits) at printsellers, Princes Street, Soho – 8d. A destructive fire broke out about 5 o'clock this morning at the Red Lion Public House, Great Wild Street, Lincolns Inn Fields, which entirely destroyed the stock in trade and furniture and must have burnt very fierce . . . Went to see it in the evening.

Nathaniel Bryceson, *Diary*, 1846

TEA ON THE STRAND

Dull and rainy, warm. Did nothing. In afternoon to Savoy Theatre ('Utopia') with Miss Collet, who had invited us. Tea afterwards in the Strand. Had to take a cab home from Waterloo, for fear little Grosbey would be left too long alone with the girl.

George Gissing, *Diary*, 1893

~ *15 October* ~

THE CLOSING OF THE GREAT EXHIBITION

Went to the Crystal Palace to witness the closing scene of the Great Exhibition. An immense crowd of thirty or forty thousand spectators. The Prince was very much applauded when entering and speaking, and on going away. I stayed some time after the ceremony, and wandered about the building, already stripped of many of its treasures; a melancholy sight!

John Cam Hobhouse, *Diary*, 1851

GERMANS VERY ACTIVE

The Germans very active last night in these parts. Besides burning out the Carlton Club, they hit the Monaco, Burton's and the church in Piccadilly, landed one in St James's Square, one at the bottom of the steps at the bottom end of Regent St, where they unfortunately killed Admiral Tower, who was my chief Naval Liaison Officer. Held a conference at St Paul's for Army Commanders lasting from 10 a.m. to 1.30 p.m. Started with Intelligence summary of invasion prospects . . . After lunch Dill came and gave an excellent talk on the world situation. Tonight the Germans are hard at it again, but up to now not quite so near as last night.

Lord Alanbrooke, *Diary*, 1940

~ *16 October* ~

SUBLIME FIRE

Good God! I am just returned from the terrific burning of the Houses of Parliament. Mary and I went in a cab, and drove over the bridge. From the bridge it was sublime. We alighted, and went into a room of a public-house, which was full. The feeling among the people was extraordinary: jokes and radicalism universal. If Ministers had heard the shrewd sense and intelligence of these drunken remarks! I hurried Mary away.

Benjamin Haydon, *Journals*, 1834

DARKNESS FALLS OVER LONDON

Theatres in the evening are mostly going to close owing to London being in darkness, by reducing street lights. Closing hours for public-houses, Clubs, restaurants for intoxicating drinks to be 10 p.m.; at Woolwich 9, but at Woolwich and Greenwich night workers may be served alcoholic drinks with meal between 1 a.m. and 2 a.m.

Viscount Sandhurst, *From Day to Day*, 1914

THE PROMENADE AT THE SERPENTINE

Before taking her to catch her train at Paddington, walked for a while in Hyde Park, joining the promenade at the Serpentine. Horses on Rotten Row, sailing dinghies, anglers casting lines. Dan inevitably falling in. Mum complained of a light breeze that ruffled her perm.

Peter Nichols, *Diary*, 1971

A HURRICANE HITS THE CAPITAL

In the grounds of Kenwood House there is devastation. Paths are almost impassable and an avenue of limes which forms one picturesque approach to the terrace in front of Kenwood has been almost totally uprooted. There is no one else around now, and being in the middle of this dreadful damage is quite eerie. One thing's for certain – the reassuring landscape I've run through for eight years has been drastically changed. It'll never be the same again. On the news I hear that Kew Gardens have suffered enormous losses, which cannot be made good within a lifetime. To dinner at Terry J's. The impressive avenue of Camberwell Grove is a shambles, with two cars completely crushed . . . Home, past the remainders of what the radio is at long last admitting was a hurricane. Britain's worst since 1703.

Michael Palin, *Diaries*, 1987

∽ 17 OCTOBER ∽

MANGLED QUARTERS

Scot, Scroop, Cook, and Jones, suffered for reward of their iniquities at Charing Cross, in sight of the place where they put to death their natural prince, and in the presence of the King his son, whom they also sought to kill. I saw not their execution, but met their quarters, mangled, and cut, and reeking, as they were brought from the gallows in baskets on the hurdle. Oh, the miraculous providence of God!

John Evelyn, *Diary*, 1660

BURNING OF THE HOUSES OF PARLIAMENT

The two Houses of Parliament were burned down last night. Both were completely consumed, but I am happy to say that Westminster Hall has escaped. Not so, however, the fine tapestry in the Painted Chamber in the House of Lords, commemorating the defeat of the Spanish Armada, which has been entirely destroyed. I visited the scene of devastation today; but what with the crowd, the smoke, the mud, and the police, who keep you at a respectful distance, I failed in carrying away any very definite idea of how matters stand. There are acres of tottering walls and sashless windows, but whether the ruin is such as will admit of meas-

ures of repairs, or will entail the entire re-building of the structure, no person can possibly form an idea, from the point of observation to which the general public is admitted.

William Archer Shee, *My Contemporaries*, 1834

ATTITUDES TO AMERICANS IN LONDON

Read an article in the *Guardian* by a particularly paranoid American playwright, Ms Carol Gould, who's convinced London is currently a hotbed of anti-American feeling. It's taken from a right-wing website, so one should really bear that in mind.

Citing an encounter with a *London minicab driver* as an example of blanket consensus rather undermines her argument . . . I have heard the occasional anti-US arguments starting up between strangers when an American accent is overheard, but these were entirely on Night Buses, where the speakers were audibly intoxicated, and are therefore as much an index of general local feeling as the rantings of cab drivers. I for one adore the company of Americans in London. They are so less guarded and reserved than the British, so less shifty and bitter, and they have such better teeth.

Dickon Edwards, *Diary*, 2004

∼ *18 October* ∼

LONDON IN THE RAIN

Very wet morning. Went to New Tottenham Court Chapel, Grafton Street, Tottenham Court Road, in consequence of the weather preventing me going to my regular church. The rain descended in such torrents that I was obliged to wear two coats and carry umbrella likewise; even then I returned home wet, it raining without ceasing. At home all the afternoon reading history Queen Anne etc. *After tea had Ann up as usual. Carried on the same game as heretofore.** Took walk in evening with Ann through Fleet Street etc; returned home quarter past 9 o'clock.

Nathaniel Bryceson, *Diary*, 1846

* For an explanation of the italics, see page 336.

DOG WALKING AND DOUBLE LIVES IN BARNES

I took Queenie to Barnes Common by train this evening. I had never taken her to the common that way before, and it transforms the walk from prose to poetry. It sets one down in the middle of the common. One emerges through a stone entrance, like the entrance to a castle or a church, into the midst of great beeches and chestnuts: one emerges into the country. It is wonderfully romantic and pleasure is given even before one leaves the station, for a single tree, a plane tree, grows out of the centre of the middle platform. It is only one station from Putney, five minutes, and I have often thought how much I would like it to be my station, in summer to emerge into such cool green shade, in autumn, as now, to be greeted by the delicious smells from the thick carpet of fallen leaves. It is to this station that my father used clandestinely to come from time to time, on a Saturday or Sunday afternoon, from Richmond where we lived until he died in 1929. He came there because he had a second family, of which we knew nothing, a mistress and three daughters, and had housed them in Sheen, on the border of the common. When he felt he could do so without arousing suspicion he

would 'take the dogs for a walk'; the walk he took them was to Richmond station, thence by train to Barnes, a few stops farther on. No one
knew. He would emerge at this station, this tall distinguished-looking
man, and walk through the trees to the house where his mistress and
three young daughters lived. They did not know he was their father.
They never did know it while he was alive. They knew him as an uncle,
Uncle Bodger. His name was Roger. He was a strange man.

J. R. Ackerley, *Diary*, 1948

THE ASKING PRICE

Another house – perhaps. 44 Southwood Lane, Highgate. It's a 1780
peasant's cottage, very small, but pretty. £7,500.

John Fowles, *Journals*, 1963

∼ *19 OCTOBER* ∼

NOT NEAT ENOUGH FOR LIMEHOUSE

At the office all the morning, and at noon Mr. Coventry, who sat with
us all the morning, and Sir G. Carteret, Sir W. Pen, and myself, by coach
to Captain Marshe's, at Limehouse, to a house that hath been their
ancestors for this 250 years, close by the lime-house which gives the
name to the place. Here they have a design to get the King to hire a
dock for the herring busses, which is now the great design on foot, to
lie up in. We had a very good and handsome dinner, and excellent wine.
I not being neat in clothes, which I find a great fault in me, could not
be so merry as otherwise, and at all times I am and can be, when I am
in good habitt, which makes me remember my father Osborne's rule
for a gentleman to spare in all things rather than in that. So by coach
home, and so to write letters by post, and so to bed.

Samuel Pepys, *Diary*, 1661

A WOUNDED MAN ON THE DOORSTEP

Returning home* from dinner with Madame de Stael, I found a man sleeping upon the doorsteps; our servants called to the watchman to take charge of him. The threshold of the door was all covered with blood, which had been running from the wounds in his head. The poor man had been ill-treated in the streets, he had knocked loudly at our door for assistance, having seen a light. At last the watchmen carried him away upon a stretcher, that I made them make of a door which our men had given them.

Mary Berry, *Journal*, 1813

* To North Audley Street, Mayfair.

～ 20 OCTOBER ～

THE LOT OF LONDON POSTMEN

My car arrived at 8.15 a.m. and I was at the Office by 8.40, hours before anyone else. Appointments had been made with several more directors. Mr George Downes, Director, London Postal Region, has 52,000 postmen under him and of course has felt the main impact of the recent pay dispute. We discussed the need for improved working conditions for London postmen, which he said were very bad in parts. He also said it was the custom to ask the Lord Mayor of London and the Sheriffs to Mount Pleasant just before Christmas.

I said I was in favour of also inviting the Chairman of the LCC [London County Council] and would like to do this. The Director General, who was sitting in, said this might not be popular with the Lord Mayor.

Tony Benn, *Diary*, 1964

～ *21 OCTOBER* ～

VERDANT BLACKFRIARS

Rode over Battersea Bridge and across the fields to Blackfriars.

William Windham, *Diary*, 1797

LONDON IMPROVING

Mr Dowie, the American evangelist, tells his audiences that London is the wickedest city the world has ever known, and that it becomes more ribald and drunken every day. He knows nothing about it. I have frequently noticed that London improves year by year. It is a perfect fairyland compared with ten years ago. I remember when Tottenham Court Road and the Strand were impossible after eight p.m. I walked with D'Oyly Carte from the Grand Hotel at Charing Cross at nine o'clock last night (Saturday), as far as Savoy Hill, always the worst part of the Strand. We counted only nine men and five women who were unsteady with drink, and in not one instance were we molested; which shows that London is improving instead of going backward.

R. D. Blumenfeld, *R.D.B.'s Diary*, 1900

～ *22 OCTOBER* ～

SPIES AND CEMENT FLOORS

Looked in at Devonshire House to see D. about motors. London agog between German waiters and Zeppelins. The Admiralty have charge of air guarding. Some apprehension that while Zeppelins may do some damage, Winston shells in pursuit may do more. There is one big gun in Green Park in front of the Turf Club . . .

The town is mad about cement floors and spies. One near Marble Arch reported at Cinema Show place and found to have been laid by the Lord Chamberlain's architect providing for possible concerts . . .

All the Germans in Hotel Restaurants having been discharged, there are 2,000 of them unemployed in and about Shaftesbury Avenue.

Viscount Sandhurst, *From Day to Day*, 1914

∼ *23 October* ∼

A PROPOSAL FOR LISMORE CIRCUS

At 8.00 I went to a Gospel Oak meeting. There are quite a number of consultative meetings held in and around Oak Village, as the whole area is being subjected to such massive redevelopment. In 1951 the first redevelopment in Gospel Oak was Barrington Court – by Powell and Moya. It's a long, ten-storey block, but it is as good as many present-day designs, and better than most. The West Kentish Town development followed in the 1950s – it's not picturesque, but it is low-rise and friendly.

Then a progressive deterioration of architectural standards, which reached its nadir in the appalling block that borders Mansfield Road and is known locally as the Barracks. It is without charm, without style, without any beauty whatsoever – it is essentially a mathematical achievement, a result of juggling a lot of people with a little money, stymied as the Camden planners are now by the general abandonment of high-rise blocks.

Some of the new occupants were at the St Martin's Church Hall tonight to hear proposals for Lismore Circus renovation and for the next part of the Gospel Oak scheme.

The meeting was entirely staffed by stereotypes. If one had written a play with these characters in it would have been called facile and uninventive. Mr and Mrs Brick of Kiln Place – a physically formidable pair and both with plenty to say forcibly and clearly. The popularist vicar, who couldn't resist occasional semantic jokes; the hard-line Marxist in a nondescript coat but with a fine, strong, lean face, worn hard and lined in struggles for the proletariat. The woolly-headed liberals, the gentle, embarrassed architect, and even the local hippy, a squatter who berated the platform from the back of the room for being cynical and hypocritical in even having this meeting at all.

Notes that stuck in the mind – a small Andy Capp-like figure telling the platform with a feeling of frustrated sadness, 'Living round here is bloody terrible.' The soft-voiced, inoffensive architect taking on the wrath of the gathering as well as its repartee. He was talking of how, even when the builders were working, 'Lismore Circus retained its trees, its flowers, even squirrels . . .' – 'and rats' came a voice from the audience. The lack of enthusiasm for the plans from the audience was understandable, but very, very sad. For here was an enlightened borough, with a good and humane record, selling something that people didn't want in the most democratic way possible.

Michael Palin, *Diary*, 1972

∿ 24 OCTOBER ∿

CARVING OUT A DATE FOR DINNER

Had bread and cheese dinner at the Gun Tavern, Pimlico. Tap room lately fitted up with seats and partitions; cut date 1846 in the partition.

Nathaniel Bryceson, *Diary*, 1846

A DAY'S WALK

Went to Mark Lane by train, then walked over the Tower Bridge, and back along Lower Thames Street to London Bridge, up to Whitechapel, St Paul's, Fleet Street, and Charing Cross, and so home.

Near Reilly's Tavern, I saw a pavement artist who had drawn a loaf with the inscription in both French and English: 'This is easy to draw but hard to earn.' A baby's funeral trotted briskly over the Tower Bridge among Pink's jam waggons, carts carrying any goods from lead pencils and matches to bales of cotton and chests of tea.

In the St Catherine's Way there is one part like a deep railway cutting, the whole of one side for a long way, consisting of the brick wall of a very tall warehouse with no windows in it and beautifully curved and producing a wonderful effect. Walked past great blocks of warehouses and business establishments – a wonderful sight; and everywhere bacon factors, coffee roasters, merchants. On London Bridge, paused to feed the sea-gulls and looked down at the stevedores. Outside Billingsgate Market was a blackboard on an easel – for market prices – but instead some one had drawn an enormously enlarged chalk picture of a cat's rear and tail with anatomical details . . .

Loitered at a dirty little Fleet Street bookshop where Paul de Kock's *The Lady with the Three Pairs of Stays* was displayed prominently beside a picture of Oscar Wilde.

In Fleet Street, you exchange the Whitechapel sausage restaurants for Taverns with 'snacks at the bar,' and the chestnut roasters, with their buckets of red-hot coals, for Grub Street camp followers, selling *L'Indépendance Belge* or pamphlets entitled *Why We Went to War.*

In the Strand you may buy war maps, buttonhole flags, etc., etc. I bought a penny stud. One shop was turned into a shooting gallery at three shots a penny where the Inner Temple Barristers in between the case for the defence and the case for the prosecution could come and keep their eye in against the time the Germans come.

Outside Charing Cross Station I saw a good-looking, well-dressed woman in mourning clothes, grinding a barrel organ . . .

W. N. P. Barbellion, *The Journal of a Disappointed Man*, 1914

∼ 25 October ∼

LAYING THE FOUNDATION STONE
FOR THE MANSION HOUSE

I afterwards put on the Scarlet Gown and went to Stocks Market, attended by several Gentlemen of the Committee appointed to erect a Mansion House for the Lord Mayor of this City, in their Gowns, preceded by the City Musick and my Officers, with the Sunday Sword and Mace, and laid the chief corner stone of the said Mansion House, and placed therein a copper plate with an inscription engraved thereon, and afterwards returned home.

Micajah Perry, *Lord Mayor Perry's Diary*, 1739

DEATH OF GEORGE II

His Majesty George II died 1760 at Kensington, in the 77th year of his age, and 34th of his reign, taken from a people by whom he was sincerely loved, fortunately for himself, at the most shining period o' his life. 'Twas astonishing to see the amazing consternation, bustle, and confusion an event like this, quite unexpected, made in a metropolis such as London. I happened to be out that morn before it was known: it was published about twelve, when instantly the streets were in a buzz, the black cloth carrying about, and in half an hour every shop was hung with the appendages of mourning . . .

Mrs Philip Lybbe Powys, *Diary*, 1760

A POET WALKS A LADY HOME

Since I wrote thus far I have met with that same Lady again, whom I saw at Hastings and whom I met when we were going to the English Opera. It was in a street which goes from Bedford Row to Lamb's Conduit Street. – I passed her and turned back: she seemed glad of it – glad to see me, and not offended at my passing her before. We walked on towards Islington, where we called on a friend of hers who keeps a Boarding School . . . As we went along, sometimes through shabby, sometimes through decent Streets, I had my guessing at work, not knowing what it would be, and prepared to meet any surprise. First it ended at this House at Islington: on parting from which I pressed to attend her home. She consented, and then again my thoughts were at work what it might lead to, though now they had received a sort of genteel hint from the Boarding School. Our Walk ended in 34 Glouces-ter Street, Queen Square – not exactly so, for we went upstairs into her sitting-room, a very tasty sort of place with Books, Pictures, a bronze Statue of Buonaparte, Music, æolian Harp, a Parrot, a Linnet, a Case of choice Liqueurs, etc. etc. She behaved in the kindest manner – made me take home a Grouse for Tom's dinner. Asked for my address for the purpose of sending more game . . . I expect to pass some pleasant hours with her now and then: in which I feel I shall be of service to her in matters of knowledge and taste: if I can I will . . . Notwithstanding your Happiness and your recommendation I hope I shall never marry.

Though the most beautiful Creature were waiting for me at the end of a Journey or a Walk; though the Carpet were of Silk, the Curtains of the morning Clouds; the chairs and Sofa stuffed with Cygnet's down; the food Manna, the Wine beyond Claret, the Window opening on Winander mere, I should not feel – or rather my Happiness would not be so fine, as my Solitude is sublime.

John Keats, Letter to George and Georgiana Keats, 1818

～ 26 OCTOBER ～

YOUNG BLOODS AT THE BURLINGTON ARCADE

Shopkeepers in the Burlington Arcade are again complaining about the obstruction caused at the Piccadilly entrance by the young bloods from Tufnell Park and Acton and Tooting Bec, who congregate there after five o'clock in the afternoon, all dressed up in frock coats, highly polished hats and lavender gloves. They stand tightly wedged together leaning on their gold- and silver-mounted sticks, looking bored and imagine that they give the impression to passers-by that they are all heirs to peerages and great estates and are just out for an airing. This afternoon I saw young X, one of our clerks, in the languid group. Now I know why he is always so anxious to get away before five. A strange fad.

R. D. Blumenfeld, *R.D.B.'s Diary*, 1900

～ 27 OCTOBER ～

FIVE ONE-ARMED MEN

Bought coffee at Fortnum & Mason's and took a book at the London Library (a novel, Cooper's Pathfinder – I ought to be ashamed of myself, but I'm not). On the way home I left a card at the Farrers. The King's Road was enlivened by a party of five men, all young and well-looked, all dressed in snow-white Linen jackets, all having lost an arm, and all singing a doleful ditty, for hapence! Taking them for victims of 'the Russian war', I stopt in an effervescence of mingled pity and patriotism to give them – sixpence? – or a shilling? – (the moment was to decide which) – ; and while I was getting out my purse, Mr C chanced to come up, and asked one of the five: 'What are you at all? Are you soldiers?' 'No, Sir – we are factory-men – were all hurt by the explosion of a boiler.' The man's continuance was so prepossessing, that I believed him, – just for the moment: but is it credible that the explosion of a boiler should have blown off five arms, to five men, without doing them any other apparent damage? I should have liked to bring these five one-armed men home with me and to make them tell their histories . . .

Jane Welsh Carlyle, *Diaries*, 1855

A DEMONSTRATION AT GROSVENOR SQUARE

E and I went down the Chancery at one o'clock where we met . . . other personnel, to spend the next seven hours. Consuming sandwiches and Bloody Marys, we listened to the radio and television to somewhat meagre accounts of what was taking place. A crowd that congregated at the Embankment had got underway in the early afternoon toward Hyde Park, to the number of 30,000 or more people. A break-away dissident column left the large body, to make entry into Grosvenor Square, there to attack our Embassy. There seemed to be about 5,000 of them against a thousand police and 40 horsemen. The control exercised by the police was superb. In spite of every form of provocation, we, who had a bird's eye view of proceedings, witnessed not a single example of so-called brutality or even the use of a club by these sorely pressed officers, some of whom were badly beaten up during charges by wild looking, yelling creatures tossing banner poles, fireworks and coins at them. In some places, the cordon of police was twelve deep. There were the usual attempts to charge the officers with attacking civilians. One fellow we saw from the window covered himself in red paint and screamed with vocal assist from others, he had been beaten up. It was an interesting, instructive, not edifying sight, except for the courage and the skill of the police. When we left the scene at 8:30, a couple of hundred so-called anarchists and Maoists were still milling around the Square, but were making no attempt to break through the police lines.

David Bruce, *Diary*, 1968

～ *28 October* ～

AN EVENING WITH PSYCHOGEOGRAPHERS

It's Friday evening, and I'm at the Bishopsgate Institute, a building people might notice when walking from Liverpool St Station to Spitalfields Market.

The event is a discussion promoting the paperback release of *London, City of Disappearances*, a new anthology of musings on the capital. The book is edited by Mr Sinclair and features contributions from Alan Moore and Michael Moorcock, and all three are here to talk about it.

I've seen the indelible Alan Moore before; the leonine explosion of hair (tonight tamed in a ponytail), the Old Testament beard, the deadpan Midlands accent, the Rasputin eyes. Moorcock is also bearded, but less wildly so. I've seen younger photos of him looking like, well, Alan Moore, and I wonder if that has something to do with his more reined-in length today. Perhaps you can only have one author looking like that at one time, or the universe will explode.

Moorcock talks about having 'a good Blitz', when to wake up in London and find the landscape changed from day to day was exciting rather than frightening. He mentions how it used to be possible to walk from the old Port of London to the West End in no time at all, because the buildings in between were just not there.

Though you have to be careful with Michael Moorcock's London. He likes to re-imagine whole parts of the city, notably Brookgate, his fictional district based on Holborn. Iain Sinclair interjects that people who've read the hardback version of *City of Disappearances* have approached him and reminisced vividly about the places Moorcock mentions. Places which never existed.

'We are living in text,' points out Moore. 'We live by manipulating language.' And it's this line of thinking that really connects with me. I think about the askew glance of the flâneur. Marks on paper becoming bricks and mortar and back again. The language of property deeds: text as possession of the unpossessable. Cities as thought, changed by thought, with text as both the means and the process.

It helps that Moore also likes to entertain as much as provoke thought: 'London is essentially a fantasy invented by the Midlands.'

Dickon Edwards, *Diary*, 2007

~ *29 October* ~

THE LORD MAYOR'S SHOW

We went to my Lord Mayor's Show, four of us in the Duchess of Shrewsbury's coach, and two with the Prince's Lords in one of the King's coaches. We stood at a Quaker's, over against Bow Church. I thought I should have lost the use of my ears with the continual noise of huzzas, music, and drums; and when we got to the hall the crowd was inconceivably great. My poor Lady Humphreys made a sad figure in her black velvet, and did make a most violent bawling to her page to hold up her train . . .

Mary, Countess Cowper, *Diary*, 1714

THE ERECTION OF PRINCE ALBERT

John Henry Foley [designer of the Albert Memorial] was very kind and affable and shewed us through his studio. The model of the Statue of Prince Albert for the Hyde Park monument was there. He says when the Queen came to see it, she liked the expression of the face so much that she desired it might not even be touched by him any further, and so, though he had not considered it quite finished he had complied with her request and left it as it was. The statue, to be in bronze gilt, had been so long in execution, because in the hurry to get it done, the molten metal had been poured into the mould before the latter was thoroughly dry, so that the generated steam had exploded and destroyed it. Thus to save a week, they had lost 6 months at least for the extra work required to make a second mould.

Alfred Domett, *Diary*, 1873

A KNOCKOUT IN SOUTHWARK

Yesterday at The Ring in Blackfriars Road I had a very nice conversation with Ted Broadribb, the boxing manager. He lives in Walworth, not far from me. He is probably the most famous bloke in my district. We talked boxing pretty near 15 minutes. He says that if I see him around-like with a boxer of note and I am too shy to ask the said boxer for his autograph Mr Broadribb will get it for me. This is the first time anyone has ever offered to help me with my hobby. I also met Seaman Nobby Hall, the lightweight champion boxer of Europe. I was ever so clumsy, my boot grazed the highly polished surface of his left shoe. He was naturally angry and very nearly gave me his Hall mark – a knockout.

I am still working in the carpentry shop opposite The Camberwell Palace at Camberwell Green. I hate it. What is the prospect, what is the future in being a slave to a horrible planing machine?

Fred Bason, *Diary*, 1922

～ 30 October ～

BURNT ALIVE

Elizabeth Hare, lately condemned for high treason in clipping his majesties coin, was, according to her sentence, burnt alive in Bunhill Field.

Narcissus Luttrell, *Diary*, 1683

ON STRAWBERRY HILL

Sir William Stanhope, brother to the Earl of Chesterfield, now lives in Mr Pope's house on the banks of the Thames; you pass over his grotto, immediately under the common highway, as you come from the town of Twickenham to Mr Walpole's house of Strawberry Hill. Next to it is the house belonging to the late Earl of Radnor, which is the last house on the Thames bank next to Strawberry Hill, a road going by the Thames-side to Kingston Bridge, being between the river and Mr Walpole's garden, which, however, is within a furlong or two of the river, and his own meadows go quite down to the banks of it, and nothing to obstruct the view of that most beautifying fluid, which makes everything handsome that is within its influence. From the garden you discover the elegant Chinese Temple, being the last building on the bank of the Thames, and close to my Lord Radnor's house or garden wall – though the house belonging to it is on the other side of the road, and is the last house on that side next to Strawberry Hill, and is an handsome new square building – I say, from this garden of Mr Walpole you discover the Chinese summer house in which, about last August, Mr Isaac Fernandez Nunez, a Jew, shot himself through the head, on the loss of the Hermione, a rich French ship which he had insured, and by that means ruined his fortune and family. His house and furniture were sold by auction while I was at Strawberry Hill, and I was at the sale for a few minutes.

From Mr Walpole's garden and house you have the most beautiful and charming prospect of Richmond, with variety of fine villas and gardens on the banks of the Thames, which river alone would sufficiently recommend any situation; though when I was there last, viz., in October and the beginning of November, 1762, the excessive rains which had lately fell had so swelled the river that it caused such inundations as were never known in the memory of man; insomuch that during my stay there, two islands just before the garden were totally covered by the waters and could not be seen. The floods did infinite mischief all over England, and particularly in Essex. At Cambridge it was within six inches of the highest flood ever known or recorded there, of which a mark is cut in the wall of King's College Senior Fellows Garden, on the river's bank; and the waters came into the cellars of Queens' College in such a torrent that the butler had not time to go in to stop up the vessels, they having just newly filled their cellars for the year; by which means the water got in, and spoiled all their beer.

Reverend William Cole, *Diary*, 1762

～ *31 October* ～

JACKSON THE BRUISER

At 8 o'clock left Cambridge in the Telegraph Coach & got to Fetter Lane ¼ before 4 o'clock. Jackson the bruiser was an outside Passenger. He had been to Cambridge to instruct the Marquiss of Tavistock & other young men of rank, who take him much into their association. He has a room in the Albany building, Piccadilly where he gives lessons in pugilism, & is supposed to make 4 or 500 a year.

Joseph Farington, *Diary*, 1807

BUCKINGHAM PALACE ENLARGED

Had the unpleasant job to discharge James Hollingsworth from his employment as screener through repeatedly absenting himself. But he saw and promised the master better attendance in future, upon which a reconciliation was effected and he was permitted to resume his employment.

The front of Buckingham Palace presents a different appearance, being encircled with boarding which extends round the front rails as far distant as the semi-circular pathway. The Palace is to be enlarged, which, from the continued cart loads of rubble taken away and the cart loads of bricks taken in, appears that the alterations to be undertaken will be very extensive.

The exterior and interior of St James's Church Piccadilly is now undergoing a thorough repair and beautifying, the windows of which are nearly half fresh glazed, which suffered extensively from the effects of the late storm. The foundation of the new rectory house on the same site as the old one is just commenced.

Nathaniel Bryceson, *Diary*, 1846

ACTIVISTS IN GOSPEL OAK

To an Oak Village Residents' Association Meeting.

The chairperson took me aside at the start of the meeting, before I went in, to warn me about certain 'activists' on the Association and their dangerous work. Armed with these fears, and ever watchful, I approached the hall to find about six people sitting there. None of them really seemed to fit the bill as 'activists'.

Anyway, I spoke up, rather insistently, about the appalling state of Lismore Circus and have undertaken to gather signatures about it. I was almost voted on the committee at one point, when Bruce Robertson proposed me, amidst uproar, after one lady had questioned the necessity for a committee at all and the chairperson had been accused of 'intolerable restriction of debate'.

All excellent entertainment. I made a good friend out of the admirable Bruce Robertson, and I've also lumbered myself with the job of organizing next summer's street party.

Michael Palin, *Diary*, 1979

November

∼ 1 NOVEMBER ∼

PRETTY SOBER

My Governor and I went to Mr. Brown's the Distiller where we met with a very honest set of neighbours. As usual was exceeding merry till about 11, then I took one of the company under the arm and walk'd as far as the Crown Tavern. The rest follow'd and we renew'd our mirth, ate boil'd mutton and pork griskin, drank about a bottle a piece more, came home about one in the morning, call'd in at Mr. Lamb's a baker where we flung flower in one another's faces and upon one another's cloaths — but as to myself I escap'd damage by flying the danger. Got home between one and two and went to bed pretty sober.

John Baptist Grano, *Diary*, 1728

ACCOSTED IN PANCRAS LANE

Rose at 7 o'clock, breakfasted and went and took a turn in St Paul's Cathedral, and from thence to St Mary-at-Hill. Returning home through Pancras Lane, I met a man who accosted me in a peculiar manner telling a distressing tale and prevailed in getting a penny out of me, I, by his manner, believing him to be true. After dinner went to meet Ann with the intent of going to St Paul's, but, after waiting till it was too late, I proceeded alone to St Anne's Soho, looked over the tablets and stopped while prayers. Had Ann up in the evening. Took walk with Ann over Westminster Bridge, and after the outside of the Abbey etc, returned home about half past 9 o'clock. Saw the 2d omnibuses running for the first time in Trafalgar Square north side.

Nathaniel Bryceson, *Diary*, 1846

EDEN MUST GO

Burgo arrived in the evening, talking and thinking hard about the crisis, or war, or what Eden prefers to call 'Armed Conflict'. He was in Parliament Square last night where a huge crowd, mostly young, were shouting 'Eden must Go!' and being charged by mounted police with batons. Military veterans crawl out of holes and talk about 'pockets of resistance' and 'mopping up'.

Frances Partridge, *Diary*, 1956

~ 2 NOVEMBER ~

THE DAY THE QUEEN ARRIVED

In the afternoon I went forth and saw some silver bosses put upon my new Bible, which cost me 6s. 6d. the making, and 7s. 6d. the silver, which, with 9s. 6d. the book, comes in all to L1 3s. 6d. From thence with Mr. Cooke that made them, and Mr. Stephens the silversmith to the tavern, and did give them a pint of wine. So to White Hall, where when I came I saw the boats going very thick to Lambeth, and all the stairs to be full of people. I was told the Queen* was a-coming; so I got a sculler for sixpence to carry me thither and back again, but I could not get to see the Queen; so come back, and to my Lord's, where he was come; and I supt with him, he being very merry, telling merry stories of the country mayors, how they entertained the King all the way as he come along; and how the country gentlewomen did hold up their heads to be kissed by the King, not taking his hand to kiss as they should do. I took leave of my Lord and Lady, and so took coach at White Hall and carried Mr. Childe as far as the Strand, and myself got as far as Ludgate by all the bonfires, but with a great deal of trouble; and there the coachman desired that I would release him, for he durst not go further for the fires. So he would have had a shilling or 6d. for bringing of me so far; but I had but 3d. about me and did give him it. In Paul's church-yard I called at Kirton's, and there they had got a mass book for me, which I bought and cost me twelve shillings; and, when I came home, sat up late and read in it with great pleasure to my wife, to hear that she was long ago so well acquainted with it. So to bed. I observed this night very few bonfires in the City, not above three in all London, for the Queen's coming; whereby I guess that (as I believed before) her coming do please but very few.

Samuel Pepys, *Diary*, 1660

* Henrietta Maria, wife of Charles I, was returning to England from exile on the Continent since her son was now safely on the throne as Charles II.

A KNOCKOUT OF A MAYOR

After dinner, at 10, or thereabout, I drove to 'Wonderland', in Whitechapel, to see some boxing at this the well-known centre of pugilism in the East End of London. Some of my friends urged me not to go; all of them begged me not to wear my badge. Sir William Dunn and Sir Ernest Flower accompanied me, and a strong detachment of police was on duty outside the hall. I took my badge and brought it safely home again, and a cheque for £50 for my Fund. I made a speech to about 3,000 very rough-looking young men; they seemed very cheerful and happy, and very sympathetic. As I walked through the crowd of these men, inside the building, one of them said: 'God bless you, governor; you're a fair old knock-out!'

W. P. Treloar, *A Lord Mayor's Diary*, 1907

～ 3 NOVEMBER ～

£500 A YEAR IN PLEASURE

And now I've found a house 35 Woburn Square. Yes, shall I write that address often? Certainly I hope so. For me it would be worth £500 a year in pleasure. Think of the music I could hear, the people I could see, easily, unthinkingly. And then comes before me the prospect of walking through the city streets; starting off early, some day L.'s at the office, & walking say to Wapping; & then to tea at the office. Why this so obsesses my mind I don't know. It was a beautiful clear November day yesterday, when I went up & past our house (with green doors opposite the mews) & the squares with their regular houses, & their leafless trees, and people very clearly outlined filled me with joy.

Virginia Woolf, *Diary*, 1923

STOPPING OFFICE BUILDING

Cabinet was almost entirely devoted to the secret plan George Brown and I had worked out for stopping all office building in London. This was suddenly presented to Cabinet. George spoke. I gave details on the factual case for doing it, and despite the predictions in my Ministry that there would be tremendous opposition there was none at all. Nobody in a Labour Cabinet is going to object to an action which is extremely popular outside London and which will only ruin property speculators; actually, it probably won't even do that because a lot of them will make money out of the rising rents paid now for offices already in existence. It all went with a bang, and we got through comfortably.

Richard Crossman, *Diary*, 1964

A MOMENT TO FREEZE IN TIME

The sun, low, clear and brilliant, encourages me out of the house again, this time to take Rachel to the zoo. The tigers pace disturbingly and continually. The ostriches and emus and cassowaries are in poor housing and look rather seedy . . .

Then we walk up Primrose Hill together. Though it is very cold, the leaves are still on the trees and the great glowing gold sun picks out the fading colours with breathtaking richness. We pause at the top of the hill and marvel. With Rachel beside me, in her fashionable and elegant navy blue coat, it's one of those moments when you wish you could freeze time.

Michael Palin, *Halfway to Hollywood*, 1985

~ *4 November* ~

A GREAT FRAY

The fourth day of November began a great fray at Charing cross at viii
of the clock at night between the Spaniards and Englishmen, the which
through wisdom there were but a few hurt, and after the next day there
were certain taken that began it; one was a blackamoor, and was brought
afore the head officers by the knight-marshal's servants.

Henry Machyn, *Diary*, 1554

PLENTY OF POLICE

Last night, in order to enliven a drowsy liver, I walked the streets of the
West End, for three hours, 8.30 to 11.30, from Tottenham Court Road
to Hyde Park Corner; and noted nothing beyond the extraordinary
number of policemen, stationed every few score yards on either side of
the road, in Coventry Street and neighbouring thoroughfares. Everything was quiet and I puzzled in vain to account for them. Only the fear
of a snub prevented me from inquiring of one of them direct.

Arnold Bennett, *Journal*, 1896

SO FAR ABOVE THE WORLD

Today we took over Alexander Fleming House, the great skyscraper at
the Elephant and Castle. I have a long room in a suite of offices on the
seventh floor with magnificent but not very pretty views of modern
skyscrapers. Still, it is exhilarating up there and when the door from
my Private Office is shut and I sit alone I am totally insulated. That's
the first thing I notice. I'm not in an ivory tower but a steel tower miles
away from Westminster and Whitehall, with double glazing to give a
sense of absolute silence, so far up above the world that nothing seems
to be relating to me.

Richard Crossman, *Diary*, 1968

∼ 5 NOVEMBER ∼

TALKING TO AN ACTRESS

Up Holborn and walked St James's Park half an hour or more; on going out saw the King get into his chaise and 4 black horses. I went to Blue Posts – had beef steak etc. then to Covent Garden, 'Beggar's Opera' and 'Commissary'; found the Pit not one fifth full, and on the 4th bench from Orchestra orange woman showed me Pol. Kennedy alias Mrs Bivon,* on which I went and sat immediately before her and talked with her much during the play.

John Baker, *Diary*, 1773

* A well-known actress of the day.

WHAT DO THE CONVICTS THINK?

Saw a van full of convicts pass London Bridge. What must they have thought, shut up in their confinement, of the noise and rattle and bustle without them; for, though the bells of a steeple close to me were ringing, their sound was drowned in the noise of passing vehicles. If there was a penitent man amongst them, how must he have envied the freedom and cheerfulness of the crowd that were hurrying past him to their respective duties.

Sir Michael Connal, *Diary*, 1836

A BELGIAN MAKES A BET

I held the stake to-day, £5 a-side, in a wager between Monsieur Van Branteghem, that strange little Belgian diplomat-financier, who wears a golden bracelet, a gold-rimmed monocle, and an enormous gold watch chain, and Marcus Mayer, who was Patti's manager for many years. The bet was that Van Branteghem could walk all the way on the kerb side of Regent Street from Verreys to Piccadilly and that he would not have more than three mud splashes from passing horses' hoofs on his collar.

When we reached Swan and Edgar's corner the little Belgian had five blobs on his high collar and three for luck on his face. To-day was Guy Fawkes' Day. I have never seen so many guys in the streets.

R. D. Blumenfeld, *R.D.B.'s Diary*, 1900

~ 6 NOVEMBER ~

LIGHT ON THE THAMES

I passed a considerable time this morning in studying the effect of light upon the scenery of the River Thames. I walked over Blackfryars Bridge & proceeded upon the banks of the river towards London Bridge & studied the effect of light, haze, & colour upon St. Paul's & the buildings on the London side of the River. I afterwards walked along the Bank above Blackfryars Bridge for the same purpose.

Joseph Farington, *Diary*, 1812

A HOUSE IN A DANGEROUS CONDITION

Whilst mending a pen this morning, the knife slipped and gave me a very nasty cut on the middle finger. I hastened to the chemist and bought a pennyworth sticking plaster. In evening strolled into Richmond's Auction Rooms, Rathbone Place. Moore the toyman's house in a very dangerous condition propped up with deals, the inhabitants being obliged to make a hasty quittal, the foundations having gave way and the front wall bulging forward, which, but for the support offered to it, would in all probability before this time have been level with the ground.

Nathaniel Bryceson, *Diary*, 1846

FIRST TRIP ON THE TUBE

To Hatton Garden by the Metropolitan Railway to get me a stronger pair of spectacles. Never saw the underground rail before; it gives one the idea of going into an immense, tidy coal cellar, did not strike cold but smelt rather sepulchral.

Louisa Bain, *Diary*, 1863

~ 7 November ~

THE PARLIAMENTARIANS
DEFEND THE CITY

They do not cease to provide with energy for the defence of London, or for the means of reinforcing Essex. They have sent a number of parliamentarians to the surrounding provinces with instructions to get together the largest number they can of their trained bands, with the intention of despatching these subsequently to where the remains of the parliamentary army are quartered. They have brought a number of the companies of these trained bands of the country into this city. All the troops are kept constantly at arms. There is no street, however little frequented, that is not barricaded with heavy chains, and every post is guarded by numerous squadrons. At the approaches to London they are putting up trenches and small forts of earthwork, at which a great number of people are at work, including the women and little children. They have issued a new manifesto to the people full of the usual representations against the present procedure of the king, for the purpose of arousing their enthusiasm still more in the support of this cause.

Giovanni Giustiniani, Letter to the
Doge and Senate of Venice, 1642

PREACHING AGAINST MARTIN LUTHER

Wandered down to the Needle on the Embankment. I regarded it with interest, but without any sense of reverence, and yet that may grow as I realize its antiquity . . . Went to the Aquarium; saw the seals, etc. The acrobatic performances sensational. I did not care to look at them. Then wandered for five or ten minutes into Westminster Abbey; the transept crowded with monuments; the service just finishing. Impressed with the grandeur of the Abbey. Went to Hyde Park to see Albert Memorial; magnificent . . . On Sabbath morning wandered over Westminster Bridge to Stamford Street. Remembered the stifling heat in my lodgings forty-three years ago and more. Came over Blackfriars Bridge and went to St. Paul's. As Mr. Kennedy and I said, there could be little more culti-vated there than a devout spirit, for the place was too large to hear distinctly. The singing fine, but on the whole I felt it was foreign to spiritual worship. The altar decorated with flowers and cross, and the existence of a side chapel perplexing and almost Roman Catholic . . . Saw a Roman Catholic woman, with a thick cable round her neck, preaching against Martin Luther, under the arches of the railway.

Sir Michael Connal, *Diary*, 1878

WHERE HAVE ALL THE KIPPERS GONE?

A terrible night! Guns never seemed to cease. Many bombs. No chance to go up the road. Slept at office until All Clear after 7 a.m. Not very refreshing to sleep in one's clothes, but the lovely bath helps a bit. Every district of London got it last night . . . Very difficult to get any eggs . . . almost impossible. Not a kipper to be had for a long time. Can't think what have they done with them.

Vere Hodgson, *Diary*, 1940

~ 8 NOVEMBER ~

THE FATAL VESPERS

The next day after I wrote last here fell out a pittiful accident in the black friers, where the papists had hired a house next to the French Ambassadors (that so they might be as it were under his protection) to hold their assemblies, say masse, meet at sermons, and perform all other their exercises and rites after the Romish manner; a great multitude beeing met there on the 26th of the last month to heare father Drurie a famous Jesuite among them preach in an upper roome, the floore sunke under them, or rather the beames and joysts not able to beare the weight brake in the midst. Many perished, partly battered and bruised, but most part smothered, for the first floore fell with such violence that it brake down a second under it. A number were hurt maimed and lost their limmes, which found litle helpe or comfort at first, our people beeing growne so savage and barbarous that they refused to assist them with drinck, aqua vitae or any other cordials in their necessitie, but rather insulted upon them with taunts and gibes in their affliction as they were carried away all that evening and the night following, and even in Cheapside where they shold be more civill they were redy to pull and teare them out of the coaches as they passed to their lodgings, or to the surgeons; but there was as much goode order taken as might be on the sodain to represse the insolencie and inhumanitie of the multitude, and for reliefe of the distressed.

John Chamberlain, Letter to Dudley Carleton, 1623

THE CITY AT DAWN

Lovely dawn. A fierce north-westerly gale, torn grey rags of cloud and riffs of very clear white, lemon and tawny sky. London a vast sparkle of light, orange and blue, pearl-towers, diamonds; the tall blocks shadowy, the downs and hills around all visible, the wind had swept things clean. The whole dawn city sparkling and as lovely as a young woman in the new light and wind.

John Fowles, *Journals*, 1963

∽ 9 NOVEMBER ∽

LONELY IN LONDON

Lord-Mayor's Day. Got nearly squeezed to death among a set of the lowest of the low. So much for the gratification of curiosity. Since my arrival in the Metropolis, having no companion up to about this time, I am in some measure solitary. My evenings are spent in my garret, reading or writing. I have chalked out no plan of study yet. Often melancholy, I have wandered about the streets, gazing in at windows, or listening to a poor little boy playing on a stringed instrument. Lamps lighted – streets crowded – grand equipages – misery – destitution – vice.

Sir Michael Connal, *Diary*, 1835

BEING POKED IN THE CRANIAL RIBS

Dined at the Devonshire Club in St. James's Street, W., with Dr. H— and Mr.—, the latter showing the grave symptomatic phenomena of a monocle and spats. A dinner of eight courses. Only made one mistake – put my salad on my dish instead of on the side dish. Horribly nervous and reticent. I was apparently expected to give an account of myself and my abilities – and with that end in view, they gave me a few pokes in my cranial ribs. But I am a peculiar animal, and, before unbosoming myself, I would require a happier *mise-en-scène* than a West End Club, and a more tactful method of approach than ogling by two professors, who seemed to think I was a simple penny-in-the-slot machine. I froze from sheer nervousness and nothing resulted.

W. N. P. Barbellion, *The Journal of a Disappointed Man*, 1910

AN EXTRA HALF-HOUR IN BED

We are filming now at the empty, recently sold A1 Dairy in Whetstone High Street. The immediate significance of filming in Whetstone is that, for once, it favours those who live in North London – i.e. G. Chapman and myself – who have long since had to leave earlier than anyone else to reach location in Ealing, Walton-on-Thames and points south. Now we reap an additional benefit of Hampstead living – half an hour extra in bed – and when I am being collected at 7.30 each day, in darkness, the half hour is very welcome.

Michael Palin, *The Python Years*, 1970

∼ 10 NOVEMBER ∼

AN ARTIST SAVES A SERVANT'S FORTUNE

Should the circumstance of a fire in Charlotte Street appear in any of the papers, it is possible you may meet with it; and I write this hasty line or two, that you may not be uneasy on my account. The fire did in fact happen on the premises I inhabit; but I have lost nothing. We shall suffer a temporary inconvenience; but Mr. Watts has kindly ordered me a bed in his house, and a neighbour, Mr. Henderson, in Charlotte Street, has allowed me a room to paint in while the house is under repair. We were put to some alarm and bustle, but no one was hurt; and I hope Mr. Weight's insurance will cover his loss. The fire began in a workshop at the back of the house, about four o'clock in the morning, and spread so very fast, that at one time we thought of saving ourselves only. I, however, secured my most valuable letters; and we went to work removing whatever we could into the street . . . I found the poor woman-servant, who had lately nursed Mrs. Weight, in great distress, as all her fortune was in the garret, and in her pockets which were under her pillow; there was no time to be lost, I ran up stairs, and she was overjoyed to see me return with them, through the smoke, quite safe. It was now that the engines arrived, and fortunately succeeded in putting a stop to the flames.

John Constable, Letter to Miss Bicknell, 1812

A RIOT FOR REFORM

It was expected last night that there would be a great riot, and preparations were made to meet it. Troops were called up to London, and a large body of civil power put in motion. People had come in from the country in the morning, and everything indicated a disturbance. After dinner I walked out to see how things were going on. There was little mob in the west end of the town, and in New Street, Spring Gardens, a large body of the new police was drawn up in three divisions, ready to be employed if wanted. The Duke of Wellington expected Apsley House to be attacked, and made preparations accordingly. He desired my brother to go and dine there, to assist in making any arrangements that might be necessary. In Pall Mall I met Mr. Glyn, the banker, who had been up to Lombard Street to see how matters looked about his house, and he told us (Sir T. Farquhar and me) that everything was quiet in the City. One of the policemen said that there had been a smart brush near Temple Bar, where a body of weavers with iron crows and a banner had been dispersed by the police, and the banner taken. The police, who are a magnificent set of fellows, behave very well, and it seems pretty evident that these troubles are not very serious, and will soon be put an end to. The attack in Downing Street the night before last, of which they made a great affair, turned out to be nothing at all. The mob came there from Carlile's lecture, but the sentry stopped them near the Foreign Office; the police took them in flank, and they all ran away.

Charles Greville, *Journal of the Reigns of King George IV and King William IV*, 1830

∼ 11 NOVEMBER ∼

A FEMINIST THROWS HERSELF IN THE THAMES

Mrs. Imlay, (late Mrs Wolstencraft) Authoress of the Rights of Women, married Mr. Imlay, an American, in Paris, & has one child. Imlay came to England with her & pretended he had been married before, and proposed to Mrs. Imlay to live in the same house with his first wife, (who in fact is only his mistress). She was so much affected by this usage, that one day the last summer she took a boat and was rowed to Putney, where going on shore & to the bridge, she threw herself into the water. Her cloaths buoyed her up & she floated, & was taken up senseless abt. 200 yards from the bridge, and by proper applications restored to life. Her mind is now calm; she is separated from Imlay, and visits her friends as usual, & does not object to mention her attempt.

Joseph Farington, *Diary*, 1796

A LOATHSOME ENDING TO THE WAR

I got to London about 6.30 and found masses of people in streets and congested Tubes, all waving flags and making fools of themselves – an outburst of mob patriotism. It was a wretched wet night, and very mild. It is a loathsome ending to the loathsome tragedy of the last four years.

Siegfried Sassoon, *Diary*, 1918

A PANDEMONIUM FOR PEACE

Peace! London to-day is a pandemonium of noise and revelry, soldiers and flappers being most in evidence. Multitudes are making all the row they can, and in spite of depressing fog and steady rain, discords of sound and struggling, rushing beings and vehicles fill the streets.

Beatrice Webb, *Diary*, 1918

∼ *12 November* ∼

THE PRICE OF A SHAVE

To Drury Lane Theatre: 'King Lear,' by Garrick. Agreed with the barber for shaving me at 6s. a quarter.

William Bray, *Diary*, 1757

ARRIVING AT EUSTON

We left the Lime Street Station for London at 2 p.m. in one of those dinky little compartments. The country looked very peaceful and attractive and we arrived at Euston Station, London at 7 p.m. They have the most pernicious system of carrying baggage. You have to get your own baggage put in the van and when we arrived in London everyone made a wild rush for the baggage van and there was a regular riot for a while. Everyone scrambling to get their trunks, etc. and when you found your luggage you had to then find a porter and when you found him you had to hunt a cab. After wearing yourself out you finally have a cab with your luggage all over it and can go to a hotel. I never saw so much tipping. Everybody who looks at you has his hands out for a tip. I finally arrived at the Savoy Hotel and Stewart, Turney and myself have a suite together. We took dinner at Simpson's and I am now going to bed as the last few days have worn me out.

Alfred A. Cunningham, *Diary*, 1917

PYTHONS IN A PET SHOP

Shooting at a pet shop in the Caledonian Road. It's a grey, wet, messy day and this part of the Caledonian Road is a grey, wet, messy part of the world. In the pet shop there is scarcely room to move, but the angel fish and the guppies and the parrots and the kittens and the guinea pigs seem to be unconcerned by the barrage of light — and the continually discordant voices. The shop is still open as we rehearse. One poor customer is afraid to come in, and stands at the door, asking rather nervously for two pounds of Fido. 'Two pounds of Fido,' the cry goes up and the message is passed by raucous shouts to the lady proprietor. 'That's 15/-,' she says. '15/-,' everyone starts to shout.

We've finished by 5.30. Outside the shop is a little boy whose father, he tells us, is coming out of the nick soon.

'What'll you do when he comes out?'

'Kill him.'

'Why?'

'I hate him.'

'Why do you hate him?'

'He's a ponce.'

All this cheerfully, as if discussing what kind of fish fingers he likes best. As I walk back to the caravan a battered-looking couple argue viciously in a doorway.

Michael Palin, *The Python Years*, 1970

∼ *13 November* ∼

A REGENCY PICKPOCKET

In the evening I set out on a walk which proved an unlucky one. As I passed in the narrow part of the Strand, near Thelwall's, I entered incautiously into a crowd. I soon found myself unable to proceed, and felt that I was pressed on all sides. I had buttoned my greatcoat. On a sudden I felt a hand at my fob. I instantly pressed my hands down, recollecting I had Mrs. Wordsworth's watch in my pocket. I feared making any motion with my hands, and merely pressed my waistband. Before I could make any cry, I was thrown down (how, I cannot say).

I rose instantly. A fellow called out, 'Sir, you struck me!' I answered, 'I am sorry for it, – I'm robbed, and that is worse.' I was uncertain whether I had lost anything, but it at once occurred to me that this was a sort of protecting exclamation. I ran into the street, and then remarked, for the first time, that I had lost my best umbrella. I felt my watch, but my gold chain and seals were gone. The prime cost of what was taken was about eight guineas. On the whole, I escaped very well, considering all circumstances. Many persons have been robbed on this very spot, and several have been beaten and ill-treated in the heart of the City – and in the daytime. Such is the state of our police! My watch-chain was taken from me, not with the violence of robbery, or the secrecy of theft, but with a sort of ease and boldness that made me for a moment not know what the fellow meant. He seemed to be decently dressed, and had on a white waistcoat.

Henry Crabb Robinson, *Diary*, 1820

A VICTORIAN EXECUTION

I was a witness of the execution at Horsemonger Lane this morning. I went there with the intention of observing the crowd gathered to behold it, and I had excellent opportunities of doing so, at intervals all through the night, and continuously from day-break until after the spectacle was over . . . I believe that a sight so inconceivably awful as the wickedness and levity of the immense crowd collected at that execution this morning could be imagined by no man, and could be presented in no heathen land under the sun. The horrors of the gibbet and of the crime which brought the wretched murderers to it faded in my mind before the atrocious bearing, looks, and language of the assembled spectators. When I came upon the scene at midnight, the shrillness of the cries and howls that were raised from time to time, denoting that they came from a concourse of boys and girls already assembled in the best places, made my blood run cold. As the night went on, screeching, and laughing, and yelling in strong chorus of parodies on negro melodies, with substitutions of 'Mrs. Manning' for 'Susannah', and the like, were added to these. When the day dawned, thieves, low prostitutes, ruffians, and vagabonds of every kind, flocked on to the ground, with every variety of offensive and foul behaviour. Fightings, faintings, whistlings, imitations of Punch, brutal jokes, tumultuous demonstrations of indecent delight when swooning women were dragged out of the crowd by the police, with their dresses disordered, gave a new zest to the general entertainment. When the sun rose brightly – as it did – it gilded thousands upon thousands of upturned faces, so inexpressibly odious in their brutal mirth or callousness, that a man had cause to feel ashamed of the shape he wore, and to shrink from himself, as fashioned in the image of the Devil. When the two miserable creatures who attracted all this ghastly sight about them were turned quivering into the air, there was no more emotion, no more pity, no more thought that two immortal souls had gone to judgement, no more restraint in any of the previous obscenities, than if the name of Christ had never been heard in this world, and there were no belief among men but that they perished like the beasts.

Charles Dickens, Letter to *The Times*, 1849

∼ *14 November* ∼

A MENAGERIE IN THE STRAND

Two nights ago I saw the tigers sup at Exeter 'Change . . . Such a conver-
sazione! — There was a 'hippopotamus,' like Lord Liverpool in the face;
and the 'Ursine Sloth' hath the very voice and manner of my valet —
but the tiger talked too much. The elephant took and gave me my
money again — took off my hat — opened a door — *trunked* a whip —
and behaved so well, that I wish he was my butler. The handsomest
animal on earth is one of the panthers . . .

Lord Byron, *Journal*, 1813

UNRULY KNIGHTS

On Saturday night the Knights of the Bath were entertained by the
Lord Mayor at Drapers Hall with a supper and a play, where some of
them were so rude and unruly and carried themselves so insolently
divers wayes, but specially in putting citizens' wifes to the squeake, so
far forth that one of the Sheriffes brake open a doore upon Sir Edward
Sackville, which gave such occasion of scandall, that they went away
without the banket, though it were redy and prepared for them.

John Chamberlain, Letter to Dudley Carleton, 1616

A SEETHING PALACE OF TOYS

A day in London, partly to do a little Christmas shopping. Hamleys was
a seething palace of toys; egotistic children were dragging their elders
towards expensive things they coveted, while others just lay back in
their push-chairs and bawled. Grandparents lovingly stroked the silk
fur of monster Teddy bears. I felt stifled, and hurried away to a very
different atmosphere — an exhibition of paintings by Francis Bacon.

Frances Partridge, *Diary*, 1949

～ *15 November* ～

A FAMOUS DUEL

Before this comes to your hands, you will have heard of the most terrible accident that hath almost ever happened. This morning, at eight, my man brought me word that the Duke of Hamilton had fought with Lord Mohun, and killed him, and was brought home wounded. I immediately sent him to the Duke's house, in St. James's Square; but the porter could hardly answer for tears, and a great rabble was about the house. In short, they fought at seven this morning. The dog Mohun was killed on the spot; and while the Duke was over him, Mohun, shortening his sword, stabbed him in at the shoulder to the heart. The Duke was helped toward the cake-house by the Ring in Hyde Park (where they fought), and died on the grass, before he could reach the house; and was brought home in his coach by eight, while the poor Duchess was asleep. Maccartney, and one Hamilton, were the seconds, who fought likewise, and are both fled. I am told that a footman of Lord Mohun's stabbed the Duke of Hamilton; and some say Maccartney did so too. Mohun gave the affront, and yet sent the challenge. I am infinitely concerned for the poor Duke, who was a frank, honest, good-natured man. I loved him very well, and I think he loved me better. He had the greatest mind in the world to have me go with him to France, but durst not tell it me; and those he did, said I could not be spared, which was true. They have removed the poor Duchess to a lodging in the neighbourhood, where I have been with her two hours, and am just come away. I never saw so melancholy a scene; for indeed all reasons for real grief belong to her; nor is it possible for anybody to be a greater loser in all regards. She has moved my very soul. The lodging was inconvenient, and they would have removed her to another; but I would not suffer it, because it had no room backward, and she must have been tortured with the noise of the Grub Street screamers mentioning her husband's murder to her ears.

Jonathan Swift, *The Journal to Stella*, 1712

A WALK IN THE DOCK

I went a little way into St Katharine's Dock, and found it crowded with great ships; then, returning, I strolled along the range of shops that front towards this side of the Tower. They have all something to do with ships, sailors, and commerce; being for the sale of ships' stores, nautical instruments, arms, clothing, together with a tavern and grog-shop at every other door; bookstalls, too, covered with cheap novels and song-books; cigar-shops in great numbers; and everywhere were sailors, and here and there a soldier, and children at the doorsteps, and women showing themselves at the doors or windows of their domiciles.

Nathaniel Hawthorne, *English Notebooks*, 1857

~ 16 *November* ~

AN EARLY LOTTERY

State lottery being to be drawn, curiosity led me to Guildhall, where a gallery for spectators is erected with seats, one of which I obtained for sixpence. The first object that struck me was a great number of clerks writing down the numbers of tickets and quality as they were proclaimed. The wheels were placed on either hand upon a stage raised about six feet from the floor, at the bottom of the hall under Beckford's statue; between were seated the commissioners at a long table, and a boy at each wheel. After delivering the ticket, the boy raises his hand above his head with fingers displayed open, and after two flourishes thrusts it into the wheel, delivering the tickets severally to the man on either side, who on cutting the tickets open, being tied and sealed, declares the number. To prevent future pranks from boys employed to draw out the numbers, a commissioner sits in a box directly opposite each boy and near him; who besides is obliged on taking out each number to raise up his hand, holding the ticket between his fore finger and thumb, delivering it to the man, who after cutting it open announces its fate or fortune.

Samuel Curwen, *Journal*, 1780

AN ARTIFICIAL GARDEN

Went to Mr Ewer's, at Clapham, for a week. We went one morning to town, and saw the 'artificial flower-garden', a pretty invention, worth seeing once; all kinds of flowers in paper, put into beds of earth, and box edging, sand walks between.

Mrs Philip Lybbe Powys, *Diary*, 1786

∼ *17 November* ∼

MAKING MERRY FOR THE QUEEN

Between 11 and 12 a' forenoon, the lady Elizabeth was proclaimed queen Elizabeth, queen of England, France and Ireland, and defender of the faith, by divers heralds of arms and trumpeters, and dukes, lords ... the which was there present, the duke of Norfolk, the lord treasurer, the earl of Shrewsbury, and the earl of Bedford, and the lord mayor and the aldermen, and divers other lords and knights. The same day, at afternoon, all the churches in London did ring, and at night did make bonfires and set tables in the street, and did eat and drink and made merry for the new queen Elizabeth, queen Mary's sister.

Henry Machyn, *Diary*, 1558

∼ *18 November* ∼

A MADMAN IN PALL MALL

Coming home at seven, a gentleman unknown stopped me in the Pall Mall, and asked my advice; said he had been to see the Queen (who was just come to town), and the people in waiting would not let him see her; that he had two hundred thousand men ready to serve her in the war; that he knew the Queen perfectly well, and had an apartment at Court, and if she heard he was there, she would send for him immediately;

that she owed him two hundred thousand pounds, etc., and he desired my opinion, whether he should go try again whether he could see her; or because, perhaps, she was weary after her journey, whether he had not better stay till to-morrow. I had a mind to get rid of my companion, and begged him of all love to go and wait on her immediately; for that, to my knowledge, the Queen would admit him; that this was an affair of great importance, and required despatch: and I instructed him to let me know the success of his business, and come to the Smyrna Coffee-house, where I would wait for him till midnight; and so ended this adventure. I would have fain given the man half a crown; but was afraid to offer it him, lest he should be offended; for, beside his money, he said he had a thousand pounds a year.

Jonathan Swift, *The Journal to Stella*, 1711

THE DUKE'S FUNERAL

To-day I witnessed the Duke of Wellington's funeral. Never saw London in such a bustle or so visibly excited in all parts as on this occasion. E., with the Sayers, secured a seat opposite St Dunstan's Church, and I hired a seat in a window near, but on going to take possession found the house belonged to some swindlers who kept a betting house, and that the seats had been sold over and over again, and were filled by the first claimants among the many who had bought tickets. However, I got a very good standing place in Fleet Street, and saw everything well. Most of the windows had been fitted up with seats. We went to Fleet Street about eight. The procession commenced about half-past ten. The effect of the military music very fine indeed. The funeral car heavy and gaudy and not effective. Perhaps the old horse of the departed Duke, led by its old groom, was the most touching part of the spectacle. I have often met the Duke on horseback and been honoured by a salute from him in return to the one I tendered. The last time I saw him was at the Great Exhibition, where he was a frequent visitor.

George Harris, *Autobiography*, 1852

～ 19 NOVEMBER ～

THE BRITISH MUSEUM READING ROOM

A long morning at the British Museum reading up *Jewish Chronicle* and suchlike. The Reading Room has a 'homey feeling'; it was there in the spring of '85 that I first recovered my thirst for knowledge and again felt the passion for Truth overcoming all other feeling. It is filled with ugly nonentities – the 'failures of life'; but for the most part they seem mesmerized by the atmosphere of untold knowledge and unfathomable experience (which haunts the home of millions of books) – into a list-less content. There you see decrepid men, despised foreigners, forlorn widows and soured maids – all knit together by a feeling of fellowship with the great immortals . . .

Beatrice Webb, *Diary*, 1888

LONDON WATER

I am better in health, avoiding all fermented liquors, and drinking nothing but London water, with a million insects in every drop. He who drinks a tumbler of London water has literally in his stomach more animated beings than there are men, women, and children on the face of the globe.

Sydney Smith, Letter to the Countess Grey, 1834

'A COUSENING PRANCKE'

I must not forget to tell you of a cousening prancke of one Venner, of Lincoln's Inne, that gave out bills of a famous play on Satterday was sevenight on the Banckeside, to be acted only by certain gentlemen and gentlewomen of account. The price at comming in was two shillings or eighteen pence at least; and, when he had gotten most part of the mony into his hands, he wold have shewed them a faire paire of heeles, but he was not so nimble to get up on horseback, but that he was faine to forsake that course and betake himselfe to the water, where he was pursued and taken, and brought before the Lord Chiefe Justice, who wold make nothing of it but a jest and a merriment, and bounde him over in five pound to appeare at the sessions. In the meane time the common people, when they saw themselves deluded, revenged themselves upon the hangings, chaires, stooles, walles, and whatsoever came in theire way, very outragiously, and made great spoil.

John Chamberlain, Letter to Dudley Carleton, 1602

∼ 20 NOVEMBER ∼

A MUSICIAN FROM THE MARSHALSEA

Took a walk out into the Borough* with my Governor; call'd at the Crown . . . After that stept in at Mr. Brown's where Mr. Lamb and Mr. Levi call'd. Mr. Levi treated his friend with some rasbury brandy but I refus'd his kind offer. Mr. Lamb invited us to dine with him but my Governor said he was oblig'd to dine at home . . . We went to dinner a little after one and had an excellent piece of boyl'd beef and turnips as also a little pretty belly piece of pork. After dinner we sate a good while and I sounded now and then with the mute in the trumpet. My Governor went out about 5 and then my Governess order'd tea, which she gave me leave to partake with her. After that, we convers'd a good while, and when exhausted of conversation I read a Tatler or two and then took my leave, came to our chamber, practis'd a while on the flute and trumpet etc. After the people were lock'd up, I went to St. James's, call'd at Rudd's Coffee House, spoke to Mr. Smith, engag'd the hands and a harpsichord, then went to Mr. Colville — left some tickets, for he could not see, being engag'd with a lady. Came back to the Coffee House, drank my share of a bottle of wine with Mr. Phil Potts and Mr. Christ. Festing, left St. James's about 12, took a link boy in Charing Cross, got at the Crown by one in the morning, ate a stake and drank my share of a bottle, then came home and went to bed about 2.

John Baptist Grano, *Diary*, 1728

* Grano was imprisoned for debt in the Marshalsea but, as he bears witness, those who had access to money and/or influential friends could come and go more or less as they pleased, as long as they returned to the prison at night.

A CLOSE ENCOUNTER WITH SOME LIONS

Dined at Brookes's alone: and having received a message from Drury Lane Theatre, to say that if I would come to the stage-door there would be a person waiting to receive me, set off there accordingly, and had my choice of private boxes given me. In the course of the piece was joined by Bunn, and went behind the scenes with him, where the mixture of materials, both human and bestial, was, to be sure, most astounding. In one place was a troop of horse from Astley's, with the riders all mounted, and about and *among* them were little children with wings, practising their steps, while some maturer nymphs were pirou-etting, and all looking as grave, — both riders, urchins, and nymphs, — as if the destiny of the world depended upon their several operations. A few steps further you came upon the lions, which I did rather too closely, and was warned off by Bunn. While I stood looking at them, there was also another gentleman, a grave and respectable looking young man, standing with his arms folded, and contemplating them in silence, while the animals were pacing about their cage without minding any of us. This, to my surprise, (I found from Bunn) was Mr. Van Amburgh, their tamer; and having heard since that he is under the impression he will one day or other be the victim of one of these animals (the lesser lion, I think), I must say that the grave earnestness with which he stood silently looking at them that night was such as one might expect from a person prepossessed with such a notion.

Thomas Moore, *Diary*, 1838

∼ *21 November* ∼

A FAT PIG AND A SEA-BEAR

We went right through Southwark and St George's Fields, an open field between Southwark and Westminster Bridge, where the Thames makes a large curve. On the way to the bridge we went to see an enormous pig, which could not move for fat, and was also of an exceptional size, as big as a small horse, and had therefore been brought to London to be shown. Not far from this spot we found a quantity of outlandish animals, such as a large, white-haired, four-footed water animal, which we took for a sea-bear from Greenland, a camel, a quantity of monkeys, eagles, civet-cats, etc.

Count Frederick Kielmansegge,
Diary of a Journey to England, 1761

LIVING AT A BRAZIER'S SHOP

We have left the Temple . . . Our rooms were dirty and out of repair, and the inconveniences of living in chambers became every year more irksome, and so at last we mustered up resolution enough to leave the good old place that so long had sheltered us – and here we are, living at a Brazier's shop, No. 20, in Russell Street, Covent Garden, a place all alive with noise and bustle, Drury Lane Theatre in sight from our front and Covent Garden from our back windows. The hubbub of the carriages returning from the play does not annoy me in the least – strange that it does not, for it is quite tremendous. I quite enjoy looking out of the window and listening to the calling up of the carriages and the squabbles of the coachmen and linkboys. It is the oddest scene to look down upon, I am sure you would be amused with it. It is well I am in a chearful place or I should have many misgivings about leaving the Temple.

Mary Lamb, Letter to Dorothy Wordsworth, 1817

AN INDELICATE POSTAL CODE

I knew a woman who could not bear to say 'W.C.' for the London postal district because of its indelicate associations and always said 'West Central'.

Evelyn Waugh, Letter to Nancy Mitford, 1955

AT THE BARBICAN

Walking through the foyer first thing in the morning, it's like some futuristic city mysteriously depopulated. A pair of automatic doors have quietly gone mad during the night and can't stop opening and closing.

Anthony Sher, *The Year of the King*, 1983

∽ 22 *November* ∽

NEWS OF AN ASSASSINATION

Just as I was leaving home to speak in Acton the phone rang and Hilary answered it and it was one of his friends. When he rang off he said that Kennedy had been shot and I didn't believe it. But we switched on the television and there was a flash saying that he was critically ill in Dallas. I drove to Acton and heard the 7.30 bulletin, just before going into the meeting, which announced that Kennedy had died. It was the most stunning blow and at the beginning of the meeting we all stood in silence for a moment in tribute.

Tony Benn, *Diary*, 1963

NOSTALGIC CAMP

Thelma and I had lunch at Biba's, the chic new department store that's replaced Derry and Toms. The original Art Deco foyers and lifts are the pretext for a new look of chromium counters and geometric armchairs. We whizzed up in a brown lift, right out of an Astaire film, to the Rainbow Restaurant where marble floors and a white baby-grand give promise of being attended by Eric Blore. But the waiters weren't old enough to expostulate like him, only camp boys with bell-bottomed trousers that explained how the floor was kept so shiny. The arrival of a Zigeuner trio (with boots, balalaika and tambourine) showed that the design motif was Lyons'-Corner-House Revival, though with far better food. Later we went downstairs to look at clothes but it was too dark to risk buying things we could hardly see. Real 1930s shops were at least decently lit. With this and a retrospective of Mary Quant at the London Museum, nostalgic camp has now reached the limit.

Peter Nichols, *Diary*, 1973

∾ 23 NOVEMBER ∾

HEADING FOR THE CRIMEA

Another division of the Guards marched on Friday to the London Bridge station to embark in the Royal Albert at Portsmouth for the Crimea. They were most enthusiastically cheered on their march, and plied with drink by immense crowds of people.

Henry Greville, *Diary*, 1854

∾ 24 NOVEMBER ∾

HALF STRANGLED IN THE STREETS

Garrotte robberies are so shamefully frequent that no one feels safe; even in the streets of London people are being half strangled as well as robbed, and that quite early in the evening.

Louisa Bain, *Diary*, 1862

THE THRALDOM OF LANDLADIES

You will be amazed to hear that I have taken a three years' lease of a good set of chambers in Marylebone Road and I have found a decent woman who will come in daily to do work. I fear I shall not be able to take possession till Christmas. The rooms are in a huge block called Cornwall Residences. I shall be free from the thraldom of landladies and what is more settled for a good long time.

George Gissing, Letter to his brother Algernon, 1884

TURTLE SOUP AND BONY DUCK

I have luncheon at Kettners off the Charing Cross Road – and for the first time ever in my life I had *Turtle Soup*. I believe that the snobs and the so called important people at Guildhall Banquets start with this here soup. Well, they are lucky people if it's prepared the same way as it is at Kettners, for their soup was proper lovely and went down me a treat as it was hot and tasty. And then I had *duck* and green peas. I've had peas lots of time because one of my own simple luxuries in life is a tin of hot peas all to myself. They gives me wind, but I love 'em. And so I had 'em. But this was the first time I'd ever eaten duck. There was a lotta bone but what duck was there was jolly tasty and I enjoyed it. This lunch was paid for by my lawyer, Stanley Rubinstein. (I have not got any law, but I have a lawyer just in case: it sounds so nice to have a lawyer).

There cannot be a more generous hearted man in London than Mr Rubinstein. He don't say to me, 'Come to lunch,' and then look down the list and say, 'am having fish and chips, that would do you good and it's the cheapest thing on the Bill of Fare.' He don't do anything like that; he just hands the foreign language menu over and you just picks out. Well, diary, you *know* how I picks out what I want. I don't read the blooming things cause I don't know what on earth they stand for. I just reads *the prices*. If there is something at 7s 6d and something at 5s 6d, I of course has the 7s 6d cause Kettners, Verrys or anywhere else would not have the impudence to charge 7s 6d for a thing that was only worth 4s; and it stands to commonsense that the 7s 6d must be pretty good, not only because of the price, but because of the prominence it's displayed on the me and you. One of these days I may see meself in the Ritz. I hope that I do not there choose something marked 9s and find it's the Head waiter or something equally startling.

Fred Bason, *Diary*, 1954

～ 25 November ～

A COMMODIOUS AERIAL CONVEYANCE?

Attended among the rest of expectants to have a sight of the air-balloon discharged from the Artillery-ground, at one o'clock; it rose moderately, and in a southerly direction; was in sight ten or twelve minutes; its appearance to my eye, after it diminished to four or five inches in diameter, was like three round balls in contact, in shape of a triangular body with obtuse angles. I should think the numbers in Moorfields exceeded fourscore thousand. The sight was amusing; perhaps posterity may improve on this newly investigated subject, and make what is now only a pleasing show, a commodious, perhaps pernicious, aerial conveyance.

Samuel Curwen, *Journal*, 1783

SUNRISE IN THE PARK

In the morning it was so beautiful on the way to Turnham Green, the chestnut trees and clear blue sky and the morning sun were reflected in the water of the Thames, the grass was gloriously green and everywhere all around the sound of church bells. The day before I'd gone on a long journey to London, I left here at 4 in the morning, arrived at Hyde Park at half past six, the mist was lying on the grass and leaves were falling from the trees, in the distance one saw the shimmering lights of street-lamps that hadn't yet been put out, and the towers of Westminster Abbey and the Houses of Parliament, and the sun rose red in the morning mist – from there on to Whitechapel, that poor district of London, then to Chancery Lane and Westminster . . .

Vincent Van Gogh, Letter to his brother Theo, 1876

SO KNIGHTSBRIDGE AND NO INTELLECT

Prudey's new flat is over the Covent Garden market. You fight your way through baskets of fruit and vegetables to a small opening in the wall of the warehouse, squeeze through and find yourself at the bottom of dark stone stairs leading to the studio. She spends the day there and sleeps on the floor at the Players Theatre during air-raids. The studio is entirely brown. Brown corduroy chairs, a big modelling stand, a model's throne used as a table with a big bowl of oranges on it. Also scattered around are abstracts by the Baron, very phallic, but Prudey is having special shelves built in the lavatory to accommodate them.

She was looking great in scarlet dungarees, with her hair done up in a handkerchief. We sat in her blue and red bedroom with a big window overlooking the market and drank coffee round the stove. She has a new lower-class lover who is decorating the flat for her while the Baron is away. She also goes around with a 'set', the one that sleeps at the Players every night. I wish I had a set.

While we were drinking our coffee (which I put sugar into, although Prudey said I shouldn't), I showed her Rupert's letter and pumped her about his sex life with S. 'Well,' Prudey said, 'I don't want to depress you darling, but Rupert used to sleep with Squirrel a hell of a lot! You see, whatever else one can say against her she had one great thing, she was simply wonderful in bed. Rupert says it's because she was Fiji. He was always telling me about how she used to put salt on his cock and how thrilling it was, and so on. And just because she's terrific in bed he'll probably never give her up.'

'But she's terrible,' I said. 'She's so Knightsbridge, and she has no intellect.'

'Oh I know, but Rupert always has to have two girlfriends, one for sex and the other to talk to. I suppose that one was you,' she added rather tactlessly . . .

Joan Wyndham, *Love Lessons: A Wartime Diary*, 1940

⁓ 26 NOVEMBER ⁓

SWANSON THE DANE

Last night, Swanson the Dane, (who stole one Mrs. Rawlins, an heiresse, and forced her to marry him,) and one Mrs. Bainton, his pretended sister, who assisted, were convicted of felony at the Queens Bench bar.

Narcissus Luttrell, *Diary*, 1702

AN ASSEMBLY IN SOHO

We went to Court, and in the evening to an assembly at Soho. This consists of a concert and a ball, which take place every fortnight in a fine room, which has been much improved this year. Several ladies have a book, in one of which every one signs his name, paying five guineas for twelve nights. In order that only those people may be subscribers who are known to one of the ladies, the subscription books are kept by the ladies only, and the power to admit or to exclude whom they like is confined to them, and is not given to the owner of the rooms, who is an Italian of the name of Cornelia. The rooms in which they play, as well as the large ballroom, are very fine and beautifully lighted, and exceedingly well furnished. The vocal and instrumental music, by an orchestra at the end of the room, begins at seven o'clock and lasts until nine; dancing afterwards goes on until one or two. Tea, lemonade, and cake are served in two rooms. As at first we did not know how long we should be able to remain in England, and as we did not feel inclined to spend ten guineas perhaps for nothing, and also as my deep mourning* did not allow me to dance, we did not subscribe. But as every subscriber who is prevented from attending may give his ticket away, we got tickets from friends and went with my Lady Howe's youngest son.

Count Frederick Kielmansegge,
Diary of a Journey to England, 1761

* For his wife.

～ 27 NOVEMBER ～

THE GREAT STORM

About one this morning a terrible storm arose, which continued till past 7, the wind south west; the like not known in the memory of man; blew down a vast number of the tops of houses, chimnies, &c.; the damage incredible, the lady Nicholas and a great many people killed, and many wounded; most of the boats and barges forced ashore; an East India ship cast away near Blackwall, besides several merchant ships and colliers; divers of the great trees in St James Park, Temple, Grayes Inn, &c. blown down; and we are apprehensive we shall hear of great losses at sea.

Narcissus Luttrell, *Diary*, 1703

A VISIT TO NEWGATE

I went (conducted by Mr. Carver, the ordinary) into Newgate, where I had never been before, to see a poor Jewess, Alice Abraham, who had been my client in the late case of the gold-dust robbery. There was nothing very remarkable about her except her intense grief, less for herself than her father, Mouny (i.e. Emanuel) Moses, who was tried and convicted with her. I was much struck with the cleanliness, neatness, and propriety which prevail in the prison, so different from the scenes of depravity I have been used to read of, and that horrible state of filth and neglect, which, even up to recent times, produced, among many other maladies, the gaol distemper. All this wonderful improvement is the work of Mrs. Fry. An odd coincidence: in passing through one of the yards, Mr. Carver told me some of the executed criminals were buried there. 'Here,' said he, 'is G for Greenacre, there is T for Thistlewood.' Very odd. I prosecuted one and defended the other.

John Adolphus, *Journal*, 1839

SMUG CHELSEA FANS

I am looking forward to today; not only are we at home to Chelsea but it is Lyndsey's and my 22nd Wedding Anniversary. As a treat I have booked a pre-match anniversary meal in 'Legends' Restaurant in the North Stand. 'I know how to treat a girl.' I am still harbouring hopes that we can produce a repeat of the storming performance that saw us beat Chelsea 4–2 last season, on Boxing Day, but unlike last season, I don't honestly believe we are capable of doing it . . . All our hopes evaporated when within five minutes of the start of the second half we were 0–3 down . . . This was our sixth scoreless game out of fifteen. Off to 'The Ship' to be gloated at by our smug Chelsea chums, I can't wait! In the pub it's a good turnout of deflated Charlton fans ready to take our medicine, but to be fair to the Chelsea boys (not something that comes easily), they don't gloat too much; in fact they patronisingly try to console us.

Russ Wilkins, *Diary of a Common Fan*, 2004

～ 28 NOVEMBER ～

DR JOHNSON IN FAILING HEALTH

Last Thursday, my father set me down at Bolt-court, while he went on upon business. I was anxious to again see poor Dr. Johnson, who has had terrible health since his return from Lichfield. He let me in, though very ill. He was alone, which I much rejoiced at; for I had a longer and more satisfactory conversation with him than I have had for many months. He was in rather better spirits, too, than I had lately seen him, but he told me he was going to try what sleeping out of town might do for him.*

'I remember,' said he, 'that my wife, when she was near her end, poor woman, was also advised to sleep out of town, and when she was carried to the lodgings that had been prepared for her, she complained that the staircase was in very bad condition – for the plaster was beaten off the wall in many places. "Oh," said the man of the house, "that's nothing but by the knocks against it of the coffins of the poor souls that have died in the lodgings.'"

He laughed, though not without apparent secret anguish, in telling me this. I felt extremely shocked, but, willing to confine my words at least to the literal story, I only exclaimed against the unfeeling absurdity of such a confession.

'Such a confession,' cried he, 'to a person then coming to try his lodgings for her health, contains, indeed, more absurdity than we can well lay our account for.'

Fanny Burney, *Diary*, 1784

* Johnson died in his house in Bolt Court, Fleet Street, a few weeks later.

A BOMB NEAR HARRODS

All London is excitement on account of a Zeppelin raid which took place in the small hours of this morning. Four Zeppelins participated and two were brought down. Late at noon, a German seaplane dropped a bomb just in front of Harrods . . .

Frank Hurley, *Diary*, 1916

∼ 29 NOVEMBER ∼

FEARS OF THIEVES IN THE NIGHT

Waked about seven o'clock this morning with a noise I supposed I heard, near our chamber, of knocking, which, by and by, increased: and I, more awake, could distinguish it better. I then waked my wife, and both of us wondered at it, and lay so a great while, while that increased, and at last heard it plainer, knocking, as if it were breaking down a window for people to get out; and then removing of stools and chairs; and plainly, by and by, going up and down our stairs. We lay, both of us, afeard; yet I would have rose, but my wife would not let me. Besides, I could not do it without making noise; and we did both conclude that thieves were in the house, but wondered what our people did, whom we thought either killed, or afeard, as we were. Thus we lay till the clock struck eight, and high day. At last, I removed my gown and slippers safely to the other side of the bed over my wife: and there safely rose, and put on my gown and breeches, and then, with a firebrand in my hand, safely opened the door, and saw nor heard any thing. Then (with fear, I confess) went to the maid's chamber-door, and all quiet and safe. Called Jane up, and went down safely, and opened my chamber door, where all well. Then more freely about, and to the kitchen, where the cook-maid up, and all safe. So up again, and when Jane come, and we demanded whether she heard no noise, she said, 'yes, and was afeard,' but rose with the other maid, and found nothing; but heard a noise in the great stack of chimnies that goes from Sir J. Minnes through our house; and so we sent, and their chimnies have been swept this morning, and the noise was that, and nothing else.

Samuel Pepys, *Diary*, 1667

THE AIR AT KNIGHTSBRIDGE

I removed with my family to town on account of my daughter Helena's cough and feverish disposition, for which I sent her to Knightsbridge for the air two days before, and that Dr. Hollings might have more convenience to visit her than whilst she was at Charlton. I dined at my house in Pall Mall. In the evening Dr. Hollings came to acquaint my wife that Helena will do well.

Earl of Egmont, *Diary*, 1735

～ 30 NOVEMBER ～

RUMINATIONS WITH REGARD TO LODGINGS

I thought my present lodgings too dear, and therefore looked about and found a place in Crown Street, Westminster, an obscure street but pretty lodgings at only £22 a year. Much did I ruminate with regard to lodgings. Sometimes I considered that a fine lodging denoted a man of great fashion, but then I thought that few people would see it and therefore the expense would be hid, whereas my business was to make as much show as I could with my small allowance. I thought that an elegant place to come home to was very agreeable and would inspire me with ideas of my own dignity; but then I thought it would be hard if I had not a proportionable show in other things, and that it was better to come gradually to a fine place than from a fine to a worse. I therefore resolved to take the Crown Street place, and told my present landlord that I intended to leave him.

James Boswell, *London Journal*, 1762

STEALING BODIES IN THE NIGHT

At night went and got 3 Bunhill Row, sold to Mr. Cline, St. Thomas's Hospital.

Joseph Naples, *The Diary of a Resurrectionist*, 1811

DECEMBER

~ 1 December ~

SKATING IN ST JAMES'S PARK

Having seen the strange and wonderful dexterity of the sliders on the new canal in St James's Park performed before their Majesties by divers gentlemen and others with skates, after the manner of the Hollanders, with what swiftness they pass, how suddenly they stop in full career upon the ice, I went home by water, but not without exceeding difficulty, the Thames being frozen, great flakes of ice encompassing our boat.

John Evelyn, *Diary*, 1662

THE UNIVERSAL PROVIDER

Bought our Christmas supplies at Whiteley's Westbourne Grove. He now sells everything, provisions of all kinds included. They say it is impossible to ask for anything he can't supply; his neighbours are very angry, and on last Guy Fawkes day burnt him in effigy.

Louisa Bain, *Diary*, 1874

GIGGLING AT VAGUE ADVANCES

Have just been out with one of the men and had two half-pints of beer – am feeling unwontedly cheerful in consequence. Have walked up Whitehall and down again in the pitch black out, feeling rather a devil and listening to his account of his wife's nerves. Stood on Westminster Bridge for a few minutes and giggled away his vague advances, thinking sententious thoughts about the Thames being the same in spite of war – except for the strands of coloured lights of peace/business/war advertisements.

Olivia Cockett, *Diary*, 1940

RUDLAND & STUBBS FISH RESTAURANT

Yellow light, wooden panelling, sawdust on the floor . . . The head waiter tells us after Richard Gere ate here a few nights ago many of the waitresses and some of the waiters made a beeline for his chair – which has since disappeared . . . We leave the restaurant about half one. Smithfield Market is coming noisily to life. Giant lorries trundle into the floodlights. Men in bloody aprons, breath steaming in the cold night air, carrying carcasses into the great hall. Inside I glimpse rows of meat hooks and a man stirring a boiling cauldron, stripping the flesh off a few heads.

Anthony Sher, *The Year of the King*, 1983

∼ 2 DECEMBER ∼

A CHRISTENING WITH GOOD PLAIN COMPANY

Up, and to church, and after church home to dinner, where I met Betty Michell and her husband, very merry at dinner, and after dinner, having borrowed Sir W. Pen's coach, we to Westminster, they two and my wife and I to Mr. Martin's, where find the company almost all come to the christening of Mrs. Martin's child, a girl. A great deal of good plain company. After sitting long, till the church was done, the Parson comes, and then we to christen the child. I was Godfather, and Mrs. Holder (her husband, a good man, I know well), and a pretty lady, that waits, it seems, on my Lady Bath, at White Hall, her name, Mrs. Noble, were Godmothers. After the christening comes in the wine and the sweetmeats, and then to prate and tattle, and then very good company they were, and I among them. Here was old Mrs. Michell and Howlett, and several married women of the Hall, whom I knew mayds. Here was also Mrs. Burroughs and Mrs. Bales, the young widow, whom I led home, and having staid till the moon was up, I took my pretty gossip to White Hall with us, and I saw her in her lodging, and then my owne company again took coach, and no sooner in the coach but something broke, that we were fain there to stay till a smith could be fetched, which was above an hour, and then it costing me 6/- to mend. Away round by the wall and Cow Lane, for fear it should break again; and in pain about the coach all the way. But to ease myself therein Betty Michell did sit at the same end with me . . .

Samuel Pepys, *Diary*, 1666

～ *3 December* ～

FAILED HIGHWAYMEN

Two highwaymen were this morning taken in Clare Market, being discovered by a butcher whom they robbed: they offered to discharge their pistolls, but did not goe off; 2 soldiers forc'd them to yield.

Narcissus Luttrell, *Diary*, 1692

SUDDENLY ALONE

Walked up the Strand, when to my surprise I found myself all alone, not a person within sight, not a coach to be seen or heard; which, considering the hour, (five p.m.), was singular. In this predicament I walked on a hundred yards or more; arrived at Spring Garden Coffee-House, and over a dish of tea read the Morning Post.

Samuel Curwen, *Journal*, 1780

WALKING INTO TOWN

Breakfasted at the inn at Wimbledon; walked from thence to Putney bridge, where I got into a boat and went as far as Chelsea bridge, from whence I walked to the Haymarket.

William Hervey, *Journals*, 1799

~ *4 December* ~

MEETING THE WORDSWORTHS

I breakfasted early, and soon after nine walked to Dr. Wordsworth's, at Lambeth. I crossed for the first time Waterloo Bridge. The view of Somerset House is very fine indeed, and the bridge itself is highly beautiful; but the day was so bad that I could see neither of the other bridges, and of course scarcely any objects. I found Mr. and Mrs. Wordsworth and the Doctor at breakfast, and I spent a couple of hours with them very agreeably. We talked about poetry. Wordsworth has brought MSS. with him, and is inclined to print one or two poems, as it is the fashion to publish small volumes now . . .

Henry Crabb Robinson, *Diary*, 1817

ETHER SOAP UP THE BOTTOM

Rowena rings to say, in a dead sort of voice, 'The worse has happened, Billy Bolitho says I am definitely pregnant. Can you lend me fifteen quid till Saturday?' I said I could give her six, which is all I had, because I know just how she feels, and if she doesn't have an abortion before Saturday it will be too late. I met her in Dean Street and we wandered down to Duran's in the icy cold for a *delicious* lunch. Christ their pastries are good! Poor Rowena couldn't eat anything. She says her only other chance is to put lots of ether soap up her bottom for ten days. Billy Bolitho says it's tough going but infallible, but R says, 'How will I keep it from my Mum if I go around smelling like an operating theatre?'

Joan Wyndham, *Love Lessons: A Wartime Diary*, 1940

~ 5 DECEMBER ~

VISITING A NEW THEATRE

Having never seen the Royalty theatre, determined this day should be devoted to that purpose. Passed along Cheap-side, Lombard-street, Fenchurch-street, and down the Minories, until I arrived at Tower-hill, and afterwards by a circuitous rout, found myself in Wellclose-Square — I more than encompassed it. I saw a poor woman with grey locks, but whose face did not quite correspond with them, stoop down, pick up two or three small crumbs of bread, and put them into her mouth. I called her back, gave her a trifle, and was angry with myself afterwards, that it was not more. I feel assured that she was not an imposter . . . It being yet early, went into a pastry cook's shop, and being almost at a loss what to ask for, bought something more than a pound of plum cake, and eat two jellies. Quitting the shop, I sauntered about; went into a public house, called for a pint of porter which I just tasted, and found the tap room in which I was sitting was frequented by thieves, as the landlady said she was obliged to remove the fire-side furniture, and that the lead of the clock had been recently stolen.

The doors of the theatre still remaining closed, I went to another tap, opposite to it. There were two foreign sailors smoking, and two or three other foreigners, I believe Germans — it seemed a foreign house. I here called for a glass of brandy and water, which I never tasted. At length I crossed the street, and as I reached the box door, Mr. John Astley had just got out of a hackney coach. I entered the house with him . . . The theatre is very plain, but neat; the house seemed to me something larger than the Hay-market; the pit is small but I was told, the middle gallery would contain a thousand people . . . The performance consisted of singing, dancing, and pantomimic exhibitions, in one of which Mrs. Astley performed. At the conclusion, I returned by Rosemary lane, and re-trod the streets I had passed in the morning, and arrived at King-street, about half past eleven.

George Frederick Cooke, *Journal*, 1806

OPENING PEACE WEEK

Put finishing touches to a peace speech, then drive down to Camberwell, via the picture-framers in Islington. Brief glimpse of the nightmare world of bottled-up traffic on the way through London. Unmoving lines of huge lorries in the drizzle. Dark, enormous, steaming, hissing, hostile and hugely out of scale with the buildings and streets they clog . . . Then I drive up to Camden Institute where I deliver my five-minute piece on peace to open Peace Week there. A small but appreciative audience of middle-aged, grey-haired intellectuals, students, slightly dog-eared supporters of the cause and people who look a little mad.

Michael Palin, *Halfway to Hollywood*, 1983

∼ 6 *December* ∼

HEADS ON TEA CHESTS

Francis Dann and Will Arnold were yesterday executed for Murder. They were the first Malefactors conveyed to the new Surgeon's Hall in Lincoln's Inn Fields. They were conveyed in a cart, their Heads supported by Tea-Chests for the public to see – I think contrary to all decency and the Laws of Humanity in a Country like this; I hope it will not be repeated.

George Macaulay, *The War Diary of a London Scot*, 1796

A STRANGE ABSENCE

All these days, since my last date, have been marked by nothing very well worthy of detail and description. I have walked the streets a great deal in the dull November days, and always take a certain pleasure in being in the midst of human life, – as closely encompassed by it as it is possible to be anywhere in this world; and in that way of viewing it there is a dull and sombre enjoyment always to be had in Holborn, Fleet Street, Cheapside, and the other busiest parts of London. It is human life; it is this material world; it is a grim and heavy reality. I have never had the same sense of being surrounded by materialisms and hemmed in with the grossness of this earthly existence anywhere else; these broad, crowded streets are so evidently the veins and arteries of an enormous city. London is evidenced in every one of them, just as a megatherium is in each of its separate bones, even if they be small ones. Thus I never fail of a sort of self-congratulation in finding myself, for instance, passing along Ludgate Hill; but, in spite of this, it is really an ungladdened life to wander through these huge, thronged ways, over a pavement foul with mud, ground into it by a million of footsteps; jostling against people who do not seem to be individuals, but all one mass, so homogeneous is the street-walking aspect of them; the roar of vehicles pervading me, – wearisome cabs and omnibuses; everywhere the dingy brick edifices heaving themselves up, and shutting out all but a strip of sullen cloud, that serves London for a sky, – in short, a general impression of grime and sordidness; and at this season always a fog scattered along the vista of streets, sometimes so densely as almost to spiritualize the materialism and make the scene resemble the other world of worldly people, gross even in ghostliness. It is strange how little splendour and brilliancy one sees in London, – in the city almost none, though some in the shops of Regent Street.

Nathaniel Hawthorne, *English Notebooks*, 1857

~ 7 December ~

RADICALS IN MARYLEBONE

The London Corresponding Society having signified an intention to meet in Marybone fields to-day; at one o'clock, I went into the new road where great numbers of people were passing to and from those fields. In the second field from the road, on the right hand of the Jews Harp, three slips of hustings were erected in different parts of the field; and before each, a crowd of people were assembled, as at fairs, when a quack Doctor exhorts a mob . . . Of all the orators, Jones appeared to me to have most genius: but he labours under a constitutional disadvantage, which seems to oblige him often to pause . . . Citizen Jones is a tallish, slender man; his complexion pale, & face thin. He was without powder, his hair dark. He is afflicted with a paralytic affection, which causes, excepting when he is exerting himself, an almost constant convulsive twitching of his head, shoulders, & arms. He was dressed in a green coat, & had halfboots on; and on the whole presented a figure such as is usually called shabby genteel. He seems to be about 3 or 4 & thirty years old. He has an excellent voice; sharp, clear and distinct; and his harangues at different periods were well calculated for catching his auditory; and many passages ingenious enough . . . He spoke with great inveteracy against Pitt, and of his being brought to publick execution . . . Many respectable people were in various parts of the field: but they all appeared like myself, spectators of the proceedings of the day. No tumult took place: nor was any offence given to such as did not hold up hands or join in the plaudit. I was in every part, & where the crowd was greatest; yet never held up my hand or expressed approbation.

Joseph Farington, *Diary*, 1795

A FIRE IN HAYMARKET

The Queen's Theatre in the Haymarket was burnt down last night. James and Tom had gone to bed, and happily for them the wind blew the flames away from their side of the street. The heat was so intense that they could not remain at their windows; they both got on the roof and poured water over it and the window frames as Mr. Kinnaird did over the roof of the Bank next door. All the block of houses in the centre of which the Opera House stood are more or less burnt; it has been an awful fire. The ground is covered with snow which continues to fall at intervals.

Louisa Bain, *Diary*, 1867

EXTREMES OF TEMPERATURE

The registering thermometer outside a window, looking east, at the Athenaeum Club showed this morning a difference of nearly a hundred degrees between the maximum and minimum temperature of the night, and the minimum was not far from the freezing point. The great fire which destroyed Her Majesty's Theatre in the Haymarket had occurred during the night. A pane of glass in a window of the drawing-room, a few yards nearer to the source of heat, was cracked.

Sir Frederick Pollock, *Diary*, 1867

A NEW OLIVE DRESS

Saturday, so up late and went to call for E at her flat in Markham Square to take her out to lunch. She had on a new olive green dress, which she had just bought at Harvey Nichols. We went to a new restaurant in the King's Road – Alvaro's, was it? Cheerful, crowded and noisy – just the place for a grim December day, and then to the film about the mongoloid killer.*

Charles Ritchie, *Diary*, 1968

* *Twisted Nerve*, starring Hayley Mills and Hywel Bennett.

～ 8 DECEMBER ～

ACTING IN WOOLWICH

Arose at eight. Breakfasted at nine. I had promised Mr. Beverley, of Theatre Royal, Covent Garden, to act a night for him at Woolwich, where he had a company at present stationed. A little after ten he called upon me, and about half past we set out together in a post-chaise, through Greenwhich and New Charleton. We alighted at Mr. Beverley's lodgings, near the theatre, and were received by Mrs. Beverley. A little after twelve I went to the theatre, and rehearsed Sir Pertinax McSycophant* – afterwards took a slight refreshment; and the day, which had been very wet, clearing up, I walked with Mr. B. to the Royal arsenal, formerly called the Warren. I was introduced to Mr. White, a gentleman belonging to the place, who very obligingly showed us as much as our short stay would permit us to view. The arsenal covers a very large space of ground. There are several handsome buildings, and a large new store-house is now erecting, upon piles. Next to the river there is a long handsome wharf, and we saw many convicts with irons on, variously employed – they sleep on board hulks, are put in classes, and rewarded according to their behaviour . . . Dined heartily at Mr. B's, and about six, went with Mrs. B. to the theatre – acted Sir Pertinax; the play was very perfect, and better acted than I have known it by much larger companies, and better actors. The audience genteel and numerous. Fifty pounds is the utmost which the house (which is a very neat one) can contain: and Mr. B. told me the receipt was 47l. 16s. exclusive of some free people.

George Frederick Cooke, *Journal*, 1806

* The oddly named central character in a once-popular play by the eighteenth-century actor and dramatist Charles Macklin.

BEGGING ON THE BRIDGE

Richard Briers tells me how he was going up the steps from the National on to Waterloo Bridge when he was accosted, as one invariably is, by someone sitting on the landing, begging. 'No, I thought,' said Richard – 'not *again*, and walked on. Only then I heard this lugubrious voice say, "Oh. My favourite actor." So I turned back and gave him a pound.'

That particular pitch is known to be very profitable, partly because of actors and playgoers being more soft-hearted than the general run. The beggars have got themselves so well organized as to ration the pitch to half an hour apiece on pain of being beaten up. I find it easiest to think of Waterloo Bridge as a toll bridge, and resign myself to paying at least 50p to get across, thus sidestepping any tiresome questions about need or being taken advantage of.

Alan Bennett, *Diary*, 1990

∾ 9 December ∾

A BEAR'S REVENGE

The sam day at after-non was a bere-beytyn on the Banke syde, and ther the grett blynd bere broke losse, and in ronnyng away he chakt a servyng man by the calff of the lege, and bytt a gret pesse away, and after by the hokyll-bone, that with-in iij days after he ded.

Henry Machyn, *Diary*, 1554

BLESSED BE SHAKESPEARE

Went to see *Much Ado About Nothing* at the Lyceum. The play was most charming. We had a big side box, where I at once secured the worst seat (and then felt my conscience at rest). Irving has unpleasant mannerisms, but when he acts it makes an impression upon you. I never saw him look so well as he does as Benedick. Ellen Terry was charming as Beatrice. Beatrice is certainly a most delightful girl — there is nothing stagey about Beatrice . . . The *mise-en-scène* & the dresses were splendid. It is astonishing how well that play acts. Blessed be Shakespeare.

Mary, Lady Monkswell, *Journal*, 1882

POWER CUTS

The lights have just come on after another power cut, resulting from electrical workers striking for a 30 per cent rise, after turning down 10 . . . the power cuts have brought a return of Dunkirk spirit. Candles change hands at high prices. Long queues at filling-stations for petrol and in Blackheath Village for paraffin.

Peter Nichols, *Diary*, 1970

∼ *10 December* ∼

HANGED FOR COUNTERFEITING

Rafe Egerton, of London, being one of my Lord Chancellor's servants, and one Thomas Herman, sometime servant with Fleetwood, one of my Lord Chancellor's gentlemen, were drawn from the Tower of London to Tyburn, and there hanged and quartered for counterfeiting the King's Great Seal.

Charles Wriothesley, *Chronicle*, 1541

THE FATE OF SWANSON THE DANE

Yesterday the Dane, who stole Mrs. Rawlins and married her by force, was executed in Southwark.

Narcissus Luttrell, *Diary*, 1702

DRUNK AND STEALING BODIES

Intoxsicated all day: at night went out and got 5 Bunhill Row, Jack all most buried.

Joseph Naples, *The Diary of a Resurrectionist*, 1811

A PAIL ON THE STAIRS

We went looking at private hotels today. Quite horrified by a decent one in Queen's Gate. Pail on stairs. Yet comfortable. But too horribly ugly and boarding-house-y. I had begun by putting cost at £40 a month. I then dropped it to £25, under M's influence. It must now go up to £30 or £35. Lunched at Harrods Stores, crammed; had to wait a minute for a table. Home in petrole-ous omnibus. This morning I walked 5 or 6 miles through Roehampton and Barnes. Impressed by the cleanliness, order, and sober luxury of all the dwellings I saw.

Arnold Bennett, *Journal*, 1907

WELCOME HOME, MRS PANKHURST

I went yesterday to Mrs. Pankhurst's welcome home meeting in London. She has returned from America, where she seems to have had a very successful tour. The Albert Hall was full up, and as usual the audience was most enthusiastic. Mrs. Pankhurst informed us that her fine had been paid by someone anonymously, so she will not go to prison. I believe the Government has got something to do with it, as in several cases lately Suffragettes' fines have been paid by someone unknown.

Katherine Roberts, *Pages from the Diary of a Militant Suffragette*, 1909

~ *11 December* ~

DOWNING STREET NO LONGER A NEST OF FILTH

I was much hurried during my stay in London; the improvements ever since I was last there surprised me, particularly the Treasury and Downing Street, especially the latter, which was a nest of filth, dirt, and thieves.

General William Dyott, *Diary*, 1827

PING-PONG AT THE ROYAL AQUARIUM

I took half an hour after dinner last night, on my way to the office, and looked in at the Royal Aquarium* to watch the big ping-pong tournament. There was a crowd around the eight tables. Some of the play was shocking. I could have done better on a kitchen table . . . The Aquarium was terribly cold and draughty in this dreadful wintry weather. Two rival ping-pong associations are now in full swing, and it threatens to become one of the national pastimes.

R. D. Blumenfeld, *R.D.B.'s Diary*, 1901

* The Royal Aquarium, built in 1876, stood opposite Westminster Abbey. It was demolished a few years after Blumenfeld's visit.

DOWNTOWN DOCKLANDS

This offer arrived out of the blue. A letter came from Olympia & York, the huge Canadian international property developers, asking would I act as a design consultant . . . It had been pointed out to them that, being a Canadian firm with five American architects, they needed a UK input . . . Nigel [Brockes] took me round the whole Docklands area, puffing a cigar in the front of his grey Rolls-Royce and purring with pleasure, as well he might, at the resurrection of this vast eight-mile scene of desolation. It was an odd mixture. I can see how people said why wasn't there a masterplan, but it would never have happened at all. As it is, it is a mixture of restored old warehouses, post-modernist buildings and constructions for businesses, restored yuppie old houses, acres of crumbling decay, eruptions of deadly council housing (over 80% of the population live in this, mainly the real East End working class, left from the days when we had a port) and occasionally a church with a spire.

Canary Wharf has quite a history and I have been brought in post Olympia & York buying out the previous developers. The project is to build what can be described as the Docklands 'downtown' area, a huge formal working and retail centre which would act as a focus for the whole, in the same way that London falls into areas like Kensington, Chelsea, the West End and the City. The concept includes a grand series of formal squares and circuses, high-rise buildings constructed with linking design modules. All this can happen without reference to anyone as Docklands is a development zone.

Sir Roy Strong, *Diary*, 1987

∼ 12 December ∼

AS OLD AS THE FIRE

In the afternoon, went from Charing Cross to Cannon Street by rail, and thence walked up to certain old bookshops, beyond Finsbury Square. On my way back I rambled through the old-fashioned streets about Cripplegate; attracted first by the fine massive antique tower of Cripplegate church, which is a-repairing. In the quiet of a Saturday afternoon, when offices are closed and busy men departed, the world of modern life disappears for a moment, and these old 17th & 18th century streets and alleys, these deserted old churches, bring back something of the interest and delight with which one wanders through a medieval street abroad. Far better it is to ramble here, at such a time, than in some bustling suburb, mean, newfangled, fashionable or vulgar. I went, probably for the last time, through the mazes of old Newgate market: long low alleys, glazed in of late years, but walled on both sides with butchers' shops nearly as old as the Fire: open sheds, with massy beams and rafters and blocks, browned and polished by age and friction. Many of the alleys were closed and dark, for the butchers had removed to the new Market in Smithfield: but two or three were lighted up & busy with buyers and sellers – long rude vistas of meat and men.

Arthur Munby, *Diary*, 1868

∼ 13 December ∼

ANTI-CATHOLIC RIOTS

On Tuesday night there was an alarm, occasioned by burning the Papists' Lincoln's Inn Fields Chapel; they did the like to the Chapels of St. John's Clerkenwell, and Lime-street, but not easily breaking into the latter, cried they would down with it, were it as strong as Portsmouth. And, accordingly, having levelled them, they carried all the trumpery in mock procession and triumph, with oranges on the tops of swords and staves, with great lighted candles in gilt candlesticks, thus victoriously passing of the Guards that were drawn up. And after having bequeathed these trinkets to the flames, they visited Harry Hills' Printing House, which they served in like manner. But, what is most ungrateful, their execution reaching to the Spanish Ambassador's House, which they plundered of all its rich furniture, plate, money, and three coaches, to the value as is computed of £20,000. All sober people are extraordinarily concerned at this horrid violation of the Law of Nations, and the Lords are said to have assured his Excellency that they will study some means to make him satisfaction.

Anon., Letter to John Ellis, 1688

GLADSTONE TELLS A JOURNALIST
TO GO AWAY

Just as I came out of Charles Street into St. James's Square I spied the Prime Minister walking round by the iron railings opposite, apparently bent on an after-lunch walk. He had a big grey shawl over his shoulders, and appeared to be talking to himself. The usual Scotland Yard 'shadow' was not there, so I concluded the P.M. was only out for a few minutes. But it appeared to me to be providential, and so, since Mr. Gladstone knows me well and is always most friendly to me, I stepped across, and, raising my silk hat, said: 'Good-day, Prime Minister. I . . .' 'Go away,' said the P.M., without looking up, and walked on. I stepped alongside, and said: 'But, Mr. Gladstone, you don't appear to know me. I am Blumenfeld, of the New York Herald, and I would like . . .' The old man stood still and glared like a ferocious lion. 'Go away, I tell you,' he added. 'I don't know you. Don't bother me,' and stumped on. The old apple woman sitting beside her basket opposite the Duke of Norfolk's house jeered at me. A cabman on his hansom cracked his whip at me; and I sneaked across to the club. I am sure that to-morrow I shall have a postcard from the P.M. asking me to overlook it.*

R. D. Blumenfeld, *R.D.B.'s Diary*, 1892

* Poor snubbed Blumenfeld later reports that he never got his note of apology from Gladstone.

～ 14 December ～

AN ENORMOUS BABEL

Of this enormous Babel of a place I can give you no account in writing: it is like the heart of all the universe; and the flood of human effort rolls out of it and into it with a violence that almost appals one's very sense. Paris scarcely occupies a quarter of the ground, and does not seem to have the twentieth part of the business. O that our father saw Holborn in a fog! with the black vapour brooding over it, absolutely like fluid ink; and coaches and wains and sheep and oxen and wild people rushing on with bellowings and shrieks and thundering din as if the earth in general were gone distracted. To-day I chanced to pass through Smithfield, when the market was three fourths over. I mounted the steps of a door, and looked abroad upon the area, an irregular space of perhaps thirty acres in extent, encircled with old dingy brick-built houses, and intersected with wooden pens for the cattle. What a scene! Innumerable herds of fat oxen, tied in long rows, or passing at a trot to their several shambles; and thousands of graziers, drovers, butchers, cattle-brokers with their quilted frocks and long goads pushing on the hapless beasts; hurrying to and fro in confused parties, shouting, jostling, cursing, in the midst of rain and *shairn* [dung] and braying discord such as the imagination cannot figure. Then there are stately streets and squares, and calm green recesses to which nothing of this abomination is permitted to enter. No wonder Cobbett calls the place a Wen! It is a monstrous Wen! The thick smoke of it beclouds a space of thirty square miles; and a million of vehicles, from the dog- or cuddy-barrow to the giant waggon, grind along its streets forever. I saw a six-horse wain the other day with, I think, Number 200,000 and odd upon it!

There is an excitement in all this, which is pleasant as a transitory feeling, but much against my taste as a permanent one. I had much rather visit London from time to time, than live in it. There is in fact no *right* life in it that I can find: the people are situated here like plants in a hot house, to which the quiet influences of sky and earth are never in their unadulterated state admitted.

Thomas Carlyle, Letter to his brother Alick, 1824

A FENIAN OUTRAGE

Yesterday afternoon a most horrid attempt was made to blow up the wall of the Prison at Clerkenwell in order to rescue Burke, the Fenian leader. A truck attended by three men and one woman was drawn up to the wall of the prisoners' exercise ground, on it was what looked like a 36 gallon beer barrel. In an instant the bung was out and a match lighted; they all four ran off, while the barrel, which contained 500 lbs. of gunpowder, blew up, and forty feet of the prison wall was blown down, and many houses on the other side of the way were reduced to ruins. Above sixty people, mostly women and children, are at the Hospitals with ghastly wounds, and some are crushed to death; a more cruel outrage was never perpetrated.

Louisa Bain, *Diary*, 1867

～ 15 DECEMBER ～

A TRUE ENGLISH DAY

The enemies of the people of England who would have them considered in the worst light represent them as selfish, beef-eaters, and cruel. In this view I resolved today to be a true-born Old Englishman. I went into the City to Dolly's Steak-house in Paternoster Row and swallowed my dinner by myself to fulfill the charge of selfishness; I had a large fat beef-steak to fulfil the charge of beef-eating; and I went at five o'clock to the Royal Cockpit in St. James's Park and saw cock-fighting for about five hours to fulfill the charge of cruelty.

A beefsteak-house is a most excellent place to dine at. You come in there to a warm, comfortable, large room, where a number of people are sitting at a table. You take whatever place you find empty; call for what you like, which you get well and cleverly dressed. You may either chat or not as you like. Nobody minds you, and you pay very reasonably. My dinner (beef, bread and beer and waiter) was only a shilling . . .

I then went to the Cockpit, which is a circular room in the middle of which the cocks fight. It is seated round with rows gradually rising. The pit and the seats are all covered with mat. The cocks, nicely cut

and dressed and armed with silver heels, are set down and fight with amazing bitterness and resolution. Some of them were quickly dispatched. One pair fought three quarters of an hour. The uproar and noise of betting is prodigious. A great deal of money made a very quick circulation from hand to hand. There was a number of professed gamblers there. An old cunning dog whose face I had seen at Newmarket sat by me a while. I told him I knew nothing of the matter. 'Sir,' said he, 'you have as good a chance as anybody.' He thought I would be a good subject for him. I was young-like. But he found himself balked. I was shocked to see the distraction and anxiety of the betters. I was sorry for the poor cocks. I looked round to see if any of the spectators pitied them when mangled and torn in a most cruel manner, but I could not observe the smallest relenting sign in any countenance. I was therefore not ill pleased to see them endure mental torment. Thus did I complete my true English day, and came home pretty much fatigued and pretty much confounded at the strange turn of this people.

James Boswell, *London Journal*, 1762

A DIFFICULT CASE

I spent several hours at the Clerkenwell Sessions. A case came before the court ludicrous from the minuteness required in the examination. Was the pauper settled in parish A or B? The house he occupied was in both parishes, and models both of the house and the bed in which the pauper slept were laid before the court, that it might ascertain how much of his body lay in each parish. The court held the pauper to be settled where his head (being the nobler part) lay, though one of his legs at least, and a great part of his body, lay out of that parish. Quod notandum est!

Henry Crabb Robinson, *Diary*, 1815

~ 16 DECEMBER ~

CUTTING A LEG OFF UNNECESSARILY

I went to the Westminster Infirmary, being one of the Governors, upon a summons to hear a complaint of Serjeant Dickins against one Hawkins and one Wilkie, subordinate surgeons to the hospital. The serjeant being one of the superior surgeons and as such vested with an inspection into the good behaviour of these inferior ones, complained of those gentlemen for acting in a late case without his knowledge, whereby they had proceeded to cutting off a poor woman's leg, which he apprehended needed not have been done in case his advice when he saw the woman had been followed, which was to clap a poultice of bread and milk to her leg and wait the issue for a day or two; but contrary to this, they, when his back was turned, run a knife into the leg and cut and slashed her in such a manner that a mortification had ensued if they had not in time cut the leg off. Hawkins said in his justification that he imagined there was matter gathered, which if so, it was fit as early as could be to search for it, and give it vent; that accordingly the event proved him in the right, for upon the excision above half a pint of matter came away, as was testified by an affidavit of five pupil surgeons which he produced.

Earl of Egmont, *Diary*, 1737

OVERRATED TERRORS

Morning with Blake around the city. Afternoon to Madame Tussauds.
This huge waxworks display I found very disappointing. The terrors of
the Chamber of Horrors are absurdly overrated . . . Blake is woman-
mad and gives me the pip.

Frank Hurley, *Diary*, 1916

MUSIC IN A HAWKSMOOR CHURCH

With Louise and Dan to a carol concert in St Alfege's Church beside
the main traffic-circuit of Greenwich. Their music master, Turner, is
an enterprising teacher. At their last prize-giving his choir gave Britten's
Golden Vanitie. Now he directed the older children in a Jazz Chorale
with bits of contemporary reportage stuck in – comparing the fortunes
of babies born in Lewisham and an African township, UFOs sighted
over Salisbury Plain, the inevitable starving Indians. Vague assurance
of goodwill and some magic for good measure. Piano, choir, percussion,
recorders, a parade of huge masks made and worn by the children. But
the interior of this Hawksmoor church, with its Gibbons carvings and
Thornhill murals, has the worst sight-lines and some of the hollowest
acoustics of any I've known. We had to sit on the pew-backs to see
anything. These buildings were for the congregation to see *each other.*

Peter Nichols, *Diary*, 1971

～ *17 December* ～

VISITING WILLIAM BLAKE

A short call this morning on Blake. He dwells in Fountain Court, in the
Strand. I found him in a small room, which seems to be both a working-
room and a bedroom. Nothing could exceed the squalid air both of the
apartment and his dress; yet there is diffused over him an air of natural
gentility. His wife has a good expression of countenance. I found him
at work on Dante. The book (Cary) and his sketches before him. He

showed me his designs, of which I have nothing to say but that they evince a power I should not have anticipated, of grouping and of throwing grace and interest over conceptions monstrous and horrible . . .

We spoke of the Devil, and I observed that, when a child, I thought the Manichean doctrine, or that of two principles, a rational one. He assented to this, and in confirmation asserted that he did not believe in the omnipotence of God. The language of the Bible on that subject is only poetical or allegorical. Yet soon afterwards he denied that the natural world is anything. 'It is all nothing; and Satan's empire is the empire of nothing.'

He reverted soon to his favourite expression, 'My visions.' 'I saw Milton, and he told me to beware of being misled by his "Paradise Lost". In particular, he wished me to show the falsehood of the doctrine, that carnal pleasures arose from the Fall. The Fall could not produce any pleasure.' As he spoke of Milton's appearing to him, I asked whether he resembled the prints of him. He answered, 'All.' – 'What age did he appear to be?' – 'Various ages – sometimes a very old man.' He spoke of Milton as being at one time a sort of classical Atheist, and of Dante as being now with God. His faculty of vision, he says, he has had from early infancy. He thinks all men partake of it, but it is lost for want of being cultivated. He eagerly assented to a remark I made, that all men have all faculties in a greater or less degree. I am to continue my visits, and to read to him Wordsworth, of whom he seems to entertain a high idea.

Henry Crabb Robinson, *Diary*, 1825

A DESERTED HOUSE OF COMMONS

Today we had the Department of Employment carol service . . . I only can properly enjoy carol services if I am having an illicit affair with someone in the congregation. Why is this? Perhaps because they are essentially pagan, not Christian, celebrations. Next, thoroughly disillusioned with everything, and in foul mood, I traipsed around the precincts of the Palace of Westminster looking for Alison in order to seek his advice on how I should convey to the PM that I wanted 'out'. He was nowhere to be seen. His office was sterile-tidy, deserted. I switched objectives and searched for Tristan. But he had flown. Off, already, to Spain. The House is emptying fast. It echoes, and workmen have appeared, smelling of nicotine and perspiration.

Alan Clark, *Diaries*, 1985

～ 18 DECEMBER ～

A QUARREL IN A COFFEE-HOUSE

Dining in the City with six gentlemen of quality, coming away with two of them after dinner, they quarrelled in a coffee-house, where we stayed to drink coffee; and though I did what I could to reconcile them, went presently out and drew in the street, and made a pass one at the other, but missing one another, closed. By this time I got into them and broke one of their swords, and so they were parted. The one of them, which was Major Orbe, eldest son of Sir Thomas Orbe, of Lincolnshire (the other's name was Bellengeambe, of the North, the chief of that family), not thinking this full satisfaction, notwithstanding all my endeavours to make them friends, challenged Bellengeambe a second time; and taking coach, and I with them, bought new swords by the way, and came towards Hyde Park to fight. As we came by the way, I offered to be second, since they would fight, to either of them, and the other should look out for another to be his. Mr. Orbe chose me, and bid Bellengeambe seek his friend. Bellengeambe said he never would make use of any second, but would decide it presently by moonshine, for it was nine o'clock at night and very light, and would confide in my honour to see fair play done between them; which at the last I accepted at both their entreaties. By the mercy of heaven, missing one another's bodies as they passed against one another the second time, and closing together, I came in to part them, and Mr. Orbe's footman doing the same, we held their swords so as no mischief was done; only Mr. Orbe had a slight prick in the thigh, Mr. Bellengeambe had a raze on the forehead, and myself a slight hurt as I came in to part them. After this we went all to supper, and parted good friends.

Sir John Reresby, *Diary*, 1683

∼ *19* DECEMBER ∼

AN AIR RAID IN THE FIRST WORLD WAR

To Turkish Baths. I was wakened out of my after-bath sleep by news of impending air-raid. This news merely made me feel gloomy. I didn't mind missing dinner at flat, or anything – I was merely gloomy. As soon as I got out into Northumberland Avenue I heard guns. Motors and people rushing. Then guns very close. I began to run. I headed for Reform Club, and abandoned idea of reaching the flat. Everybody ran. Girls ran. However, I found that after the Turkish bath I couldn't run much in a heavy overcoat. So I walked. It seemed a long way. Guns momentarily ceased. So I didn't hurry and felt relieved. But still prodigiously gloomy. I reached the Club. Hall in darkness. No girls in coffee room. The menservants manfully tackled the few diners. Nothing could be had out of kitchen as kitchen under glass and deserted.

Arnold Bennett, *Journal*, 1917

∼ *20* DECEMBER ∼

A PLAN FOR A BRIDGE

Telford came about his plan and model for a bridge of one arch over the Thames instead of London Bridge.* Vansittart wrote to desire the use of one of the rooms at the Royal Academy for the model to be set up in.

Charles Abbot, Lord Colchester, *Diary*, 1800

* Telford's proposal of a single iron arch was later rejected in favour of the more conventional design by John Rennie.

A PROFUSION OF BONBONS

The shops in London begin to show some tokens of approaching Christmas; especially the toy-shops, and the confectioners', – the latter ornamenting their windows with a profusion of bonbons and all manner of pygmy figures in sugar; the former exhibiting Christmas-trees, hung with rich and gaudy fruit.

Nathaniel Hawthorne, *English Notebooks*, 1857

∽ 21 DECEMBER ∽

SLEEPING IN A GARRET

In a garret at the Black Lion, Water Lane, London. Having made half a dinner at Queen's Square Place, drove off furiously to the White Horse, Piccadilly, to be in time for the Oxford stage. Having waited half an hour and the coach not come, the weather cool, went in to warm. Having warmed half an hour, and wondering at the delay, went out to see. The coach had been gone twenty minutes. My honest coachman, as well to be sheltered from the storm as for repose, had got inside and was sound asleep. Drove to Gloucester Coffee-house to take the mail. Was advised to go to the Golden something, Charing Cross. Thither went. The mail was full, inside and out. Thence to the Saracen's Head. Thence to Fister Lane. Coach full. To the Black Lion, Water Lane, Fleet – full, inside and out. To the Old Crown, Holborn – no coach hence till Friday. To the Bolt Inn, where found a seat in a coach to go at 7 tomorrow, but no bed to be had. Went to the nearest inn, being the same Black Lion, where I am occupant of a garret room, up four flights of stairs, and a very dirty bed.

Aaron Burr, *Journal*, 1808

CHRISTMAS SHOPPING

We came to London for a couple of days' shopping; that is to say, Sophia came for shopping and I for the pleasure of coming ... We started in a fog which promised fine weather in town, and we were not disappointed. London was as full as it could hold; the streets were full, the shops over-full; to buy a penny stamp at the Post Office it was necessary to take your place in a long queue. But everybody seemed in good spirits; matronly dames, puffing papas, tall serious sisters were letting themselves be tugged down every street by apple-cheeked schoolboys; nursemaids smiled as they pushed their perambulators through the thickest of the crowd; the poor tired shop-girls smiled under the fostering eye of the shop-walker; even the sombre pavement artist chose subjects that smacked of the season, high-coloured roast beef of Old England, plum pudding crowned with no mortal holly; and the mechanical people who touch their hats at street corners and give five sweeps if you drop in a penny were keeping holiday, and cheerfully overlooked the mud at their crossings.

H. C. Beeching, *Pages from a Private Diary*, 1896

HOW FINE THIS WOULD HAVE BEEN

Oh dear – How agitating life is – What *I* think of when I walk down the Strand is: how fine this would have been if Wren's plans for rebuilding London after the Great Fire had been adopted. Steps to the river, and all that – and a broad thoroughfare – I've got lots to say but it must wait –

Vita Sackville-West, Letter to Virginia Woolf, 1926

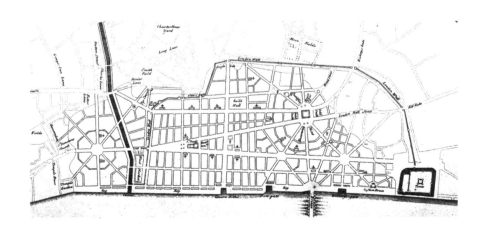

～ 22 December ～

A REMARKABLE FOG

Accidents occurred all over London, from a remarkable fog. Carriages ran against each other, and persons were knocked down by them at the crossings. The whole gang of thieves seemed to be let loose. After perpetrating their deeds, they eluded detection by darting into the fog. It was of an opake, dingy yellow. Torches were used as guides to carriages at mid-day, but gave scarcely any light through the fog. I went out for a few minutes. It was dismal.

Richard Rush, *Residence at the Court of London*, 1818

THE P.M.'S PLEASURE SPOILED

Bertram Mills gives a luncheon for 1,100 people at Olympia. I am about to enter when I hear a voice behind me. It is Ramsay MacDonald. He says, 'Well, this is my one holiday in the year. I love circuses.' At that moment they hand him a telegram. He opens it. He hands it to me with the words, 'Keep this, my dear Harold, and read it if ever you think you wish to be Prime Minister.' It is a telegram from some crank society abusing him for attending a luncheon in honour of a circus proprietor – since performing animals are cruel. He is disgusted and his pleasure spoiled.

Harold Nicolson, *Diary*, 1930

～ 23 December ～

RIDING DANGEROUSLY

Never felt so much danger on horseback as riding down to Fulham, my horse not being frost-shod.

William Windham, *Diary*, 1784

PRINCE OF WALES IN A PANIC

Hayes called and gave me some directions respecting my cold. He told me that the late murders of Mr. Marr's, & Mr. Williamson's families in Ratcliffe Highway,* & Gravel Lane, have so much alarmed the Prince Regent as to cause him to give orders to Col. Bloomfield not to allow any stranger to be admitted to Carlton House after 8 o'clock at night. This has occasioned great disappointment to the Prince's servants who had made preparations for entertaining their friends at Christmas.

Joseph Farington, *Diary*, 1811

* The notorious Ratcliffe Highway murders caused much anxiety among ordinary families in the East End but it seems unlikely that the Prince Regent had much to worry about.

A MYSTERIOUS ASSURANCE

An alarm from Emma . . . Started back as far as Islington to see after the nurse . . . Took 'bus myself to the Archway, Highgate, in distress of mind at not being able to afford a cab in such an emergency; and so walked home four miles, racked with anxiety about Emma, the most beautiful duck in existence. With 18s. 9d. in hand, to last at least three weeks, how *could* I take a cab? and this was all that remained me this evening. As I walked down the Grove, and very tired with a weak foot, I felt that mysterious assurance that all was right which I have before felt when nearing some dreaded event that has eventually turned out all right. I got home at eight p.m., and found dear Emma still in expectation . . .

Ford Madox Brown, *Diary*, 1854

∼ 24 December ∼

A CATHOLIC CHRISTMAS EVE

Up, and all the morning at the office, and at noon with my clerks to dinner, and then to the office again, busy at the office till six at night, and then by coach to St. James's, it being about six at night; my design being to see the ceremonys, this night being the eve of Christmas, at the Queen's chapel. But it being not begun I to Westminster Hall, and there staid and walked, and then to the Swan, and there drank and talked . . . and so to White Hall, and sent my coach round, I through the Park to chapel, where I got in up almost to the rail, and with a great deal of patience staid from nine at night to two in the morning, in a very great crowd; and there expected, but found nothing extraordinary, there being nothing but a high masse. The Queen was there, and some ladies. But, Lord! what an odde thing it was for me to be in a crowd of people, here a footman, there a beggar, here a fine lady, there a zealous poor papist, and here a Protestant, two or three together, come to see the shew. I was afeard of my pocket being picked very much . . . Their musique very good indeed, but their service I confess too frivolous, that there can be no zeal go along with it, and I do find by them themselves that they do run over their beads with one hand, and point and play and talk and make signs with the other in the midst of their masse. But all things very rich and beautiful; and I see the papists have the wit, most of them, to bring cushions to kneel on, which I wanted, and was mightily troubled to kneel. All being done, and I sorry for my coming, missing of what I expected; which was, to have had a child born and dressed there, and a great deal of do: but we broke up, and nothing like it done: and there I left people receiving the Sacrament: and the Queen gone, and ladies; only my Lady Castlemayne, who looked prettily in her night-clothes, and so took my coach, which waited, and away through Covent Garden, to set down two gentlemen and a lady, who come thither to see also, and did make mighty mirth in their talk of the folly of this religion. And so I stopped, having set them down and drank some burnt wine at the Rose Tavern door, while the constables come, and two or three Bellmen went by.

Samuel Pepys, *Diary*, 1667

SHOPS ON CHRISTMAS EVE

Being the day before Christmas, there was more display in the shops than usual. I did not get back until candle-light. The whole scene began to be illuminated. Altogether, what a scene it was! the shops in the Strand and elsewhere, where every conceivable article lay before you; and all made in England, which struck me the more, coming from a country where few things are made, however foreign commerce may send them to us; then, the open squares, and gardens; the parks with spacious walks; the palisades of iron, or enclosures of solid wall, wherever enclosures were requisite; the people; the countless number of equipages, and fine horses; the gigantic draft horses; – what an aspect the whole exhibited! what industry, what luxury, what infinite particulars, what an aggregate!

Richard Rush, *Residence at the Court of London*, 1817

～ 25 December ～

WHEN CHRISTMAS WAS BANNED

I went to London with my wife, to celebrate Christmas-day, Mr. Gunning preaching in Exeter chapel, on Micah vii. 2. Sermon ended, as he was giving us the Holy Sacrament, the chapel was surrounded with soldiers, and all the communicants and assembly surprised and kept prisoners by them, some in the house, others carried away. It fell to my share to be confined to a room in the house, where yet I was permitted to dine with the master of it, the Countess of Dorset, Lady Hatton, and some others of quality who invited me. In the afternoon, came Colonel Whalley, Goffe, and others, from Whitehall, to examine us one by one; some they committed to the marshal, some to prison. When I came before them, they took my name and abode, examined me why, contrary to the ordinance made, that none should any longer observe the superstitious time of the nativity (so esteemed by them), I durst offend, and particularly be at common prayers, which they told me was but the mass in English, and particularly pray for Charles Stuart; for which we had no Scripture. I told them we did not pray for Charles Stuart, but for all Christian kings, princes, and governors. They replied, in so doing we prayed for the king of Spain, too, who was their enemy and a Papist, with other frivolous and ensnaring questions, and much threatening; and, finding no color to detain me, they dismissed me with much pity of my ignorance. These were men of high flight and above ordinances, and spoke spiteful things of our Lord's nativity. As we went up to receive the Sacrament, the miscreants held their muskets against us, as if they would have shot us at the altar; but yet suffering us to finish the office of Communion, as perhaps not having instructions what to do, in case they found us in that action. So I got home late the next day; blessed be God.

John Evelyn, *Diary*, 1657

A SOLITUDE À DEUX

George and I spent this lovely day together – lovely as a clear spring day. We could see Hampstead from the Park so distinctly that it seemed to have suddenly come nearer to us. We ate our turkey together in a happy *solitude à deux*.

George Eliot, *Journal*, 1857

THE USUAL XMAS AMENITIES

Having had some lunch I went by the 2.30 train to Ealing & thence to the Fentons, where we exchanged the usual Xmas amenities. Dinner passed off very quietly – Present, Mr & Mrs Fenton, Clara Dall, Viv: Mrs & Miss Crawford, a heavy sort of German named Schimmellman, & myself, perhaps equally heavy. Miss Crawford chiefly distinguished herself by not eating any dinner with the exception of half a slice of tongue, & a plum at dessert – She I believe affects loss of appetite, but looks well on the same – The evening too passed away very quietly – there was a little singing by way of change.

Rafe Neville Leycester, *Diary*, 1865

⌁ 26 December ⌁

A SPECIAL CASE OF MIRACULOUS CURE

I made a particular inquiry into the case of Mary Special, a young woman, then in Tottenham-Court-Road. She said, 'Four years since, I found much pain in my breasts, and afterward hard lumps. Four months ago my left breast broke, and kept running continually. Growing worse and worse, after some time, I was recommended to St. George's Hospital. I was let blood many times, and took hemlock thrice a day, but I was no better; the pain and the lumps were the same, and both my breasts were quite hard, and black as soot. When, yesterday se'nnight, I went to Mr. Owen's, where there was a meeting for prayer, Mr. Bell saw me, and asked, "Have you faith to be healed?" I said, "Yes." He prayed for me; and, in a moment, all my pain was gone; but the next day, I felt a little pain again. I clapped my hands on my breasts, and cried out, "Lord, if thou wilt, thou canst make me whole." It was gone; and from that hour I have had no pain, no soreness, no lumps, or swelling, but both my breasts were perfectly well, and have been ever since.'

John Wesley, *Journal*, 1761

CATASTROPHE AT COVENT GARDEN

On Boxing Night I was at Covent Garden. A dull pantomime was 'worked' (as we say) better than I ever saw a heavy piece worked on a first night, until suddenly and without a moment's warning, every scene on that immense stage fell over on its face, and disclosed chaos by gaslight behind! There never was such a business; about sixty people who were on the stage being extinguished in the most remarkable manner. Not a soul was hurt. In the uproar, some moon-calf rescued a porter pot, six feet high (out of which the clown had been drinking when the accident happened), and stood it on the cushion of the lowest proscenium box, P.S., beside a lady and gentleman, who were dreadfully ashamed of it. The moment the house knew that nobody was injured, they directed their whole attention to this gigantic porter pot in its genteel position (the lady and gentleman trying to hide behind it), and roared with laughter. When a modest footman came from behind the curtain to clear it, and took it up in his arms like a Brobdingnagian baby, we all laughed more than ever we had laughed in our lives. I don't know why.

Charles Dickens, Letter to W. C. Macready, 1860

∼ 27 DECEMBER ∼

A POOR FELLOW IN FLEET DITCH

As I went into the city the people at Fleet Ditch were all looking at a poor fellow that had fallen in last night or this morning, and lay dead there; unhappy accident!

John Byrom, *Journal*, 1727

SURVIVING A BEGGAR'S CURSE

I wonder how you would have taken a thing that befell me last Wednesday? I was waiting before a shop in Regent Street for some items of stationery; and a young woman, black-eyed, rosy-cheeked, with a child in her arms, thrust herself up to the carriage window and broke forth in a paroxysm of begging: refusing to stand aside even when the shopman was showing me envelopes. Provoked at her noise and pertinacity, I said: 'No, I will give you not a single penny as an encouragement to annoy others as you are annoying me.' If there be still such a thing as the evil eye, that beggar-woman fixed the evil eye on me, and said slowly, and hissing out the words: 'This is Wednesday, lady; perhaps you will be dead by Christmas Day, and have to leave all behind you! Better to have given me a little of it now!' and she scuttled away, leaving me with the novel sensation of being under a curse.

Would you have minded that after the moment? I can't say I took it to heart. At the same time, I was rather glad when, Christmas Day being over, I found myself alive and just as well as before.

Jane Welsh Carlyle, Letter to Mrs Russell, 1864

~ 28 December ~

THE GASES AND THE PHANTASMAGORIA

Shelley and Clara out all the morning. Read *French Revolution* in the evening. Shelley and I go to Gray's Inn to get Hogg; he is not there; go to Arundel Street; can't find him. Go to Garnerin's. Lecture on electricity; the gases, and the phantasmagoria; return at half-past 9. Shelley goes to sleep. Read *View of French Revolution* till 12; go to bed.

Mary Shelley, *Journal*, 1814

A SWISS PEASANT IN HAVERSTOCK HILL

A dense fog. E. went to Olympia for the day. In the afternoon I went by invitation to see A. J. Smith at his brother Watson's house, 34 Upper Park Road, Haverstock Hill. Watson's wife originally a Swiss peasant; now a strong, amiable, energetic woman, with seven children.

George Gissing, *Diary*, 1893

A HOTBED OF INFAMY

London is at present a hotbed of infamy and immorals. This of course has developed through the war, which has stirred the dormant animal passions of man. Prostitutes appear to have flocked to the city, where in powder and attire, no doubt they present meretricious attractions to those who have returned from the thunder of battle. It is a deplorable state of affairs. So hard is it to discriminate between the respectable and the irresponsible, that I find it more satisfactory to keep aloof . . . London appears to be thriving under the influences of war. This is occasioned of course by the vast number of Colonials and Imperials, who spend their 10 days' leave here. Their accumulated back money burns and quickly goes, so that one sees no demonstrations of poverty, but overstocked and busy shops. Rarely even does one hear the war talked of − generally it is theatres.

Frank Hurley, *Diary*, 1916

〜 *29* DECEMBER 〜

A TRIP TO ST PAUL'S

Carlyle and I in omnibus. Rain, so we did not alight at Charing Cross, and I suggested our going into St. Paul's − to which, to my surprise, he agreed. He had not been there for many years. We ascended the west steps and went in by right-hand door. C. immediately pulled off his broad hat and we soon, arm-in-arm, turned into centre aisle. The Cathedral was lighted up and a sermon going on under the Dome.

C. said, 'Ah, this is a fine place!'

I found seats on the edge of the seated congregation, where we had a good view up into the dim dome and along the vista of the choir. We could hear the preacher's voice but not the words. I tried to keep him till the end and the organ music.

'There is no doubt a very fine organ,' he said, 'and the Amen comes like nothing else in the world.' But by and by he became impatient: 'We can hear nothing − let us go.' So we glided out of our places, and went to look at the Wellington Monument, but he declared he could make out nothing of it.

He was full of praises of Wren and his work − 'the grandest Cathedral he had ever seen,' − and spoke of his first day in London.

He arrived by water from Leith, and went up to Islington to Edward Irving whose guest he was. In the evening he found himself in view of

St. Paul's, and has never forgotten the sight of it rising above the crowd of little houses.

We walked up and down St. Paul's Churchyard, and looked up at the dome – 'Ay, it's a bonny thing.'

William Allingham, *A Diary*, 1878

YELLING FIREMEN

The fire brigade came dashing down the Strand at Wellington Street to-day with the usual wild cries of 'Hi! yi! hi! yi!' which always creates a sensation in the streets. One of the engine horses came down on the slippery pavement, but the men had the team going in an incredibly short time. The suggestion so often made that the firemen should abandon their wild and alarming cries and substitute a gong is bitterly opposed by the firemen. They have always yelled 'Hi! yi!' and they always will do so.

R. D. Blumenfeld, *R.D.B.'s Diary*, 1901

GUARDING A POWER STATION

My first day's duty (as a Special Constable) has gone off all right. I was a little afraid last night I should have a snow storm to patrol in! It snowed and blew furiously after dinner but the morning was clear and bright. I got there at 9.45, received my whistle, truncheon and badge and paraded and started off with Larken to follow a senior man to our post which is outside a power station in Holland Park. There we arrived at 10.15 and stayed till we were relieved at 2.20. There is a hut for shelter (one at a time) and two police mackintosh capes for us to use if we want them. Our duty is to allow no one to enter the power station who is not known to the caretaker, and I insisted on stopping her son till she acknowledged him!

John Cann Bailey, Letter to his wife, 1914

~ 30 December ~

A CROSSING SWEEPER AT CHARING CROSS

A girl named Margaret Cochrane is a crossing-sweeper at Charing Cross, and has been so, to my knowledge for several years. She says she is but fourteen, but she looks much older – quite a young woman, indeed. She sweeps a path from King Charles's statue to Spring Gardens; the densest part of the wide throng of hurrying carriages. She plies her daring broom under the wheels, which bespatter her with mire as they fly; she dodges under the horses' heads, and is ever ready to conduct the timid lady or nervous old gentleman through the perils of the crossing; she is wet through her thin clothing when it rains; she is in the street all day, the lowest and least protected of that roaring buffeting crowd. And she is a well-grown and really pretty girl; with a delicate complexion and refined features and bright eyes: her mud-stained frock and bonnet are neat, though shabby; and even in her dirt she is attractive, as she drops you a quiet curtsy and says 'Please Sir,' holding out her hand and leaning

The smallest donation thankfully received!

on her well-worn broom. Yet I never – and I have often watched her among her companions – saw any rudeness, levity, nor immodesty in her behaviour: nor did I ever see her insulted by any passerby. Tonight in giving her a penny I asked her if she meant to remain a crossing sweeper; and she said 'No Sir – I think I shall take to selling oranges when I grow up.' Whether it be modesty or love of change, it is the fact that crossing-sweeper girls seldom stay at their calling after they pass the age of puberty.

Arthur Munby, *Diary*, 1862

A BOOK HUNT

Little doing. In the morning Hooper and I went for a book hunt in Charing Cross Road. In the evening I went down to the nativity and mystery plays by the girls at Camberwell. A poor show but amusing.

Evelyn Waugh, *Diary*, 1919

～ *31 December* ～

SO LITTLE DAYLIGHT

The fog was so thick that the shops in Bond Street had lights at noon. I could not see people in the street from my windows. I am tempted to ask, how the English became great with so little daylight?

Richard Rush, *Residence at the Court of London*, 1817

MAKING A NIGHT OF IT

Last day of the Old Year. May we both have a very happy 1956 – and by happiness I mean seeing each other, being together, as much as possible. Oh I do pray, that may be so . . .

   London feels very ghostly without you. I realize that it had come to be, for me, simply a place I come to see you. It's a brilliantly fine pale sunny day – or rather has been; it's about 5 p.m. now. I am writing this in bed, in the course of an afternoon rest, in my funny little tiny doll-house room at 170 Ebury Street. It has a paper striped in two shades of dark green, and a bed with a very ducal crimson-brocaded head. The electric fire is full on, the window looks out (at the back) over dusky gardens, and I can hear the trains rumbling in the distance. For the afternoon, I have this tiny house to myself . . . Tonight we are going to make a NIGHT of it — going to the opening of the ballet at Covent Garden, then on to Quaglino's . . .

Elizabeth Bowen, Letter to Charles Ritchie, 1955

MILLENNIAL DISAPPOINTMENT

My whole life I thought I'd be at a wild party at the end of the millennium. Instead, I was queuing outside Stratford tube station. It was the only way to get to the Dome. Our friends Keith Khan and Catherine Ugwu were staging the New Year's Eve show, and they'd worked on it for ten years. We queued for hours. The police and London Underground apologised for any inconvenience caused by the unexpectedly large crowds. How could the crowds be unexpected? It was the millennium. Although the police knew 10,000 people would be travelling to the Dome via Stratford, they only brought *one* X-ray machine. London Underground weren't blameless either. There was a forty minute wait for the first train — even though they'd had a thousand years to get it on the platform.

Oona King, *Diary*, 1999

THE RIVER THAMES
CHELSEA REACH

GREEN PARK

HYDE PARK

REGENT'S PARK

THE MONUMENT

This Pillar was set up in perpetual remembrance of a most
dreadfull Burning of this City.
An.no 1666, on three sides of the
Pedestal are Inscriptions which
give an account the reof on
the other there are proper
Hieroglyphick figures car-
ved in Relievo, and at Top
there is Golden flames proceeding out of an Urn: the
Monument stands on a large
Vault of Stone Arched over,
the Pedestal is 21 foot and
square and 27 foot high, the

the Column is of the Dorick
Order and measure 15 foot
15 in Circumference, 10 Diameter
from out to out is 15 foot, and
9 foot within, its height from
the Pedestal to the Balcony
is 133 foot, and from the Balcony to the top of ye Flame
is thirty eight foot, so that
the height of the Monument
from the ground is 202 foot,
the whole of it is a curious
piece of Workmanship and
cost upwards of 13,700 Pounds
in Building.

Fish Street Hill

∽ CONTRIBUTORS ∽

Anonymous *Pages 500–1*

Charles Abbot, Lord Colchester (1757–1829)
Born in Abingdon, the son of a vicar, he was educated at Westminster School and Christ Church, Oxford. A lawyer and Tory MP, he was Speaker of the House of Commons from 1802 to 1817. His *Diary and Correspondence* were published in three volumes in 1861. *Pages 250, 297, 509*

J. R. Ackerley (1896–1967)
Editor of *The Listener* for many years, he was also the author of several idiosyncratic memoirs including *Hindoo Holiday* and *My Dog Tulip*. Ackerley made little secret of being gay even at a time when homosexuality was illegal in the UK. His diaries were published posthumously as *My Sister and Myself* in 1982. The J. R. Ackerley Prize for Autobiography has been awarded each year for the past three decades. *Pages 419, 428–9*

John Adolphus (1768–1845)
A barrister who acted for the defence in a number of notorious cases in Regency London, including the Cato Street Conspiracy, he was also a historian who published volumes on England in the eighteenth century and the French Revolution. Selections from his journal were published in a biography in 1871. *Page 479*

James Agate (1877–1947)
Born near Manchester, Agate became the most influential drama critic of the 1920s and 1930s, working for the *Sunday Times* and the BBC. His diaries, filled with theatrical gossip, literary opinion and personal anecdote, were published in nine volumes, entitled *Ego, Ego 2, Ego 3* etc., between 1935 and 1948. *Pages 42, 62, 83–4, 191, 222, 246, 303, 367–8, 369, 371, 373, 381, 382, 395, 410*

Lord Alanbrooke (1883–1963)
Chief of the Imperial General Staff, or head of the British Army, for much of the Second World War, he was one of the most significant contributors to the ultimate success of the Allies in the fight against Hitler. His relationship with Churchill was hugely important to the war effort, although, as his diaries show, it was rarely an easy one. The diaries, in an abridged version, were first published in the 1950s. *Pages 375, 397, 424*

Fanny Allen (1781–1875)
A member of the extended family network of Allens, Wedgwoods and Darwins which was so important to English intellectual life in the nineteenth century, Fanny Allen was sister-in-law to the second Josiah Wedgwood and aunt by marriage to Charles Darwin. Her letters, together with those of other family members, were published in two volumes in 1915. *Page 253*

William Allingham (1824–89)
Irish poet, diarist and man of letters, he was a friend of many of the major literary figures of the Victorian era including Tennyson, Carlyle and Dante Gabriel Rossetti. His best-known poem, unfortunately for his reputation, remains 'The Fairies' with its opening lines, 'Up the airy mountain/Down the rushy glen/We daren't go a-hunting/For fear of little men.' *Pages 218–19, 256, 331–2, 347, 520–21*

Lindsay Anderson (1923–94)
A film critic and film director, he came to prominence in the Free Cinema documentary movement of the 1950s and, over the next thirty years, went on to make a series of well-known, often controversial, feature films including *This Sporting Life, If . . ., O! Lucky Man* and *Britannia Hospital*. His diaries were published a decade after his death. *Pages 196, 405*

Elias Ashmole (1617–92)
The man who gave his name to the Ashmolean Museum in Oxford, he was an antiquary, astrologer and student of alchemy. A collector himself, he inherited in controversial circumstances the huge collection of specimens and curiosities gathered together by the Tradescants, father and son botanists from Lambeth. He gave this to the University of Oxford in 1677. *Page 150*

Mary Bagot (1790–1869)
The unmarried daughter of a Staffordshire clergyman, she wrote a journal from which extracts were published in a family history of 1901. These extracts include some short accounts of visits to London. *Page 301*

John Cann Bailey (1864–1931)
A well-connected example of the now vanished breed of 'men of letters', he published books on Milton and Dr Johnson and wrote hundreds of unsigned reviews for *The Times Literary Supplement*. He edited the diary of Lady Frederick Cavendish and extracts from his own diaries and letters were published soon after his death. *Pages 64, 521*

Louisa Bain (1803–83)
Married into a family involved in bookselling in London for several genera-
tions, she kept a diary in the second half of the nineteenth century. Extracts
from it were published in a history of the family business in 1940. *Pages 31,
40, 88, 124–5, 249, 256, 262, 409, 452–3, 474, 486, 493, 503*

John Baker (1712–79)
The son of a Chichester grocer, Baker studied to become a lawyer at the Middle
Temple and practised initially as a barrister in London. On the death of his
first wife, he moved to the West Indies, where he married a local heiress and
became Solicitor General of St Kitts. He came back to Britain when he was
in his forties. His diary, excerpts from which were first published in 1931, is
considered particularly valuable by cricket historians because Baker regularly
mentions the matches he attended. *Pages 204, 219, 235, 251, 451*

W. N. P. Barbellion (1889–1919)
One of the most compelling diarists of the twentieth century, Bruce Frederick
Cummings took the elaborate *nom de plume* of Wilhelm Nero Pilate Barbel-
lion when he published *The Journal of a Disappointed Man* just six months
before his early death from multiple sclerosis. He worked at the Natural
History Museum until the progress of his illness made it impossible. *A Last
Diary* was published the year after he died. *Pages 42, 67, 79, 89–90,
129–31, 248, 295, 313–14, 358, 433–4, 456*

J. M. Barrie (1860–1937)
The author of *Peter Pan* kept up an extensive correspondence for all his adult
life. Born in Scotland, he moved to London after his first literary success and
his love for the city emerges in a number of his letters. *Pages 205, 376, 387–8*

Fred Bason (1908–73)
Bason was born in Walworth and became a dealer in secondhand books when
he was still in his teens. Through bookselling he came to know authors such
as Arnold Bennett, Somerset Maugham and James Agate and he ran a bookshop in Camberwell throughout the 1930s. His own writings included
hundreds of articles for the press, BBC talks, books on theatre-going and
collecting cigarette cards, and four volumes of diaries, published in the 1950s.
Pages 15, 18, 34, 86, 105, 111–12, 197, 217, 234–5, 243, 355, 393–4, 400, 440, 475

Cecil Beaton (1904–80)
Beginning as a photographer of the Bright Young Things of the twenties and
thirties, Cecil Beaton went on to become famous for fashion photography and
society portraits. He was also an award-winning costume designer for stage

and screen. Six volumes of his diaries were published during his lifetime. *Pages 202, 225, 420–1*

James Beattie (1735–1803)
Born in the north of Scotland and educated at the University of Aberdeen, he published *Essay on the Nature and Immutability of Truth* in 1776, which established his reputation as a philosopher; his long poem *The Minstrel* was highly praised by Dr Johnson. The diary he kept on a visit to London in 1773 was published in 1946. *Pages 223, 270*

Henry Beeching (1859–1919)
A poet and clergyman, he wrote satirical verses about university characters while at Oxford and published several volumes of his poetry in the 1880s and 1890s. After entering the church, he worked in Liverpool before becoming Dean of Norwich. Extracts from his diaries appeared anonymously in 1898. *Pages 223, 270*

Tony Benn (born 1925)
One of the most significant figures in the post-war history of the Labour Party, Benn was Minister of Technology in Harold Wilson's first government and Secretary of State for Industry and Secretary of State for Energy in his second. A controversial standard bearer for the Left, he kept extensive diaries which have been published in several volumes. *Pages 50, 65, 213, 253–4, 296–7, 414–5, 430, 473*

Alan Bennett (born 1934)
Alan Bennett first came to public attention as a member of the cast of *Beyond the Fringe* in 1960. In the decades since then he has built a reputation as playwright, performer, writer and all-round national treasure. His plays include *Forty Years On, The Madness of King George, The History Boys* and (most recently) *People*. Since the early 1980s he has been publishing extracts from his diaries in the *London Review of Books* and many of these have also appeared in collections of his writings. *Pages 15–16, 28, 41, 75, 86–7, 110, 210–11, 215–16, 237, 268–9, 352, 495*

Arnold Bennett (1867–1931)
Most of his best-known novels (*Clayhanger, The Card, Anna of the Five Towns*) are set in the Potteries where he grew up but Arnold Bennett himself wasted no time as a young man in heading for London. He lived and worked there (or in Paris) for most of the rest of his life, producing a steady stream of novels, plays and journalism. He kept a journal from 1896 until the end of his life. *Pages 16–17, 20, 34, 49, 52, 70, 72, 136, 180, 222, 256, 257, 274, 335, 359, 399, 412–13, 450, 497, 509*

A. C. Benson (1862–1925)

An academic and writer, Benson was the son of Edward White Benson, Archbishop of Canterbury from 1882 to 1896, and the brother of E. F. Benson, author of the Mapp and Lucia novels. He edited Queen Victoria's letters, published ghost stories, literary essays and memoirs but his most familiar work today consists of the words to the patriotic song, 'Land of Hope and Glory'. His diaries run to millions of words and only selections of them have been published. *Pages 123, 354*

Mary Berry (1763–1852)

According to Horace Walpole, their friend in his old age, Mary Berry and her sister were 'the best-informed and most perfect creatures I ever saw'. When he died in 1797, he left them substantial bequests. The sisters lived into the middle of the nineteenth century and Mary devoted much energy to the editing and publication of Walpole's work. Volumes of her own diaries and correspondence were published in the decade after her death. *Pages 115, 153–4, 170, 176, 181, 226–7, 253, 261, 284, 430*

John Betjeman (1906–84)

Poet laureate between 1972 and his death, he was born in London and was a great lover of the city and its buildings. The statue of him in St Pancras Station is a tribute to his importance in the successful 1960s campaign to save it from demolition. The letter quoted in this book shows his nostalgic appreciation for London's past. *Pages 170–1, 383*

R. D. Blumenfeld (1864–1948)

Born in Wisconsin, Ralph Blumenfeld came to Britain to report on Queen Victoria's Golden Jubilee in 1887 and eventually settled in London seven years later. He worked for a number of newspapers before joining the *Daily Express* in 1902. He became its editor in 1909 and remained in the job for two decades. Selections from his diary, covering the years between the Jubilee and the First World War, were published in 1930, the year after he retired from the paper. *Pages 82, 155, 265, 268, 410, 413, 431, 436, 451–2, 498–9, 501, 521*

James Boswell (1740–95)

For many years after his death, Boswell stood in the shadow of Dr Johnson, the man whose biography he wrote. In the 1920s, however, the discovery of a large cache of his private papers enabled him to speak out more clearly in his own voice. His *London Journal*, first published in 1950, covers the years 1762 and 1763, just before and just after his original meeting with Johnson, when he was a boozing, womanising young-man-about-town. *Pages 21, 145–6, 199–200, 208–9, 305, 328–9, 483, 503–4*

Elizabeth Bowen (1899–1973)
An Anglo-Irish novelist, her two best-known novels (*The Death of the Heart* and *The Heat of the Day*) are both set largely in London. Her love affair with the diary-writing Canadian diplomat Charles Ritchie, which began during the war and lasted until her death, is reflected in their correspondence, published as *Love's Civil War* in 2009. *Pages 32–3, 42–3, 99, 132, 212, 325, 348, 378, 523–4*

William Bray (1736–1832)
Bray was a lawyer and antiquary with a particular interest in the history of Surrey, his native county. He was the first person to produce an edition of John Evelyn's *Diary*. Extracts from his own diary were printed for members of his family several decades after his death. *Pages 31, 168, 211, 459*

Peter Briggins (c. 1660–1717)
Little is known about this prosperous London merchant other than the information to be gleaned from the brief entries in his diary, first published in 1895. Briggins was a Quaker and was active in the reign of Queen Anne when he owned a house in Bartholomew Close and several other properties in the city. *Pages 41, 285–6, 290, 314, 320, 324, 338–9*

Vera Brittain (1893–1970)
Best known for *Testament of Youth*, her haunting memoir of her experiences during the First World War, Vera Brittain was also a novelist, pacifist, feminist and the mother of the politician Shirley Williams. She kept diaries for long periods of her life, and extracts from her journals during both world wars have been published since her death. *Page 389*

Ford Madox Brown (1821–93)
An artist associated with the Pre-Raphaelites, although he was never an official member of their Brotherhood, his best known paintings are *Work*, a street scene in Hampstead, and *The Last of England*, a study of two emigrants leaving the country to start a new life in Australia. He kept a diary for extended periods of his life, selections from which were published after his death. *Pages 370, 414, 513*

Elizabeth Barrett Browning (1806–61)
Author of *Aurora Leigh* and *Sonnets from the Portuguese* and one of the best-known poets of the Victorian era, she is also famous for her elopement from the family home in Wimpole Street with fellow poet Robert Browning. They travelled to Italy where they lived for most of the rest of her life. She died in Rome at the age of fifty-five. *Page 348*

David Bruce (1898–1977)
Born in Maryland, Bruce was a career diplomat who served as US Ambassador to France after the Second World War and to West Germany in the 1950s. In 1961, John F. Kennedy appointed him US Ambassador to London, where Bruce had spent time during the war. He remained in the post until 1969. His diaries record his time in 1960s London and the anti-Vietnam War demonstrations of that decade. *Pages 125, 152, 205, 248, 286, 308, 373–4, 394, 412, 437–8*

Nathaniel Bryceson (1826–1911)
Born in Marylebone in 1826, Bryceson was the son of Mary Bryceson, a widow, and Nathaniel White, a pauper in the local workhouse. His diary, which covers just the one year of 1846, was written when he was a nineteen-year-old clerk, working for Lea's Coal Wharf in Pimlico. Bryceson went on to become an accountant in Islington and he died, at the age of eighty-five, in Mile End. His diary is preserved in the Westminster City Archives and can be accessed online. *Pages 17, 30, 58–9, 64, 80, 96, 122, 149, 188, 210, 216, 234, 237, 277–8, 336, 349, 372, 391, 403, 408, 423, 428, 433, 442–3, 446, 452*

George Buchanan (1904–89)
The son of a vicar in County Antrim, he became a journalist in London and published both fiction in the 1930s and poetry in the 1970s and 1980s. He edited what was subtitled 'An Intelligent Person's Guide to London' just before the Second World War and his two volumes of journals, which appeared in 1932 and 1936, reflect his life in the city. *Pages 225, 307, 316*

Fanny Burney (1752–1840)
The daughter of the musicologist Charles Burney, she published her first novel *Evelina* in her twenties. She became, as she records in her diaries, a confidante of the ageing Dr Johnson and took up a position at the court of George III and Queen Charlotte in 1786. She resigned from it five years later to concentrate on her writing and published *Camilla* in 1796. She married General Alexandre D'Arblay in 1793. Her diaries were published in several volumes after her death. *Pages 334, 480–1*

Aaron Burr (1756–1836)
The third vice-president of the United States, serving under Thomas Jefferson, Burr saw his career end in disgrace and exile when he killed a political rival in a duel. Travels in the American West led to a trial for treason. He was acquitted but fled to Europe. He lived in London for several years but returned to the US to practise as a lawyer. His private journal, published two years after his death, covers his time in Europe. *Pages 65, 510*

John Byrom (1692–1763)

A poet, hymn-writer and creator of his own system of shorthand, John Byrom was born in Manchester and educated there and at Cambridge. He spent long periods of time in London, arranging the publication of his verses and promoting his shorthand system. Extracts from his journal were published in the middle of the nineteenth century. *Pages 140, 220, 518*

Lord George Gordon Byron (1788–1824)

The Romantic poet, author of *Don Juan*, kept a journal for brief periods of his tumultuous life and was a lively and prolific letter-writer. His early journals and correspondence, written before scandal and a taste for riotous living drove him abroad, show him making the most of London society. *Pages 131, 330, 339, 463*

Thomas Campbell (1733–95)

Born in County Tyrone and educated at Trinity College, Dublin, Thomas Campbell was a clergyman in the Church of Ireland. In the years between 1775 and 1795, he made several long trips to London where he met many of the most famous people of the day, including Dr Johnson. He died in London on the last of these visits. His diary of his times in London was discovered in Australia in the mid-nineteenth century, where it had been taken by the nephew who had inherited it, and was first published in Sydney in 1854. *Pages 104–5, 106, 114–15, 120, 128, 148, 166–7*

Henry Carey, 1st Baron Hunsdon (1526–96)

The son of Sir William Carey, a Tudor courtier, and Mary Boleyn, sister of Henry VIII's unfortunate second wife, he is best remembered as the patron of the Lord Chamberlain's Men, the theatrical company in which Shakespeare had a major stake. Because his mother was, like her sister, one of Henry VIII's lovers, some historians have suggested that Henry Carey was the king's illegitimate son. *Page 415*

Jane Welsh Carlyle (1801–66)

Born in Haddington in Scotland, Jane Welsh married Thomas Carlyle in her mid-twenties and moved with him to London in 1834. The marriage was not a happy one. The writer Samuel Butler once remarked that, 'It was very good of God to let Carlyle and Mrs Carlyle marry one another, and so make only two people miserable and not four.' While her husband forged a career as one of the great intellectual figures of his age, Jane became a witty, gossipy and prolific correspondent, described by a later biographer as 'the greatest woman letter writer in English'. *Pages 192, 283, 327–8, 342–3, 369, 436–7, 518–9*

Thomas Carlyle (1795–1881)
The Sage of Chelsea, as he was sometimes known, was born in Ecclefechan in Dumfriesshire and was a schoolteacher in Scotland before moving to London in 1834. He lived in a house in Cheyne Row, which is now open to the public as a museum, for the rest of his life. *Sartor Resartus* and *The French Revolution*, though infrequently read today, established his reputation as one of the greatest thinkers and historians of the Victorian era. *Pages 259–60, 502*

Dora Carrington (1893–1932)
A painter who studied at the Slade, Carrington became involved in a *ménage à trois* with the gay Bloomsbury writer Lytton Strachey (whom she loved) and Ralph Partridge (who loved her). She married Partridge but was devastated by Strachey's death in 1932 and committed suicide two months later. Her own art has been rediscovered in recent years and her complicated life has been the subject of biographies and a feature film. *Page 329*

Julia Cartwright (1851–1924)
A successful writer on Renaissance art and history, Julia Cartwright published books on Mantegna, Botticelli and Raphael, as well as a number of novels. Extracts from the diaries which she kept for much of her life were published in 1989. *Page 99*

Carl Gustav Carus (1789–1869)
A painter who studied under Caspar David Friedrich, a scientist who came up with an idea that was later used by Darwin in the formulation of the theory of evolution, a psychologist who was credited by Jung with pioneering insights into the unconscious, Carus was also, for a number of years, physician to the King of Saxony. In that role, he travelled with his royal master to England in 1844 and kept a journal of what he saw. *Pages 238, 245*

Lady Frederick Cavendish (1841–1925)
Born Lucy Lyttelton, she married Lord Frederick Cavendish, a son of the Duke of Devonshire, in 1864. Her husband, appointed Chief Secretary for Ireland, was assassinated by Irish Nationalists in Phoenix Park, Dublin, in 1882. She became a pioneer of women's education: Lucy Cavendish College, Cambridge, is named after her. Her diaries span the period from the mid-1850s to the death of her husband. *Pages 75, 109, 157–8, 188–9, 293, 310–11*

Anne Chalmers (1813–91)
She grew up in Edinburgh where her father was a professor of theology and a leading member of the Free Church of Scotland. At the age of seventeen, having (in her own words) 'reached a most venerable antiquity', she began to

keep a diary. It includes lively accounts of her experiences on an 1830 visit to London with her father and other members of her family. *Pages 191, 194, 195, 201, 218, 230–1*

John Chamberlain (1553–1628)
The son of a wealthy London ironmonger, who left him enough money to live as a gentleman of leisure, Chamberlain would be long forgotten today if it were not for the letters he wrote over a period of thirty years. Addressed to various friends, many of them living abroad, they provide valuable insights into London life in the late Elizabethan and Jacobean periods. *Pages 23, 113, 116, 297, 454–5, 463, 469*

Alan Clark (1928–99)
The son of the art historian Kenneth Clark, he published works of military history (*The Donkeys*, *The Fall of Crete*) before entering Parliament as a Conservative MP in February 1974. He went on to become Minister for Trade and Minister for Defence Procurement in Margaret Thatcher's government but is more likely to be remembered for what one reviewer called his 'staggeringly, recklessly candid' diaries. *Pages 48, 147, 160, 239, 273, 288–9, 507–8*

Ossie Clark (1942–96)
A Warrington-born fashion designer, Clark was a familiar figure in Swinging Sixties London and designed clothes for icons of the era including Mick Jagger, Marianne Faithfull and the Beatles. He and his then wife Celia Birtwell are the subjects of a famous portrait by David Hockney. His later career was not so successful and he was living in a council flat in Chelsea when he was fatally stabbed by his lover. *Pages 132, 297, 299*

Lady Anne Clifford (1590–1676)
The daughter of the Earl of Cumberland, Lady Anne Clifford became the Countess of Dorset through her first marriage and the Countess of Pembroke through her second. She survived both husbands. A major patron of the arts and literature, she kept a diary as a young woman and wrote an autobiography when she was in her sixties. *Page 414*

Henry Fynes Clinton (1781–1852)
An MP for twenty years, Clinton's main interest in life was the history and literature of Ancient Greece and Rome and he published several books on these subjects. His journal, much of which records his prodigious and carefully planned reading of classical authors, covers the years from 1819 to his death. *Pages 131, 172*

Olivia Cockett (1912–98)

In the summer of 1939, just before the outbreak of the Second World War, the social research organisation Mass Observation recruited hundreds of ordinary people to record their everyday lives in diaries. One of these was Olivia Cockett, an unmarried clerk at the Ministry of Works living with her parents in a London suburb. Cockett's diary, first published in 2008, is one of the liveliest and most revealing of the Mass Observation journals. *Page 486*

Lady Jane Coke (1706–61)

The eldest daughter of the Marquis of Wharton, she was married at the age of nineteen, widowed at twenty-three and married for a second time (to Derbyshire landowner Robert Coke) at twenty-seven. Her letters to a friend in Derbyshire were mostly written after she was widowed for a second time and was a regular visitor to London. *Pages 55, 161–2*

Reverend William Cole (1714–82)

Born in Cambridgeshire and educated at Eton and King's College, Cambridge, Cole was a clergyman who devoted far more time to antiquarian studies than to parochial duties. A close friend and correspondent of Horace Walpole, Cole wrote multi-volume histories of his college and of Cambridgeshire and kept a diary in the 1760s, from which extracts were published in 1931. *Pages 441–2*

John Payne Collier (1789–1883)

Collier was an erudite scholar of Shakespearean drama who, in the 1840s and 1850s, claimed to have found new documents relating to the playwright's life and emendations to his plays written by one of Shakespeare's contemporaries. Other scholars soon argued that Collier's discoveries were forgeries and, although he has had his defenders in recent years, it seems likely that most of his finds were fabricated. He published excerpts from a diary towards the end of his long life. *Pages 275–6, 315–16, 324–5*

Sir Michael Connal (1817–93)

Connal was a Glaswegian businessman whose diary, first published two years after his death, covers nearly sixty years of his life. He spent three years in London as a young man in the 1830s and returned regularly for visits. *Pages 183, 188, 451, 453–4, 455–6*

John Constable (1776–1837)

Best known for paintings of his native Suffolk such as *The Haywain*, Constable moved to London when he was a young man and actually spent most of his life in the city. He lived for a long time in Hampstead and is buried in the graveyard of St John-at-Hampstead church. His surviving letters provide a vivid account of an artist's life in the early nineteenth-century city. *Pages 62–3, 284, 356, 457*

George Frederick Cooke (1756–1812)
An early example of the actor as hellraiser, Cooke began his career on stage at Brentford but rapidly became a star in more prestigious London theatres. His tours around the country and, later, in America were punctuated by disasters and disappearances brought on by his bouts of prodigious drinking. Excerpts from his journal were first published in a biography that appeared the year after his death. *Pages 38, 490, 494–5*

Duff Cooper (1890–1954)
Educated at Eton and Oxford, he was a diplomat and Conservative politician who served in the governments of Stanley Baldwin and Neville Chamberlain. Opposed to appeasement of Hitler, he resigned from the post of First Lord of the Admiralty the day after the Munich Agreement. Cooper was also a biographer and historian. Extracts from his diaries, edited by his son John Julius Norwich, were published in 2005. *Pages 163, 404*

Noël Coward (1899–1973)
Born in Teddington, he began to write for the stage as a teenager and achieved a *succès de scandale* with his 1924 play *The Vortex*. He went on to write dozens of plays including *Blithe Spirit*, *Private Lives* and *Design for Living*. When his style of drama went out of fashion in the 1950s, he reinvented himself as an international cabaret star. Selections from his diaries were published after his death. *Pages 253, 265*

Mary, Countess Cowper (1685–1724)
Mary Clavering was a Durham heiress who, at the age of twenty, became the second wife of the successful lawyer and politician William Cowper. The year after the marriage, her husband was raised to the peerage as Baron Cowper and he went on to become Lord High Chancellor of Great Britain. She was a Lady of the Bedchamber to the Princess of Wales from 1714 to 1720 and, for some of that time, she kept an entertaining, gossipy diary of life at court. *Pages 109, 151, 439*

Thomas Creevey (1768–1838)
A politician who was a Whig MP for thirty years and twice held minor offices in government, Creevey would be almost entirely forgotten today if it were not for his gossipy, often malicious letters and journals, first published as *The Creevey Papers* in 1903. 'That old mischief-brewer', as one fellow politician called him, wrote indiscreetly and memorably about the political and social world in which he lived. *Pages 214–5*

Richard Crossman (1907–74)
An Oxford don in the 1930s, he entered Parliament as Labour MP for Coventry East in the 1945 General Election and retained the seat until his death. Firmly on the Left, he served in Harold Wilson's first government as Minister of Housing and, later, Secretary of State for Health. Despite attempts by James Callaghan's government to prevent publication, his controversial diaries began to appear in 1975. *Pages 64, 449, 450*

Alfred A. Cunningham (1881–1939)
Born in Atlanta, Georgia, Alfred Cunningham was an early enthusiast for flying and a pioneer of aviation in the American armed services. He became the first director of the US Marines Aviation Corps. His diary of his service in the First World War records his reactions to London when he passed through the city *en route* to the Flanders battlefields. *Pages 459–60*

Samuel Curwen (1715–1802)
Born in Salem, Massachusetts, and educated at Harvard, Curwen supported British rule in America and left the country just before the outbreak of the American War of Independence. He came to London and remained there as an exile for nearly a decade before returning to his native land in 1784. His journal was first published in 1842. *Pages 84–5, 102, 152, 263, 266, 365, 370, 402–3, 465, 476, 488*

Emma Darwin (1808–96)
Granddaughter of the potter Josiah Wedgwood, she married her cousin Charles Darwin, future author of *On the Origin of Species*, in 1839. Their marriage lasted for forty-three years and Emma survived her husband by a further fourteen years. An extensive collection of her family letters was published in 1915. *Page 69*

John Dee (1527–1608)
Born in London into a Welsh family, Dee became one of the greatest scholars of the Elizabethan era. He was adviser to the Tudor queen on astrological and scientific matters before embarking on a peripatetic life around the courts of central Europe, trying to persuade various rulers of the importance of his communications with angels. He spent his last years in poverty in Mortlake. His private diary was first published in the nineteenth century. *Pages 32, 422*

Charles Dickens (1812–70)
The greatest of London novelists kept a diary for only the briefest of periods, but he was a voluminous correspondent whose collected letters, in their most recent scholarly edition, occupy a dozen volumes. *Pages 19, 295–6, 461–2, 517–8*

George Bubb Dodington (1691–1762)
Born George Bubb, this eighteenth-century politician acquired an extra surname when his uncle, George Dodington, died in 1720 and bequeathed a fortune to him. An MP for nearly fifty years, he was created 1st Baron Melcombe on the accession of George III. His diary was first published in 1784. *Pages 113–4*

Alfred Domett (1811–87)
A poet and friend of Robert Browning, he emigrated to New Zealand in 1842 and became that country's fourth Prime Minister twenty years later. He returned to England in 1871, published an epic poem of Maori life entitled *Ranolf and Amohia* and kept a diary which was published nearly seventy years after his death. *Pages 228, 359, 398, 440*

Mountstuart E. Grant Duff (1829–1906)
The son of an administrator in the Raj, his own career was closely linked to the sub-continent. As an MP he was Under-Secretary of State for India and he spent five years in Madras as its governor. He published a dozen volumes of diaries, covering his time in India, his extensive travels throughout Europe and his years in London literary and political society. *Pages 139, 139–40, 181, 260, 374*

General William Dyott (1761–1847)
A career soldier who served in Ireland, Nova Scotia and the West Indies, Dyott was a brigade commander in the epically disastrous Walcheren expedition during the Napoleonic Wars. In England, he led troops to suppress the Luddite Riots in Nottinghamshire in 1811. As a young man he was a friend of the future William IV (he records a dinner during which he, the then Prince and 18 other friends polished off 63 bottles of wine) and went on to become an aide-de-camp to George III. He kept his diaries for more than sixty years. *Pages 180, 251, 498*

Maria Edgeworth (1768–1849)
Born in Oxfordshire but brought up in Ireland where her father had an estate, Maria Edgeworth became a novelist. Her most famous work is probably *Castle Rackrent*, published in 1800. Her letters include descriptions of her regular trips to London. *Pages 150–1*

Edward VI (1537–53)
Edward VI came to the throne in 1547 aged nine. During his short reign, the Protestant Reformation in England gathered pace and the precociously intellectual Edward was in favour of the reforms instituted largely by his Archbishop of Canterbury, Thomas Cranmer. The young king fell ill in February

1553 and died that summer, a few months short of his sixteenth birthday. His diary, one of the earliest English examples to survive, was first published in the nineteenth century. *Pages 227, 262–3, 293*

Dickon Edwards (born 1971)
In his own words, Dickon Edwards is a 'writer, dysfunctional dandy, flâneur, lyricist, DJ, dilettante, boulevardier, valetudinarian, imbiber'. He was a founding member of the indie bands Orlando and Fosca and played guitar for Spearmint on one of their albums. He has kept an online diary since 1997. *Pages 47, 50–51, 90, 213–4, 229, 236, 291–2, 379–80, 421, 427, 438–9*

Earl of Egmont (John Perceval) (1683–1748)
An Irish baronet who was educated in England, John Perceval was a member of the Irish House of Commons for many years. He served as an English MP from 1727 and was created Earl of Egmont in 1733. He was a leading figure in the establishment of Georgia as an American colony. His diaries, first published nearly two centuries after his death, are a valuable source for parliamentary and social history in the reign of George II. *Pages 50, 103–4, 119, 147–8, 150, 181, 199, 282, 314, 483, 505*

George Eliot (1819–80)
The novelist Mary Ann Evans, author of *Middlemarch, Adam Bede* and *Silas Marner*, moved to London from her native Warwickshire in 1850 after the death of her father. For many years she lived with the married philosopher and critic George Lewes in a relationship that scandalised some in Victorian society. Three volumes of her letters and journals were published in 1885, edited by John Cross, who became her husband after Lewes's death. *Pages 34, 198, 235, 312, 516*

Brian Eno (born 1948)
Regarded as one of the most innovative musicians in rock history, Eno first came to fame as the keyboards player of Roxy Music during the 1970s. A pioneer of Ambient music, his varied artistic career has ranged from producing best-selling albums by Talking Heads, U2 and Coldplay to designing multimedia installations and apps for mobile phones. He published a volume of his diaries in 1996. *Pages 17, 77, 420*

John Evelyn (1620–1706)
Born in Wotton, Surrey, Evelyn was a royalist during the Civil War, an exile in Europe for a period under Cromwell and a founding member of the Royal Society after the Restoration of Charles II. He was a friend of Samuel Pepys, the other great diarist of seventeenth-century London. His book *Fumifugium or The Inconvenience of the Aer and Smoak of London Dissipated* was an early

attempt to provide a solution to the problem of the city's pollution and he was one of those whose plans for the rebuilding of London after the Great Fire proved too costly to implement. His diaries, which cover a much longer period of time than those of Pepys, were first published in the early nineteenth century. *Pages 25, 32, 69–70, 87–8, 122, 148, 166, 236–7, 249, 306, 333, 353, 366–7, 386, 395, 411, 416–7, 426, 486, 515–6*

Michael Faraday (1791–1867)
Appointed a laboratory assistant by the chemist Sir Humphry Davy in 1813, Faraday went on to become one of the great figures in nineteenth-century science, famous for his experiments with electricity and electromagnetism. In a letter to *The Times*, Faraday was one of the first people to draw attention to the appallingly polluted state of the Thames. *Pages 290–1*

Joseph Farington (1747–1821)
A landscape painter from Lancashire, Farington moved to London while still in his teens and was elected a Royal Academician in 1785. He became heavily involved in the administration of the Academy and was a member of the committee which chose the paintings to hang in its exhibitions. His diary, which covers the period from 1793 to 1821, provides an insider's view of the art world of the time. It was first published in sixteen volumes in the 1920s, just over a century after Farington's death. *Pages 36, 83, 121, 146, 242, 275, 307, 317–18, 342, 354, 355–6, 390, 442, 452, 458, 492–3, 513*

Henry Fielding (1707–54)
A magistrate who, together with his half-brother, established the Bow Street Runners, arguably London's first police force, he is better remembered as a novelist, the author of *Tom Jones*. His *Journal of a Voyage to Lisbon* is an account of his journey to that city in search of a cure for his chronic ill-health and records his departure from London in vivid detail. *Pages 273, 278–80*

Annie Elizabeth Fisher (fl. 1857)
Born in France, Annie Elizabeth Fisher spent most of her adult life in Cambridge, where she died. Twice widowed, in later life she 'sought refuge in opiates'. As a young woman kept a journal recording her experiences of everyday life in Victorian England, extracts from which were published in a short-lived magazine called *The British Diarist* in 2004. *Pages 37–8*

William Fleetwood (c. 1525–94)
A member of a Lancashire family which had settled in London, William Fleetwood studied at Oxford but left without a degree. After training as a lawyer in the Middle Temple, he became an MP and represented several constituencies over a period of more than thirty years. He was Recorder of

London, one of the city's chief judges, between 1571 and 1592. In that capacity he wrote a number of letters to Lord Burghley, Elizabeth I's chief adviser, detailing criminal activity in London. *Page 289*

John Fowles (1926–2005)
The author of *The Magus* and *The French Lieutenant's Woman* lived in London for ten years, working mostly as a teacher of foreign languages at a college in Hampstead. The success of his first novel *The Collector*, and the sale of its film rights, meant he was able to give up the job and move out of the capital in 1965. His journals record, among many other things, his attempts to buy a house in London. *Pages 359, 420, 429, 455*

Caroline Fox (1819–71)
A member of a prominent Quaker family from the West Country, Caroline Fox kept a journal for much of her life (her brother and her sister were also diarists). Although her home was in Cornwall, she travelled frequently to London and, through family connections, knew many of the leading intellectual figures of the Victorian era, including John Stuart Mill, Thomas Carlyle and the scientist and inventor Charles Wheatstone. *Pages 209–10, 239–40*

Henry Fox, 4th Baron Holland (1802–59)
Born at Holland House, he was a member of a prominent family of Whig politicians and served briefly as an MP in his twenties. He went on to work as a diplomat in Italy, Russia and Austria. Selections from the journal he kept as a young man were published in 1923. *Pages 298, 304*

Elizabeth Freke (1642–1714)
Born in Wiltshire, she eloped with a distant cousin to London but the resulting marriage was not successful. Her diary, which she describes as 'some few remembrances of my misfortuns have attended me in my unhappy life since I were marryed', was published recently in a scholarly edition by Cambridge University Press. *Pages 303, 355*

Elizabeth Fry (1780–1845)
The daughter of a wealthy Quaker banker, Elizabeth Gurney married Joseph Fry of the confectioner's family in 1800. Her comfortable, upper-middle-class life was dramatically changed when she paid a visit to Newgate prison in 1813 and witnessed the conditions in which women prisoners were held. She became a lifelong campaigner for the improvement of their lot. Extracts from her journals, which she kept from her teenage years, were first published in a memoir edited by her daughters two years after her death. *Pages 106–7*

Frederic Gershow (fl. 1602)
Little is known about Gershow other than that he was secretary to the Duke
of Stettin-Pomerania during the latter's two-month visit to England in 1602.
He kept a diary which includes observations on early seventeenth-century
London as it appeared to an intelligent foreign visitor. *Pages 383–4, 387*

George Gissing (1857–1903)
Gissing's promising academic career was brought to an abrupt end when he
was imprisoned for theft in Belle Vue Gaol, Manchester, in 1876. After his
release he moved briefly to America and then settled in London where he
began a precarious career as a freelance writer and novelist. As his letters and
diaries reveal, he knew very well the kind of poverty and misery of late Victorian London which he described in many of his novels. *Pages 26, 52, 56, 66,
96–7, 142, 182, 198–9, 209, 228, 243, 245, 321, 322, 340, 393, 398, 400, 423, 474, 519*

Giovanni Giustiniani (fl. 1642)
Member of a family prominent in Venice since the thirteenth century, Gius-
tiniani was his city's ambassador to the court of Charles I during a crucial
period in English history. His frequent despatches to the Doge and Senate of
Venice include fascinating glimpses of London on the brink of the Civil War.
Page 453

Lord Ronald Gower (1845–1916)
Often identified as the model for Sir Henry Wotton in Oscar Wilde's *The
Picture of Dorian Gray*, the aristocratic Gower (son of the Duke of Sutherland) was a politician, sculptor and writer. His statue of Shakespeare
surrounded by four of his best-known characters can be seen in Stratford-
upon-Avon. He published selections from his diaries in 1902 which were
blandly unrevealing of his private life but were an interesting record of the
arts and the upper classes. *Pages 196, 211–12*

John Baptist Grano (c. 1692–c. 1748)
The son of French parents who had emigrated to London, Grano was born in
Pall Mall where his father ran a haberdasher's. For most of his adult life, he
worked as a trumpeter and flautist in various theatre orchestras in the city
and he was well known to more famous musicians of his day, including George
Frederick Handel. Grano's diary dates to 1728–9 during his incarceration in
the Marshalsea prison for a debt of £99. *Pages 332, 446, 469–70*

Graham Greene (1904–91)
Author of many novels including *Brighton Rock*, *The Power and the Glory*
and *The End of the Affair*, Greene was one of the best-known and most

admired English writers of the twentieth century. His published letters include many passages which brilliantly evoke the London he knew immediately before, during and after the Second World War. *Page 405*

Ireland Greene (1728–95)
The unusually named daughter of a Lancashire lawyer and landowner named Isaac Greene, she kept a brief diary in the late 1740s. First published in 1921, it includes descriptions of two visits to London, one in the spring of 1748 and one in the following year. *Pages 124, 180*

Joseph Greenhalgh (fl. 1662)
A London schoolmaster of whom little is known, Greenhalgh's letter to a friend about visiting a Jewish synagogue was preserved in a manuscript collection in the British Museum and first published in 1825. *Pages 173–4*

Charles Greville (1794–1865)
A member of an aristocratic family (one grandfather was the Earl of Warwick and the other the Duke of Portland), Greville was educated at Eton and Oxford. In his twenties he was granted the position of Clerk of the Council in Ordinary, equivalent to a senior Civil Service post today, and he continued to hold it for the next forty years. As his diaries reveal, Greville knew everybody who was anybody in politics and high society. The publication of his diaries, soon after his death, was seen by many as a serious breach of confidence: Queen Victoria condemned his 'indiscretion, indelicacy, ingratitude . . . and shameful disloyalty towards his Sovereign'. *Pages 39, 73, 80, 159–60, 251–2, 329, 457–8*

Henry Greville (1801–72)
Like his elder brother Charles (see above), Henry Greville was a diarist who recorded the life of the upper classes in nineteenth-century England. He was a diplomat in Paris in the 1830s and 1840s and became an official at Queen Victoria's court on his return. Extracts from his diaries were first published in two volumes in 1883–4. Further volumes followed twenty years later. *Pages 41, 121, 156, 192–3, 474*

Alec Guinness (1914–2000)
The actor first became a star in Ealing comedies such as *Kind Hearts and Coronets* (in which he played eight different roles) and in films of Dickens novels directed by David Lean (*Great Expectations* and *Oliver Twist* in which he played Fagin). He won fame with another generation as Obi-Wan Kenobi in the *Star Wars* movies. Volumes of his diaries were published both just before and just after his death. *Page 166*

Sir William Hardman (1828–90)
Born in Lancashire and educated at Cambridge, Hardman qualified and practised as a barrister but he was best known for his association with the Tory
newspaper *The Morning Post*, which he edited from 1872 until his death. His
letters about London life to a Cambridge friend who had emigrated to
Australia formed the basis for his book *A Mid-Victorian Pepys*, published in
1923. *Page 48*

Thomas Hardy (1840–1928)
The poet and novelist, author of *Tess of the D'Urbervilles, Far from the
Madding Crowd* and *The Mayor of Casterbridge*, kept diaries throughout
much of his life. His second wife used carefully chosen selections from them
to produce her life of her husband which was published soon after his death.
Pages 24, 85, 189, 193, 227

George Harris (1809–90)
A lawyer and writer, Harris published his *magnum opus, A Philosophical Trea-
tise on the Nature and Constitution of Man*, in 1878. He had been working on
it intermittently for more than forty years and, although it received some
respectful reviews, it was generally considered to be outdated, and has since
been almost entirely forgotten. His *Autobiography*, published two years before
his death, consists largely of the diaries which he kept for many decades. *Pages
173, 467–8*

Colonel Peter Hawker (1786–1853)
Educated at Eton, Hawker joined the Royal Dragoons in 1801 and was severely
wounded at the Battle of Talavera during the Peninsular War. Invalided out
of the army, he became famous as the author of works on field sports such as
shooting and fishing. His *Advice to Young Sportsmen* was first published in
1814 and was still in print well into the twentieth century. His diary, although
filled with his records of slaughtering birds, also contains many brisk and
lively entries about his life in town. *Pages 40, 59, 107, 124, 126, 127, 158, 292–3,
298, 319*

Nathaniel Hawthorne (1804–64)
The American novelist, author of *The Scarlet Letter*, lived in England for
several years in the 1850s after he had been appointed Consul in Liverpool by
his old college friend, Franklin Pierce, 14th President of the USA. He came
to know London well and wrote about the city in his *English Notebooks*, first
published six years after his death. *Pages 135, 333, 373, 385, 465, 491–2, 510*

Benjamin Haydon (1786–1846)

A painter of huge canvases on biblical and historical subjects, Haydon suffered financial difficulties throughout his life and was imprisoned for debt several times. In 1846, when he exhibited his work at the Egyptian Hall in Piccadilly, the American dwarf General Tom Thumb drew large crowds while his paintings attracted very few visitors; he was so distressed that he killed himself. His diaries provide a vivid portrait of literary and artistic life in London (he was a friend of Keats, Wordsworth and other leading figures of the Romantic Movement) and of Haydon's own troubled personality. *Pages 272–3, 288, 425*

Thomas Hearne (1678–1735)

An antiquarian and scholar who spent much of his life in Oxford, Hearne was a librarian at the Bodleian Library but he lost his job because he refused to take the required oath of allegiance to George I. He was the editor of many volumes of early English chronicles. In his diaries, he is an occasional, usually horrified, recorder of life in early eighteenth-century London. *Page 140*

William Hervey (1732–1815)

A soldier who entered the army in his twenties as a lieutenant and ended up as a general in the 1790s, Hervey served in Canada during the Seven Years' War and returned to become MP for Bury St Edmunds for five years. His journals record his extensive travels in Britain and the rest of Europe. *Pages 121, 337, 489*

John Cam Hobhouse (1786–1869)

As a young man, Hobhouse was a close friend of Byron and was his companion on a journey to Greece and Turkey between 1809 and 1811. He entered Parliament as a Radical MP in 1820 and served as a minister in the Whig governments of Grey, Melbourne and Lord John Russell. He kept a journal for much of his adult life. Extracts from it were published in a multi-volume memoir edited by his daughter after his death. *Pages 38, 63, 68–9, 78, 172–3, 277, 282, 294, 324, 372, 423*

Vere Hodgson (1901–79)

Born in Edgbaston, Vere Hodgson read history at the University of Birmingham. She taught in Italy during the 1920s and ran a charity in Notting Hill in the 1930s and during the Second World War. She kept diaries for much of her life and published extracts from her wartime journal in 1976. *Page 454*

James Hogg (1770–1835)

Best known for his novel of 1824, *The Private Memoirs and Confessions of a Justified Sinner*, Hogg was born near Ettrick in Scotland and, as a young man, worked as a farm labourer and shepherd. Through his poetry and ballads, he came to the attention of Walter Scott and became a familiar figure in Scottish literary life. He visited London towards the end of his life and delivered his unfavourable opinion of the city in letters written to his wife back in Scotland. *Page 27*

Robert Hooke (1635–1703)
One of the great polymaths of late seventeenth-century England, Hooke was interested in everything from microscopy to architecture, astronomy to palaeontology. He was curator of experiments at the Royal Society for many years and assisted Sir Christopher Wren in the reconstruction of London after the Great Fire. His diary was edited and published in 1935. *Pages 14, 55, 68, 221, 229, 263, 418*

J. W. Horsley (1845–1921)
A London clergyman with a wide range of interests (he published books on place-names, folklore and British snails, among other subjects), Horsley was best known in the late Victorian era as an advocate of penal reform. His book *Jottings from Jail* includes his diary of a month spent as chaplain at Clerkenwell Prison. *Pages 328, 334, 340, 346*

George Howard, 7th Earl of Carlisle (1802–64)
A Yorkshire MP from 1826 until 1848 when he succeeded his father as Earl of Carlisle and entered the House of Lords, he served as Chief Secretary for Ireland in Lord Melbourne's government and Lord Lieutenant of Ireland under Lord Palmerston. His sister published extracts from his journals after his death. *Pages 96, 119, 132, 155–6, 186–7, 271, 387, 418*

Frank Hurley (1885–1962)
An Australian photographer who participated in the Imperial Trans-Antarctic Expedition of 1914–17, he was one of the men stranded on Elephant Island while Ernest Shackleton travelled to South Georgia to summon help. In later life, he worked as a documentary film-maker and was an official war photographer during the Second World War. His diaries record his responses to London when he arrived there after his experiences in the Antarctic. *Pages 481, 506, 519–20*

William Ralph Inge (1860–1954)
Nicknamed 'The Gloomy Dean' by the press because of his largely pessimistic views on human nature and society, W. R. Inge was one of the best known English churchmen of the first half of the twentieth century. Born in Yorkshire and educated at Eton and Cambridge, he was an academic theologian in his early career but became a public figure after he was chosen to be Dean of St Paul's in 1911. Selections from his diary were published a few years before his death. *Pages 22, 27, 47, 129*

Sir Justinian Isham (1687–1737)
The fifth baronet of Lamport in Northamptonshire, Sir Justinian Isham was a Tory MP for the county from 1730 until his death. He wrote diaries from his teens to the time of his election to Parliament and extracts from them were published in the nineteenth century. *Page 179*

Sir Thomas Isham (1656–81)
A baronet from Lamport in Northamptonshire, his short life ended when he contracted smallpox and died in London at the age of twenty-five. He is remembered only for the brief diary he kept as a teenager. On the instructions of his father who wished him to improve his grasp of the language, it was written in Latin, and first translated and published in the nineteenth century. *Page 49*

Henry James (1843–1916)
American-born novelist and author of *Portrait of a Lady*, *The Golden Bowl* and *The Turn of the Screw*, he settled in London in 1876 and lived in the city for the next twenty years. After moving to Rye in Sussex he continued to return to London for extended visits. London, he wrote, 'is not a pleasant place; it is not agreeable, or cheerful, or easy, or exempt from reproach. It is only magnificent.' *Page 117*

Derek Jarman (1942–94)
Director of one of the very few movies to be made in Latin with subtitles (the homoerotic *Sebastiane*), he was one of the most imaginative and creative figures in the British film industry for more than twenty years. His other films include *Jubilee*, *Caravaggio* and *Edward II*. His diaries were published in two volumes, in 1991 and 2000. *Pages 190, 243–4*

John Keats (1795–1821)
The Romantic poet was a Londoner, born in Moorgate, and he lived in the city for most of his short life before travelling to Italy, in search of a better climate for his consumptive lungs, where he died in Rome. The house in Hampstead where he was staying when he fell in love with Fanny Brawne and where he wrote some of his finest letters is now a museum. *Pages 435–6*

Count Frederick Kielmansegge (1728–1800)
Kielmansegge was a German nobleman who, together with his brother, travelled to England soon after George III came to the throne. A century after his death, his manuscript diary of his travels was found in the library of the family home and was translated and published in English. *Pages 58, 390, 396–7, 471, 478*

Oona King (born 1967)
The second black female MP to be elected to the House of Commons, she served as Labour MP for Bethnal Green and Bow between 1997 and 2005. She has been a life peer (Baroness King of Bow) since 2011. Her diaries cover her years as an MP. *Pages 56, 95, 132, 217, 524*

Charles Lamb (1775–1834)
Born in the Temple, where his father was a lawyer's clerk, Lamb loved London and his writings, particularly his *Essays of Elia*, are imbued with his sense of the city's past and present. He was a close friend of the poets Coleridge and Wordsworth. For many years, he worked as a clerk at the East India House in Leadenhall Street. *Pages 53–4, 313, 365–6*

Mary Lamb (1764–1847)
The elder sister of Charles Lamb, her life and that of her brother were shaped by the terrible events of 22 September 1796 when, suffering from mental illness, she stabbed her mother to death. She suffered from periodic bouts of mania and depression for much of the rest of her life, and spent time in asylums. When she was well, she lived with her brother and together the two wrote *Tales from Shakespeare*, first published in 1807. *Page 472*

James Lees-Milne (1908–97)
An architectural historian, Lees-Milne worked for The National Trust just before and after the Second World War. More than anybody else, he was responsible for the transfer of many country houses from private hands into the ownership of the Trust. He is now best known for his many volumes of diaries, in which he turned a cool, witty and often acerbic eye on the society in which he lived. *Pages 76, 86, 97, 156–7, 165, 196–7, 320, 399*

Rafe Neville Leycester (1843–??)
Leycester was a young clerk in Victorian London. Nothing is known of his life beyond what is recorded in the two volumes of diaries he wrote which cover the years from 1859 to 1865. *ages 33, 238, 302, 311, 337–8, 516*

Clayton Littlewood (born 1963)
Co-owner of a fashion shop in Old Compton Street, he published *Dirty White Boy: Tales of Soho* in 2008. It was followed four years later by *Goodbye to Soho*. In an interview, Littlewood remarked, 'I was interested in writing about the real Sohoites. The street people. The pimps. The rent boys. The bag ladies. The hookers. The trannies. The old queens. All those on the outside I guess.' *Pages 72–3, 94, 134–5, 139, 203–4*

Narcissus Luttrell (1657–1732)
Born in Holborn, he trained as a lawyer and was briefly an MP on two occasions in the 1680s and 1690s. His diary is a record of parliamentary proceedings and of political and social events in Britain and abroad rather than of personal experience (Luttrell very rarely uses the first person pronoun) but, in its own way, it is as revealing of London life as Pepys or Evelyn. *Pages 19, 21, 32, 33, 96, 311, 338, 374, 441, 478, 479, 488, 497*

George Mackenzie Macaulay (1750–1803)
Born in the Outer Hebrides, Macaulay arrived in London at the age of fifteen. He soon gained success in business. By the time he was in his twenties, he was a member of one of the city's livery companies. He was elected as an Alderman in 1786; four years later, he was Sheriff of the City of London. His (slightly misleadingly titled) *The War Diary of a London Scot*, covering a period of just over a year in 1796–7, was first published, long after his death, in 1916. *Pages 44, 126, 270–1, 319, 491*

Thomas Babington Macaulay (1800–59)
Historian and polymath ('I wish I was as cocksure of anything as Tom Macaulay is of everything,' it was once said), he was a politician and Indian administrator but is best remembered for his *History of England from the Accession of James II*, published in several volumes from 1848. His original intention was to take his narrative to the time of George III but, at his death, five volumes had covered only seventeen years. His letters were published after his death. *Page 352*

Michael MacDonagh (1862–1946)
Born in Limerick, MacDonagh moved to London as a young man and worked as a political journalist for *The Times*. He published books on the history of Parliament, a biography of Daniel O'Connell and two volumes recording the experiences of Irish soldiers during the First World War. His diary of the home front between 1914 and 1918 was published in 1935. *Page 408*

Henry Machyn (1496?–1563)
Little is known of Machyn except that he was a respectable and relatively prosperous London merchant. Because of the frequency with which his diary refers to funerals, it is often assumed that his business involved the supply of clothing and trappings for funeral processions. The diary, which survives in manuscript form in the British Library (although it was damaged in a fire in the early eighteenth century), was first published in 1848. *Pages 124, 157, 177, 186, 282, 294–5, 450, 466, 496*

Helen G. McKenny (fl. 1885–88)
The daughter of the last Methodist minister to live in John Wesley's House in City Road before it was turned into a museum, she wrote a diary during her time in the house and extracts from it were published in 1978. *Pages 46, 47, 98, 255*

William Charles Macready (1793–1873)
The most successful English actor of his generation, Macready made his first London appearance in 1816 and became famous for his interpretation of Shakespearean roles such as Richard III, King Lear and Macbeth. He toured extensively in Britain and America where his visit of 1849 was marked by rivalry with the American actor Edwin Forrest and by riots which ended in the deaths of 23 people. He retired from the stage two years later. His diaries were published after his death. *Pages 163, 183, 248, 254–5, 257, 274, 304, 348*

Reverend William MacRitchie (1754–1837)
Born in Perthshire and educated at the Universities of St Andrews and Edinburgh, MacRitchie was ordained in 1784 and became a minister in the parish of Clunie in his native county, where he stayed for the rest of his life. His only journey outside Scotland took place in 1795 when he travelled south into England. His diary recording his experiences, including a visit to London, was edited by one of his descendants and published just over a century after it had been written. *Pages 308–9, 321, 326–7*

Sir Frederick Madden (1801–73)
An antiquarian who worked for the British Museum for many years, he edited and published a number of works in Middle English and medieval Latin. Because of a quarrel with colleagues, he left his papers not to the Museum but to the Bodleian Library in Oxford. They include his diary, which he kept from 1819 until just before his death; it runs to nearly four million words, but only short extracts have been published. *Page 37*

John Manningham (c. 1576–1622)
An undistinguished lawyer in the courts of Jacobean England, Manningham is remembered today because of the diary he kept intermittently between 1601 and 1603 when he was studying in the Middle Temple. It was preserved among the Harleian Manuscripts, one of the collections which formed the basis of what is today the British Library, and was first published in the Victorian era. It records a number of incidents and anecdotes of London life in the period from the performance of a Shakespeare play to responses to the death of Elizabeth I. *Pages 68, 133*

Gideon Mantell (1790–1852)
Mantell was a doctor in his home town of Lewes for much of his working life but his claim to fame lies in the discoveries he made in palaeontology. He published *The Fossils of the South Downs* in 1822 and was the first person to describe what he called an iguanodon, an early dinosaur. His diary records frequent visits to London to meet and compare notes with his scientific peers. *Pages 30, 48, 119, 154, 320, 333*

Hallie Eustace Miles (c. 1870–c. 1940)
The daughter of the rector of St Clement Danes, Hallie Killick married the sportsman and writer Eustace Hamilton Miles in 1906. Together with her husband, she ran a vegetarian restaurant and pioneering health food centre near Charing Cross. Her diary of London life during the First World War was published in 1930. *Pages 97, 388, 400–2, 409*

Lady Mary Monkswell (1849–1930)
The daughter of Joseph Hardcastle, a Liberal MP, she married another politician, Robert Collier, 2nd Baron Monkswell, in 1873. Extracts from her diary, which begin with her marriage and cover the next twenty years of her life, were published by a descendant in 1944. *Pages 288, 496*

Thomas Moore (1779–1852)
Born in Dublin, he was a poet, singer and writer of songs (including 'The Minstrel Boy' and 'The Last Rose of Summer') whose fame and popularity in his own lifetime have not lasted. He may now be best known as a friend of Lord Byron and one of the literary executors who agreed to the burning of the poet's reputedly scandalous memoirs. His own more decorous memoirs, together with extracts from his journals and correspondence, were published in a multi-volume edition immediately after his death. *Pages 49, 154–5, 205, 209, 255–6, 294, 417, 470*

Karl Philip Moritz (1756–93)
Born in Hamelin, Moritz began his working life as a hatter's apprentice but became a writer and philosopher whose works were quoted with approval by Goethe. As well as a series of semi-autobiographical novels, he published accounts of his travels in Italy and in England. His description of his visit to London is in the form of a journal. *Page 239*

Chris Mullin (born 1947)
Editor of two volumes of speeches by Tony Benn and author of the political thriller *A Very British Coup*, he worked as a TV journalist before becoming Labour MP for Sunderland South in 1987, which he represented until he retired in 2010. His three volumes of diaries provide an entertaining, revela-

tory account of the rise and fall of New Labour from the perspective of an independently minded supporter of the party. *Pages 30–31, 43, 60, 309*

Arthur Munby (1828–1910)
A minor poet and man of letters in Victorian England, Munby is now best remembered for his diary which reveals his obsessive interest in working-class women. In 1873, he secretly married out of his class and became the husband of a domestic servant named Hannah Culwick. His diary also paints a remark-ably rich and memorable portrait of Victorian London. *Pages 26, 74, 102, 149, 169, 178, 200–1, 234, 235, 248, 266–7, 298–9, 306, 310, 345–6, 398, 500, 522–3*

Joseph Naples (c. 1775–1840?)
The son of a stationer and bookbinder, Naples went to sea as a young man and served on one of the ships that took part in the Battle of St Vincent in 1797. After his discharge from the Navy, work was difficult to find and he became a 'resurrection man', supplying illegally obtained bodies to London hospitals. His brief diary of his body-snatching activities in 1811 and 1812 came into the possession of the Royal College of Surgeons and was published in 1896. *Pages 483, 497*

Peter Nichols (born 1927)
Born in Bristol, he trained as an actor and worked as a teacher before becoming a playwright. His best-known works for the stage include *A Day in the Death of Joe Egg* (1967) and *Privates on Parade* (1977). In 2000, he published extracts from his diaries, covering the period from 1969 to 1977. *Pages 95, 187–8, 202, 213, 254, 258, 326, 379, 395–6, 413, 418–9, 425, 473, 496, 506*

Harold Nicolson (1886–1968)
A diplomat who represented Britain at the Paris Peace Conference in 1919, he went on to become a historian and politician, entering the House of Commons in 1935. He was a staunch opponent of appeasement and served briefly in Churchill's wartime government. With his wife Vita Sackville-West, he created the famous gardens at Sissinghurst Castle. Selections from his diaries, recording the world of politics, high society and the arts in which he lived, were first published in the 1960s. *Pages 23, 24, 76, 164, 512*

William Oldys (1696–1761)
An antiquarian and bibliographer, he was the illegitimate son of a wealthy man but he lost much of the money he inherited in the South Sea Bubble. Forced to earn a living, he worked for booksellers and publishers in London. In his fifties, he was appointed Norroy King of Arms at the College of Arms. His short diary, consisting largely of notes about books and manuscripts, was published in the nineteenth century. *Pages 104, 411*

George Orwell (1903–50)
The journalist, essayist and novelist, author of *The Road to Wigan Pier*, *Animal Farm* and *1984*, kept diaries intermittently in the 1930s and 1940s. His diaries during the Second World War are particularly revealing of life in London during the Blitz. *Pages 102–3, 165, 252, 318, 361*

Edward Oxnard (1747–1803)
Born in Boston and educated at Harvard, Oxnard was another American loyalist who went into exile in England during the years of the American War of Independence. Like several of his fellow exiles, he kept a journal which was published several decades after his death. Oxnard lived in London until 1785 when he travelled back across the Atlantic, first to Nova Scotia and then, the following year, to the newly created United States. *Pages 137, 392, 397*

Michael Palin (born 1943)
Famous for his work on *Monty Python's Flying Circus*, for his appearances in films such as *The Missionary*, *A Private Function* and *A Fish Called Wanda*, and for travels around the world for BBC documentaries, Michael Palin has kept diaries for much of his adult life. Selections from them, covering the years from 1969 to 1988, have recently been published. *Pages 35, 40, 71, 79, 158, 159, 249, 302, 391, 416, 417, 425–6, 432–3, 443, 449, 456, 460, 491*

Frances Partridge (1900–2004)
In the last few years of her long life, Frances Partridge was the only survivor from the Bloomsbury Group of writers and artists which had exercised such an influence on English culture in the twentieth century. In 1978, she published *A Pacifist's War*, a selection from the diaries she kept during the Second World War. She went on to publish six more volumes of post-war diaries. *Pages 76–7, 207, 312, 447, 463*

Sir Robert Peel (1788–1850)
Prime Minister briefly in 1834–5 and again in 1841–46, Peel is best remembered for his creation in 1829 of the Metropolitan Police. As Home Secretary, he established a force of police officers who are still occasionally known as 'bobbies' or 'peelers'. *Page 418*

Samuel Pepys (1633–1703)
The most famous of all English diarists was born in London and spent most of his life there. He began his diary in 1660, just before he secured a position as Clerk of the Acts to the Navy Board, and brought it to an end nine years later because he believed (mistakenly) that his eyesight was deteriorating so badly that he risked blindness. After he ceased to keep the diary, he went on

to a distinguished career as an MP and naval administrator. *Pages 14, 39, 91, 127, 137, 175–6, 269, 292, 318, 342, 343, 346–7, 351, 371, 422, 429, 447–8, 481–2, 487–8, 514*

Micajah Perry (c. 1695–1753)
A merchant who became Master of the Worshipful Company of Haber-dashers, Micajah Perry was elected Lord Mayor of London in 1738 and laid the first stone of the Mansion House. For fourteen years he was also one of the City's four MPs. His unusual name derives from a minor Biblical character. His diary, together with that of a more recent Lord Mayor, was first published in 1920. *Pages 250, 353, 434*

John Thomas Pocock (1814–76)
Born into a prosperous family in Leadenhall, Pocock emigrated to South Africa at the age of twenty where he became a successful businessman. The diary which he kept as a London schoolboy between 1826 and 1830 was first published a hundred and fifty years after he made the last entry in it. *Pages 54, 61, 83, 214, 306*

Sir Frederick Pollock (1815–88)
The son of a Tory politician who was Attorney General in the government of Sir Robert Peel, Sir Frederick Pollock was a distinguished lawyer. From 1874 to 1886, he was Queen's Remembrancer, taking an ancient judicial position which had first been created by Henry II in the middle of the twelfth century. His translation of Dante's *Divine Comedy* appeared in 1853. The two-volume autobiography that was published the year before he died included extracts from his journals. *Pages 89, 116–17, 122–3, 345, 493–4*

Mrs Philip Lybbe Powys (1739–1817)
Born Caroline Girle, the daughter of a Berkshire landowner, she married the owner of Hardwick House in Oxfordshire. She kept a diary for more than fifty years which reveals much about the life and habits of the eighteenth-century upper classes. Selections from it were first published eighty years after her death. *Pages 163–4, 361, 435, 466*

Thomas Raikes (1777–1848)
The son of a one-time Governor of the Bank of England, Raikes was educated at Eton where he met Beau Brummell. Like Brummell, Raikes grew up to be a famous dandy, a habitué of gentlemen's clubs such as White's and a regular traveller in Europe. Selections from the journals which he kept in the 1830s and 1840s were published after his death. *Pages 108, 134, 204, 261–2, 327*

Sir John Reresby (1634–89)
Born in Yorkshire, Reresby was a Royalist who exiled himself to Europe in the aftermath of the English Civil War. After the Restoration of Charles II, he returned to England and entered Parliament. His *Memoirs*, written in the form of a diary, were first published in 1734, one hundred years after his birth. *Pages 199, 508*

Sophie Richmond (born 1952)
Malcolm McLaren's secretary during the heyday of the Sex Pistols, Sophie Richmond was the partner of the artist and graphic designer Jamie Reid. Extracts of her diaries from the punk period appeared in *The Sex Pistols: The Inside Story*, published in 1978. *Page 24*

Charles Ritchie (1906–95)
Ritchie was a Canadian diplomat, born in Nova Scotia, who spent long periods of his career in London. He was in the city for much of the Second World War and, after periods as ambassador to West Germany, the United Nations and the USA, he returned as Canadian High Commissioner in the late sixties. His diaries have been published in four volumes. His letters to the writer Elizabeth Bowen, with whom he conducted an intermittent love affair from 1941 until her death in 1973, have also been published. *Pages 31, 195, 368, 404, 494*

Katherine Roberts (fl. 1910)
Nothing is known about the author of *Pages from the Diary of a Militant Suffragette* which recounts the introduction of an ordinary middle-class woman to the ideas and campaigns of the suffragettes. Katherine Roberts may well have been a pseudonym. *Page 498*

Henry Crabb Robinson (1775–1867)
Born in Bury St Edmunds, Crabb Robinson was first a journalist and then a lawyer but he is remembered today for his extensive diary which records his friendships and meetings with many of the most famous figures in art and literature of his time. He knew Coleridge, Wordsworth and Charles Lamb well and was acquainted with William Blake. All of them make appearances in the pages of his diary. *Pages 71, 78, 182–3, 189, 220, 337, 380–1, 461, 489, 505, 506–7*

William Michael Rossetti (1829–1919)
Brother of poet and painter Dante Gabriel and poet Christina, W. M. Rossetti was one of the founding members of the Pre-Raphaelite Brotherhood. He edited the movement's magazine *The Germ* in 1850 and went on to combine a career in the civil service with work as a literary critic and biographer. He produced a collection of Pre-Raphaelite letters and diaries in 1900. *Page 134*

Richard Rush (1780–1859)
Born in Philadelphia, the son of one of the signers of the Declaration of Independence, Rush became a leading diplomat and politician in early nineteenth-century America. He was appointed American Minister to the Court of St James in 1817 and lived in London for eight years. He published selections from his journals covering that period in 1833 and 1845. *Pages 22, 108, 512, 515, 523*

Lady John Russell (1815–98)
Daughter of the Earl of Minto, Frances Elliott was born in Roxburghshire in Scotland and, in 1841, became the second wife of the Whig politician Lord John Russell. Her husband was twice Prime Minister, in 1846–52 and 1865–66. Extensive selections from her diaries and correspondence were included in a memoir of her which was published in 1910. *Pages 63, 65–6, 83*

Dudley Ryder (1691–1756)
An MP for twenty years, Ryder was appointed Attorney General in 1737 and was one of the founding governors of the Foundling Hospital in Bloomsbury. He became Lord Chief Justice two years before his death. As a young law student at the Middle Temple in 1715 and 1716, he kept a diary in shorthand which records his family and social life, his intellectual and artistic interests and his attachments to women. *Page 357*

Vita Sackville-West (1892–1962)
A poet and author, who created the gardens at Sissinghurst Castle, now owned by The National Trust, she became famous after her death for her unconventional marriage to the diplomat and diarist Harold Nicolson. Both of them had (mostly same-sex) love affairs outside the marriage. Vita's passionate relationship with Virginia Woolf is celebrated in the letters of both women. *Pages 411–12, 511*

Ignatius Sancho (c. 1729–80)
A writer and composer, Sancho was born a slave and brought to England as a child. He gained his freedom as a young man and became a well-known figure in Georgian London. Gainsborough painted his portrait, and his friends included the actor David Garrick and the novelist Laurence Sterne. In his later years, he ran a grocery store in Mayfair. *The Letters of the Late Ignatius Sancho, an African*, published two years after his death, became a bestseller. *Pages 241–2, 356–7*

William Sancroft (1617–93)
Born in Suffolk and educated at Emmanuel College, Cambridge, Sancroft, a Royalist, was an exile abroad during the Commonwealth. On Charles II's Restoration in 1660, he returned to favour and became Archbishop of Canterbury in 1677. He continued in the post under James II but refused to take the oath to William and Mary after the Glorious Revolution and was replaced. *Pages 177–8*

Viscount Sandhurst (William Mansfield) (1855–1921)
A Liberal politician, he served as a minister under Gladstone and was then despatched to India to become Governor of Bombay from 1895 to 1900. On his return he continued to occupy minor posts in the Liberal governments of Asquith and Lloyd George. He was appointed Viscount Sandhurst in 1917. His diaries of the First World War years were published in two volumes after his death. *Pages 24, 85, 202–3, 208, 330, 425, 431–2*

Siegfried Sassoon (1886–1967)
Decorated for bravery as a soldier in the First World War, he was a poet whose verses revealed the horrors of the fighting and satirised the pretensions and incompetence of the high command. After the war he wrote a trilogy of autobiographical novels. His diaries, written in the war and in the 1920s, were published after his death. *Pages 250, 459*

Sir Walter Scott (1771–1832)
The poet and historical novelist, author of books including *Ivanhoe*, *Rob Roy* and *The Heart of Midlothian* which were astonishingly popular throughout most of the nineteenth century and beyond, kept a diary for the last eight years of his life. It has been called 'perhaps the most valuable, certainly the most moving, of all his productions'. It was first published in 1890. *Page 168*

George Selwyn (1719–91)
An MP for 44 years, George Selwyn never once made a speech in the House of Commons. Outside Parliament, he was renowned as a wit, a leading member of the infamous Hellfire Club and a man with an unhealthily obsessive interest in death and executions. *Pages 319, 339*

Keshub Chandra Sen (1838–84)
Born in Kolkata, he was a Bengali philosopher and social reformer who aimed to find common ground between Hindu thought and Christianity. In 1870, he travelled to England and stayed for six months, lecturing and expounding his ideas about the underlying unity of religious beliefs. He kept a journal throughout his time in the country. *Pages 128–9, 136, 149, 168*

George Bernard Shaw (1856–1950)
The Irish dramatist, author of *Pygmalion*, *Saint Joan* and *Back to Methuselah*, was a regular writer of (often very funny) letters to the press on subjects ranging from vaccination and vivisection to the employment of children on the stage and the censorship of his plays. His views on proper dress at the opera are reprinted here. *Pages 284–5*

William Archer Shee (1810–99)
The son of a well-known portrait painter who became President of the Royal Academy, Shee was born in Dublin and became a successful barrister. Extracts from his diary from 1830 to 1870 were published a few years before he died and record details of literary, artistic and social life in mid-Victorian London. *Pages 264–5, 426–7*

Mary Shelley (1797–1851)
Author of *Frankenstein* which, famously if possibly inaccurately, is said to have been inspired by a nightmare she experienced while staying with her husband, the poet Percy Bysshe Shelley, and his friend Lord Byron at the Villa Diodati on the shore of Lake Geneva. She kept a journal intermittently throughout her life and excerpts from it were first published in a nineteenth-century biography. *Pages 261, 422, 519*

Anthony Sher (born 1949)
Born in South Africa, the actor began his career in Britain at the Everyman Theatre, London, and went on to great acclaim in productions for the Royal Shakespeare Company and the National Theatre. He has also appeared frequently on TV and in films. His own plays have been staged at the Almeida and at the National. *Year of the King* was a volume of diaries covering the period when he was preparing for his groundbreaking performance as Richard III in 1984. *Pages 472, 487*

Emily Shore (1819–39)
She began her journal at the age of eleven when she was living at the family home in Bury St Edmunds and kept it until her death eight years later in Madeira, where she had been taken in the hope that the climate would improve her consumption. Published by her sisters in 1891, it includes her descriptions of family visits to London in the 1830s. *Pages 215, 286–7, 364*

Louis Simond (1767–1831)
Born in France, he emigrated to America before the Revolution where he settled in New York and became a successful merchant. In 1810–11, he travelled to Britain and later published his impressions of the country in his *Journal of a Tour and Residence in Great Britain. Pages 29, 45, 81–2, 375*

Elizabeth Smart (1913–86)
A Canadian poet and novelist who lived for many years in London, Elizabeth Smart is best known for her work of prose poetry *By Grand Central Station I Sat Down and Wept*, first published in 1945. The book, once described by Angela Carter as 'like *Madame Bovary* blasted by lightning', was inspired by her long, tormented love affair with the English poet George Barker. Her journals were published in two volumes in 1987 and 1997. *Pages 98, 110–11*

Sydney Smith (1771–1845)
A clergyman, Smith moved to London from Edinburgh in 1803 and became widely known as an author, preacher and society wit. Although obliged to spend time in exile in the country during his career ('My living in Yorkshire,' he once wrote, 'was so far out of the way that it was actually twelve miles from the nearest lemon'), he was happiest in the city and his letters reflect his enjoyment of the metropolis. *Page 468*

Thomas Sopwith (1803–79)
Grandfather of the man who created the pioneering Sopwith Aviation Company, he was a mining engineer who turned to work on the railways with George and Robert Stephenson. He was responsible for surveying and engineering thousands of miles of railway lines both in Britain and on the Continent. Born in Newcastle-upon-Tyne, he spent much of his life in the north-east but was a regular visitor to London. *Pages 141–2*

Stephen Spender (1909–95)
Spender was associated with Auden, Cecil Day-Lewis and Louis MacNeice as one of the 'Thirties Poets' and went on to play a leading role in English literary life for another sixty years. His letters to his friend, the novelist Christopher Isherwood, were first published in 1980. *Page 44*

Nils Stevenson (1953–2002)
A pioneering punk, he worked with Malcolm Maclaren at the time the Sex Pistols were launched on an unsuspecting nation and went on to manage Siouxsie and the Banshees. Together with his brother Ray, a photographer, he published his punk diary in 1999. *Pages 23, 145*

Sir Roy Strong (born 1935)
Initially coming to public attention as the flamboyant and innovative director of the National Portrait Gallery and then the Victoria & Albert Museum, Roy Strong went on to become a writer and broadcaster on the arts and creator of a much-admired garden in Herefordshire. His diaries, bitchily and entertainingly revealing of the art world, were published in 1997. *Pages 105–6, 118, 301, 499*

Jonathan Swift (1667–1745)
The author of *Gulliver's Travels* lived for long periods in London during the reign of Queen Anne before being obliged by circumstances to return unwillingly to his native Dublin where he remained for the rest of his life. During his time in London, he wrote a series of letters to a friend, Esther Johnson, whom he called Stella. The letters, which take the form of journal entries, were published posthumously in 1766. *Pages 25–26, 103, 114, 207, 386, 464, 466–7*

William Tayler (1807–92)
Born into a farming family in Oxfordshire, Tayler went into service in London as a young man, ending his career as a butler. At the time he wrote his diary, he was working for Mrs Prinsep, the widow of an MP, who lived in Great Cumberland Place, near Marble Arch. *Pages 20, 37, 46*

William Johnston Temple (1739–96)
A clergyman in Cornwall for much of his career, Temple had been at the University of Edinburgh with James Boswell and remained a close friend of the biographer. His diaries, first published in 1929, record visits to the capital and his experiences in London literary society. *Pages 193, 224*

Ralph Thoresby (1658–1725)
An antiquarian, merchant and scholar, he wrote the first history of his native Leeds. As he records in his diary, which he kept for much of his adult life, Thoresby spent long periods in London, examining manuscripts that interested him and gathering material for his own collection of coins, medals and other antiquities. *Pages 162, 179, 300, 317, 385*

John Tillison (fl. 1665–77)
Tillison worked for William Sancroft (q.v.), Dean of St Paul's and later Archbishop of Canterbury. He addressed a number of letters to his employer about life in London and the affairs of the Church which survive in the Bodleian Library and British Museum. *Page 384*

Sir William Treloar (1843–1923)
A prominent businessman in Victorian London and head of the family haberdashery firm, Treloar was knighted in 1900 and chosen as Lord Mayor in November 1906. His diary of his year in office was published in 1920. The Treloar Trust, a charity which provides education and training for young people with physical disabilities, is named after him. *Pages 46, 115, 126, 128, 448*

John Tyler (1742–1823)
Born in Wallingford, Connecticut, Tyler was educated at Yale and Columbia and travelled to London in the summer of 1768 to be ordained. He returned to America in September that year and took up a post as minister of a church in Norwich in his home state where he remained for the rest of his life. His short journal of his visit to London was published in 1894. *Pages 298, 315*

Kenneth Tynan (1927–80)
A theatre critic who championed the Angry Young Men of the 1950s, the man who famously first used the word 'fuck' on British television (during a 1965 interview) and literary manager of the National Theatre while Laurence Olivier was its artistic director, Tynan was a distinctive presence in British cultural life for most of his adult life. His diaries, edited by John Lahr, were published in 2001. *Pages 271–2*

Vincent Van Gogh (1853–90)
The Dutch Post-impressionist painter spent some time in London as a young man. He worked for the art dealer Goupil in the city between 1873 and 1875, lodging in Brixton and Kennington and commuting to the company's offices in the Strand. In 1876, he was employed as a teacher in Isleworth. His letters home to his family and friends, particularly his younger brother Theo, describe his London life. *Pages 415–6, 476*

Peter Van Schaack (1747–1832)
A lawyer born in Kinderhook, New York, and educated at Columbia University, Van Schaack was one of the many Americans who went into exile in England because they were loyal to the crown and opposed independence. During his seven years in England, he kept a diary, extracts from which were published in a biography of 1842. He returned to America in 1785 and practised as a lawyer for the rest of his life. *Pages 318–19, 371*

Queen Victoria (1819–1901)
The longest-serving British monarch kept a journal from 1832, when she was thirteen years old and Princess Victoria of Kent, to the time of her death, when she ruled over a vast empire on which the sun allegedly never set. The journals have recently been put online in their entirety. *Pages 206–7*

Sophie Von La Roche (1730–1807)
Author of *The History of Lady Sophie Sternheim*, one of the earliest novels in German written by a woman, she was the hostess of a literary salon attended by the young Goethe. In the 1780s and 1790s she published several volumes of journals recounting her travels around Europe, including a visit to London. *Pages 378–9*

Thomas Wale (1701–96)
Wale was an East Anglian merchant who lived and traded for many years in the countries now known as Latvia and Estonia. He also spent part of his long life in London. His papers, including many diary entries, provided the basis for *My Grandfather's Pocket-Book*, a volume edited by one of his grandsons and published in 1883. *Page 220*

Horace Walpole (1717–97)
The youngest son of the first prime minister, Sir Robert Walpole, Horace Walpole entered parliament as a young man and was an MP from 1741 to 1768. However, he is best remembered as the author of *The Castle of Otranto*, the creator of Strawberry Hill, a Gothic villa at Twickenham, and as a voluminous letter-writer. His letters, most recently published in 48 volumes by Yale University Press, provide a witty, detailed and memorable portrait of upper-class eighteenth-century life. *Pages 60, 88–9, 107, 117–18, 144–5, 167, 222–3, 240–1, 246–7, 280, 300, 343, 364, 368–9, 409*

Thomas Asline Ward (1781–1871)
Ward was a prominent citizen of Sheffield who took an active part in the government of his native town and was, for many years, editor of a local newspaper. He kept diaries throughout most of his life and, in one of them, he recorded his impressions of London during a visit as a young man. *Pages 344, 349, 350–1*

Evelyn Waugh (1903–66)
The author of *Decline and Fall, Scoop* and *Brideshead Revisited* kept witty and acerbic diaries for much of his life. The entries from the 1920s are particularly revealing of the hedonistic London lives of those members of the post-war generation known as the Bright Young Things. *Pages 208, 268, 276, 376, 391–2, 404–5, 472, 523*

Beatrice Webb (1858–1943)
Beatrice Potter was a pioneering sociologist who worked with Charles Booth on his survey of London slums in the 1880s. In 1892 she married Sidney Webb and together they went on to become leading figures in the history of the Labour Party, and co-founders of the London School of Economics. She kept journals throughout most of her life which are now in the LSE archives. *Pages 59, 194, 331, 459, 468*

Harry Wedgwood (1799–1885)
The grandson of the famous potter Josiah Wedgwood and Charles Darwin's brother-in-law, Harry Wedgwood became a London barrister. He wrote a chil-

dren's book, *The Bird-Talisman: An Eastern Tale*, which was still in print as recently as the 1970s. His letters have appeared in collections of Wedgwood and Darwin family correspondence. *Page 221*

Joshua Wingate Weeks (1738–1806)
Rector of a church in Marblehead, Massachusetts, Weeks was one of those many Americans loyal to the crown who travelled to England during the American War of Independence. His journal of his experiences while staying in London was first published in 1916. *Pages 52–3, 160–1, 190–1*

Denton Welch (1915–48)
Born and brought up in China, where his father was a wealthy English merchant, Welch was an art student at Goldsmith's College when he was severely injured in a road accident. Complications from his fractured spine led to his early death thirteen years later. In the years after his accident, he wrote prolifically, producing three novels, more than fifty shorter pieces and the journal that was published posthumously. One admirer of his work was William Burroughs, who dedicated one of his novels to his memory. *Pages 360, 382*

John Wesley (1703–91)
The founder of Methodism kept a journal for most of his adult life which records his extraordinary journeys around the country. (During his career as an evangelist, Wesley is supposed to have travelled something like 250,000 miles and preached close to 40,000 sermons.) The journal throws light on his life and work in London and its surrounding suburbs. *Pages 33, 68, 79, 182, 351–2, 380, 517*

Walter White (1811–93)
After leaving school at the age of fourteen, White worked as a cabinet-maker in Reading before travelling in the USA as a young man. On his return to Britain, he became a writer and, for more than forty years, a librarian at the Royal Society. Through his work at the Royal Society, he came to know many of its more famous members, including Darwin, Tennyson and Carlyle. Selections from his journals were published in 1898, five years after his death. *Page 194*

Russ Wilkins
Born in London, where he still lives and works, Russ Wilkins is a fan of Championship football team Charlton Athletic. In 2005, he published *The Diary of a Common Fan*, a record of the club's centenary season from a supporter's perspective. *Pages 78, 480*

J. Williams (1793–??)
A young Londoner whose Christian name is not known but whose journal, kept during a few months when he was in his twenties, survives. Extracts from it were published in the magazine *Notes & Queries* in 1903. *Page 162*

Kenneth Williams (1926–88)
A comic actor, his nasal drawl and camp demeanour were familiar to millions in the 1950s and 1960s in radio programmes such as *Hancock's Half Hour* and *Round the Horne*. One of the regular performers in the *Carry On* films, he was also in demand as a raconteur on chat shows and panel games. His diaries, published after his death (possibly by suicide), reveal a more melancholy, indeed depressive personality than his public image suggested. *Pages 21, 28, 35, 98, 217, 231, 272, 389–90, 393*

William Windham (1750–1810)
A Whig politician and contemporary of Charles Fox and William Pitt the Younger, he was renowned for his parliamentary oratory in an age when the ability to make a fine speech was much admired. He was Secretary at War in Pitt's government for seven years during the war against revolutionary France. Selections from his diary were first published in 1866. *Pages 61, 221, 225–6, 392, 395, 431, 512*

Anthony Wood (1632–95)
A scholar and antiquary who spent most of his life in Oxford, he wrote extensive diaries. They are particularly revealing of university politics and personalities of the time, but often included news of events in London. *Page 198*

James Woodforde (1740–1803)
Woodforde led a largely uneventful life as a country parson in Somerset and Norfolk but he recorded it in a diary which he kept for more than forty years. When extracts from it were first published in the 1920s, it was hailed as a remarkable account of everyday eighteenth-century life. Woodforde visited London on a number of occasions and recorded his experiences there. *Pages 229, 230, 270*

Virginia Woolf (1882–1941)
The modernist writer and novelist, author of *To the Lighthouse*, *Mrs Dalloway* and *A Room of One's Own*, kept diaries for much of her life. A multi-volume selection, beginning in 1915 and ending with her suicide by drowning in 1941, was edited by her nephew Quentin Bell and his wife, and published in the 1970s and 1980s. *Pages 138, 154, 176–7, 203, 205, 376–7, 448–9*

Dorothy Wordsworth (1771–1855)
The sister of the Romantic poet was an inveterate keeper of journals, most of which record their life in the Lake District. Some of the journals describe travels further afield, including visits to London. *Page 321*

Sir Henry Wotton (1568–1639)
A poet and diplomat, Wotton once defined an ambassador as 'an honest man sent to lie abroad for the good of his country'. He was ambassador for James I for many years, most notably in Venice. On his return to England in 1624, he became an MP and Provost of Eton. Selections from his chatty and gossipy letters to friends were published after his death. *Pages 224–5, 283*

Charles Wriothesley (1508–62)
Born in London where both his father and his grandfather were heralds in the College of Arms, he was educated at Cambridge and, thanks to family influence, began his own career as a herald at the age of sixteen. His *Chronicle of England During the Reign of the Tudors* is a largely day-by-day record of the chief events from the time Henry VII came to the throne to the accession of his granddaughter, Elizabeth I. *Pages 126, 153, 158, 183, 350, 364, 497*

Joan Wyndham (1921–2007)
A member of the bohemian world of wartime Fitzrovia when she was a young woman, Joan Wyndham became known to a wider public after her diaries (*Love Lessons, Love Is Blue*) were published in the 1980s. Memorably described in one newspaper as 'a latterday Pepys in camiknickers', Wyndham wrote with wit and exuberance of her love affairs, London during the Blitz and her encounters with the likes of Dylan Thomas and Julian Maclaren-Ross. *Pages 287, 340–1, 388–9, 477, 489*

John Yeoman (1748–1824)
Yeoman was a Somerset potter who made two business trips to the capital when he was in his twenties. He kept a diary, recording his experiences there, which was edited and published in 1935. *Pages 141, 147*

~ BIBLIOGRAPHY ~

Abbot, Charles, Lord Colchester, *Diary and Correspondence*, 3 vols., John Murray, 1861

Ackerley, J. R., *My Sister and Myself: The Diaries of J. R. Ackerley* (ed. Francis King), Hutchinson, 1982

Adolphus, John, *Recollections of the Public Career and Private Life of the Late John Adolphus, with Extracts from his Diaries* by Emily Henderson, Cautley Newby, 1871

Agate, James, *Ego*, 9 vols., Harrap, 1935–48

Alanbrooke, Lord, *The War Diaries of Field Marshal Lord Alanbrooke* (ed. Alex Danchev), Weidenfeld & Nicolson, 2001

Allingham, William, *A Diary*, Macmillan, 1907

Altick, Richard, *The Shows of London*, Harvard University Press, 1978

Anderson, Lindsay, *The Diaries* (ed. Paul Sutton), Methuen, 2004

Ashmole, Elias, *The Lives of those Eminent Antiquaries Elias Ashmole and William Lilly, Written by Themselves*, T. Davies, 1774

Bagot, Mrs Charles, *Links with the Past*, Edward Arnold, 1901

Bailey, James Blake, *The Diary of a Resurrectionist 1811–1812*, Swan Sonnenschein, 1896

Bailey, John Cann, *Letters and Diaries*, John Murray, 1935

Bain, James S., *A Bookseller Looks Back: The Story of the Bains*, Macmillan, 1940

Baker, John, *The Diary of John Baker, barrister of the Middle Temple, solicitor-general of the Leeward Islands*, 1931

Barbellion, W. N. P., *The Journal of a Disappointed Man*, Chatto & Windus, 1919

Barrie, J. M., *Letters of J. M. Barrie* (ed. Viola Meynell), Peter Davies, 1942

Bason, Fred, *Fred Bason's Third Diary* (ed. Michael Sadleir), André Deutsch, 1955; *The Last Bassoon: From the Diaries of Fred Bason* (ed. Noël Coward), Max Parrish, 1960

Beaton, Cecil, *The Wandering Years: Diaries 1922–39*, Weidenfeld & Nicolson, 1961; *The Years Between: Diaries 1939–44*, Weidenfeld & Nicolson, 1965

Beattie, James, *James Beattie's London Diary*, Aberdeen University Press, 1946

Beeching, H. C., *Pages from a Private Diary*, Smith, Elder, 1898

Bell, Amy Helen, *London Was Ours: Diaries and Memoirs of the London Blitz*, I. B. Tauris, 2008

Benn, Tony, *Out of the Wilderness: Diaries 1963–67*, Hutchinson, 1987; *Office Without Power: Diaries 1968–72*, Hutchinson, 1988

Bennett, Alan, *Writing Home*, Faber, 1994

Bennett, Arnold, *The Journals of Arnold Bennett*, Cassell, 1932

Benson, A. C., *The Diary of Arthur Christopher Benson* (ed. Percy Lubbock), Hutchinson, 1927

Berry, Mary, *Extracts of the Journal and Correspondence of Miss Berry 1783–1852*, 3 vols., Longman, Green, 1865

Betjeman, John, *Letters* (ed. Candida Lycett Green), 2 vols., Methuen, 1994–95

Birch, Thomas (ed.), *The Court and Times of James I, Illustrated by Authentic and Confidential Letters*, 2 vols., Henry Colburn, 1848

Blumenfeld, R. D., *R.D.B.'s Diary*, William Heinemann, 1930

Boswell, James, *Boswell's London Journal 1762–1763* (ed. Frederick A. Pottle), Yale University Press, 1950

Bowen, Elizabeth and Charles Ritchie, *Love's Civil War: Elizabeth Bowen and Charles Ritchie, Letters and Diaries* (ed. Victoria Glendinning), Simon & Schuster, 2009

Bray, William, *Extracts from the Diary of William Bray*, privately printed, 1876

British Diarist, The, Issue 4, Paul Minet, 2004

Browning, Elizabeth Barrett, *The Letters of Elizabeth Barrett Browning* (ed. Frederick Kenyon), 2 vols., Macmillan, 1898

Bruce, David, *Ambassador to Sixties London: The Diaries of David Bruce 1961–1969*, Republic of Letters, 2009

Bryceson, Nathaniel, *Diary*, City of Westminster Archives, online

Buchanan, George, *Passage through the Present*, Constable, 1932

Burney, Fanny, *The Diary and Letters of Madame D'Arblay*, 3 vols., Vizetelly, 1891

Burr, Aaron, *The Private Journal of Aaron Burr During His Residence of Four Years in Europe* (ed. Matthew Davis), 2 vols., Harper Brothers, 1838

Byrom, John, *The Private Journal and Literary Remains of John Byrom*, Chetham Society, 1854

Byron, George Gordon, *Letters and Journals* (ed. Rowland Prothero), 2 vols., John Murray, 1898

Calendar of State Papers Relating to English Affairs in the Archives of Venice, vol. 26, HMSO, 1925

Campbell, Thomas, *Diary of a Visit to England in 1775*, in *Johnsoniana* (ed. Robina Napier), Bell & Sons, 1889

Carlyle, Jane Welsh, *Letters and Memorials of Jane Welsh Carlyle* (ed. J. A. Froude), 3 vols., Longmans Green, 1883

Carlyle, Thomas, *Early Letters of Thomas Carlyle* (ed. Charles Eliot Norton), Macmillan, 1886

Carrington, Dora, *Carrington: Letters and Extracts from her Diaries*, Jonathan Cape, 1970

Cartwright, Julia, *A Bright Remembrance*, Weidenfeld and Nicolson, 1989

Carus, C. G., *The King of Saxony's Journey Through England and Scotland*, Chapman & Hall, 1846

Cavendish, Lady Frederick, *The Diary of Lady Frederick Cavendish* (ed. John Cann Bailey), 2 vols., John Murray, 1927

Chalmers, Anne, *Letters and Journals of Anne Chalmers*, The Chelsea Publishing Co., 1923

Chamberlain, John, *A Jacobean Letter Writer: The Life and Times of John Chamberlain* by Edward Phillips Statham, Kegan Paul, 1920

Clark, Alan, *Diaries*, Weidenfeld & Nicolson, 1993

Clark, Ossie, *The Ossie Clark Diaries* (ed. Lady Henrietta Rous), Bloomsbury, 1998

Clifford, Lady Anne, *The Diary of Lady Anne Clifford* (ed. Vita Sackville-West), Heinemann, 1924

Clinton, Henry Fynes, *Literary Remains of Henry Fynes Clinton*, Longman, 1854

Cockett, Olivia, *Love and War in London: The Mass Observation Diary of Olivia Cockett* (ed. Robert Malcolmson), History Press, 2008

Coke, Lady Jane, *Letters from Lady Jane Coke to her Friend Mrs Eyre 1747–58* (ed. Mrs Ambrose Rathborne), Swan Sonnenschein, 1899

Collier, John Payne, *An Old Man's Diary*, privately printed, 1871–2

Connal, Sir Michael, *Diary of Sir Michael Connal 1835–93* (ed. J. C. Gibson), James MacLehose, 1895

Constable, John, *Memoirs of the Life of John Constable, Esq. R.A., Composed Chiefly of His Letters* (ed. C. R. Leslie), Longman, Brown, Green & Longmans, 1845

Cooke, George Frederick, *Memoirs of the Life of George Frederick Cooke* by William Dunlap, 2 vols., Longworth, 1813

Cooper, Duff, *The Duff Cooper Diaries 1915–51* (ed. John Julius Norwich), Weidenfeld & Nicolson, 2005

Coward, Noël, *The Noël Coward Diaries* (ed. Graham Payn and Sheridan Morley), Weidenfeld & Nicolson, 1982

Cowper, Mary, Countess, *Diary of Mary, Countess Cowper: Lady of the Bedchamber to the Princess of Wales 1714–1720*, John Murray, 1864

Creevey, Thomas, *The Creevey Papers* (ed. Sir Herbert Maxwell), 2 vols., John Murray, 1903

Croker, John Wilson, *The Croker Papers* (ed. Louis Jennings), 3 vols., John Murray, 1884

Crossman, Richard, *The Crossman Diaries: Selections from the Diaries of a Cabinet Minister 1964–70* (ed. Anthony Howard), 1979

Cunningham, Alfred A., *Marine Flyer in France: The Diary of Captain Alfred A. Cunningham*, US Marine Corps, 1974

Curwen, Samuel, *The Journal and Letters of Samuel Curwen: An American in England from 1775–1783*, C. S. Francis, 1842

Darwin, Emma, *Emma Darwin: A Century of Family Letters 1792–1896* (ed. H. Litchfield), 2 vols., John Murray, 1915

Dee, John, *The Private Diary of Dr. John Dee* (ed. J. A. Halliwell), The Camden Society, 1842

Dickens, Charles, *The Letters of Charles Dickens*, 3 vols., Chapman & Hall, 1880–2

Dodington, Bubb, *The Diary of the Late George Bubb Dodington*, G. & T. Wilkie, 1784

Domett, Alfred, *The Diary of Alfred Domett 1872–1885* (ed. E. A. Horsman), Oxford University Press, 1953

Duff, M. E. Grant, *Notes from a Diary*, 14 vols., John Murray, 1897–1905

Dyott, William, *Dyott's Diary* (ed. Reginald W. Jeffery), 2 vols., Constable, 1907

Edgeworth, Maria, *The Life and Letters of Maria Edgeworth* (ed. Augustus Hare), 2 vols., Edward Arnold, 1894

Edward VI, *Literary Remains of King Edward the Sixth* (ed. J. G. Nichols), 2 vols., Roxburghe Club, 1857

Edwards, Dickon, *The Diary at the Centre of the Earth*, http://dickonedwards.co.uk/diary/

Earl of Egmont, *Manuscripts of the Earl of Egmont* (ed. R. A. Roberts), 3 vols., HMSO, 1920–23

Eliot, George, *George Eliot's Life as Related in her Letters and Journals* (ed. J. W. Cross), 3 vols., Blackwood & Sons, 1885

The Eliot Papers (ed. Eliot Howard), 2 vols, E. Hicks, 1895

Ellis, Sir Henry (ed.), *Original Letters Illustrative of English History*, 11 vols., Richard Bentley, 1824–6

Eno, Brian, *A Year with Swollen Appendices*, Faber, 1996

Essex Institute Historical Collections, vol. 52, 1916

Evelyn, John, *The Diary of John Evelyn*, 2 vols., Dent, 1907

Farington, Joseph, *The Farington Diary* (ed. James Greig), 8 vols., Hutchinson, 1924–28

Fielding, Henry, *The Journal of a Voyage to Lisbon*, Chiswick Press, 1892

Fisher, Annie, unpublished diary, *The British Diarist*, May 2004

Fowles, John, *The Journals: Volume I*, Jonathan Cape, 2003

Fox, Caroline, *Memories of Old Friends: Being Extracts from the Journals and Letters of Caroline Fox*, Smith, Elder, 1882

Fox, Henry Edward, *The Journals of Henry Edward Fox*, Thornton Butterworth, 1923

Freke, Elizabeth, *The Remembrances of Elizabeth Freke 1671–1714* (ed. Raymond Anselment), Cambridge University Press, 2002

Fry, Elizabeth, *Memoir of the Life of Elizabeth Fry with Extracts from her Letters and Journal*, 2 vols., Gilpin, 1847

Gissing, George, *Letters of George Gissing to Members of His Family*, Constable, 1931

Gower, Lord Ronald, *Old Diaries 1881–1901*, John Murray, 1902

Grano, John Baptist, *Handel's Trumpeter: The Diary of John Grano* (ed. John Ginger), Pendragon Press, 1998

Greene, Graham, *Graham Greene: A Life in Letters* (ed. Richard Greene), Little, Brown, 2007

Greene, Ireland, *Isaac Greene: A Lancashire Lawyer of the Eighteenth Century, with the Diary of Ireland Greene* by Ronald Stewart-Brown, privately printed, 1921

Greville, Charles, *A Journal of the Reigns of King George IV and King William IV*, 3 vols., Longman Green, 1874; *A Journal of the Reign of Queen Victoria*, 3 vols., Longman Green, 1885

Greville, Henry, *Leaves from the Diary of Henry Greville*, Smith, Elder, 1883

Guinness, Alec, *My Name Escapes Me: The Diary of a Retiring Actor*, Hamish Hamilton, 1996

Hardman, William, *A Mid-Victorian Pepys*, Cecil Palmer, 1923

Hardy, Florence, *The Life of Thomas Hardy*, 2 vols., 1928

Harris, George, *The Autobiography of George Harris*, privately printed, 1888

Hawker, Peter, *The Diary of Colonel Peter Hawker*, 2 vols., Longmans, Green, 1893

Hawthorne, Nathaniel, *Passages from the English Notebooks*, 2 vols., Fields, Osgood, 1870

Haydon, Benjamin, *The Autobiography and Journals* (ed. Malcolm Elwin), Macdonald, 1950

Hearne, Thomas, *Reliquiae Hearnianae: The Remains of Thomas Hearne* (ed. Philip Bliss), 2 vols., John Russell Smith, 1869

Hervey, William, *Journals in North America and Europe*, Paul & Mathew, 1906

Hobhouse, John Cam, *Recollections of a Long Life, with Additional Extracts from his Private Diaries*, 6 vols., John Murray, 1909–11

Hodgson, Vere, *Few Eggs and No Oranges*, Persephone Press, 1999

Hogg, James, *Memorials of James Hogg*, Alexander Gardner, 1904

Hooke, Robert, *The Diary of Robert Hooke* (ed. H. W. Robinson and Walter Adams), Taylor & Francis, 1935

Horsley, J. W., *Jottings from Jail: Notes and Papers on Prison Matters*, Fisher Unwin, 1887

Howard, George, 7th Earl of Carlisle, *Extracts from Journals*, privately printed, 1864

Hurley, Frank, *The Diaries of Frank Hurley 1912–1941*, Anthem Press, 2011

Inge, William Ralph, *Diary of a Dean*, Hutchinson, 1949

Isham, Thomas, *The Diary of Thomas Isham of Lamport (1658–81)*, Miler & Leavins, 1875

James, Henry, *The Letters of Henry James* (ed. Percy Lubbock), 2 vols., Macmillan, 1920

Jarman, Derek, *Modern Nature: Journals of Derek Jarman*, Century, 1991

Keats, John, *Letters of John Keats to his Family and Friends* (ed. Sidney Colvin), Macmillan, 1891

Kielmansegge, Frederick, *Diary of a Journey to England in the Years 1761–1762*, Longmans Green, 1902

King, Oona, *The Oona King Diaries: House Music*, Bloomsbury, 2007

Lamb, Charles, *The Letters of Charles Lamb, to which are Added Those of His Sister Mary Lamb* (ed. E. V. Lucas), 3 vols., J. M. Dent, 1935

Lees-Milne, James, *Prophesying Peace: Diaries 1944–45*, Chatto & Windus, 1977; *Holy Dread: Diaries 1982–84*, John Murray, 2001; *The Milk of Paradise: Diaries 1993–1997*, John Murray, 2005

Leycester, Rafe Neville, *Diary*, online at www.day-books.com

Littlewood, Clayton, *Goodbye to Soho*, DWB Press, 2012

Luttrell, Narcissus, *A Brief Historical Relation of State Affairs*, 6 vols., Oxford University Press, 1867

Macaulay, George Mackenzie, *The War Diary of a London Scot*, Alexander Gardner, 1916

Macaulay, Thomas, *The Life and Letters of Lord Macaulay* (ed. George Otto Trevelyan), 2 vols., Longman Greens, 1876

MacDonagh, Michael, *In London during the Great War*, Eyre & Spottiswoode, 1935

Machyn, Henry, *The Diary of Henry Machyn, Citizen and Merchant Taylor of London* (ed. John Gough Nichols), Camden Society, 1848

McKenny, Helen G., *A City Road Diary 1885–1888*, World Methodist Historical Society, 1978

Macready, William Charles, *The Diaries of William Charles Macready 1833–1851* (ed. William Toynbee), 2 vols., Putnam's, 1912

MacRitchie, Reverend William, *Diary of a Tour through Great Britain in 1795*, Elliott Stock, 1897

Madden, Frederic, Diary, 1844, quoted in Richard D. Altick, *The Shows of London*, Harvard University Press, 1978

Manningham, John, *Diary of John Manningham of the Middle Temple*, Camden Society, 1868

Mansfield, William, Viscount Sandhurst, *From Day to Day 1914–15*, Edward Arnold, 1928

Mantell, Gideon, *The Unpublished Journal of Gideon Mantell*, online

Miles, Hallie Eustace, *Untold Tales of Wartime London: A Personal Diary*, Cecil Palmer, 1930

Mitford, Nancy and Evelyn Waugh, *The Letters of Nancy Mitford & Evelyn Waugh* (ed. Charlotte Mosley), Hodder & Stoughton, 1996

Monkswell, Lady Mary, *A Victorian Diarist* (ed. Hon. E. C. F. Collier), John Murray, 1944

Moore, Thomas, *Memoirs, Journal and Correspondence of Thomas Moore*, 8 vols., Longmans, Green, 1853–6

Moritz, Karl Philipp, *Travels in England in 1782*, G. G. & J. Robinson, 1797

Mullin, Chris, *Decline and Fall: Diaries 2005–2010*, Profile, 2010

Munby, Arthur, *Munby: Man of Two Worlds* by Derek Hudson, John Murray, 1972

Nichols, Peter, *Diaries 1969–1977*, Nick Hern, 2000

Nicolson, Harold, *Diaries and Letters 1930–39*, Collins, 1966; *Diaries and Letters 1939–45*, Collins, 1967; *Diaries and Letters 1945–62*, Collins, 1968

Notes & Queries, 9th Series, volume XII, 1903

Oldys, William, *A Literary Antiquary: Memoir of William Oldys Esq., Together with his Diary*, Spottiswoode & Co, 1862

Orwell, George, *The Orwell Diaries*, Penguin, 2010

Oxnard, Edward, *A Sketch of His Life and Extracts from his Diary* (ed. Edward S. Moseley), Clapp & Sons, 1872

Palin, Michael, *The Python Years: Diaries 1969–1979*, Orion, 2006; *Halfway to Hollywood: Diaries 1980–1988*, Orion, 2009

Partridge, Frances, *Everything to Lose*, Gollancz, 1985

Pepys, Samuel, *The Diary of Samuel Pepys* (ed. Henry Wheatley), George Bell & Sons, 1893

Pocock, John Thomas, *The Diary of a London Schoolboy 1826–1830*, Camden History Society, 1980

Pollock, Sir Frederick, *Personal Remembrances*, 2 vols., Macmillan, 1887

Powys, Mrs Philip Lybbe, *Passages from the Diaries of Mrs Philip Lybbe Powys* (ed. Emily Climenson), Longmans Green, 1899

Raikes, Thomas, *A Portion of the Journal Kept by Thomas Raikes from 1831 to 1847*, 4 vols., Longman, 1856

Reresby, Sir John, *The Memoirs of Sir John Reresby* (ed. James J. Cartwright), Longmans, Green, 1875

Ritchie, Charles, *The Siren Years*, Macmillan, 1974

Roberts, Katherine, *Pages from the Diary of a Militant Suffragette*, Garden City Press, 1909

Robinson, Henry Crabb, *Diary, Reminiscences and Correspondence* (ed. Thomas Sadler), 3 vols., Macmillan, 1869

Rossetti, William Michael (ed.), *Preraphaelite Diaries and Letters*, Hurst and Blackett, 1900

Rush, Richard, *A Residence at the Court of London*, Richard Bentley, 1833

Russell, Lady John, *Lady John Russell: A Memoir with Selections from her Diaries and Correspondence* by Desmond McCarthy, Methuen, 1910

Ryder, Dudley, *The Diary of Dudley Ryder*, Methuen, 1939

Sackville-West, Vita, *The Letters of Vita Sackville-West to Virginia Woolf* (ed. Louise Salvo and Mitchell A. Leaska), Hutchinson, 1984

Sancho, Ignatius, *Letters of the Late Ignatius Sancho, An African*, 2 vols., J. Nichols, 1782

Sancroft, William, *The Life of William Sancroft* by George D'Oyly, John Parker, 1840

Sassoon, Siegfried, *Diaries 1915–1918*, Faber, 1983; *Diaries 1920–1922*, Faber, 1981

Scott, Sir Walter, *The Journal of Sir Walter Scott*, David Douglas, 1890

Selwyn, George, *George Selwyn: His Letters and His Life* by E. S. Roscoe and Helen Clergue, T. Fisher Unwin, 1899

Sen, Keshub Chandra, *Diary in England*, Brahmo Tract Society, 1894

Shaw, George Bernard, *The Letters of Bernard Shaw to 'The Times'* (ed. Ronald Ford), Irish Academic Press, 2007

Shee, William Archer, *My Contemporaries*, Hurst & Blackett, 189

Shelley, Mary Wollstonecraft, *The Life and Letters of Mary Wollstonecraft Shelley* by Mrs Julian Marshall, 2 vols., Bentley & Son, 1889

Sher, Anthony, *The Year of the King*, Chatto & Windus, 1985

Shore, Emily, *Journal of Emily Shore*, Kegan Paul, 1891

Simond, Louis, *Journal of a Tour and Residence in Great Britain During the Years 1810 and 1811*, 2 vols., Constable, 1815

Smart, Elizabeth, *Necessary Secrets: The Journals of Elizabeth Smart* (ed. Alice van Wart), Grafton Books, 1991

Smith, Sydney, *A Memoir of the Reverend Sydney Smith with a Selection from his Letters*, 2 vols., Longman, Brown, Green and Longmans, 1855

Sopwith, Thomas, *Thomas Sopwith: With Excerpts from his Diary of Fifty-seven Years* by Benjamin Ward Richardson, Longmans, 1891

Spender, Stephen, *Letters to Christopher* (ed. Lee Bartlett), Black Sparrow Press, 1980

Stettin, Duke of, 'Diary of the Duke of Stettin's Journey through England' by Frederic Gershow, *Transactions of the Royal Historical Society*, New Series, vol. 6, 1892

Stevenson, Nils and Ray, *Vacant: A Diary of the Punk Years 1976–79*, Thames & Hudson, 1999

Strong, Roy, *The Roy Strong Diaries 1967–87*, Weidenfeld & Nicolson, 1997

Swift, Jonathan, *The Journal to Stella* (ed. George Aitken), Methuen, 1901

Tayler, William, *Diary of William Tayler, Footman* (ed. Dorothy Wise), St Marylebone Society Publications, 1962

Temple, William Johnston, *The Diaries of William Johnston Temple* (ed. Lewis Bettany), Oxford University Press, 1929

Thackeray, W. M., *A Collection of Letters of W. M. Thackeray 1847–1855*, Smith, Elder, 1887

Thoresby, Ralph, *The Diary of Ralph Thoresby*, 2 vols., Colburn & Bentley, 1830

Treloar, W. P., *A Lord Mayor's Diary*, John Murray, 1920

Tyler, John, *The Reverend John Tyler's Journal*, privately printed, 1894

Tynan, Kenneth, *The Diaries of Kenneth Tynan* (ed. John Lahr), Bloomsbury, 2001

Van Gogh, Vincent, *The Letters of Vincent Van Gogh*, Allen Lane, 1996

Van Schaack, Peter, *The Life of Peter Van Schaack*, Appleton, 1842

Vermorel, Fred and Judy, *The Sex Pistols: The Inside Story*, Star, 1978

Queen Victoria, *Journals*, online at www.queenvictoriasjournals.org

Von La Roche, Sophie, *Sophie in England* (trans. Clare Williams), Jonathan Cape, 1933

Wale, H. J., *My Grandfather's Pocket-book*, Chapman & Hall, 1883

Walpole, Horace, *Correspondence with the Reverend William Cole*, Yale University Press, 1937; *The Letters of Horace Walpole*, 9 vols., Richard Bentley, 1891

Ward, Thomas Asline, *Peeps Into the Past: Being Passages from the Diary of Thomas Asline Ward* (ed. Robert Leader), W. C. Leng, 1909

Waugh, Evelyn, *The Diaries of Evelyn Waugh* (ed. Michael Davie), Weidenfeld & Nicolson, 1976

Webb, Beatrice, *The Diary of Beatrice Webb*, 2 vols., Virago, 1983

Welch, Denton, *Journals* (ed. Michael De-La-Noy), Allison & Busby, 1983

Wesley, John, *The Journal of the Reverend John Wesley*, 4 vols., Dent, 1906

White, Walter, *The Journals of Walter White*, Chapman & Hall, 1898

Wickham, Glynne et al, *English Professional Theatre 1530–1660*, Cambridge University Press, 2000

Wilkins, Russ, *The Diary of a Common Fan: My Year During Charlton AFC's Centenary Season 2004/5*, Blaisdon Publishing, 2005

Williams, Kenneth, *The Kenneth Williams Diaries* (ed. Russell Davies), Harper Collins, 1993

Windham, William, *The Diary of William Windham 1784–1810* (ed. Mrs Henry Baring), Longmans Green, 1866

Wood, Anthony, *The Life and Times of Anthony Wood, Antiquary of Oxford* by Andrew Clark, Oxford University Press, 1891

Woodforde, James, *Passages from the Diary of a Country Parson*, Oxford University Press, 1935

Woolf, Virginia, *The Diaries of Virginia Woolf* (ed. Anne Olivier Bell), 5 vols., The Hogarth Press, 1977–84; *The Letters of Virginia Woolf* (ed. Nigel Nicolson and Joanne Trautmann), 5 vols., The Hogarth Press, 1975–79

Wordsworth, Dorothy, *Journals of Dorothy Wordsworth* (ed. William Knight), 2 vols., Macmillan, 1904

Wotton, Sir Henry, *The Life and Letters of Sir Henry Wotton* (ed. Logan Pearsall Smith), 2 vols., Oxford University Press, 1907

Wriothesley, Charles, *A Chronicle of England During the Reigns of the Tudors* (ed. William Douglas Hamilton), 2 vols., Camden Society, 1875

Wyndham, Joan, *Love Lessons: A Wartime Diary*, Heinemann, 1985; *Love Is Blue: A Wartime Diary*, Heinemann, 1986

Yeoman, John, *The Diary of the Visits of John Yeoman to London in the years 1774 and 1777* (ed. Macleod Yearsley), Watts & Co, 1934

∼ *Acknowledgements* ∼

We would both like to thank everyone at Frances Lincoln but especially Andrew
Dunn and Jane Havell for their tireless work in guiding this book from proposal to
print. This book was only possible with the help of numerous diarists, publishers,
agents, executors and estates. Thank you all.

T.E. and N.R.

A full list of thanks would probably prove longer than the book itself so I will
restrict myself to raising a glass to all the staff and librarians at the London
Metropolitan Archives in Clerkenwell, the local history units at both Southwark
and Finsbury libraries, The British Library in St Pancras, The London Library
in St James's and especially Mr Richard Boon of Stoke Newington Library, who
helped supply the various diaries that were duly pilfered for *A London Year*. In
addition I would like to thank: Dickon Edwards, Mike Jones, Pam Berry, Bob
Stanley, Pete Wiggs, Martin Kelly, Sarah Cracknell, Paul Kelly, Debsey Wykes,
Cathi Unsworth, Max Décharné, Marc Glendening and all the Sohemians, Liz
Vater, Pete Brown, Mark Mason, Joe Kerr, Charles Holland, Raz at the Betsey,
Guy Sangster Adama, Alex Mayor and my beautiful and brilliant wife, Emily Bick.

T.E.

My love and thanks go to my wife Eve who has spent more time than she can have
expected to do in the last year reading London diaries. Many of the best entries in
this book were found by her and I am very grateful for her efforts in unearthing
them. Other people who have provided encouragement and help (sometimes
unwittingly) during the research on the book include Anita Diaz, my sister Lucinda
Rennison, Andrew Holgate, Susan Osborne, Hugh Pemberton, my mother Eileen
Rennison, Kevin Chappell, Ion Mills, John, Michael and Andrew Thewlis, Gordon
Kerr and Kathy Crocker.

N.R.

Various publishers and Estates have generously given permission to use extracts
from the following copyright works:
J. R. Ackerley, *My Sister and Myself*, Hutchinson, 1982. Reproduced by permission
    of David Higham Associates Ltd
Lord Alanbrooke, *War Diaries of Field Marshal Lord Alanbrooke* (ed. Alex
    Danchev), Weidenfeld & Nicolson, 2001. Reproduced by permission of David
    Higham Associates

© Lindsay Anderson, *The Diaries* (ed. Paul Sutton), Methuen Drama, an imprint of Bloomsbury Publishing, 2004

Cecil Beaton, *The Wandering Years: Diaries 1922–39*, Weidenfeld & Nicolson, 1961; *The Years Between: Diaries 1939–44*, Weidenfeld & Nicolson, 1965. Reproduced by permission of the Literary Executor and Rupert Crew Limited

Alan Bennett, *Writing Home*, Faber, 1994. Reproduced by permission of Faber and Faber in the UK

© John Betjeman by permission of The Estate of John Betjeman

Vera Brittain, *Wartime Chronicle*. Extract included by permission of Mark Bostridge and T. J. Brittain-Catlin, Literary Executors for the Estate of Vera Brittain 1970

Alan Clark, *Diaries*, Weidenfeld & Nicolson, 1993. Reproduced by permission of Orion Books

© Ossie Clark, *The Ossie Clark Diaries* (ed. Lady Henrietta Rous), Bloomsbury Publishing Plc, 1998

Duff Cooper, *The Duff Cooper Diaries 1915–51* (ed. John Julius Norwich), Weidenfeld & Nicolson, 2005. Reproduced by permission of Orion Books

Noël Coward, *The Noël Coward Diaries* (ed. Graham Payn and Sheridan Morley), Weidenfeld & Nicolson, 1982. Reproduced by permission of Orion Books

Brian Eno, *A Year with Swollen Appendices*, Faber, 1996. Reproduced by permission of Faber and Faber in the UK

John Fowles, *Journal*. Reproduced by permission of Aitken Alexander Associates

Alec Guinness, *My Name Escapes Me: The Diary of a Retiring Actor*, Hamish Hamilton, 1996. Reproduced by permission of David Higham Associates

Frank Hurley, *The Diaries of Frank Hurley 1912–1941*, Anthem Press, 2011

Derek Jarman, *Modern Nature: Journals of Derek Jarman*, copyright © University of Minnesota Press, 2009

© Oona King, *The Oona King Diaries: House Music*, 2007, Bloomsbury Publishing

James Lees-Milne, *Prophesying Peace: Diaries 1944–45*, Chatto & Windus, 1977; *Holy Dread: Diaries 1982–84*, John Murray, 2001; *The Milk of Paradise: Diaries 1993–97*, John Murray, 2005. Reproduced by permission of David Highham Associates Ltd

© Clayton Littlewood, *Goodbye to Soho*, DWB Press, 2012

Chris Mullin, *Decline and Fall: Diaries 2005–2010*, Profile, 2010. Reproduced by permission of Profile Books

© Peter Nichols, *Diaries 1969–77*, Nick Hern, 2000. Reprinted with permission of Nick Hern Books (www.nickhernbooks.co.uk)

© George Orwell, *The Orwell Diaries*, Penguin, 2010. Reprinted by permission of Bill Hamilton as the Literary Executor of the Estate of the Late Sonia Brownell Orwell

Michael Palin, *The Python Years: Diaries 1969–1979*, Orion, 2006; *Halfway to Hollywood: Diaries 1980–1988*, Orion, 2009. Reproduced by permission of Orion Books

© Frances Partridge, *Everything to Lose*, Gollancz, 1985. Reproduced by permission of the author's Estate c/o Rogers, Coleridge & White Ltd, 20 Powis Mews, London, W11 1JN

Siegfried Sassoon, *Diaries 1915–1918*, Faber, 1983; *Diaries 1920–1922*, Faber, 1981.
    Reproduced by permission of Faber and Faber
Anthony Sher, *The Year of the King*, Chatto & Windus, 1985. Reprinted with
    permission of Nick Hern Books (www.nickhernbooks.co.uk)
Stephen Spender, *Letters to Christopher: Stephen Spender's Letters to Christopher
    Isherwood*, © 1980. Reprinted by kind permission of the Estate of Stephen
    Spender
© Nils and Ray Stevenson, *Vacant: A Diary of the Punk Years 1976–79*, 1999,
    reprinted by kind permission of Thames & Hudson Ltd, London
© Roy Strong, *The Roy Strong Diaries 1967–87*, Weidenfeld & Nicolson, 1997.
    Reproduced by permission of Felicity Bryan Literary Agency and the author
Diary of William Tayler, Footman (ed. Dorothy Wise), 1962. Reproduced by
    permission of St Marylebone Society Publications
© *Kenneth Tynan, The Diaries of Kenneth Tynan* (ed. John Lahr), 2001.
    Bloomsbury Publishing
The Diaries of Evelyn Waugh (ed. Michael Davie), Weidenfeld & Nicolson, 1979.
    © The Estate of Laura Waugh. Reproduced by permission of The Wylie
    Agency
The Diary of Beatrice Webb, Virago, 1983. British Library of Political and
    Economic Science, LSE, Passfield Papers
Denton Welch, *Journals* (ed. Michael De-La-Noy), Allison & Busby, 1983.
    Reproduced by permission of David Highham Associates Ltd
The Diary of Virginia Woolf (ed. Anne Olivier Bell), volumes 1–5. Copyright
    © 1977, 1978, 1982, 1984 by Quentin Bell and Angelica Garnett. Reprinted
    by permission of Houghton Mifflin Harcourt Publishing Company in the US
    and of The Random House Group Limited and The Society of Authors in the
    UK. All rights reserved
The Letters of Virginia Woolf (ed. Nigel Nicolson and Joanne Trautmann), 5 vols.,
    The Hogarth Press, 1975–79. Reprinted by permission of The Random House
    Group Limited and The Society of Authors in the UK

Permission has been sought for several extracts which are not cited above. Every
effort has been made to secure these permissions before this book went to print.
Anyone we have not been able to reach is invited to contact the publishers so that
a full acknowledgement may be given in subsequent editions.

The publishers would like to thank Nikki Braunton and Jenna Collins at the
Museum of London for their help in providing the majority of the illustrations
used in this book. All are © Museum of London except for pages 26 © Esther
M. Zimmer Lederberg Memorial Website; 51 and 138 © Mike Jones; 107; 167; 222;
276; 287; 365; 416 © Pam Berry, and the last endpaper © Eric Fischer, using data
from the Flickr search API and the Twitter streaming API. Further credits can
be found in the Illustrations list.

~ *ILLUSTRATIONS* ~

~ INDEX ~

See Contributors (pages 529–69) for index entries for the contributing authors. They have further entries here only if they are mentioned in the writings of others.

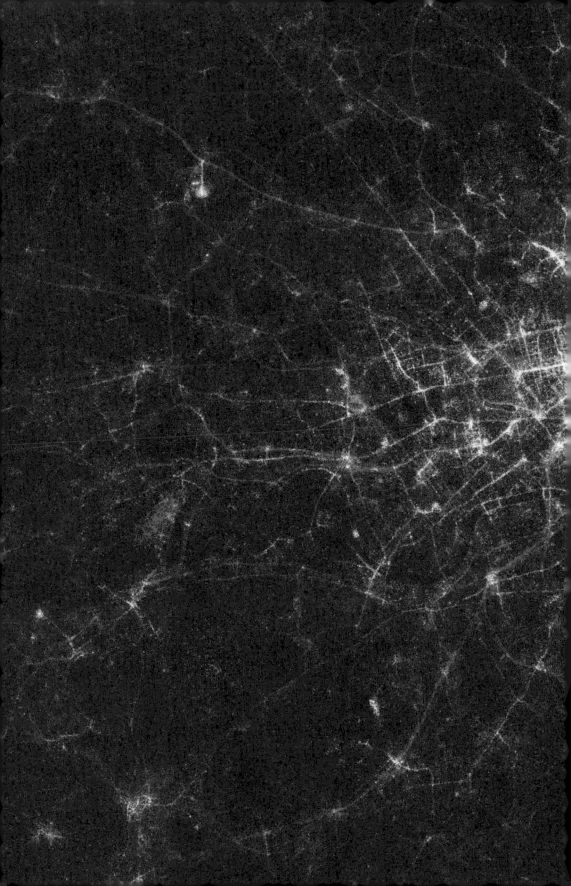